Count

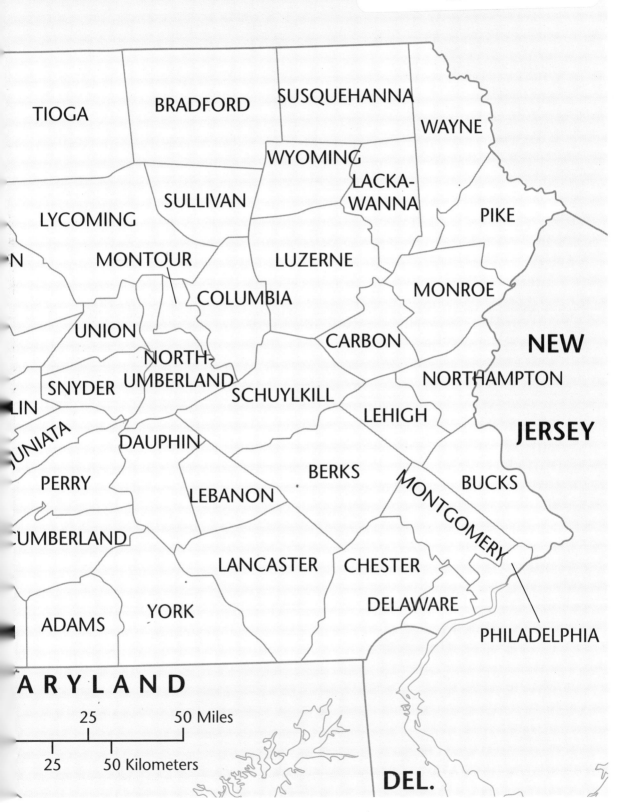

TIOGA

BRADFORD

SUSQUEHANNA

WAYNE

WYOMING

SULLIVAN

LACKA-
WANNA

LYCOMING

PIKE

N

MONTOUR

LUZERNE

COLUMBIA

MONROE

UNION

CARBON

NEW

NORTH-
UMBERLAND

SNYDER

NORTHAMPTON

LIN

SCHUYLKILL

LEHIGH

JERSEY

JUNIATA

DAUPHIN

PERRY

BERKS

MONTGOMERY

BUCKS

LEBANON

CUMBERLAND

LANCASTER

CHESTER

YORK

DELAWARE

ADAMS

PHILADELPHIA

M A R Y L A N D

25   50 Miles

25   50 Kilometers

DEL.

Trees of Pennsylvania

TREES OF PENNSYLVANIA

A Complete Reference Guide

ANN FOWLER RHOADS AND
TIMOTHY A. BLOCK

Drawings by Anna Aniśko

Morris Arboretum of the University of Pennsylvania

UNIVERSITY OF PENNSYLVANIA PRESS
Philadelphia

10 9 8 7 6 5 4 3 2 1

Published by
University of Pennsylvania Press
Philadelphia, Pennsylvania 19104-4011

Library of Congress Cataloging-in-Publication Data
Rhoads, Ann Fowler.
  Trees of Pennsylvania : a complete reference guide / Ann Fowler Rhoads and
Timothy A. Block ; drawings by Anna Aniśko
    p. cm.
  ISBN 0-8122-3785-4 (cloth : alk. paper)
  Includes bibliographical references and index.
  1. Trees—Pennsylvania—Identification. 2. Trees—Pennsylvania—Pictorial
works. I. Block, Timothy A. II. Aniśko, Anna. III. Title
QK183 .R562   2004
582.16'09748—dc22   2004055464

Text design by George Lang

Frontispiece: Canadian hemlock

Contents

Acknowledgments

We extend thanks to James Macklin for assistance and advice in dealing with the hawthorns and for the loan of specimens from the Academy of Natural Sciences of Philadelphia Herbarium; Jim Bissell for the loan of specimens from the Cleveland Museum of Natural History Herbarium and the photo of the bark of pumpkin ash; Miles Arnott for specimens from the Bowmans Hill Wildflower Preserve; the Darlington Herbarium, West Chester University, for the loan of *Populus heterophylla* specimens; and Jeff Stuffle of the Pennsylvania Bureau of Forestry, Valley Forge District, for access to the database of big trees of Pennsylvania. We also thank Bird-in-Hand Consignment Shop of Chestnut Hill for their support.

Introduction

Trees dominate the natural landscape of Pennsylvania; homeowners plant trees to enhance their properties, and municipalities invest in shade trees to make communities more attractive. Although changes have occurred since William Penn named the state for its forest resources, trees are still a dominant element throughout. This book contains information about the 134 native trees of Pennsylvania and 62 additional species that have escaped cultivation and inserted themselves into the natural landscape.

This book is a field guide and natural history of all the native and naturalized trees that grow in Pennsylvania. It contains descriptions of growth form, leaves, twigs, buds, bark, flowers, and fruits. Additional information includes blooming and fruiting times and fall leaf color. Distribution in Pennsylvania and beyond is shown on range maps for each native species.

Also included is information on pollination, seed dissemination, and wildlife value, including larval food sources and nectar for moths and butterflies. Ecological relationships and economic importance are described, as are traditional uses by Native Americans and early settlers.

Chapter 1. What Is a Tree?

Defining a tree is not as easy as it might seem at first; growth form, not size, is the major factor we considered. We included woody species that tend to be single-stemmed, or at least grow that way some of the time. Not all "trees" fit the pattern. Some, such as gray birch, typically grow as a cluster of stems but are considered trees. Shrubs, on the other hand, are almost always multistemmed from the ground. Despite efforts at definition, there was clearly some subjectivity involved in deciding what to include as a tree.

GROWTH

The growth of trees is determined by two processes. The increase in height or branch length occurs through the action of active cell division regions (apical meristems) located at the tip of each twig and rootlet. These points elongate each season that the tree is alive, making trees indeterminate in their growth; that is, they continually increase in size until they die. The life span of Pennsylvania trees ranges from 20 or 30 years to 700 years, depending on the species and the growing conditions. Because of differences in environmental conditions, it can be hard to estimate the age of a tree by observing its size. Many of the largest specimens recorded are trees in cultivated settings.

Wood

Each year trees also increase in diameter (girth) due to activity of the vascular cambium, which forms a cylinder between the bark and the woody interior of each trunk, branch, and root. Cell division in the cambium layer produces a new layer of wood (xylem) each year. New xylem, known as sapwood, transports water from the roots to the leaves. Heartwood, usually of a darker color, develops in the center of the trunk or larger limbs.

Wood (mature xylem) becomes part of the structural support for the tree, it contains few if any living cells and so requires little or no energy to maintain it. Variations in the size of xylem cells produced early in the year versus those that form later in a given season create a pattern of annual growth rings

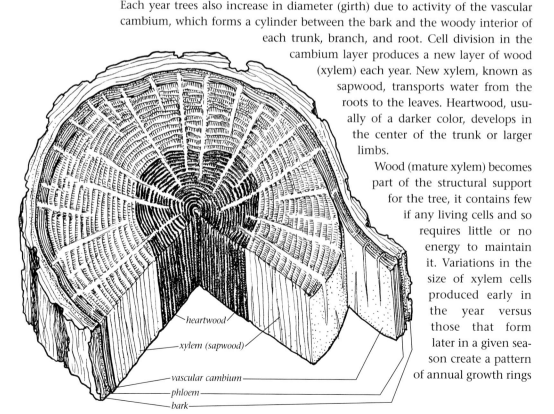

heartwood
xylem (sapwood)
vascular cambium
phloem
bark

by which the age of a stem can be determined. Weather variations and other environmental changes are recorded in the growth rings as variations in width that can be used to recreate past climate through the science of dendrochronology.

The vascular cambium also is the source of phloem, the tissue that transports sugars made in the leaves to other areas of the tree where energy is needed or where storage will occur. Phloem is located between the cambium and the bark, and does not accumulate the way xylem does.

Bark

Tree trunks, branches, and roots are covered with a protective layer of bark, the pattern and texture of which is characteristic for each species. Bark is produced by another cambium layer known as the bark cambium. Both the vascular cambium and the bark cambium must expand as the girth of a stem increases. Bark protects the phloem, which lies just beneath it on the surface of the wood. When bark is damaged, the phloem is often also affected. The term girdling refers to the removal of the bark, including the phloem and the vascular cambium, all the way around the entire circumference of a stem. Partial or complete girdling isolates the roots from their only source of energy (sugar from photosynthesis) and will kill a tree in a year. Early settlers used girdling to kill trees when clearing the land. Bark and an intact vascular cambium also protect the xylem from attacks by insects and wood-decaying fungi. Healing of small wounds occurs when callus or wound tissue forms from the exposed edges of the cambium. Larger wounds, however, often become infected before they heal over, leading to internal wood decay.

Young stems with thin bark usually have corky raised areas known as lenticels, which allow for movement of gases in and out of the stem. The shape and orientation of lenticels is a useful characteristic for tree identification. Birches and cherries for instance, are known for their prominent horizontal lenticels.

Growth Patterns

Growth patterns of various species achieve the overall goal of maximizing exposure to the sun while balancing the need for water, minerals, gas exchange, and support. Growth of individual branches in the crown of a tree is controlled by hormones that respond to light and other environmental clues to maintain coordinated growth. In some species hormones produced by the tip of the main stem establish a pattern of dominance over side branches that creates a strong conical shape, as in many conifers. Pin oaks and sweetgums also show strong apical dominance when young.

Different species have characteristic patterns of branching that are especially noticeable when the bare branches are silhouetted against the winter sky. Trees growing close together in the forest often do not show as well-developed patterns of branching due to crowding. Tree structure has also evolved in response to environmental stress such as wind, snow, and ice by maintaining a blend of strength and flexibility. The conical form of conifers allows them to shed snow thus avoiding breakage.

Short Shoots and Long Shoots

Some trees have two types of branches: those that elongate normally from the tip and short, stubby side branches. Short shoots or spurs as the small side branches are known, usually bear both leaves and flowers. On trees that produce short shoots, flowers and fruits are found only on these modified branches, the long shoots support leaves only. In some trees short shoots may regain the ability to elongate normally after a few seasons. Some examples of trees that have short shoots include larch, ginkgo, blackgum, apple, honey-locust, and hawthorn.

Juvenility

The first few years of growth of most trees is a juvenile period when flowering does not occur. In some species the juvenile period can be as long as 20 to 30 years. The retention of dry, brown leaves through the winter in beech, hophornbeam, and many oaks is a juvenile characteristic. Even when the trees are older, leaves cling to central portions of the crown that represent the juvenile growth period. Leaf shape, and even leaf arrangement differ between the juvenile and adult stages of some trees. The production of spines can also be affected by maturity. Osage-orange trees are spiny in the juvenile stage and lack spines in the adult part of their life cycle.

LEAVES

Leaves are the primary sites of photosynthesis, the process by which green plants use the energy from sunlight to produce sugar. Deciduous trees lose their leaves in the autumn and grow new ones the following spring. Those that keep their leaves through the winter are termed evergreen. Most gymnosperms are evergreen, but in our flora the larches and ginkgo are exceptions. In our climate, most broad-leaved trees are deciduous.

In addition to photosynthesis, leaves are the site of evapotranspiration, the process by which water evaporates from the leaves into the atmosphere. Evapotranspiration drives the flow of water through a plant, exerting a pull on the tiny columns of water in the xylem cells of the vascular system. Water must continually move through plants to maintain life. Some trees shed leaves during periods of extreme drought slowing evaporation and preventing more serious damage. Regions of the earth that do not have enough water cannot support trees.

Fall Leaf Color

The leaves of many deciduous trees undergo color changes in the fall. Brilliant shades of red, yellow, orange, and purple attract viewers to the woods in October. Recent research suggests that color change may be important in prolonging the period during which trees can withdraw sugars and minerals from the leaves in a last ditch salvage effort before the leaves are shed.[1] It has also been suggested that brilliant autumn leaf color helps to advertise the presence of ripe fruits on some species, thereby attracting birds and other potential seed dispersal agents.

ROOTS

Roots are hard to observe, but vitally important to the functioning of trees. Roots have been found to extend well beyond the branch tips to achieve their dual role of anchoring and holding erect a structure that may stand more than 100 feet tall and weigh many tons. Roots are also responsible for absorbing the water and dissolved mineral elements required for tree growth. Most active absorption takes place in the top six inches of the soil, although some roots extend deeper. In forests, roots proliferate in the humus-rich upper soil layers.

Root Partners

Fungi are active partners with most trees, forming mycorrhizal structures that combine root and fungus tissue to enhance absorption of water and nutrients. The fungi benefit by obtaining sugar from the host plant in a symbiotic relationship. Plants such as alders and locusts have other types of root symbionts that fix atmospheric nitrogen, making it available to the trees.

FLOWERS, FRUITS, AND SEEDS

Conifers

Sexual reproduction in trees results in the formation of seeds. In the gymnosperms seed is formed in woody cones (except ginkgo, in which the seeds are naked except for a fleshy outer covering). Initially two types of cones are present, male or pollen cones and female or seed cones. The male cones fall from the trees after releasing pollen that carries the sperm cells or male contribution to sexual reproduction. Pollen is blown by the wind to the female or seed cones where the egg cell is present. Following fertilization (the fusion of egg and sperm cells) seed is produced. In most conifers the seeds are dispersed by wind on release from the mature cones. In our region the gymnosperms include pine, spruce, fir, hemlock, larch, juniper, white-cedar, arbor-vitae, and ginkgo.

Angiosperms

The rest of our trees are flowering plants (angiosperms), although the flowers of many species are inconspicuous and may not be noticed by many people. In the flowering plants, pollen, the male part of the sexual cycle, and egg cells are sometimes present in a single flower, in which case the flowers are referred to as bisexual or perfect. Alternatively they may be produced in separate male and female (unisexual) flowers. If separate, male and female flowers may be produced on the same tree, in which case the tree is termed monoecious, or on different trees, a condition described as dioecious.

pistil

stamen

sepal

petal

Pollination

Many deciduous trees, including oak, ash, hickory, birch, hornbeam, and mulberry, have separate male and female flowers and are wind pollinated. Species in this category generally bloom early in the spring before the leaves have expanded and produce large quantities of pollen. For those allergic to tree pollens, these are the main perpetrators. The elms are also wind pollinated but have flowers with both male and female parts in each flower. The maples are a diverse group with both perfect and unisexual flowers known and some species that are insect pollinated.

Large, showy insect-pollinated flowers or clusters of flowers are characteristic of tuliptree, magnolia, hawthorn, shadbush, dogwood, black locust and honey-locust. Trees in this category may flower before or after leaf expansion.

Seed Dispersal

After pollination and fertilization, the female part of the flower (pistil) matures into a fruit. The fruit is technically the mature ovary of the flower and in most species has evolved a form that facilitates seed dispersal. A fruit may be a dry, hard, winged structure designed for wind dispersal, for example, the samaras of ash, maple, or elm. Other fruits have evolved to be eaten and the seeds scattered by animals as they defecate. Fleshy-fruited trees such as shadbush, dogwood, hawthorn, and crabapple are examples of this type. Still others, such as acorns and hickory nuts, are gathered and stored by squirrels and other small mammals. Even though many acorns are eaten, enough are forgotten and left to grow to make this a successful strategy benefiting both tree and consumers, who are guaranteed a continuing supply of nut trees. The seeds of several trees in the bean family are also cached by small mammals with similar results. Acorns are also eaten by large mammals including deer and bear, but those that are will never germinate.

Several Pennsylvania trees produce fruits that appear to have no extant seed dispersal agents. Some, such as osage-orange, honey-locust, Kentucky coffeetree, persimmon, and pawpaw, may be relics of a time as recent as 13,000 years ago, when large mammals, better adapted to consume the fruits and disperse their seeds, such as mastodons, giant ground sloths, or wild horses that are now extinct, roamed North America.[2]

CLONAL GROWTH

Some trees reproduce in other ways in addition to the formation of seed. Forms of asexual or vegetative reproduction include root shoots and stump sprouts; these methods produce a cluster of trees that are genetically identical to the original tree. American beech in forest settings commonly produces root shoots that form a colony around the parent tree; these clones form a mosaic in the forest, and may be much longer lived than any individual shoot. Blackgum, black locust, pawpaw, and tree-of-heaven are other species that regularly reproduce by forming root shoots. Cutting down a single trunk only stimulates more to sprout from established root systems.

Stump sprouts are another form of asexual reproduction. Oaks and red maples are particularly capable of forming stump sprouts when something happens to the main shoot. Foresters count on the stump sprouts of these species to regenerate quickly after trees have been cut for timber; an established root system allows rapid growth. Oaks are particularly effective at forming shoots from the root collar just below the ground surface, a characteristic that also allows them to recover quickly after fire. Basswood is another tree that readily forms basal shoots.

Notes

1. Lee, David W. and Kevin S. Gould. 2002. Why leaves turn red. *American Scientist* 90: 524–31.

2. Barlow, Connie. 2000. *The Ghosts of Evolution: Nonsensical Fruit, Missing Partners, and Other Ecological Anachronisms.* Basic Books, New York.

Chapter 2.
Pennsylvania's Forest Heritage

A BRIEF HISTORY OF PENN'S WOODS

The land that greeted the earliest Europeans to arrive in Pennsylvania was primarily forested, broken only by rivers, occasional wetlands, and clearings associated with Native American villages. Early accounts of the landscape of the interior of Pennsylvania contain frequent references like this descriptive passage by Fortescue Cuming while crossing Tuscarora Mountain in 1807: "view to the westward, though extensive, was cheerless and gloomy, over a broken and mountainous or rather hilly country, covered with forests, chiefly of the dark and sombre pine."[1] Other accounts describe extensive grasslands and gallery-type forests in which one could "drive a carriage unhindered," apparently the product of Native Americans' regular use of fire to manage the landscape.[2]

However, that forest is a fairly recent product of the geological evolution of Pennsylvania's landscape. Eighteen thousand years ago the northeastern and northwestern corners of the state were covered with ice (Figure 1), and tundra and boreal forests covered the rest of the state.[3] As the ice receded, species that had found refuge farther south gradually returned.

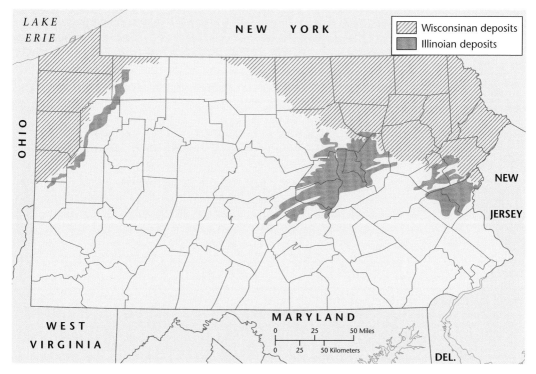

Figure 1. Glacial deposits of Pennsylvania. Adapted from Map 59, Commonwealth of Pennsylvania Department of Environmental Resources, Bureau of Topographic and Geologic Survey.

INFLUENCE OF NATIVE AMERICANS

The popular notion that European explorers and early settlers found a primeval forest free of human influence is inaccurate. Fossil pollen and charcoal preserved in bogs and lake sediments all across the eastern half of North America, as well as many of the earliest written observations, record widescale use of fire by Native Americans to manage their landscape. Evidence exists that Native Americans managed vast areas of forest with fire to create open, gallery-type forests, encourage species they prized for food, and also to clear fields where they grew corn, beans, and other crops.

The oak-dominated forests that persist today, and native grasslands, most of which disappeared soon after Native Americans were ousted from the land, almost certainly owe their existence to traditions of large-scale burning among some groups of people for centuries or thousands of years before the arrival of Europeans.[4]

Native American populations were much larger before contact with Europeans introduced smallpox and other diseases; the extent of land impacted by their management was large.[5] The first European settlers found extensive clearings created by Native Americans in the Cumberland Valley, Penns Valley in Centre County, and the Wyoming Valley as well as other sites.[6] Revealingly, later travelers in these same regions described a forested landscape apparently due to successional growth.[7]

CUTTING DOWN THE TREES

As European settlers claimed the land, taming the wilderness meant cutting down trees and eradicating some forest wildlife, especially large predators, in order to make room for farms, towns, and villages and to assure the safety of pioneer families and their livestock. Wood not needed for fuel or building material was often burned early in the process of clearing the land; after all, there was a seemingly unlimited supply.

In Pennsylvania, the clearing for farming and cutting trees for commercial uses that began with the first European arrivals had, by 1900, reduced the forest cover from 90 to 95 percent of the land area to 32 percent.[8]

Early Lumbering

Tall, straight, and suitable for masts for ships, the eastern white pine was the first large-scale target of waves of loggers who assaulted Pennsylvania's forests. Beginning in the 1760s, white pine logs 120 feet long and 4 feet in diameter (or larger) were cut in the hills of northeastern Pennsylvania, fastened together in huge rafts, and floated down the Delaware River to Philadelphia to provide masts for British ships.

A second wave of timber harvesting focused on hemlock bark, which was used in the leather tanning industry. Hemlock logs were cut and the bark stripped off and hauled to tanneries located in many parts of the state near the source of bark.

Charcoal making was another forest industry that thrived before the discovery of coal as a fuel. In areas near early iron furnaces, colliers cut trees (preferably oak or chestnut) and stacked them in conical piles built in the woods. The piles of logs were covered with earth and burned to produce charcoal that was then hauled by wagon to the iron works. Charcoal making utilized small trees and could be done on a 25-year rotation in most areas. An iron furnace required

20,000–35,000 acres of forest to support it on a sustainable basis.[9] Today, it is not unusual to come across old charcoal hearths, level areas about 40 feet in diameter, scattered throughout the forests in areas where charcoal making occurred.

The "Great Clearcut"

The invention of the geared logging locomotive set the stage for the great clearcut of Pennsylvania's forests that took place between 1890 and 1930. The railroad logging era, as it is known, allowed loggers to reach the vast interior of the state's forests. Rail beds were constructed up every hollow, far into forests unreachable when proximity to water was necessary to transport the logs to markets. Today many of the old railroad beds are the basis for a network of hiking trails.

During the railroad logging era, technology was present not only to harvest vast areas but also to utilize everything regardless of species or size. What wasn't usable as lumber was treated by slow heating and distillation in "chemical factories" that produced acetate of lime, wood alcohol, wood tar, charcoal, and gases. Wood products including barrel staves, lath, shingles, boxes, and kindling wood were produced in hastily built factories located in temporary towns that sprang up throughout the northern tier of Pennsylvania. Old photographs record the boom days at Masten, Golinza, Laquin, and many other sites that today are only names on a map, a few old foundations, or perhaps the site of a hunting camp.[10]

Clearcutting was frequently followed by fires; started by sparks from the railroads, the fires burned rapidly and fiercely through the slash left after logging. The resulting scenes of devastation generated concern by groups throughout the state and led to the formation of the Pennsylvania Forestry Association. A campaign led by Dr. Joseph Rothrock resulted in the formation of a Division of Forestry within the Pennsylvania Department of Agriculture in 1895 and the appointment of Dr. Rothrock as the first Forestry Commissioner.

Logging operations in the vicinity of Austin, Potter County, Pennsylvania, circa 1901. Photograph from
The Goodyears, an Empire in the Hemlocks *by Thomas T. Taber, III; published privately in 1971; used with permission of the author.*

Development of a system of forest reserves, now known as state forests, began in 1897 with the acquisition of abandoned cutover lands that were sold at tax sales. By 1904 the system held about half a million acres; today the state forests total 2.1 million acres.

THE FOREST TODAY

Despite the dire predictions of Rothrock and others, Pennsylvania's forests did recover in the years following the great clearcut. Trees came back not only on cutover lands, but also on abandoned farmland; today, second-growth forests cover 59 percent of the state's land area. Only a few fragments remain of the original forest. The Tionesta Scenic and Natural Area in Allegheny National Forest in northwestern Pennsylvania includes the only sizeable tract of old growth forest that remains in the state. Heart's Content, also in the Allegheny National Forest, has 100 acres of old growth hemlock and white pine forest. Fourteen other smaller fragments are preserved in state forests or state parks.

In addition to 2.1 million acres of state forests, Pennsylvania's publicly owned forest lands include another 277,000 acres in 116 state parks. State game lands, administered by the Pennsylvania Game Commission, contain another 1.4 million acres in the public domain. Pennsylvania is host to one national forest; the Allegheny National Forest contains just over half a million acres. However, the largest proportion (70 percent) of forested land in the state is privately owned.

The timber industry remains an important part of Pennsylvania's economy, totaling nearly $5 billion per year and providing about 100,000 jobs. The most valuable single product is black cherry, which is used mainly for veneer in the furniture industry. Oak and other hardwoods are also important.

RARE SPECIES

The abundance of individual tree species varies greatly from those that are found throughout the state in a variety of habitats such as red maple, beech, and red oak, to those that are very limited in their occurrence.

Rarity occurs for several reasons; some native Pennsylvania trees such as balsam fir, tamarack, and black spruce are northern species that are at their southern limit of range in Pennsylvania. Others, such as American holly, sweetbay magnolia, southern red oak, willow oak, chinquapin, and short-leaf pine, just reach the state from the south. Trees with a more western distribution that reach Pennsylvania include Shumard oak, bur oak, shingle oak, and Kentucky coffee-tree.

Others, such as chestnut and butternut, have become rare through the impact of insects or diseases. Two trees that once grew here, Atlantic white-cedar and swamp cottonwood, are extirpated (gone from the state).

The rarest native species are designated by the Pennsylvania Natural Heritage Program and protected under the Wild Plant Conservation Act. Trees listed as endangered in Pennsylvania are balsam poplar, beach plum, southern red oak, willow oak, Shumard oak, and showy mountain-ash. Allegheny plum and pumpkin ash have been recommended for endangered status. Classified as threatened are American holly, umbrella-tree, sweetbay magnolia, and hoptree. Four other tree species, short-leaf pine and three hawthorns, have been recommended for listing but a specific status has not yet been determined.

Trees classified by the Pennsylvania Natural Heritage Program

COMMON NAME	SCIENTIFIC NAME	STATUS
Atlantic white-cedar	*Chamaecyparis thyoides*	extirpated
swamp cottonwood	*Populus heterophylla*	extirpated
balsam poplar	*Populus balsamifera*	endangered
beach plum	*Prunus maritima*	endangered
showy mountain-ash	*Sorbus decora*	endangered
Shumard oak	*Quercus shumardii*	endangered
southern red oak	*Quercus falcata*	endangered
willow oak	*Quercus phellos*	endangered
Allegheny plum	*Prunus alleghaniensis*	proposed endangered
pumpkin ash	*Fraxinus profunda*	proposed endangered
American holly	*Ilex opaca*	threatened
hoptree	*Ptelea trifoliata*	threatened
sweetbay magnolia	*Magnolia virginiana*	threatened
umbrella-tree	*Magnolia tripetala*	threatened
Brainerd's hawthorn	*Crataegus brainerdii*	undetermined
downy hawthorn	*Crataegus mollis*	undetermined
Pennsylvania hawthorn	*Crataegus pennsylvanica*	undetermined
short-leaf pine	*Pinus echinata*	undetermined

FOREST SUCCESSION

With few exceptions, rainfall, temperature, and soil conditions are suitable for the growth of trees throughout Pennsylvania. Forests and the trees and other species that comprise them are constantly changing systems. Abandoned farmland, and cleared or timbered land will become forested again through a natural process known as secondary succession. Initially open land will be colonized by species such as eastern red-cedar, tuliptree, aspens, or red maple that grow well in the high light conditions of open fields. As early successional species modify the environment by increasing the organic matter and shading the forest floor, more shade tolerant species invade. Beech, sugar maple, and Canadian hemlock are so-called late successional trees because of their ability to grow and reproduce in low light conditions. The term climax forest was formerly used to describe the late successional stages of forest development. However, current interpretation is to view the forest as a constantly shifting mosaic of patches created by individual tree falls and other small-scale change.

MAJOR FOREST TYPES

Pennsylvania's climate, rainfall, and soil fertility support forest growth throughout most of the state with the exception of areas that are too wet or too rocky. The major forest types are northern hardwood forest, oak-hickory forest, Great Lakes beech-maple forest, and mixed mesophytic forest (Figure 2).

The northern hardwood forest occupies the northern third of the state and extends south at high elevations along the Allegheny Front. It also occurs farther south on north-facing slopes and cool, moist ravines. This forest type is characterized by a mixture of hardwoods and conifers and usually contains beech, birch, sugar maple, Canadian hemlock, and white pine in the canopy. Wild black cherry reaches its best development in this zone, especially in the

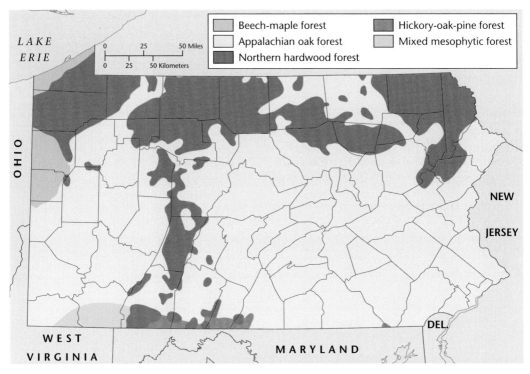

Figure 2. *Major forest types of Pennsylvania. Adapted from A. W. Kuchler (1964),* Potential Natural Vegetation of the Conterminous United States, American Geographical Society Special Publication 36.

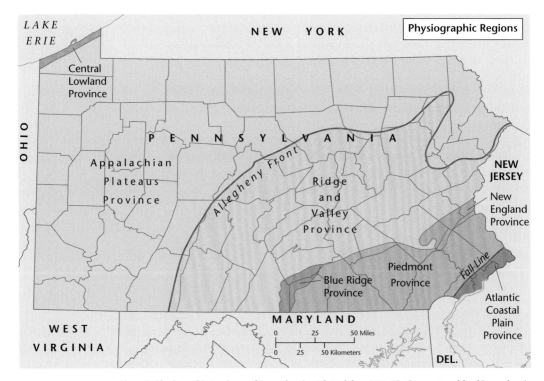

Figure 3. *Physiographic provinces of Pennsylvania. Adapted from Map 13, Commonwealth of Pennsylvania Department of Environmental Resources, Bureau of Topographic and Geologic Survey.*

northwestern part of the state. Understory trees typically include moosewood, witch-hazel, mountain holly, and shadbush.

Oak forests dominate the southern two-thirds of the state. Oak forests include red oak-mixed hardwood type on lower slopes where red and white oaks occur mixed with tuliptree, red maple, and hickories. On drier upper slopes and ridge tops throughout the central Pennsylvania, oak forests dominated by white, black, and chestnut oak are common. These forests often have a dense layer of shrubs such as mountain laurel and black huckleberry. Before 1910, American chestnut was an important component of Pennsylvania's dry oak forests, but the accidental introduction of chestnut blight in New York City in 1904 resulted in chestnut's shift from widespread canopy dominant to minor status within just a few decades.

The Great Lakes beech-sugar maple forest is represented at the western end of the state. The mixed mesophytic forests, which reach their greatest development in the Smoky Mountains, just reach southern Pennsylvania. These forests contain tuliptree, sugar maple, beech, basswood, red oak, cucumber-tree, yellow buckeye, Ohio buckeye, white ash, and black cherry. Understory trees include flowering dogwood, pawpaw, umbrella-tree, redbud, and witch-hazel. The herbaceous layer is very rich and diverse.

In the southeastern corner of the state, in a narrow sliver of the Atlantic Coastal Plain physiographic province that parallels the Delaware River, coastal plain forests contain sweetgum, willow oak, southern red oak, and sweetbay magnolia. In the northeastern and northwestern corners of the state, in areas covered by ice during the most recent glaciation, peat deposits support forests with a northern character dominated by black spruce and tamarack.

Serpentinite rock, which occurs in a band of outcrops stretching across southern Delaware, Chester, and Lancaster counties, supports forests of pitch pine or Virginia pine, coupled with eastern red-cedar, scrub oak, blackjack oak, and sassafras. Shale barrens and limestone barrens of the Ridge and Valley physiographic province contain drought-tolerant species including eastern red-cedar, Virginia pine, Table Mountain pine, yellow oak, post oak, hackberry, and sumac. See Figure 3 for a map of the physiographic provinces of Pennsylvania.

Riparian areas throughout the state, where periodic flooding is a limiting factor, are characterized by sycamore, silver maple, box-elder, American elm, slippery elm, black willow, green ash, black ash, black walnut, and red maple. River birch is common along rivers and streams in the eastern part of the state but rare in the west. Swamp forests along Lake Erie are the only locations where pumpkin ash occurs.

Sixty-two distinct tree-dominated natural community types have been described for Pennsylvania.[11]

ALTERED FORESTS

Impact of Pests and Diseases

Pennsylvania's forests have also been profoundly affected by pests and diseases introduced from different parts of the world. The chestnut blight fungus, first discovered in New York City in 1904, swept through Pennsylvania, reducing what had previously been our most abundant tree to minor status. The gypsy moth, which spread into the state following its accidental release in eastern

Massachusetts in 1869, reduced the importance of oaks through preferential feeding on members of the genus *Quercus*. Beech bark disease, which appeared in Nova Scotia about 1920, is still spreading across the northern half of the state reducing beech to groves of young sapling-size root shoots. Dutch elm disease and dogwood anthracnose have taken their toll. The most recent invader, an insect known as the hemlock woolly adelgid, is killing our state tree, the Canadian hemlock, in southern and eastern parts of the state. Mild winters have allowed the adelgid to spread rapidly.

Recent outbreaks of native insects such as elm spanworm, forest tent caterpillar, eastern tent caterpillar, and cherry scallop-shell moth have caused extensive tree death in some parts of the state. Research is ongoing to understand the cause(s) of a widespread dieback of sugar maple centered in Pennsylvania. Soil nutrient changes caused by acid rain appear to be part of the problem.[12]

Too Many Deer

Overabundant deer are a serious threat to the health of forests throughout the state. Deer have consumed the lower layers of vegetation including tree seedlings and saplings, shrubs, and herbaceous species. Fencing to exclude deer is now a standard practice on state forest lands when timber is harvested; this is necessary to allow new trees to become established and grow beyond the browse line (the height deer can reach). However, short-term fencing does not allow forest shrubs or wildflowers, which never outgrow the reach of deer, to escape devastation.

Native Versus Introduced Species

Native species are defined as those that were here before the first Europeans arrived. One hundred and thirty-five species of trees are considered native to Pennsylvania. Many others have arrived subsequently through deliberate or accidental introductions from other parts of the world. The 64 non-native trees included in this book are species that have spread into our native forests or other natural habitats. Some of them such as Norway maple, tree-of-heaven, and empress-tree have seriously impacted remnant forests in urban and suburban areas. Others including Lavalle corktree, bee-bee tree, callery pear, and mimosa are just beginning to show invasive tendencies.

Some native species such as umbrella-tree and American holly are frequently cultivated and sometimes spread into nearby woodlands from cultivated sources, making a determination of their true status more difficult.

THE VALUE OF TREES

The ecological importance of forests and trees to the well-being of the state is enormous. Trees dominate the landscape and provide habitat structure for a multitude of other plants, animals, invertebrates, and microorganisms, thereby protecting biological diversity. Like other green plants they utilize carbon dioxide and produce oxygen and sugars. They protect the soil and facilitate ground water recharge by reducing runoff and erosion. The cooling effect from transpiration and shading add to our comfort. Trees are also beautiful and restful to look at, conveying a sense of pleasure and well-being.

Notes

1. Cuming, Fortescue. 1810. *Sketches of a Tour to the Western Country, Through the States of Ohio and Kentucky; a Voyage down the Ohio and Mississipps Rivers, and a Trip Through the Mississippi Territory and part of West Florida. Commenced at Philadelphia in the Winter of 1807, and concluded in 1809*, in Reuben Gold Thwaites (ed.), 1904. *Early Western Travels 1748–1846*, Vol. IV, A. H. Clark, Cleveland; reprinted AMS Press, New York, 1966.

2. Maxwell, Hu. 1910. The use and abuse of forests by the Virginia Indians. *William and Mary Quarterly* 19: 73–103.

3. Watts, W. A. 1979. Late quaternary vegetation of central Appalachia and the New Jersey coastal plain. *Ecol. Monog.* 49 (4): 427–469; Martin, Paul S. 1958. Taiga-tundra and the full glacial period in Chester County, Pennsylvania. *American Journal of Science* 256: 470–502.

4. Russell, E. W. B. 1983. Indian-set fires in the forests of northeastern United States. *Ecology* 64: 78–88; DeSelm, Hal R. 1986. Natural forest openings on uplands of the eastern United States. Pp. 366–375 in David L. Kulhavy and Richard N. Conner (eds.). *Wilderness and Natural Areas in the Eastern United States: A Management Challenge*, Stephen F. Austin State University, Nacogdoches; Abrams, Marc D. 1992. Fire and the development of oak forests—in eastern North America, oak distribution reflects a variety of ecological paths and disturbance regimes. *BioScience* 42: 346–53; Casselberry, Samuel E. and J. Evans. 1994. The influence of Native Americans on the land. Pp. 77–101 in David A. Zegers (ed.), *At the Crossroads: A Natural History of South-central Pennsylvania*. Millersville University, Millersville.

5. Denevan, William M. 1992. The pristine myth: the landscape of the Americas in 1492. *Annals of the American Association of Geographers* 82 (3): 369–85; Dobyns, Henry F. 1966. Estimating aboriginal population I. An appraisal of techniques with a new hemispheric estimate. *Current Anthropology* 7 (4): 395–416.

6. Anonymous. 1887. *History of Franklin County, Pennsylvania*. Warner, Beers and Company, Chicago; Losensky, Brownie John, III. 1961. The great plains of central Pennsylvania. Master's thesis, Department of Forest Management, Pennsylvania State University, University Park; Cook, Frederick. 1887. *Journals of the Military Expedition of Major General John Sullivan Against the Six Nations in 1779*. Facsimile reprint, 2000. Heritage Books, Bowie, Md.; Schoepf, Johan David. 1788. *Travels in the Confederation 1783–1784*. In 2 volumes, 1968 reprint of 1911 edition translated by Alfred J. Morrison. Burt Franklin, New York.

7. Maximillan, Prince of Wied. 1832–1834. *Travels in the Interior of North America*, in Reuben Gold Thwaites (ed.). 1906. *Early Western Travels 1748–1846*, Vols. 22–25, Arthur H. Clark, Cleveland.

8. DeCoster, Lester A. 1995. *The Legacy of Penn's Woods: A History of the Pennsylvania Bureau of Forestry*. Pennsylvania Historic and Museum Commission, Harrisburg.

9. Bining, Arthur Cecil. 1987. *Pennsylvania Iron Manufacture in the Eighteenth Century*. Pennsylvania Historic and Museum Commission, Harrisburg.

10. Kline, Benjamin F. G., Jr., Walter Castler, and Thomas T. Tabor III. 1970–1978. *The Logging Railroad Era of Lumbering in Pennsylvania: A History of the Lumber, Chemical, Wood, and Tanning Companies Which Used Railroads in Pennsylvania*. Lycoming Printers, Williamsport.

11. Fike, Jean. 1999. *Terrestrial and Palustrine Forest Communities of Pennsylvania*. Pennsylvania Department of Conservation and Natural Resources, Bureau of Forestry, Harrisburg.

12. Driscoll, Charles T., Gregory B. Lawrence, Arthur J. Bulger, Thomas J. Butler, Christopher A. Cronan, Christopher Eagar, Kathleen F. Lambert, Gene E. Likens, John L. Stoddard, and Kathleen C. Weathers. 2001. Acidic deposition in the Northeastern United States: sources and inputs, ecosystem effects, and management strategies. *BioScience* 51 (3): 180–198

Chapter 3. Descriptions of Native and Naturalized Trees of Pennsylvania

The 195 native and naturalized trees that grow wild in Pennsylvania are listed here alphabetically by common name. All oaks, maples, birches, and the like are listed together under the group name and then alphabetically by common name; for example, look under "O" for oaks then alphabetically for the species, black oak, red oak, willow oak. Cross-references are provided for trees with more than one common name. Black and white illustrations were prepared by Anna Aniśko from live material or pressed herbarium specimens; they were drawn to scale and are reproduced at one-half life size unless otherwise indicated.

SOURCES

Big Trees

We obtained information on record size trees from the Pennsylvania Forestry Association's 1993 register of big trees and the database now hosted by the Pennsylvania Bureau of Forestry, Valley Forge District and the following reference (diameter measurements refer to trunk diameter at 4½ feet from the ground unless otherwise specified):

Hobaugh, Maurice. 1993. *Big Trees of Pennsylvania*. Pennsylvania Forestry Association, Mechanicsburg.

Use

Information on uses of plants by Native Americans and others is included for historical interest only; it was gleaned from the following sources. We do not recommend any attempt to self-medicate using the plants or plant parts described here.

Densmore, Frances. 1974. *How Indians Use Wild Plants for Food, Medicine and Crafts*. Dover Publications. New York.
Erichsen-Brown, Charlotte. 1989. *Medicinal and Other Uses of North American Plants: A Historical Survey with Special Reference to the Eastern Indian Tribes*. Dover Publications, New York.
Michaux, F. Andrew. 1817. *The North American Sylva, or A Description of the Forest Trees of the United States, Canada, and Nova Scotia*, in 3 volumes. Thomas Dobson-Solomon Conrad, Philadelphia.
Moerman, Daniel E. 1998. *Native American Ethnobotany*. Timber Press, Portland, Ore.
Tantaquidgeon, Gladys. 1995. *Folk Medicine of the Delaware and Related Algonkian Indians*. Anthropological Series Number 3, Pennsylvania Historic and Museum Commission, Harrisburg.

Range

The Pennsylvania Flora Database was the source of distribution information within Pennsylvania. See Figure 4 for location of Pennsylvania counties. The database, a project of the Morris Arboretum of the University of Pennsylvania,

Figure 4. Counties of Pennsylvania.

contains records of all trees and other plants that grow naturally in the state. It is based on herbarium specimens deposited in museum collections. The database and other information about the Pennsylvania Flora Project can be accessed on the internet at http://www.paflora.org or through the following books:

Rhoads, Ann Fowler and William McKinley Klein, Jr. 1993. *The Vascular Flora of Pennsylvania: Annotated Checklist and Atlas.* American Philosophical Society, Philadelphia.

Rhoads, Ann Fowler and Timothy A. Block. 2000. *The Plants of Pennsylvania: An Illustrated Manual.* University of Pennsylvania Press, Philadelphia.

Ranges beyond Pennsylvania were adapted from the following sources:

Fowells, H. A. 1965. *Silvics of Forest Trees of the United States.* Agriculture Handbook No. 271, United States Department of Agriculture, Forest Service, Washington, D.C.

Hough, Mary Y. 1983. *New Jersey Wild Plants.* Harmony Press, Harmony, N.J.

Magee, Dennis W. and Harry E. Ahles. 1999. *The Flora of the Northeast.* University of Massachusetts Press, Amherst.

Wildlife

Information on the use of trees by butterflies, moths, birds, and other wildlife was obtained from the following sources:

Allen, Thomas J. 1997. *The Butterflies of West Virginia and Their Caterpillars.* University of Pittsburgh Press, Pittsburgh.

Covell, Charles V. 1984. *Eastern Moths*. Peterson Field Guide Series, Houghton Mifflin, Boston.

McWilliams, Gerald M., and Daniel W. Brauning. 2000. *The Birds of Pennsylvania*. Cornell University Press, Ithaca, N.Y.

Merritt, Joseph F. 1987. *Guide to the Mammals of Pennsylvania*. University of Pittsburgh Press, Pittsburgh.

Scott, James A. 1997. *The Butterflies of North America*. Stanford University Press, Stanford, Calif.

Endangered, Threatened, and Rare Species

The official list of endangered, threatened, and rare plants for Pennsylvania is contained in the following reference:

Department of Conservation and Natural Resources. 1987. Pennsylvania Code, Title 17, Chapter 45. Conservation of Pennsylvania native wild plants. Pennsylvania Bulletin 17 (49). December 5, 1987. Harrisburg, Pennsylvania.

It can also be found on the World Wide Web at http://www.dcnr.state.pa.us/forestry/pndi/fullplants.asp

Other Useful References

Elias, Thomas S. 1980. *The Complete Trees of North America*. Van Nostrand Reinhold, New York.

Fike, Jean. 1999. *Terrestrial and Palustrine Plant Communities of Pennsylvania*. Pennsylvania Department of Conservation and Natural Resources, Harrisburg.

Flora of North America Editorial Committee. 1993. *Flora of North America*. Vol. 2. *Pteridophytes and Gymnosperms*. Oxford University Press, New York.

Flora of North America Editorial Committee. 1997. *Flora of North America*. Vol. 3. *Magnoliophyta: Magnolidae and Hamamelidae*. Oxford University Press, New York.

Furlow, John J. 1990. The genera of Betulaceae in the southeastern United States. *Journal of the Arnold Arboretum* 70 (5): 1-67.

Gleason, Henry A. and Arthur Cronquist. 1991. *Manual of the Vascular Plants of Northeastern United States and Adjacent Canada*. 2nd ed. New York Botanical Garden, Bronx.

Illick, Joseph S. 1923. *Pennsylvania Trees*. Bulletin 11. Pennsylvania Department of Forestry, Harrisburg.

Janzen, Daniel H. and Paul S. Martin. 1982. Neotropical anachronisms: The fruits the gomphotheres ate. *Science* 215: 19-27.

Johnson, Warren T. and Howard H. Lyon. 1991. *Insects That Feed on Trees and Shrubs*. Cornell University Press, Ithaca, N.Y.

Leopold, Donald J., William C. McComb, and Robert N. Muller. 1998. *Trees of the Central Hardwood Forests of North America*. Timber Press, Portland, Ore.

Marshall, Humphrey 1967. *Arbustum Americanum: The American Grove*. Facsimile of the edition of 1785. Hafner Publishing Company, New York.

Sinclair, Wayne A., Howard H. Lyon, and Warren T. Johnson. 1987. *Diseases of Trees and Shrubs*. Cornell University Press, Ithaca, N.Y.

Tutin, T. G., N. A. Burges, A. O. Chater, J. R. Edmondson, V. H. Heywood, D. M. Moore, D. H. Valentine, S. M. Walters, and D. A. Webb. 1993. *Flora Europaea*. Vol. 1. 2nd ed. Cambridge University Press, New York.

ALDER
ALNUS MILL.
Birch Family—Betulaceae

The alders are large multistemmed shrubs or small trees. Primarily plants of wet habitats, they occur on stream and lake shores and in other low areas where they often form dense thickets. Because alders are host to nitrogen-fixing nodules on their roots, they are important in the early stages of woody plant succession, serving to enrich the soil and setting the stage for later colonization by other species.

Alders are one of the first native plants to bloom. In the early spring the male catkins, which are visible in the bud stage all winter, elongate and shed large amounts of pollen. Female flowers are in smaller, erect catkins that mature into small pine cone-like structures in which the small, winged fruits are produced. The fruiting catkins persist long after the seeds are gone and are a distinctive feature that makes alders easy to recognize year-round.

The Pennsylvania flora include 3 native alders, one of which is more shrub-like and is not included here (mountain alder—*Alnus viridis* var. *crispa*), and one European species that is planted and occasionally naturalized.

Native Americans found many uses for alders, and early settlers brought knowledge of the properties of the European species with them. The durable wood was used for posts, pilings, and early water pipes. Black, brown, yellow, and red dyes were prepared from the outer and inner bark or the catkins for use in dying leather, quills, bark, and cloth. The leaves were used to treat wounds, swellings, fevers, and many other maladies.

Alder pollen can be a significant cause of pollen allergies. Alders are one of the favorite foods of beaver, and a larval food source for the tiger swallowtail, red-spotted purple, white admiral, mourning cloak, and green comma butterflies.

Black alder, European alder   *Alnus glutinosa* **(L.) Gaertn.**

FORM: deciduous tree to 60 feet, usually with a narrowly erect crown, a single trunk, and numerous horizontal branches

BARK: dark brown and fissured

TWIGS: young leaves, twigs, and catkins resinous and sticky

PITH: 3-angled

BUDS: stalked, resin-coated; winter buds of male catkins cylindrical and conspicuous

LEAVES: alternate, 2–4 inches long, broadly rounded or slightly notched at the end, resin-coated; margins toothed

FALL LEAF COLOR: brown

STIPULES: present when the leaves first emerge, but soon falling

LEAF SCARS: nearly rounded with 3 bundle scars

FLOWERS: unisexual (plants monoecious); staminate flowers in drooping catkins; pistillate flowers in smaller erect catkins; blooming very early in the spring before the leaves emerge; wind-pollinated

Black alder—leaf

Black alder—dormant twig

Black alder—bark

FRUIT: pistillate catkins mature into woody, cone-like structures containing numerous small 1-seeded, winged fruits

SEEDS: dispersed by wind, and possibly water

WOOD: harvested for timber in Europe

CURRENT CHAMPION: Berks County, diameter 2 feet 3 inches, height 94 feet, spread 33 feet

Native to Europe and North Africa, this small tree is frequently planted in reforestation or conservation plantings and has naturalized at scattered locations.

Smooth alder   *Alnus serrulata* (Aiton) Willd.

FORM: usually a large, multistemmed shrub, but occasionally a small tree to 20 feet

BARK: light gray and smooth with small lenticels

TWIGS: slender, smooth, brownish, covered with pale hairs

PITH: greenish-brown, 3-angled

BUDS: stalked, reddish with a rounded tip and 2 bud scales that just meet at the edges, resin-coated; flower buds visible over the winter; terminal bud not present

LEAVES: alternate, 2–4½ inches long, oval, resinous when young; margins finely single-toothed

FALL LEAF COLOR: reddish-brown

STIPULES: present when the leaves first emerge, but soon falling

LEAF SCARS: raised, triangular to half-round with 3 bundle scars

FLOWERS: as for other alders, see above

Smooth alder—leaf

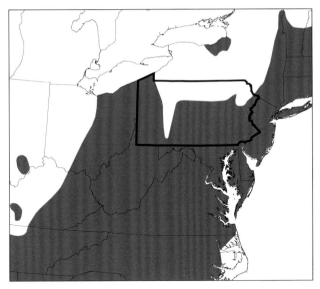

Smooth alder

Smooth alder—bark

FRUIT: small, narrowly winged samaras that are produced in woody, cone-like structures each about ½ inch long, and held in an erect position in clusters of 3–6, persisting into the winter

SEEDS: wind-dispersed

WOOD: too small to be useful

CURRENT CHAMPION: none recorded

Smooth alder is a plant of wet soils; it is the common alder of the southern two-thirds of the state where it grows in bogs and swamps, along streams, and on lake shores. Its total range extends along the Atlantic and gulf coasts from Nova Scotia and southern Quebec south to Florida, Texas and inland to southern Illinois.

Speckled alder   **Alnus incana (L.)**
Moench ssp. rugosa (Du Roi) Clausen

FORM: usually a large, multistemmed shrub, but occasionally a small tree to 30 feet

BARK: smooth, reddish-brown with conspicuous horizontal lenticels

TWIGS: slender, reddish-brown

PITH: triangular in cross section

BUDS: stalked, dark reddish-brown with 2–3 bud scales

LEAVES: alternate, oval, 2–4 inches long with 8–14 veins on each side of the midrib; upper surface veiny and wrinkled in appearance; margins double-toothed

FALL LEAF COLOR: brown

STIPULES: present when the leaves first emerge, but soon falling

LEAF SCARS: nearly round, with 3 bundle scars

FLOWERS: as for other alders, see above

FRUIT: fruiting catkins about ½ inch long, directed downward, and persisting through the winter, samaras narrowly winged

Smooth alder—leaf

Speckled alder—bark

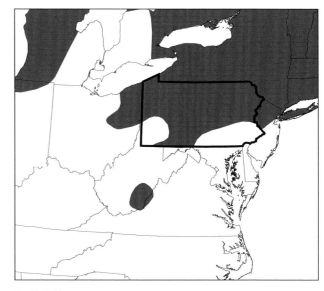

Speckled alder

SEEDS: wind-dispersed
WOOD: too small to be useful
CURRENT CHAMPION: none recorded

Speckled alder has a somewhat more northern distribution than smooth alder, although their ranges overlap across central Pennsylvania. In Pennsylvania it is common in the northern half of the state and at higher elevations along the Allegheny Front. Its total range extends from West Virginia to Wisconsin and north to Labrador and Saskatchewan.

Speckled alder—old and new female catkins

APPLE
MALUS MILL.
Rose Family—Rosaceae

Apple   *Malus pumila* **Mill.**

FORM: medium-sized tree to 40 feet with a trunk
that divides into several major limbs;
crown broad and rounded

BARK: dark grayish-brown and flaky

TWIGS: stout, densely hairy and reddish-
brown at first becoming grayish-brown and
smooth, flowers and fruit borne on short lateral
shoots

PITH: greenish-white, continuous

BUDS: terminal bud ⅛–¼ inch long, blunt and
hairy, lateral buds smaller

LEAVES: simple, alternate, 1½–4 inches long with a short
pointed tip, hairy on the lower surface; edge sharply toothed
to nearly smooth

FALL LEAF COLOR: yellow

Apple—flowers

STIPULES: falling early and leaving a short, narrow scar on each
side of the leaf base

LEAF SCARS: crescent-shaped, raised, containing 3 bundle scars

FLOWERS: in small clusters on short lateral spur branches, each flower
1–3 inches across with a hairy stalk, 5 spreading white to light pink
petals, 5 sepals, numerous stamens, and 5 styles and stigmas, pollinated by bees

FRUIT: 3–4 inches in diameter, green, yellow, or red with firm, juicy flesh, sepals
persisting on the end opposite the stem

SEEDS: brown, slightly flattened, about ⅛ inch long, disseminated by mammals
that consume the fruits

WOOD: hard, strong, and close-grained; used mainly as firewood

CURRENT CHAMPION: Bradford County, diameter 3 feet 8 inches at 3½ feet,
height 31 feet, spread 58 feet

Originally native to the mountains of Kazakhstan in Central Asia, apples have
been in cultivation since Roman times or earlier. They were carried to Europe
and from there accompanied the colonists to North America. Here their widespread distribution was aided by the famed Johnny Appleseed (John Chapman,
1774–1845), who spread apple seeds and seedlings throughout the east and Midwest. Cider, primarily in its "hard" or fermented form, was a very popular beverage in the colonies.

Apples are an important commercial fruit crop. Thousands of varieties have
been developed over the years with varied fruit shape, color, flavor, season of
ripening, and resistance to pests and diseases. Some "old-fashioned" varieties,
not now in commercial production, may persist as semiwild trees at abandoned
farm or home sites. Apple wood is hard, strong, and close-grained; however, its
main use is as firewood as it burns cleanly and produces an even, hot flame.

Apple—bark

Early settlers made vast quantities of cider and apple butter and also dried apples for winter use. The inner bark of apple trees yielded a yellow or gold dye for wool. Wild apples also provide food for birds, deer, bear, and other wildlife. Caterpillars of the promethea moth, cecropia moth, and several sphinx moths feed on the leaves. Apple leaves are also a larval food source for tiger swallowtail, viceroy, red-spotted purple, white admiral, striped hairstreak, banded hairstreak, gray hairstreak, brown elfin, and spring azure butterflies.

ARALIA
ARALIA L.
Ginseng Family—Araliaceae

These small, understory trees with huge compound leaves and late summer flowers and fruits have a form that is unlike any other plant in our flora. Confusion has arisen in the past, however, in distinguishing the native Hercules'-club, *A. spinosa*, from the Japanese angelica-tree, *A. elata*, a very similar naturalized species that is becoming increasingly common in eastern Pennsylvania. The two are most easily distinguished when in flower or fruit. The inflorescence of the native Hercules'-club has an erect central stem from which branches arise. In Japanese angelica-tree, the branches of the inflorescence radiate from the base of the inflorescence with only a very short central axis or none at all. In addition, the veins of the leaflets generally continue into the marginal teeth in Japanese angelica-tree but not in the native Hercules'-club, although this characteristic is not always consistent. Further confusion has arisen in the past because Japanese angelica-tree was mistakenly referred to as *A. chinense*.

Hercules'-club   *Aralia spinosa* L.

FORM: small, prickly, deciduous tree to 30 feet tall, unbranched when young and developing an open crown with leaves and flowers clustered at the ends of the stems

BARK: gray-brown and smooth when young, becoming ridged in age with scattered prickles

TWIGS: stout and prickly

PITH: large, white

Hercules'-club—bark

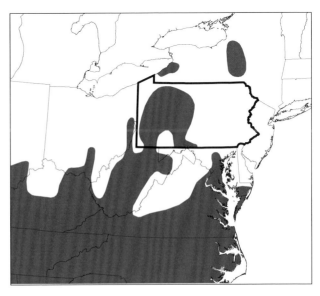

Hercules'-club

Hercules'-club—inflorescence x1/8

Hercules'-club—leaflet

BUDS: terminal bud conical, ½–¾ inch long, lateral buds smaller

LEAVES: alternate, very large, to 3–4 feet long, 2 or 3 times compound with numerous, pinnately arranged leaflets; the leaf stalks often bearing prickles

FALL LEAF COLOR: yellow tinged with red

STIPULES: not present

LEAF SCARS: broadly V-shaped, nearly encircling the twig, containing about 12 bundle scars in a curved line

FLOWERS: many, greenish-white, in a highly branched, 1- to 2-foot-long cluster at the tip of the stem or branches, insect-pollinated

FRUIT: a juicy, black berry about ¼ inch long

SEEDS: dispersed by birds and small mammals

WOOD: soft and brittle

CURRENT CHAMPION: Warren County, diameter 2 feet, height 38 feet, spread 24 feet

The native Hercules'-club is found mostly in the west-central part of the state. It is an understory tree, growing in rich, moist bottomland forests under a canopy of sugar maple, yellow birch, hemlock, and white pine. Central Pennsylvania is near the northern limit for this species, which extends to Florida, Arkansas, and eastern Texas.

Native American tribes used preparations of Hercules'-club to treat rheumatism, sore eyes, boils, and sores. The inner bark, or alternatively a tincture of berries was employed in the treatment of toothaches. Several cultural groups used an infusion of the roasted and pounded roots as a diaphoretic or emetic.

Birds and small mammals eat the fruits and disperse the seeds. In addition, the plants spread by underground runners often forming dense colonies of upright prickly stems in the forest understory.

Japanese angelica-tree   *Aralia elata* Seem.

This tree is very similar to the native Hercules'-club; see above for distinguishing characteristics. In southeastern Pennsylvania, Japanese angelica-tree began to invade the forests of Philadelphia's Fairmount Park in the early 1900s. For many years it was mistakenly identified as the native Hercules'-club, the only species mentioned in regional plant identification manuals.

In recent years Japanese angelica-tree has appeared with increasing frequency in suburban forest patches in the counties surrounding Philadelphia. It is native to China, Japan, and Korea where it grows in habitats such as forest edges, hillsides, ravines, and thickets. It has been in cultivation since 1830.

Japanese angelica-tree—leaflet

Japanese angelica-tree—bark

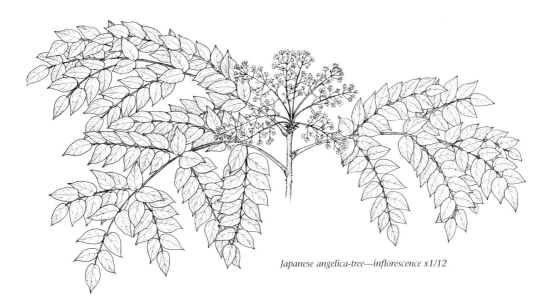

Japanese angelica-tree—inflorescence x1/12

ARBOR-VITAE
Thuja L.
Cypress Family—Cupressaceae

Arbor-vitae, northern white-cedar   ***Thuja occidentalis* L.**

FORM: narrowly columnar, evergreen, to 60 feet tall

BARK: reddish-brown or gray-brown, separating in long, narrow fibrous strips

TWIGS: covered with small, tightly clasping leaves, clusters of branchlets forming strongly flattened sprays

BUDS: buds of the next year's cones are visible on the tips of twigs in winter, otherwise the buds are hidden beneath the clasping leaves

LEAVES: yellowish-green, tiny, scale-like, in pairs clasping the twigs tightly

LEAF SCARS: inconspicuous

CONES: ⅓–½ inch long, oblong with 4 pairs of overlapping cone scales, each at right angles to the last; maturing in a single year

SEEDS: ⅛ inch, with 2 equal wings, wind-dispersed

WOOD: yellowish-brown, rot-resistant

CURRENT CHAMPION: Monroe County, diameter 3 feet 4 inches, height 57 feet, spread 41 feet

Arbor-vitae—cone x2

Although arbor-vitae occurs naturally in New York and Ohio, there is no record of native stands in Pennsylvania, but it has naturalized in a few locations. It is primarily a tree of more northern areas from Nova Scotia to Minnesota and south in the mountains to North Carolina, frequently growing in calcareous swamps and on limestone cliffs. On the Niagara escarpment in New York State, gnarled and dwarfed arbor-vitae up to 700 years old cling to the cliff face.

Because it is light and easily worked, the wood of arbor-vitae was used by Native Americans to make frames for birch bark canoes. The wood has also been used for roof shingles because of its resistance to rot. In 1535–1536, when the French explorer Jacques Cartier explored the St. Lawrence River in what is now Canada, he learned from the natives that the sap of arbor-vitae was an effective cure for scurvy, a common scourge of sailors in those days. Other medicinal uses have included treatment of dysentery and externally, in poultices to alleviate extreme pain.

Arbor-vitae— branchlets x1

Arbor-vitae—bark

Arbor-vitae was one of the few North American trees to have been grown in Europe before 1600 and may in fact have been the first such export. Today it is widely used as a landscape ornamental; dozens of named cultivars have been produced ranging from small globe-shaped shrubs to narrow, erect trees. Deer browse it heavily, especially in the winter. Red squirrels, crossbills, pine siskins, and some game birds eat the seeds.

ASH

FRAXINUS L.
Olive Family—Oleaceae

The ashes are large deciduous trees with stout twigs that usually occur in pairs at the nodes. The leaves are opposite and compound with 5–9 pinnately arranged leaflets, stipules are not produced. A true terminal bud is present.

Ash trees bloom in the early spring before the leaves have emerged; they are wind-pollinated. The flowers are unisexual; all species are dioecious, with the male and female flowers produced on separate trees. The male flowers each consist of 2–4 stamens and a small, 4-lobed calyx; they are densely clustered in a compact panicle. Female flowers, which are produced in a more open cluster, each have a small calyx at the base and single ovary with 2 stigma branches. Petals are absent. The winged fruits (samaras) mature in the fall and are wind-dispersed. The female flowers of several ash species are sometimes affected by a mite (*Eriophyes fraxinivorus*), which prevents seed formation and results in the deformed (galled) flower clusters that remain on the trees through the winter.

Ash seeds are eaten by woodducks, quail, turkey, songbirds, squirrels, and other rodents. Caterpillars of sphinx, cecropia, promethea, and polyphemus moths and tiger swallowtail, striped hairstreak, hickory hairstreak, and banded hairstreak butterflies feed on the leaves.

In addition to the species described below, blue ash (*Fraxinus quadrangulata* Michx.), has recently been reported from southwestern Pennsylvania. If confirmed, this would be the easternmost location for the species, which ranges from Ontario and Michigan to Georgia and Oklahoma.

Black ash   *Fraxinus nigra* **Marshall**

FORM: tree to 75 feet with upright branches and a narrow crown
BARK: grayish, scaly, and irregularly fissured
TWIGS: stout, hairy at first but becoming smooth
PITH: homogeneous
BUDS: opposite, black, terminal bud pointed, lateral buds blunt
LEAVES: 10–16 inches long with 9–11 sessile leaflets
FALL LEAF COLOR: brown
STIPULES: none
LEAF SCARS: crescent-shaped; bundle scars numerous, forming a curved line
FLOWERS: calyx soon falling, otherwise as described for the genus, see above
FRUIT: 1–1½ inches long, the wing extending to the base and notched at the apex
SEEDS: wind-dispersed
WOOD: soft and coarse-grained
CURRENT CHAMPION: Lancaster County, diameter 2 feet 3 inches, height 108 feet, spread 57 feet

Black ash—dormant twig

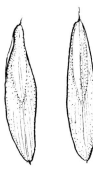

Black ash—fruit x1

Black ash—bark

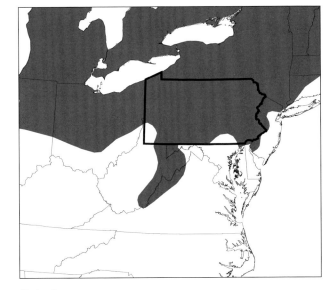

Black ash

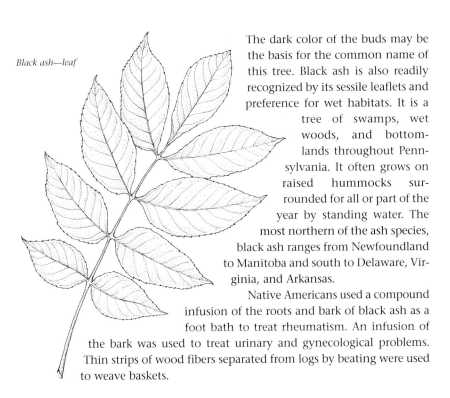

Black ash—leaf

The dark color of the buds may be the basis for the common name of this tree. Black ash is also readily recognized by its sessile leaflets and preference for wet habitats. It is a tree of swamps, wet woods, and bottomlands throughout Pennsylvania. It often grows on raised hummocks surrounded for all or part of the year by standing water. The most northern of the ash species, black ash ranges from Newfoundland to Manitoba and south to Delaware, Virginia, and Arkansas.

Native Americans used a compound infusion of the roots and bark of black ash as a foot bath to treat rheumatism. An infusion of the bark was used to treat urinary and gynecological problems. Thin strips of wood fibers separated from logs by beating were used to weave baskets.

Green ash, red ash   *Fraxinus pensylvanica* **Marshall**

FORM: tree to 75 feet with upright branches and a somewhat irregular crown
BARK: gray-brown, fissured
TWIGS: velvety or sometimes nearly smooth, gray-brown with lighter lenticels
PITH: white, solid

Green ash—bark

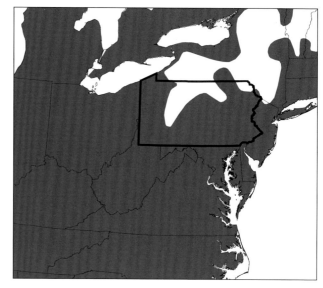

Green ash

BUDS: dark brown, hairy, terminal bud with a sharp point, lateral buds more rounded

LEAVES: 6–10 inches long with 5–9 sessile leaflets, bright green above, paler beneath, hairy to nearly smooth, tapered to a sharp tip and winged stalk, margins of the leaflets toothed or sometimes smooth below the middle

FALL LEAF COLOR: yellow grading to purple

STIPULES: none

LEAF SCARS: semicircular, straight to only slightly concave on the upper side, bundle scars numerous in a curved line

FLOWERS: as described above

FRUIT: 1–1½ inches long and winged to the middle of the seed, maturing in the fall

SEEDS: wind-dispersed

Green ash—leaf x1/4

Green ash—fruit x1

WOOD: heavy, hard, light brown, often sold as white ash

CURRENT CHAMPION: Lebanon County, diameter 6 feet 2 inches, height 88 feet, spread 90 feet

Green ash is found in alluvial woods, lowlands, stream banks, and moist fields throughout Pennsylvania. Its total range extends from New Brunswick and Manitoba and south to the Dakotas, Oklahoma, eastern Texas, and Florida.

Native Americans used an infusion of the inner bark as a tonic to treat depression and fatigue. The cambium layer was scraped from the inner bark, cooked, and eaten. Green ash lumber is marketed as white ash, which it closely resembles.

Pumpkin ash   *Fraxinus profunda* (Bush) Bush

FORM: tree to 100 feet with a narrow crown

BARK: thick, light gray, divided into broad flat or rounded scaly ridges

TWIGS: densely hairy early in the season but becoming smooth by late summer or fall

PITH: homogeneous

BUDS: blunt-tipped, light reddish-brown and hairy

LEAVES: 8–16 inches long with 7–9 leaflets; leaf stalks and under surfaces of leaflets densely hairy

FALL LEAF COLOR: yellowish-purple

STIPULES: none

LEAF SCARS: slightly raised and nearly encircling the buds

FLOWERS: as described above, stalks hairy

FRUIT: 1½–2¾ inches long, winged to the middle of the seed or beyond

SEEDS: wind-dispersed

WOOD: brown, hard, and heavy

CURRENT CHAMPION: Erie County, diameter 11 inches, height 73 feet, spread 24 feet

Pumpkin ash is a very rare tree in Pennsylvania, known only from shallow woodland ponds and wet forested flats in Erie, Crawford, and Warren Counties where it is at its northern limit of range. Only discovered to be present in the state as recently as 1992, it is classified as endangered by the Pennsylvania Natural Heritage Program. This species is primarily a tree of the southeastern Coastal Plain from North Carolina to Florida, and the Mississippi and Ohio River valleys.

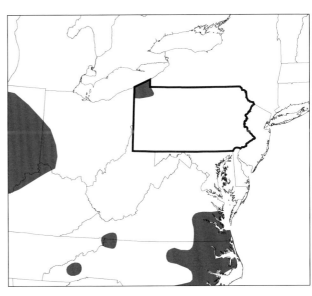

Pumpkin ash—leaf x1/4

Pumpkin ash—bark

Pumpkin ash

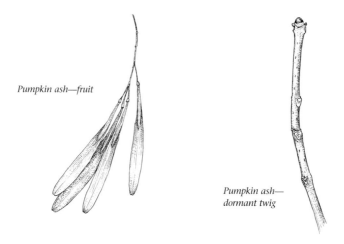

Pumpkin ash—fruit

Pumpkin ash—
dormant twig

White ash   *Fraxinus americana* L.

FORM: tree to 115 feet with upright to spreading branches and a rounded crown
BARK: grayish-brown with a regular pattern of ridges and fissures
TWIGS: stout, grayish-brown with lighter lenticels, smooth, often with a waxy coating
PITH: white, solid
BUDS: opposite, dark brown to almost black, blunt-tipped
LEAVES: 8–12 inches long with 5–9 stalked leaflets, dark green above and whitish beneath, smooth except for a few hairs along the midrib; margins slightly toothed or entire
FALL LEAF COLOR: yellow to a rich bronzy purple
STIPULES: none
LEAF SCARS: concave on the upper side, bundle scars numerous forming a curved line
FLOWERS: as for the genus, see description above
FRUIT: 1¼–2 inches long with the wing extending ⅓ the length of the seed
SEEDS: wind-dispersed
WOOD: white to light brown, strong, and hard, very desirable
CURRENT CHAMPION: Montgomery County, diameter 7 feet 1 inch, height 107 feet, spread 85 feet

White ash is common throughout Pennsylvania in forests, hedgerows, and old fields. Although it rarely forms a pure stand, as a pioneer invader in old fields white ash can be quite dense. In a forest setting it is usually mixed with other hardwoods. Excessive browsing by overabundant deer has reduced its prevalence in some areas of the state. White ash ranges from Nova Scotia and Minnesota south to Florida and Texas.

Native Americans had various medicinal uses for white ash, many of which were also taken up by European settlers. Decoctions of the bark were used as a cathartic or emetic. Branch sap was used to treat earache and a decoction of the roots was used as a poultice to treat snakebite. The seeds were thought to prevent obesity. The wood was used to make snowshoes, splints for basketry, and

White ash—bark

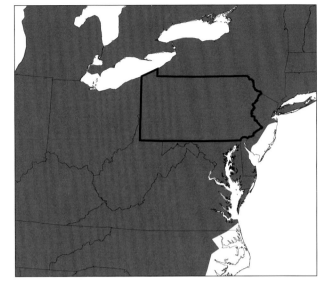

White ash

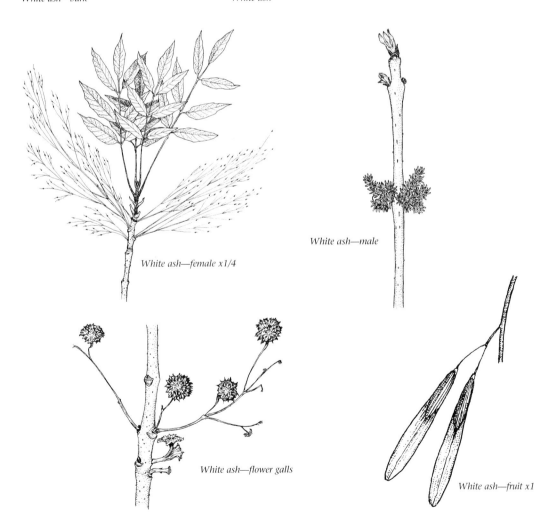

White ash—female x1/4

White ash—male

White ash—flower galls

White ash—fruit x1

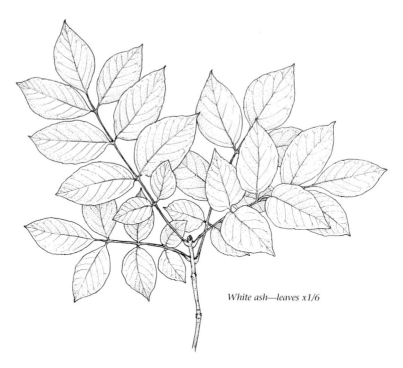

White ash—leaves x1/6

canoe frames. White ash wood remains valuable for tool handles, furniture, and interior finishing. It is also the preferred wood for baseball bats and other sports equipment such as tennis rackets, hockey sticks, and oars due to its combination of strength and light weight.

ASPEN—SEE POPLAR

BASSWOOD
TILIA L.
Linden Family—Tiliaceae

American basswood, American linden   *Tilia americana* L.

FORM: deciduous tree to 60–70 feet, or occasionally taller, with a rounded crown

BARK: dark gray, smooth when young, becoming ridged or furrowed on older trees

TWIGS: smooth, gray

PITH: white, homogeneous

BUDS: red, smooth with 3 rounded bud scales; a true terminal bud is not present

LEAVES: alternate, simple, 4–6 inches long, unequally heart-shaped at the base; edges toothed

FALL LEAF COLOR: yellow to brown

STIPULES: present but not persistent

LEAF SCARS: triangular with rounded corners, bundle scars few to many

FLOWERS: white, fragrant, in a small, drooping cluster attached to a strap-shaped bract, perfect, regular with 5 petals and 5 sepals; blooming in June after the leaves have expanded, insect-pollinated

FRUIT: a hard, fuzzy, gray nutlet about ¼–½ inch long maturing in the fall

SEEDS: 2 per nutlet, dispersed by small mammals

WOOD: light and soft, but tough, ideal for carving, white to light brown

CURRENT CHAMPION: Montgomery County, diameter 7 feet 9 inches, height 94 feet, spread 100 feet

A basswood tree in full flower is quite a spectacle, buzzing with honeybees gathering the abundant nectar from which a very desirable honey is produced. Basswood is a tree of mixed, mainly deciduous, forests often occurring on stream banks and in other most, rich sites. Sugar maple, elm, ash, and white oak are frequent associated species. In other locations it grows on forested lower slopes with birch, hemlock, and white pine.

Basswood flowers

Basswood—bark

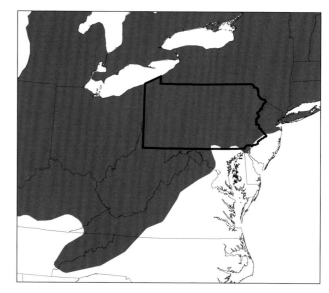

Basswood

Two varieties of basswood occur in Pennsylvania. *Tilia americana* var. *americana* has leaves that are green beneath with tufts of hairs in the vein axils; it extends from southern Canada to North Carolina and Arkansas and is found throughout Pennsylvania. *Tilia americana* var. *heterophylla*, which has leaf undersides permanently covered with fine white hairs, is primarily a tree of the southern Appalachian Mountains, and is found mainly in the southwestern corner of the state.

Basswood trees are noted for their ability to sprout prolifically from the base of the trunk; leaves on the basal shoots may be extremely large.

The tough, fibrous inner bark of basswood, known as bast, was used by Native Americans to make rope and nets. Ceremonial masks were carved from curved sections of sapwood. Today the light, soft wood of basswood is used for interior finishing, cabinetry, woodenware, toys, paper pulp, and boxes.

Quail and small mammals such as squirrels and chipmunks eat the seeds of basswood. Deer and rabbits browse the foliage. The leaves also provide food for the larvae of tiger swallowtail, red-spotted purple, white admiral, mourning cloak, and white-M hairstreak butterflies and several sphinx moths. Basswood is sometimes planted as a shade tree, but several European species including silver linden (*T. petiolaris*) and little-leaf linden (*T. cordata*) are more often used.

Basswood—fruit

BEE-BEE TREE
TETRADIUM LOUR.
Rue Family—Rutaceae

Bee-bee tree   *Tetradium daniellii* (Benn) T. G. Hartley

FORM: deciduous tree to 60 feet with spreading branches

BARK: smooth and gray with raised lenticels

TWIGS: gray-brown with prominent lenticels

PITH: white, continuous

BUDS: lateral buds small, pointed, with 1 pair of small bud scales; terminal bud rusty brown, lacking bud scales (naked)

LEAVES: opposite, 9–15 inches long, pinnately compound with 7–11 leaflets, dark green and smooth above, hairy on the veins beneath

FALL LEAF COLOR: green or yellowish-green

STIPULES: none

LEAF SCARS: broadly crescent-shaped with 3 bundle scars

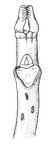

*Bee-bee tree—
dormant twig*

Bee-bee tree—fruits

Bee-bee tree—flowers x1/4

Bee-bee tree—flower x5

FLOWERS: small, white, borne in 6-inch-wide clusters in midsummer
FRUIT: a reddish cluster of 3–5 only slightly united capsule segments each of which splits open to reveal 2 black seeds
SEEDS: shiny black
WOOD: weak and splitting readily
CURRENT CHAMPION: Bucks County, diameter 2 feet, height 40 feet, spread 50 feet

The common name of this tree refers to the nectar-rich flowers, which attract numerous honeybees when they bloom in midsummer. The bee-bee tree is native to northern China and Korea. In cultivation here since 1905, it is grown mainly by beekeepers and has begun to show up as a naturalized species along roadsides and in urban and suburban forest remnants. This tree is perhaps better known by the name *Euodia daniellii* (Benn.) Hemsl. In addition, *Euodia hupehensis* Dode, at one time considered to be a separate species, is now included under the name *Tetradium danielii*.

The bee-bee tree is very similar to corktree (*Phellodendron* spp.), another non-native genus in the Rue Family. The easiest way to distinguish the two genera if neither flowers nor fruit are present, is by the buds. The base of the leaf stalk covers the lateral buds of corktree while those of the bee-bee tree are exposed. In addition corktree lacks a terminal bud whereas the bee-bee tree has a prominent naked terminal bud.

Bee-bee tree—bark

BEECH
Fagus L.
Beech Family—Fagaceae

American beech   *Fagus grandifolia* **Ehrhart**

FORM: upright tree to 60–90 feet; in the open, beech has numerous spreading branches all the way to the ground; in a forest setting, branches are limited to the upper portion of the trunk

BARK: smooth, light gray

TWIGS: slender, yellow-brown to gray

PITH: pale green

BUDS: slender, ½–¾ inch long and pointed with numerous overlapping bud scales

LEAVES: simple, alternate, 2½–5 inches long, toothed but not lobed; lateral veins unbranched and ending in a tooth

FALL LEAF COLOR: yellow to brown

STIPULES: none

LEAF SCARS: raised, crescent-shaped to elliptical, bundle scars numerous, clustered in the center

FLOWERS: unisexual; male flowers in loose, dangling, spherical heads, each flower with 6–16 stamens; female flowers in 2-flowered clusters in the axils of new leaves, each flower with distinct sepals and 3 separate ovaries; wind-pollinated

FRUITS: a pair of 3-angled nuts enclosed in a prickly husk that splits into 4 segments at maturity

SEEDS: gathered and stored by small mammals

WOOD: light in color, hard and strong

American beech—leaf

American beech   bark

American beech

American beech—
dormant twig

American beech—
fruit x1

CURRENT CHAMPION: Montgomery County, diameter 6 feet 8 inches, height 87 feet, spread 115 feet

Beech occurs throughout the state as a component of mature hardwood forests. It does best on moist soils of valley bottoms and lower slopes. Beech often grows clonally in the forest, forming patches of genetically identical trees through the formation of root sprouts. It is a tree of late successional forest communities, in part due to its ability to reproduce in dense shade. Young trees are conspicuous in the winter woods due to their tendency to retain their straw-colored leaves through the winter.

Beech bark disease, which is caused by an insect known as beech scale (*Cryptococcus fagisuga*) and a native fungus (*Nectria coccinea* var. *faginata*), has killed many native beech in northern Pennsylvania and reduced some stands to dense thickets of sapling-size root sprouts. The scale arrived in North America at Halifax, Nova Scotia, sometime prior to 1890, on imported nursery stock of European beech. The scale has now spread as far south as the Philadelphia area. Beech grows from Nova Scotia west to Wisconsin and south to eastern Texas and northern Florida.

Beech trees are nearly always accompanied by beech drops (*Epifagus virginiana*), a small purplish or yellowish, nonphotosynthetic flowering plant that parasitizes the trees' roots. Beech drops can be seen on the forest floor year round, wherever beech trees grow. In addition an eriophyid mite (*Acalitus fagerinea*) frequently causes the formation of yellowish, felt-like galls on the surface of the leaves.

Native Americans gathered beech nuts for food and extracted oil from them that was prized for cooking. They also used beech medicinally to treat frostbite, worms, consumption, burns, and heart problems. The wood, which is light-colored, hard, and strong, is used for railroad ties, fuel, crates, boxes, and veneer.

Early settlers turned their hogs loose to forage for beech nuts in the forest. The nuts are also an important component of mast, supplying food for bear, raccoon, deer, porcupine, wild turkey, grouse, and many other forms of wildlife including the now extinct passenger pigeon. Beech nuts (and hazel nuts) constitute the preferred food of larvae of the early hairstreak butterfly. Luna and cecropia moth caterpillars feed on the leaves as do those of red-spotted purple, white admiral, turquoise hairstreak, and eastern oak duskywing butterflies.

Most cultivated beech trees, including purple-leaf and cut-leaf forms, are cultivars of the European beech (*Fagus sylvatica* L.).

American beech—male flowers

American beech—young tree in winter with persistent leaves

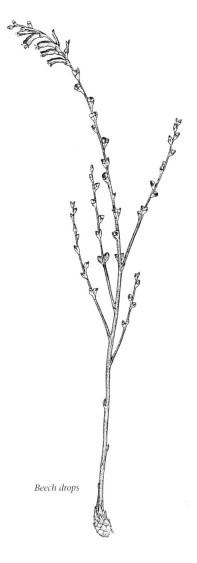

Beech drops

BIRCH
Betula L.
Birch Family—Betulaceae

The birches are best known for their papery, horizontally peeling bark, which in many species, but not all, is white. These deciduous trees have alternate, simple leaves with sharply toothed edges. First-year twigs produce a single leaf at each node, lateral branches that develop beginning in the second year are condensed short shoots with two leaves at the tip. The twigs lack a terminal bud. Birch flowers are unisexual and wind-pollinated; the male flowers are produced in drooping catkins and the female ones are in shorter erect or pendulous catkins. Flowering takes place in the spring as the leaves are emerging. Birch pollen can be a significant cause of pollen allergies. Birch fruits are small winged samaras that alternate with 3-pronged bracts in the mature female catkins. They are dispersed by the wind when the mature catkins break apart.

Deer, beaver, and porcupine feed on the twigs and bark of various species of birch, however, research has shown that phenolic compounds increase in the twigs and bark of the white-barked birches in the wintertime, presumably as a defense against browsing animals. Small mammals and songbirds eat the seeds; grouse, turkeys, and squirrels also feed on the flower buds. Several birches serve as a larval food plant for tiger swallowtail and common tortoiseshell butterflies and several species of sphinx moths.

Five species of birch are native to Pennsylvania; in addition two European species are occasionally naturalized.

Black birch, sweet birch, cherry birch   *Betula lenta* L.

FORM: tree to 60 feet (occasionally to 75 feet), crown narrow

BARK: smooth, dark reddish-brown to black, not peeling but with prominent horizontal lenticels, becoming rough and platy with age

TWIGS: smooth and shiny reddish-brown, strongly aromatic when scraped or cut

PITH: greenish-white to brown, homogeneous

BUDS: about ¼ inch long, pointed, conical and covered with 3–8 reddish-brown, overlapping bud scales

LEAVES: 2½–5 inches long with a rounded or somewhat heart-shaped base and 12–18 pairs of lateral veins

FALL LEAF COLOR: yellow

STIPULES: present, but falling early

LEAF SCARS: small, oval with 3 bundle scars

FLOWERS: see above

FRUIT: fruiting catkins erect, wings of the samaras narrower than the body

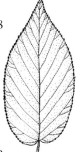

Black birch—leaf

SEEDS: mature mid-August through mid-September and are wind-disseminated from September through November

WOOD: heavy, strong, hard, dark brown with yellowish sapwood

Black birch—bark

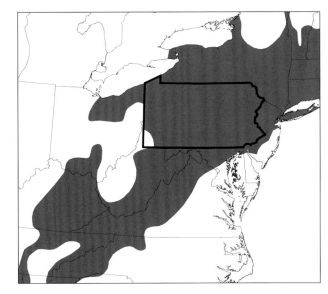

Black birch

CURRENT CHAMPION: McKean County, diameter 4 feet 2 inches, height 78 feet, spread 70 feet

It is always a delight when walking in the woods to sample the refreshing aroma of black birch twigs. In the mid- to late 1800s small distilleries were located in forested parts of northern Pennsylvania, where wintergreen oil (methyl salicylate) was extracted from black birch for use as flavoring and medicine. About 100 birch saplings were required to produce a quart of oil. Today wintergreen oil is manufactured synthetically.

Black birch is found throughout Pennsylvania in moist forests, along streams, and on rocky slopes. It is a tree of the Appalachians, extending from southern Maine to northern Georgia and only as far west as eastern Ohio and Kentucky.

Native Americans brewed a wintergreen-flavored tea from twigs. Decoctions or infusions of bark were used to treat diarrhea, pneumonia, colds, "milky urine," "bad blood," breast complaints, sores, and fever. The aromatic oil was also used to protect leather and furs from insect damage. The wood of black birch has a reddish color that deepens with age, mimicking the appearance of mahogany or cherry for which it has been substituted in the making of furniture.

Larvae of the green comma butterfly feed on the leaves of sweet birch.

Black birch—scale of fruiting catkin x5

Black birch— samara x5

Black birch— fruiting catkins

European weeping birch

Betula pendula Roth

FORM: tree to 60 feet with pendulous branches; trunks often clustered

BARK: smooth and silvery-white except toward the base where it is rough, dark, and platy; less tendency to peel than paper birch

TWIGS: not hairy, surface dotted with small resinous glands, lacking wintergreen aroma

PITH: tan

BUDS: ¼ inch long, dark brown, pointed, and covered with overlapping bud scales

LEAVES: 1½–3 inches long, triangular or rhombic in shape with 5–18 pairs of lateral veins; leaf surfaces smooth but bearing small resinous glands; leaf margins doubly toothed

FALL LEAF COLOR: yellow

STIPULES: present but falling early

LEAF SCARS: half-oval with 3 bundle scars

FLOWERS: as for other birches, see above

European weeping birch—bark

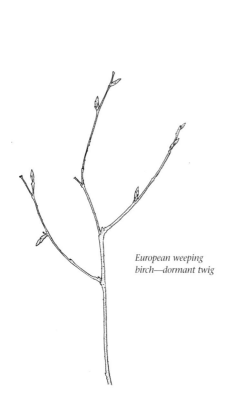

European weeping birch—dormant twig

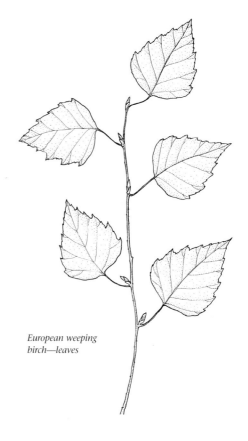

European weeping birch—leaves

FRUIT: fruiting catkins erect or pendulous; wings of the samaras much broader than the body

SEEDS: wind-dispersed

WOOD: tough and hard

CURRENT CHAMPION: Bradford County, diameter 4 feet 4 inches, height 80 feet, spread 51 feet

European weeping birch is frequently planted and many cultivars have been selected including strongly weeping, columnar, and cut-leaved forms, as well as several with yellow or purple leaves. However, the ravages of bronze birch borer (*Agrilus anxius*) have limited its usefulness as a landscape ornamental in eastern North America. European weeping birch is native to Europe and Asia Minor. It has become naturalized at a few locations in Pennsylvania, most notably at Presque Isle in Erie County.

European white birch

Betula pubescens **Ehrh.** subspecies *pubescens*

FORM: erect tree to 60 feet with a pyramidal crown and erect or spreading branches, trunks usually solitary

BARK: silvery-gray when mature, mostly remaining smooth and close

TWIGS: densely hairy when young with sparse resinous glands and without wintergreen aroma

PITH: white

BUDS: ⅜ inch long, dark reddish-brown with 4 visible bud scales

LEAVES: 1½–2 inches long, hairy, resin glands present; leaf margin coarsely toothed

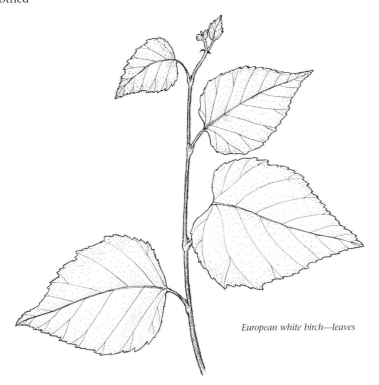

European white birch—leaves

European white birch— bark

FALL LEAF COLOR: yellow
STIPULES: present but falling early
LEAF SCARS: half-oval with 3 bundle scars
FLOWERS: as for other birches, see above
FRUIT: fruiting catkins erect or pendulous, maturing in late fall; samaras with wings as wide or wider than the body
SEEDS: wind-dispersed
CURRENT CHAMPION: none recorded

European white birch, which is native from Europe east to Siberia, is grown here as an ornamental and occasionally persists or naturalizes. As with several other birch species, its ornamental value is limited by the bronze birch borer, which causes dieback of the upper part of the crown.

Gray birch, old field birch   *Betula populifolia* Marshall

FORM: tree to 30 feet (occasionally more), trunks often in clusters, trunk slender and flexible, frequently bending to the ground with the weight of ice and snow
BARK: smooth and white with prominent black markings at the branches
TWIGS: slender, greenish to brown with a rough scaly or warty surface
PITH: greenish white to brown, homogeneous
BUDS: ⅛ inch long, sharp pointed with 3–4 somewhat resinous bud scales
LEAVES: triangular with a long slender tip, 2–3 inches long; leaf stalk dotted with black glands; leaf margins sharply toothed
FALL LEAF COLOR: yellow
STIPULES: present, but falling early
LEAF SCARS: small, half-oval with 3 bundle scars
FLOWERS: male catkins borne singly (or rarely in 2s)
FRUIT: fruiting catkins erect to nearly pendulous; scales of the mature pistillate catkins hairy; samaras broadly winged
SEEDS: maturing in the early fall
WOOD: light, soft, neither strong nor durable
CURRENT CHAMPION: Pike County, diameter 1 foot 5 inches, height 70 feet, spread 44 feet

Gray birch is the common white-barked birch of eastern Pennsylvania where it grows in dry uplands, often in sandy soil, abandoned fields, strip mine waste, and other disturbed areas. It is an early successional species, and sometimes occurs in pure stands. However, gray birch is short-lived and not at all shade tolerant; in time it is replaced by other species.

The total range of gray birch extends from Nova

Gray birch— fruiting catkin

Gray birch—flowering catkins

Gray birch—bark

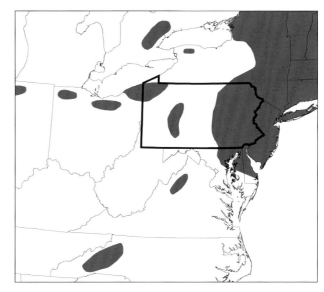

Gray birch

Scotia west to southern Quebec and Michigan, and south to New Jersey, Delaware, and Maryland. Gray birch is very susceptible to birch leaf miner (*Fenusa pusilla*), an insect introduced from Europe in the 1920s that creates conspicuous brown blotches on the leaves.

Native Americans used gray birch in many of the same ways as paper birch. In addition the inner bark was used to treat infected cuts and as an emetic.

Paper birch, canoe birch   *Betula papyrifera* Marshall

FORM: tree to 70 feet (occasionally 90); trunks usually solitary with a narrow, open crown

BARK: chalky-white with black marks at the branches, the papery outer layers peeling away to reveal salmon-pink inner bark

TWIGS: stout, sticky, and hairy, green at first becoming smooth and dark reddish-brown

PITH: small, flattened, whitish or pale tan

BUDS: about ¼ inch long, pointed with a few overlapping scales; winter buds of staminate catkins conspicuous

LEAVES: 2–3 inches long, tapered or rounded at the base; leaf stalk and lower surface covered with minute black glands; leaf margins sharply toothed

FALL LEAF COLOR: yellow

STIPULES: present, but falling early

LEAF SCARS: small, half-oval, with 3 bundle scars

FLOWERS: male catkins in clusters of 2 or 3

FRUIT: fruiting catkins pendulous, maturing in early August to mid-September

SEEDS: about ¹⁄₁₆ inch, wind-dispersed beginning in October

WOOD: light, strong, hard, light brown tinged with red

CURRENT CHAMPION: Chester County, diameter 2 feet 2 inches, height 83 feet, spread 55 feet

Paper birch—flowering catkins

Paper birch—bark

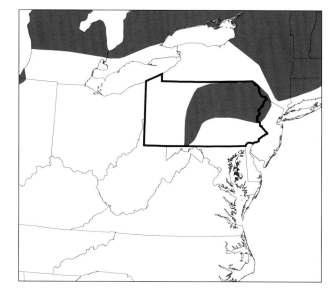

Paper birch

Paper birch—leaf

Paper birch is a northern tree the natural range of which extends across the North American continent from Newfoundland to Alaska. It extends south to Pennsylvania, the Great Lakes region, and the northern Rockies. Paper birch is the much-loved white-barked birch of New England. In Pennsylvania it is found mainly at higher elevations in the northeastern and north central parts of the state.

Paper birch is not shade tolerant and therefore is most often found in early successional forests or edges. It is not a very long-lived tree.

The waterproof bark of paper birch was very important to Native Americans of the northeast for making birch bark canoes, coverings for dwellings, baskets, and other containers. Michaux described how sheets of bark 10 to 12 feet long and nearly 3 feet wide were removed from selected trunks in the spring, stitched together with spruce roots, and sealed with spruce gum.[1] A canoe big enough to carry four people with baggage weighed only 40–50 pounds and could easily be portaged when necessary. Larger birch bark craft could carry up to 15 people. The wood of the birch provided frames for dwellings, sleds, and snowshoes as well as paddles and ribs for canoes.

This important tree also provided medicinal preparations used in the treatment of gynecological problems, stomach cramps, and teething pain in infants. Sap tapped from the trees in early spring was used as cough medicine and a preparation of the bark even served as a contraceptive.

Paper birch is a larval food source for several butterflies including viceroy, striped hairstreak, dark gray comma, and mourning cloak.

River birch, red birch   *Betula nigra* L.

FORM: tree to 80 feet with an irregular crown, frequently multistemmed

BARK: reddish-brown, peeling off in numerous filmy layers, on older trees it becomes fissured and scaly

TWIGS: slender, greenish and hairy at first becoming reddish-brown and smooth

PITH: small, angular and somewhat flattened, greenish, homogeneous

BUDS: sharp-pointed, smooth, covered with 3–7 overlapping bud scales

LEAVES: 1½–3 inches long with 6–10 pairs of lateral veins and hairy stalks; margins with large teeth alternating with smaller ones

FALL LEAF COLOR: yellow

STIPULES: present, but falling early

LEAF SCARS: small, oval with 3 bundle scars

FLOWERS: male catkins in clusters of 2–3

FRUIT: maturing May–June, samaras broadly winged, scales hairy

SEEDS: wind- and water-dispersed

River birch—leaf

WOOD: light, soft, strong, light brown with pale sapwood

CURRENT CHAMPION: Philadelphia County, diameter 5 feet 4 inches, height 85 feet, spread 84 feet

River birch occurs primarily in the eastern part of Pennsylvania, where it can be found on the banks of rivers, streams, and lakes. Its tan to reddish-brown bark that peels off in irregular papery layers is distinctive. It is unique among the birch species in the state in maturing its seeds in the late spring or early summer. Germination occurs immediately on exposed river banks and floodplains. River birch is primarily a southern tree reaching its greatest abundance in the southern Appalachians. It extends from Massachusetts to Florida and west to Minnesota and Kansas.

Native Americans chewed the leaves of river birch to counteract diarrhea, and an infusion of the bark was used to treat gastrointestinal problems. Difficulty in urination was treated with a decoction of the inner bark.

River birch—flowering catkins

This species is not significant as a timber source, but in recent years it has become a popular ornamental landscape tree. A number of cultivars have been selected of which Heritage® is perhaps the most widely grown.

River birch   bark

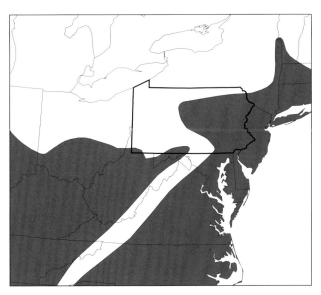

River birch

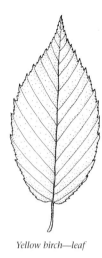

Yellow birch—leaf

Yellow birch   *Betula alleghaniensis* **Britton**

FORM: upright tree to 90 feet
BARK: yellowish-gray peeling off in irregular papery layers
TWIGS: green and hairy at first, becoming brown and smooth, aromatic when scraped or cut
PITH: green, continuous
BUDS: ¼ inch long, pointed with 3–8 overlapping bud scales
LEAVES: rounded to heart-shaped at the base with 9–12 pairs of lateral veins; margins doubly toothed
FALL LEAF COLOR: yellow
STIPULES: present, but falling early
LEAF SCARS: small, oval with 3 bundle scars
FLOWERS: as for other birches, see above
FRUIT: fruiting catkins erect, maturing in late July or August
SEEDS: dispersal is by wind beginning in October and is often facilitated by hard snow cover, which allows the seeds to blow across the surface
WOOD: heavy, strong, hard; heartwood light brown tinged with red; sapwood pale
CURRENT CHAMPION: Susquehanna County, diameter 4 feet, height 79 feet, spread 68 feet

Yellow birch is a common component of the northern hardwood forest where it grows with beech, sugar and red maple, white pine, and hemlock. It occurs in cool, moist woods throughout Pennsylvania but is more common in the northern part of the state. Yellow birch occurs from Newfoundland and Nova Scotia west to the Great Lakes region and south in the mountains to North Carolina.

Rotting logs and stumps are very important to the establishment of yellow birch seedlings and frequently result in trees that later in life appear to be perched on stilt-like roots above the forest floor.

Native Americans used compounds prepared from yellow birch to treat liver problems, gastrointestinal ailments, and blood maladies. A decoction of the plant was used to treat problems with lactation. Wintergreen oil extracted from twigs was used to flavor other medicines and a beverage made from the sap of yellow birch combined with maple sap was enjoyed. Food storage containers were made from the bark. Yellow birch saplings were preferred for making the frames of wigwams because of their strength and flexibility. Hikers and campers know that the bark of yellow birch can be used to start a campfire even when it is wet.

Yellow birch is the largest of our native birches and is an important source of hardwood lumber used for furniture, interior finishing, and tool handles. Its leaves are a larval food source for the green comma, mourning cloak, red-spotted purple, and white admiral butterflies.

Notes

1. Michaux, F. Andrew. 1817. *The North American Sylva, or A Description of the Forest Trees of the United States, Canada, and Nova Scotia*, in 3 volumes. Thomas Dobson-Solomon Conrad, Philadelphia.

Yellow birch—bark

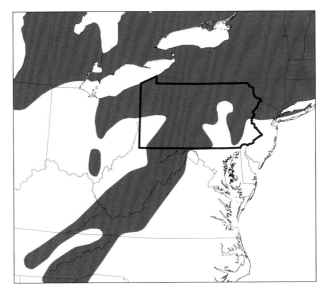

Yellow birch

Yellow birch—flowering catkins

Yellow birch fruiting catkin x1

BLACKGUM
Nyssa L.
Dogwood Family—Cornaceae

Blackgum, sourgum, tupelo   *Nyssa sylvatica* **Marshall**

FORM: deciduous tree to 80 feet or occasionally more, often forming dense clonal thickets through the formation of root shoots; branches extending at right angles from the trunk and bearing numerous short lateral spur branches; crown becoming flat-topped in age

BARK: grayish, rough and scaly, developing a blocky appearance in age

TWIGS: reddish-brown becoming gray

PITH: white, with denser green cross partitions at regular intervals

BUDS: reddish-brown, ⅛–¼ inch long with 3–5 overlapping scales, sometimes with 2–3 buds above each other (superposed); terminal bud present

LEAVES: alternate or clustered at the ends of short lateral shoots, elliptical, 2–5 inches long, dark green and very shiny on the upper surface; margin entire or occasionally with a few coarse teeth

FALL LEAF COLOR: brilliant red, starting as early as mid to late August

STIPULES: none

LEAF SCARS: broadly crescent-shaped with 3 bundle scars

FLOWERS: small, greenish-white, clustered at the end of a long stalk, unisexual and perfect, appearing in May with the leaves

FRUIT: a dark blue drupe about ⅜ inch long, often 2–3 together at the end of a long stalk

SEEDS: dispersed by birds or mammals

WOOD: light yellow, strong, and stiff but not durable, very difficult to split

CURRENT CHAMPION: Chester County, diameter 4 feet 8 inches, height 81 feet, spread 109 feet

Sourgum's glossy leaves are handsome at all times, but especially after they have turned red, which they do in late summer or early fall. Although not necessarily the largest, sourgum is one of the longest-lived native trees in the northeast; individual specimens can live 500–700 years. This versatile tree grows in low wet areas, but it is equally likely to be found on dry ridge tops, where it sometimes forms nearly pure stands. Its ability to form numerous root shoots may provide an advantage in fire-prone areas.

In Pennsylvania sourgum occurs throughout the state, but is less common in the northernmost counties. Its total range extends from Maine to Wisconsin and south to eastern Texas and Florida.

Native Americans used sourgum to treat a variety of ills including tuberculosis, intestinal worms, and diarrhea. The wood was used to make war clubs and other tools because it did not split. Early settlers, however, had little use for sourgum because the wood was so hard to split or shape. Wildlife, including many songbirds, grouse, wild turkey, mice, opossums, raccoons, and deer eat the fruits and incidentally scatter the seeds.

Blackgum—bark

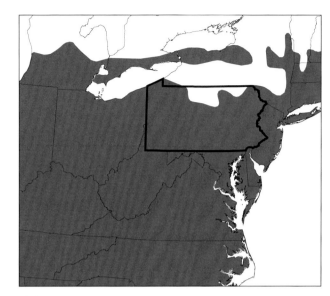

Blackgum

Blackgum—fruits

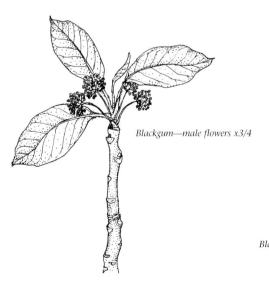

Blackgum—male flowers x3/4

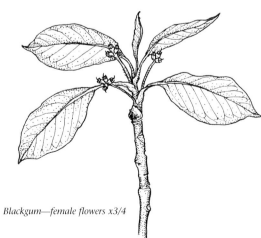

Blackgum—female flowers x3/4

BLACKHAW
Viburnum L.
Honeysuckle Family—Caprifoliaceae

Blackhaw   *Viburnum prunifolium* L.

FORM: colonial shrub or small tree to 20 feet tall

BARK: dark grayish-brown, finely divided into square plates

TWIGS: gray-brown, smooth

PITH: white, solid

BUDS: slender and pointed, about ⅛ inch long with one pair of bud scales; flower buds are larger with a broadly rounded base tapering to a slender tip

LEAVES: opposite, simple, elliptic, 1½–2½ inches long, dark green and smooth above, smooth beneath; edges finely toothed

FALL LEAF COLOR: yellow, red, or dark reddish-purple

STIPULES: none

LEAF SCARS: crescent-shaped with 3 bundle scars, each pair of leaf scars is joined around the twig by a tiny bark ridge

FLOWERS: small, white, in a 2 to 4-inch-wide, flat cluster, perfect; each with a 5-lobed, tubular corolla, 5 stamens, and a single inferior ovary

FRUIT: a black drupe, about ⅜ inch long, on branching red stalks

SEEDS: flat, black, about the size and shape of a watermelon seed, animal-dispersed

WOOD: hard, strong, and heavy; heartwood brown tinged with red; sapwood lighter, too small to be significant commercially

CURRENT CHAMPION: Montgomery County, diameter 1 foot 3 inches, height 19 feet, spread 32 feet

Blackhaw fruits provide a tasty snack in the fall woods. Common in old fields, hedgerows, edges, and successional forests in moist to dry soils, blackhaw is found throughout the southern two-thirds of Pennsylvania. Its total range extends from Connecticut to southern Wisconsin and south to Georgia and Texas.

Native Americans used the leaves of blackhaw for tea. The bark of the root was used medicinally to make a strong tea for treating chronic diarrhea and dysentery; its most valuable use, however, was the prevention of abortion or miscarriage.

Fox, deer, quail, turkey, grouse, songbirds, and various small mammals eat the fruits.

Blackhaw—fruits

Blackhaw—bark

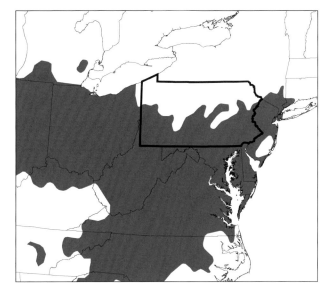

Blackhaw

Blackhaw—inflorescence

BLADDERNUT
Staphylea L.
Bladdernut Family—Staphyleaceae

Bladdernut   *Staphylea trifolia* L.

FORM: large, thicket-forming shrub or occasionally a small tree
BARK: light greenish-gray, smooth with elongate white stripes
TWIGS: greenish at first, becoming dark reddish-brown
PITH: white, solid
BUDS: rounded, greenish with several overlapping bud scales
LEAVES: opposite, pinnately compound with 3 leaflets; leaflets 2–4 inches long, dark green above, hairy beneath, finely toothed on the edge
FALL LEAF COLOR: pale yellow
STIPULES: dropping early
LEAF SCARS: raised, crescent-shaped with 3 bundle scars
FLOWERS: in drooping clusters, greenish-white, bell-shaped, about ⅓ inch long, perfect with 5 sepals, 5 petals, and 5 stamens; ovary 3-lobed
FRUIT: an inflated, 3-sided, 1¼-inch-long, papery capsule enclosing 1–3 shiny brown seeds
SEEDS: perhaps dispersed by water, the inflated capsules do float
WOOD: too small to be of commercial importance
CURRENT CHAMPION: none reported

Bladdernut is native to moist, floodplain forests and stream banks in all but the northernmost counties of Pennsylvania. It is most easily recognized by the inflated fruits, which are pale green at first, eventually becoming brown and remaining on the plant into the winter. The striped bark of the larger stems is also distinctive.

American bladdernut grows from Quebec and Ontario west to Minnesota and south to Georgia and Arkansas.

Native Americans found several uses for bladdernut. The seeds were used in gourd rattles for ceremonial dances. An infusion of the bark of the plant was employed to sedate crying children. The Iroquois also used it in a compound infusion taken for rheumatism.

The leaves are a larval food source for the giant swallowtail butterfly.

Bladdernut—flowers

Bladdernut—bark

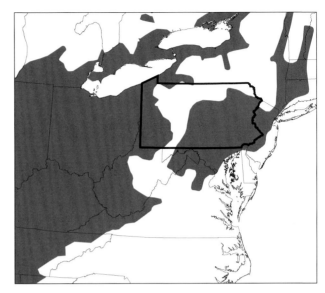

Bladdernut

Bladdernut—fruit

Bladdernut—flowers

BOX-ELDER—SEE MAPLE

BUCKEYE

AESCULUS L.

Horse-chestnut Family—Hippocastanaceae

The buckeyes and horse-chestnut (also in the genus *Aesculus*) are the only trees in our flora with palmately compound leaves. These trees are further distinguished by conspicuous clusters of showy flowers that appear in early May after the leaves have partially expanded. The flowers have an irregular, 2-lipped form, with 4 or 5 separate petals, 6–8 stamens, and a superior ovary; they are insect-pollinated. Unisexual and perfect flowers occur on a single tree. The fruit is a capsule that splits open at maturity releasing 1–3 large shiny brown seeds that look like chestnuts. Both the seeds and the young shoots contain a toxin, aesculin, and are little used by wildlife. The Pennsylvania flora includes two native buckeyes.

Ohio buckeye   *Aesculus glabra* Willd.

FORM: a small tree to 40 feet with a broad, rounded crown
BARK: grayish-brown and scaly, becoming darker and furrowed with age
TWIGS: reddish-brown to gray, hairy when young but becoming smooth later
PITH: large, light green, producing an unpleasant odor when bruised
BUDS: terminal buds present or sometimes lacking, about ⅔ inch long; outer bud scales reddish-brown but not resinous
LEAVES: opposite, palmately compound with 5 or occasionally 7 leaflets, the largest to 6 inches long
FALL LEAF COLOR: yellow or sometimes orange-red to reddish-brown
STIPULES: not present
LEAF SCARS: heart-shaped or triangular, with 3 groups of bundle scars
FLOWERS: in 5- to 6-inch-long clusters at the ends of the branches, yellowish or greenish, with the stamens extending beyond the petals; appearing in late April or early May
FRUIT: a prickly capsule 1–2 inches long containing 1–3 seeds, maturing in October
SEEDS: smooth, slightly flattened, glossy brown, 1–1¼ inches wide
WOOD: white or pale yellow, weak, soft
CURRENT CHAMPION: Cumberland County, diameter 5 feet 3 inches, height 69 feet, spread 53 feet

In Pennsylvania, Ohio buckeye is occurs naturally only in the southwestern counties of Greene, Washington, Allegheny,

Ohio buckeye—fruit

Ohio buckeye—seed

Ohio buckeye—flowers

Ohio buckeye—bark

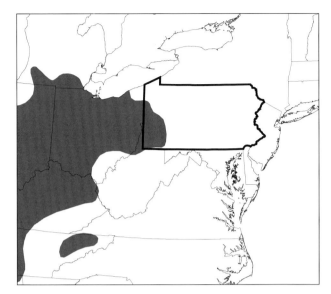

Ohio buckeye

and Beaver. Ohio buckeye is an understory tree in the rich mixed mesophytic forest community that occurs on moist stream banks and ravines, primarily on limestone soils. It has become naturalized at scattered locations in central and eastern Pennsylvania, presumably having spread from cultivated sources.

Ohio buckeye extends from western Pennsylvania to southern Ontario, Wisconsin, Iowa, and Kansas and south to Alabama and Texas. It is the state tree of Ohio, but reaches its best development in the Tennessee River valley and northern Alabama.

Native Americans carried the seeds of Ohio buckeye in their pockets to ward off rheumatism. Ground seeds mixed with oil were used to treat earaches and the pulverized seeds were also used as a poison in streams to stun fish so they could be scooped up. The wood has been used to craft artificial limbs and various items of wood-enware for which its lightness and ease of carving are an advantage.

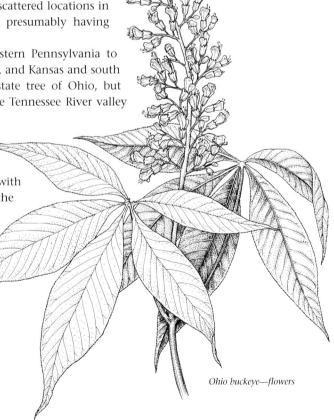

Ohio buckeye—flowers

Yellow buckeye, sweet buckeye

Aesculus flava **Sol.**

FORM: deciduous tree to 80 feet

BARK: light grayish brown, smooth when young and becoming platy with age

TWIGS: stout, hairy at first but becoming smooth, reddish-brown to grayish

PITH: large, white, and continuous

BUDS: terminal bud about ⅔ inch long with reddish-brown outer bud scales, not resinous

LEAVES: opposite, palmately compound with 5–7 leaflets, the longest to 7 inches; edges finely and irregularly toothed

FALL LEAF COLOR: yellow to orangy-brown

STIPULES: not present

LEAF SCARS: heart-shaped to triangular with 3 groups of bundle scars

FLOWERS: in 4- to 12-inch-long clusters at the ends of the branches, each flower with 4 yellow or purplish petals, the stamens no longer than the petals; blooming in May

FRUIT: a smooth capsule 2–3 inches long, maturing in September

SEEDS: smooth, shiny, reddish-brown, several per capsule, each 1½–2 inches wide

WOOD: soft and weak, light in color

CURRENT CHAMPION: York County, diameter 5 feet 8 inches, height 101 feet, spread 76 feet

As a naturally occurring forest tree, yellow buckeye, like Ohio buckeye (above), is limited to a few southwestern counties in Pennsylvania. A forest canopy species, yellow buckeye grows in rich soil along streams and bottomlands as part of a very diverse mixed mesophytic forest community. Its total range extends from southwestern Pennsylvania and southern Ohio to southern Illinois, Georgia, and Alabama. It is occasionally cultivated and naturalized elsewhere.

Yellow buckeye and Ohio buckeye often grow together in southwestern Pennsylvania, although their leaves and coarse branching pattern are similar they are readily distinguished by the following characteristics:

	BARK	FLOWERS	FRUIT
OHIO BUCKEYE	gray-brown and scaly	stamens much longer than petals	spiny
YELLOW BUCKEYE	smooth, light gray	stamens no longer than petals	smooth

Yellow buckeye—fruit

Yellow buckeye—bark

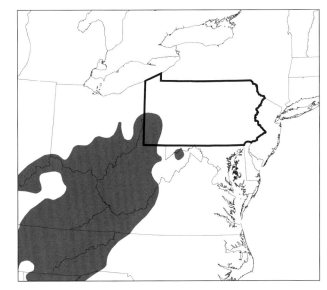

Yellow buckeye

Native Americans used the wood of yellow buckeye to make ceremonial items such as masks, carvings, and containers. It is also used for pulpwood, however, it has never been sufficiently abundant in Pennsylvania to be commercially important.

Yellow buckeye—leaf x1/4

Yellow buckeye—flowers

BUTTERNUT
JUGLANS L.
Walnut Family—Juglandaceae

Butternut, white walnut   *Juglans cinerea* L.

FORM: deciduous tree to 60 feet, usually with a short trunk, spreading branches, and a broad crown

BARK: light gray and smooth when young with dark fissures developing with age

TWIGS: stout

PITH: dark brown, chambered (containing cross partitions)

BUDS: hairy, lateral buds blunt and often occurring 2–3 at a node immediately above each other; terminal bud present

LEAVES: alternate, pinnately compound with 11–17 leaflets

FALL LEAF COLOR: drab yellow or brown

STIPULES: none

LEAF SCARS: 3-lobed or heart-shaped with a hairy fringe along the top and 3 U-shaped clusters of bundle scars

FLOWERS: unisexual, appearing as the leaves are emerging, wind-pollinated; male flowers in drooping catkins; female flowers bud-like in appearance and located on new shoots, wind-pollinated; both sexes occur on each tree making the species monoecious

FRUIT: a nut enclosed in a fibrous husk, stored and dispersed by squirrels

SEED: a rough-surfaced, cylindrical nut

WOOD: light brown, coarse-grained

CURRENT CHAMPION: Bucks County, diameter 5 feet, height 70 feet, spread 80 feet

Butternut—nut x3/4

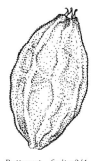

Butternut—fruit x3/4

Butternut is a tree of lowland forests and rich forested hillsides throughout most of Pennsylvania where it occurs as scattered individuals in mixed hardwood stands. The total range of butternut extends from Maine to Minnesota and south to western North Carolina, Tennessee, and Missouri. Like black walnut, the roots of butternut exude a chemical (juglone) that inhibits the growth of other plants.

The nuts of butternut are somewhat cylindrical in shape with a pointed tip and a rough furrowed shell once the outer husk is removed. The kernel is sweet tasting and oily but difficult to extract from the shell. Butternuts were an important winter food for many Native American tribes as they could be stored. The nutmeats were used to make gravy and soup and added to corn bread and puddings. In addition, as with black walnut, the sap of butternut was collected in the spring and boiled down to make syrup or "butternut molasses."

The inner bark of butternut was widely employed as a cathartic or purgative, and an infusion of the bark was used to treat diarrhea. It was used to treat dysentery during the American Revolution. Other medicinal uses of butternut included treatment of mouth ulcers, tuberculosis, and toothache. The colonists used fresh bark and husks from the nuts to prepare a yellow dye that was popular during the civil war. Squirrels, rabbits, and deer eat the nuts and the larvae of several moths and butterflies feed on the leaves.

Butternut—bark

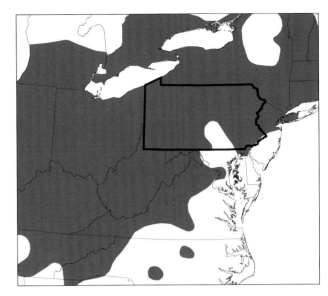

Butternut

Since the early 1900s butternut has been afflicted with a canker disease caused by a pathogenic fungus (*Sirococcus clavigignenti-juglandacearum*) that results in severe dieback. Sirococcus canker has diminished the significance of butternut as a forest tree and made it useless for lumber or landscape use.

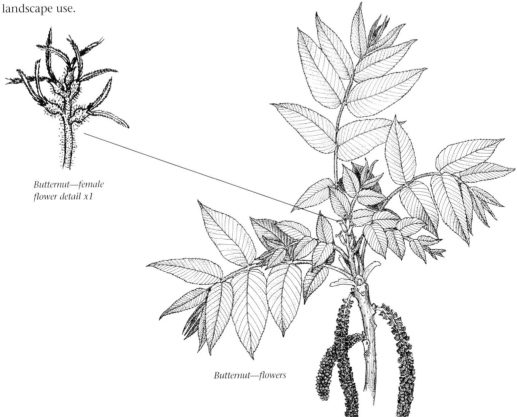

Butternut—female
flower detail x1

Butternut—flowers

CASTOR-ARALIA
KALOPANAX MIQ.
Ginseng Family—Araliaceae

Castor-aralia | ***Kalopanax septemlobus* (Thunb.) Koidz. var. *septemlobus***

FORM: spiny-stemmed deciduous tree to 60 feet

BARK: grayish-brown and smooth when young, becoming almost black with deep ridges and furrows

TWIGS: stout, yellowish-brown to whitish with numerous lenticels

PITH: large, white, and continuous

BUDS: large, $\frac{5}{16}$ inch in diameter, dome-shaped and bright, shiny green

LEAVES: alternate, simple, 7–14 inches wide with 5–7 pointed lobes

FALL LEAF COLOR: yellow or red

STIPULES: none

LEAF SCARS: V-shaped with a single row of 10–12 bundle scars

FLOWERS: small, white, grouped in large radiating clusters at the ends of the branches in July and early August, perfect, insect pollinated

FRUIT: dark brown to black, $\frac{1}{8}$ inch across, ripening in late August or early September, eaten by birds

SEEDS: disseminated by birds

CURRENT CHAMPION: Chester County, diameter 4 feet 3 inches, height 64 feet, spread 90 feet

On first glance this tree might be mistaken for sweetgum, due to the similarity in the shape of the leaves. However, the spiny stems and fleshy fruits provide a distinct difference.

Native to China, Korea, Japan, and far-eastern Russia, castor-aralia is occasionally grown as an ornamental. It seeds itself prolifically and has become naturalized in several locations in southeastern counties of Pennsylvania.

Castor-aralia—inflorescence x1/4

Castor-aralia—bark

CATALPA
CATALPA SCOP.
Trumpet-creeper Family—Bignoniaceae

Known by generations of children as johnny-smoker trees for their long slender pods, catalpas are also conspicuous because of their large yellow-green leaves and showy white flowers. The blooms are insect-pollinated, but not by just one group of insects. By day bumblebees visit catalpa flowers, guided by the yellow and purple markings (nectar guides) within; at night, production of nectar and fragrance increases and moths are attracted to the flowers.[1]

Three species of catalpa are naturalized in Pennsylvania, primarily in the southeast, but also scattered across the southern part of the state: northern catalpa, southern catalpa, and Chinese catalpa.

Catalpa wood, which is very resistant to decay, insects, and fungi, even when in contact with soil, has been used for fence posts, railroad ties, and furniture. Extracts of the wood have been tested for their ability to protect other wood from termite attack. Catalpa has been used medicinally to treat asthma and skin diseases. All three species are cultivated as fast growing ornamentals, they begin to bloom at 6–8 years of age. Catalpa is often found persisting at abandoned home sites.

The catalpa sphinx moth feeds exclusively on this genus of trees and has expanded its range as far north as New York State as catalpa has established naturalized populations. Caterpillars of the tiger swallowtail butterfly also feed on catalpa leaves.

Northern catalpa, cigartree, Indian-bean   *Catalpa speciosa* **Warder**

FORM: medium-sized tree to 50–60 feet (or occasionally taller) with spreading branches and a rounded crown

BARK: light brown, smooth when young, becoming platy with age

TWIGS: green and hairy at first

PITH: large, tan, homogeneous

BUDS: rounded and covered with overlapping, reddish-brown scales, terminal bud absent

LEAVES: in whorls of 3, or sometimes opposite, simple, 5–6 inches long and almost as wide, broadly rounded at the base with a tapering tip, smooth on the top but hairy beneath; margin entire; leaf stalk up to 6 inches long

FALL LEAF COLOR: yellow, or more often the leaves merely turn brown and drop after the first severe frost

STIPULES: none

LEAF SCARS: round to oval with a ring of bundle scars

FLOWERS: showy, 1–2 inches across with 5 spreading petals, white with yellow lines and purple spots within the tubular base; appearing in June after the leaves are fully expanded

FRUIT: a slender pod, 8–16 inches long

SEEDS: flattened, bearing 2 long fringed wings, wind-dispersed

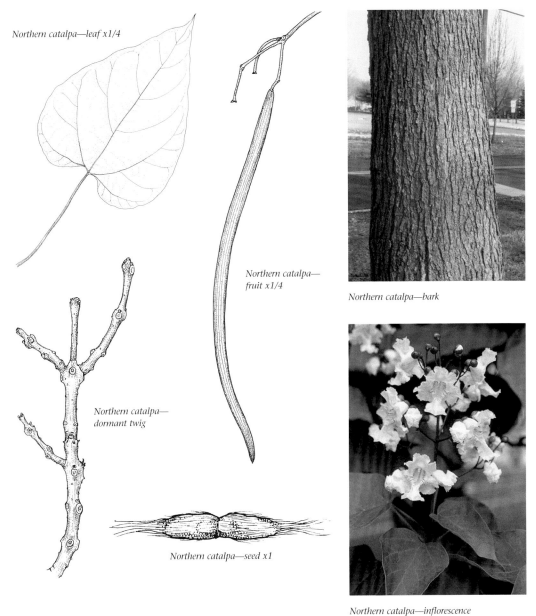

Northern catalpa—leaf x1/4

Northern catalpa—
fruit x1/4

Northern catalpa—bark

Northern catalpa—
dormant twig

Northern catalpa—seed x1

Northern catalpa—inflorescence

WOOD: light brown, soft, coarse-grained, but very durable when in contact with soil

CURRENT CHAMPION: Bucks County, diameter 6 feet 10 inches at 3 feet, height 85 feet, spread 90 feet

Northern catalpa is native to riverbanks and bottomlands in the Mississippi River drainage from central Illinois and Indiana to Arkansas and Tennessee. In Pennsylvania it is naturalized across the southern half of the state.

Southern catalpa— seed x1

Southern catalpa, cigartree, Indian-bean *Catalpa bignonioides* Walter

CURRENT CHAMPION: York County, diameter 5 feet 11 inches, height 73 feet, spread 67 feet

Southern catalpa and northern catalpa are very similar; the most easily observed differences between them are summarized in the table below.

Both southern catalpa and northern catalpa are native plants of riverbanks and bottomlands of the southeastern United States. Southern catalpa ranges from northern Florida to eastern Texas; in Pennsylvania it is widely naturalized in low, moist woods and roadsides.

	FLOWER	LEAF	FRUIT	SEED
NORTHERN CATALPA (*C. SPECIOSA*)	up to 2 inches across	with an elongate tapered tip	capsule walls thick, the halves remaining concave	fringed wings rounded at the ends
SOUTHERN CATALPA (*C. BIGNONIOIDES*)	1–1½ inches across	with a short pointed tip	capsule walls thinner, the halves becoming flattened	fringed wings narrowed to a pointed tip

Southern catalpa— leaf

Chinese catalpa   *Catalpa ovata* G. Don.

Chinese catalpa differs from northern and southern catalpa by its smaller, yellow flowers and leaves that lack hairs on the lower surface. It is native to China, and is cultivated in Japan, where its fruits are the source of a diuretic. Chinese catalpa has been found naturalized at only a few sites along the Lehigh River in northeastern Pennsylvania.

Chinese catalpa— leaf x1/4

Notes

1. Stephenson, Andrew G. and William Wayt Thomas. 1977. Diurnal and nocturnal pollination of *Catalpa speciosa* (Bignoniaceae). *Systematic Botany* 2: 191–198.

CHERRY
Prunus L.
Rose Family—Rosaceae

The cherries include both native and introduced species. They are deciduous trees with alternate simple leaves that are generally elliptical, pointed at the tip, and toothed on the edges. A distinguishing feature, shared only by some of the plums, willows, and poplars, is the presence of one or more glands on the leaf stalk or the base of the blade.

Cherry flowers have 5 white petals, 5 sepal lobes, and 15–30 stamens attached to a cup-like hypanthium that surrounds the superior ovary with its single style and stigma. All species are bee-pollinated. The fruit is a drupe characterized by a juicy outer layer and a bony inner layer (the rounded stone), which surrounds the actual seed. Fruit-eating birds and mammals disperse the seeds.

Native Americans had many uses for wild cherries. The fruits were eaten fresh, used to make beverages, added to cornbread, and dried for winter use. Infusions of the bark were used to treat coughs, chills, and fevers. A decoction of the roots was used to treat intestinal worms. Poultices of the inner bark were applied to cuts and wounds; bark was also used to treat diarrhea, gynecological problems, and as a blood tonic. Powdered root was applied to burns. The fruits were also a source of food and beverages for early European settlers.

Many species of cherry are an important food source for wildlife. Grouse, quail, pheasant, many songbirds, bear, deer, raccoon, and small mammals consume the fruit; the leaves are a larval food of tiger swallowtail, viceroy, red-spotted purple, white admiral, painted lady, coral hairstreak, woodland elfin, and spring azure butterflies and promethea, cecropia, wild cherry sphinx, and small-eyed sphinx moths.

Of the six types of cherry that can be found growing wild in Pennsylvania today, three are native and three the result of introductions from Europe and Asia.

Black cherry   *Prunus serotina* L.

FORM: upright tree to 100 feet or more with a narrow or broadly rounded crown

BARK: smooth and reddish-brown with prominent horizontal lenticels on young stems, dark with a scaly, platy surface on older trunks

TWIGS: slender, smooth, reddish-brown with large lenticels, producing a bitter odor when bruised

PITH: light brown, continuous

BUDS: ⅛ inch long, broadly triangular, smooth and shiny yellow-green to reddish-brown with overlapping bud scales

LEAVES: alternate, simple, 2–5 inches long, ovate, tapered at the tip, dark green above, pale and smooth beneath except for a narrow band of short brownish hairs on either side of the midrib near the base of the blade; edges with incurved teeth, several small glands present on the leaf stalk or the base of the blade

FALL LEAF COLOR: brilliant reddish-orange to yellow

Black cherry—bark

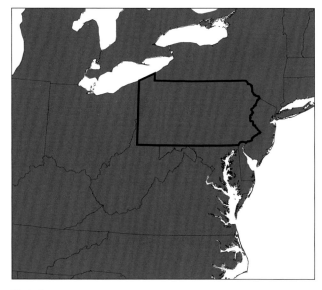

Black cherry

Black cherry—leaf with spindle galls

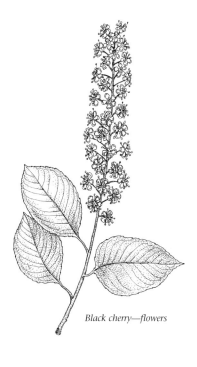

Black cherry—flowers

Black cherry—leaf

STIPULES: falling early but leaving a narrow scar on each side of the leaf base

LEAF SCARS: elliptical with 3 bundle scars, raised on a projection of the twig

FLOWERS: an elongate spreading or drooping cluster of small white flowers appearing after the leaves are fully expanded

FRUIT: drooping clusters of ⅓-inch-diameter fleshy fruits that are red at first but turn dark purple-black when fully ripe in late summer

SEEDS: spherical, about ¼ inch in diameter, disseminated by birds

WOOD: reddish brown with yellowish sapwood, hard and strong, fine grained, used for furniture, interior work, and veneer

CURRENT CHAMPION: Warren County, diameter 4 feet 10 inches, height 137 feet, spread 75 feet

Black cherry is the most important timber tree in Pennsylvania, due to its value for fine furniture, cabinetry, interior finishing, and veneers. This species reaches its maximum size and quality in the Allegheny hardwood forests of northwestern Pennsylvania and adjacent areas of New York State.

In southern Pennsylvania black cherry is usually a smaller tree of hedgerows, roadsides and successional forests. Leaves of wild black cherry are toxic to cattle and other grazing or browsing animals because of the cyanide that accumulates in wilted foliage.

In the early spring as the leaves are expanding, black cherry is often conspicuously infested with the white webs of eastern tent caterpillar. Black cherry is also a food source for the caterpillars of eastern tiger swallowtail, Canadian tiger swallowtail, coral hairstreak, and red-banded hairstreak butterflies. The red-spotted purple butterfly feeds on leaves in its larval phase and utilizes the nectar of the flowers as an adult. In addition the spring azure feeds on leaf galls of black cherry caused by eriophyid mites. These galls, known as cherry spindle or pouch gall (causal agent *Phytoptus ceraicrumena*) are a frequent feature of black cherry leaves.

Choke cherry *Prunus virginiana* L.

FORM: shrub or small tree to 25 feet with an irregular rounded crown

BARK: shiny reddish-brown on young stems, on older trunks becoming grayish and fissured

TWIGS: slender, smooth, shiny reddish-brown with conspicuous lenticels, producing a bitter odor when bruised

PITH: white, continuous

BUDS: ⅓ inch long, smooth, sharp-pointed, covered with 6–8 pale chestnut-brown, overlapping bud scales

LEAVES: alternate, simple, 2–4 inches long, oval to oblong with glands at the base of the blade, dark green and shiny above, paler and sometimes hairy beneath; edges sharply toothed

FALL LEAF COLOR: yellow to reddish

STIPULES: falling early but leaving a narrow scar on each side of the base of the leaf stalk

LEAF SCARS: elliptical with 3 bundle scars, somewhat raised on a projection of the twig

FLOWERS: small, white, in a spreading or drooping 3- to 6-inch-long cluster appearing after the leaves are fully expanded

Choke cherry—bark

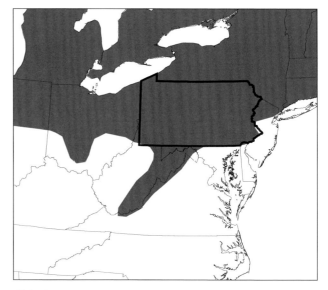

Choke cherry

Choke cherry—fruit

Choke cherry—flowers

Choke cherry—twig with black knot gall

FRUIT: red turning black, in an elongate drooping cluster, each cherry about ⅓ inch in diameter, bitter

SEEDS: spherical, about ¼ inch in diameter

WOOD: light brown, hard and heavy, but not commercially important due to the small size of the trees

CURRENT CHAMPION: Lycoming County, diameter 7 inches, height 32 feet, spread 24 feet

In Pennsylvania choke cherry is a tree of fencerows, dry slopes, stream banks, and wetland edges throughout the state. Its total range extends from Newfoundland to British Columbia and south to California and the mountains of Georgia.

The caterpillars of coral hairstreak and red-spotted purple butterflies feed on the leaves of choke cherry. The twigs are frequently seen with irregular elongate black galls caused by a disease known as black-knot (caused by the fungus: *Apiosporina morbosa*).

European bird cherry   *Prunus padus* L.

FORM: tall shrub or small tree to 45 feet with ascending or spreading branches

BARK: shiny, dark brown

TWIGS: brown, smooth, with prominent lenticels

PITH: white, homogeneous

BUDS: slender and sharply pointed with overlapping bud scales

LEAVES: alternate, simple, 2–4 inches long, oval with a pointed tip and finely toothed edge; several glands present at the top of the leaf stalk just below the blade

FALL LEAF COLOR: yellow to pinkish red

STIPULES: small, falling early

LEAF SCARS: oval with 3 bundle scars

European bird cherry—flowers

European bird cherry—bark

FLOWERS: in an elongate drooping cluster, white, fragrant, appearing after the leaves are fully expanded

FRUIT: in an elongate drooping cluster, nearly black, about ¼ inch in diameter, ripening in late summer

SEEDS: rounded with a sculptured surface, bird-dispersed

CURRENT CHAMPION: none recorded

European bird cherry is native to northern Europe. It was introduced originally as an ornamental, and now is occasionally established in thickets and along roadsides. Although the inflorescence is similar to black cherry and choke cherry, the individual flowers are larger and showier.

Higan cherry   *Prunus subhirtella* Miq.

FORM: small tree to 25 feet

BARK: brown with prominent horizontal lenticels

TWIGS: slender, often drooping, brown, hairy with raised lenticels

PITH: tan to pale greenish-white, homogeneous

BUDS: ¹⁄₁₆ inch long, brown, hairy, curved inward toward the twig, covered with overlapping bud scales

LEAVES: 1½–3 inches long with scattered hairs on the upper surface and on the veins beneath; margin sharply and doubly toothed

FALL LEAF COLOR: yellow to reddish

STIPULES: small, soon shriveling and dropping

LEAF SCARS: on raised projections on the twig, oval with 3 bundle scars

Higan cherry— leaf

Higan cherry— flowers

FLOWERS: pink, ½ inch across, blooming in the early spring before the leaves have expanded

FRUIT: ⅓ inch in diameter or less, red turning black

SEEDS: disseminated by birds

CURRENT CHAMPION: Cumberland County, diameter 3 feet, height 28 feet, spread 46 feet

Higan cherry is native to China; it has given rise to many ornamental cultivars of "Japanese flowering cherry" and is widely cultivated. It has also found its way into urban and suburban forest remnants.

Pin cherry, fire cherry   *Prunus pensylvanica* L.f.

FORM: small tree to 40 feet with ascending branches, which form a narrow crown

BARK: smooth, reddish-brown with conspicuous horizontal, orange lenticels

TWIGS: slender, smooth, glossy red with a grayish coating that is easily rubbed off, producing a bitter odor when bruised

PITH: white streaked with pale brown, continuous

BUDS: less than ⅛ inch long, smooth, pointed, with several overlapping bud scales, often clustered toward the ends of the twigs

Pin cherry—bark

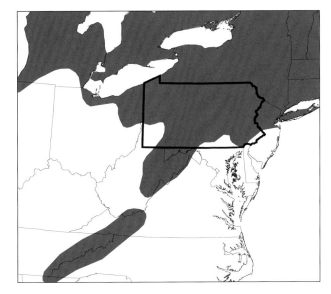

Pin cherry

LEAVES: alternate, simple, 2–4 inches long, narrow with a long pointed tip and finely toothed edges; leaf stalk with several glands below the blade

FALL LEAF COLOR: yellow to reddish-orange

STIPULES: small, falling early

LEAF SCARS: somewhat raised, crescent-shaped with 3 bundle scars

FLOWERS: white, about ½ inch wide, on long stalks arranged in clusters of 4–5, which appear when the leaves are about half expanded

Pin cherry—flowers

FRUIT: red, ¼ inch in diameter with sour flesh and an oblong stone, ripening in July

SEEDS: dispersed by birds

WOOD: light brown, soft and porous, used for firewood

CURRENT CHAMPION: Mercer County, diameter 1 foot 5 inches, height 68 feet, spread 32 feet

The common name fire cherry reflects the early successional nature of this species, which often sprouts up in great numbers in clearings created by timber harvests or forest fires. It is short-lived, soon yielding to other forest species. Pin cherry is most abundant in the mountainous areas of northern Pennsylvania. Its total range extends across Canada from Newfoundland to British Columbia and south to Minnesota and Pennsylvania; it extends further south in the mountains to North Carolina and Tennessee.

Pin cherry—fruit x3/4   Pin cherry—leaf x3/4

Sweet cherry, European bird cherry   *Prunus avium* (L.) L.

FORM: erect tree to 60 feet with a cylindrical crown

Sweet cherry—bark

BARK: tight, shiny, reddish-brown with prominent horizontal lenticels

TWIGS: stout, reddish-brown

PITH: tan, homogeneous

BUDS: clustered at the branch tips

LEAVES: alternate, simple, 2½–5 inches long, oblong with a pointed tip and coarsely toothed edge, dark green above and more or less hairy beneath; the leaf stalk bears several reddish glands just below the blade

FALL LEAF COLOR: yellow to reddish-orange

STIPULES: falling early but leaving a scar on each side of the base of the leaf stalk

LEAF SCARS: rounded to somewhat triangular with 3 bundle scars

FLOWERS: white, about 1 inch in diameter, on long stalks, borne in umbel-like clusters along the branches, appearing after the leaves have expanded

FRUIT: dark red, ½–1 inch in diameter, sweet and edible

SEEDS: rounded, bird-dispersed

WOOD: yellowish-red, strong, used for furniture and musical instruments

CURRENT CHAMPION: Chester County, diameter 6 feet 11 inches, height 85 feet, spread 60 feet

This tree is a European native that has escaped from cultivation to become widespread throughout forested areas of Pennsylvania and adjacent states. It has long been cultivated for its dark red edible fruits. Although the fruits of wild trees are smaller, many commercial sweet cherry cultivars, including "Black Tartarian." have been developed from this species.

It grows to a large size in forested areas and is also found along roadsides, woods edges, and in fencerows where it often forms dense mounded thickets through the production of root suckers.

Sweet cherry—flowers

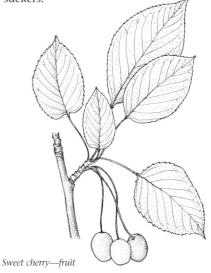

Sweet cherry—fruit

CHESTNUT
Castanea L.
Beech Family—Fagaceae

The chestnuts are deciduous trees with alternate, simple, coarsely toothed leaves. The flowers of chestnut are unisexual, but both staminate and pistillate flowers occur on each tree (monoecious). The staminate flowers of the chestnuts are arranged in semi-erect catkins and have a strong musty odor. The pistillate flowers are surrounded by a spiny husk located at the base of the uppermost catkins. The 1–4 glossy brown nuts develop inside a spiny bur. Flowers open in June after the leaves are fully expanded. The nuts, which are sweet and edible, mature in the early fall at which time the bur splits open.

Chestnut and chinquapin nuts were widely used for food by Native Americans and European settlers. They were eaten raw, or variously boiled, roasted, or pounded into flour from which bread or cakes were made, they were also made into soup or beverages. Tea made from the leaves of chestnut was used to treat whooping cough; other medicinal uses included treatments for bleeding, rheumatism, and colds. The tannin-rich wood and bark of chestnut were also useful for tanning leather. Chestnuts were a very important food source for many species of wildlife.

The Pennsylvania flora includes two native species of chestnut; in addition Chinese chestnut is frequently planted and occasionally persists or naturalizes.

American chestnut   *Castanea dentata* **(Marshall) Borkh.**

FORM: formerly a large tree 80–100 feet, but now rarely reaching more than 25–30 feet

BARK: smooth on young trunks, on older trees becoming fibrous and fissured

TWIGS: smooth, green to brown with small white lenticels

PITH: star-shaped in cross section

BUDS: ¼ inch long, pointed, covered with 2–3 smooth, brown bud scales

LEAVES: 5–8 inches long, smooth on both the upper and lower surfaces; the leaf margin bearing bristle-tipped teeth that are incurved at the tip

FALL LEAF COLOR: yellow to golden-brown

STIPULES: present, but falling early

LEAF SCARS: half-oval with numerous scattered bundle scars

FLOWERS: as described above

FRUIT: burs 2–3 inches in diameter, maturing in September–October,

SEEDS: 2–4 per bur

WOOD: yellowish-brown, durable, formerly used for paneling, beams, furniture, fence posts and rails, and railroad ties

CURRENT CHAMPION: Cameron County, diameter 1 foot 6 inches, height 85 feet, spread 48 feet

*American chestnut—
leaves and young fruit*

American chestnut—bark

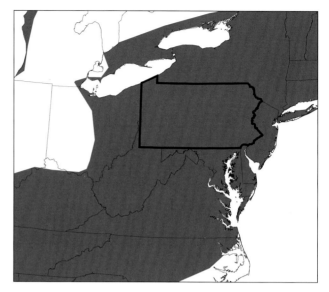

American chestnut

American chestnut was at one time the most common tree in Pennsylvania; however, chestnut blight, which spread rapidly from the New York Zoological Garden, where it was first detected in 1904, has nearly obliterated this once magnificent tree. Recognizing the potential impact of the disease on Pennsylvania's forests, the governor appointed a Commission for the Investigation and Control of the Chestnut Tree Blight Disease in Pennsylvania in 1911.[1] But despite numerous scientific studies of the disease and the fungus that causes it (*Cryphonectria parasitica*), conducted over the next few years, the damage continued to mount.[2] By 1950 the blight had reduced American chestnut to minor status throughout its range. The trees persist, still sprouting from old root crowns, but stems rarely reach more than a few inches in diameter before they too, are affected by the disease. It is rare today to find a fruiting tree and even rarer to find one that produces fully formed nuts.

The impact extended to wildlife also, because with the demise of chestnut a valuable source of mast was lost. In addition, caterpillars of several butterflies including striped hairstreak, hickory hairstreak, banded hairstreak, and banded dusky wing feed on chestnut leaves as do larvae of the polyphemus moth.

In Pennsylvania chestnut grew just about anywhere except on very wet soils or on limestone. The dry, acidic slopes and ridges where chestnut dominated before the blight, now support forests of chestnut oak, pitch pine, black locust, sweet birch, black oak, pignut hickory, and Virginia pine. On more moist sites tuliptree, red maple, white pine, white ash, and red and white oaks have filled the gap.[3]

The full range of American chestnut extended from southern Maine to Georgia, it reached its greatest development in the southern Appalachians.

In 1912 the total value of chestnut products in Pennsylvania was estimated at $70 million, an indication of the importance of chestnut to the state's timber industry. The wood, which has a warm yellow-brown color and fine grain was used for furniture and interior paneling. In addition, its extreme durability made it useful for fence posts, railroad ties, and construction.

American chestnut, Curwensville, Clearfield County, undated photograph from the collection of the Pennsylvania State Archives, Record Group 6, Records of the Department of Forests and Waters

American chestnut, undated photograph from the collection of the Pennsylvania State Archives, Record Group 6, Records of the Department of Forests and Waters.

Chinese chestnut
Castanea mollissima Blume

FORM: spreading tree to 60 feet

BARK: gray-brown, strongly ridged and furrowed

TWIGS: hairy when young

PITH: star-shaped in cross section

BUDS: ¼ inch long, gray-brown, hairy with 2 or 3 overlapping bud scales

LEAVES: 3–6 inches long, hairy beneath; leaf margin with incurved, bristle-tipped teeth

FALL LEAF COLOR: yellow to bronze

STIPULES: present, but falling early

LEAF SCARS: half-oval with scattered bundle scars

FLOWERS: as for other chestnuts, see above

FRUIT: bur 2–3½ inches in diameter

SEEDS: 2–3 per bur

CURRENT CHAMPION: Chester County, diameter 3 feet 10 inches, height 50 feet, spread 65 fet

Chinese chestnut—bark

Since the demise of the American chestnut, this native of China and Korea is frequently grown here for its edible nuts. It is resistant to chestnut blight disease, and is most easily distinguished from American chestnut by the hairy lower surface of the leaves.

Chinese chestnut—flowers

Chinquapin
Castanea pumila (L.) P. Miller

FORM: small understory tree or large shrub to 30 feet

BARK: fissured and broken into plate-like scales

TWIGS: slender, hairy at first, becoming smooth, with numerous lenticels

PITH: star-shaped in cross section

BUDS: ⅛ inch long, covered with fuzzy red bud scales

LEAVES: 3–5 inches long, smooth above and whitish-hairy beneath; margin with shallow bristle-tipped teeth

FALL LEAF COLOR: yellow

STIPULES: present, but falling early

LEAF SCARS: half-oval with scattered bundle scars

FLOWERS: as described above

Chinquapin—bark

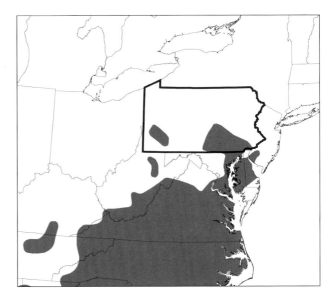

Chinquapin

FRUIT: a spiny bur 1½ inches in diameter
SEEDS: 1–2 per bur, glossy dark grayish-brown, about ½ inch long
WOOD: hard, strong, and durable
CURRENT CHAMPION: none recorded

Chinquapin is limited to a few counties in south central Pennsylvania, its range extends south to Florida, eastern Oklahoma, and Texas. Resistant to chestnut blight, it grows on moist to dry wooded slopes under a canopy of mixed oaks, blackgum, sweet birch, red maple, and hemlock.

Valued for its ornamental quality and its edible nuts, chinquapin also provided native Americans with treatments for headache, fever, chills, and cold sweats in the form of an infusion of dried leaves. The wood is of limited commercial significance due to the small size of the trees, however it was occasionally used for fence posts and railroad ties.

Chinquapin—flowers

Chinquapin—fruits

Notes

1. Anonymous. 1912. The Chestnut Blight Disease. Bulletin No. 1. Pennsylvania Chestnut Blight Commission, Harrisburg.

2. Heald, F. D. 1913. The Symptoms of Chestnut Tree Blight and a Brief Description of the Blight Fungus. Bulletin No. 5. Pennsylvania Chestnut Blight Commission, Harrisburg; Anderson, Paul J. and D. C. Babcock. 1913. Field Studies on the Dissemination and Growth of the Chestnut Blight Fungus. Bulletin No. 3. Pennsylvania Chestnut Blight Commission, Harrisburg.

3. Ceck, Franklin. 1986. American chestnut (*Castanea dentata*), replacement species and current status. In Shyamal K. Majumdar, Fred J. Brenner, and Ann F. Rhoads (eds.), *Endangered and Threatened Species Programs in Pennsylvania and Other States: Causes, Issues, and Management*, Pennsylvania Academy of Science, Easton.

CHINESE-CEDAR
Cedrela L.
Mahogany Family—Meliaceae

Chinese-cedar, Chinese toon　　　　　*Cedrela sinensis* Juss.

FORM: deciduous tree to 50 feet, crown upright; trees spreading by root shoots to form clonal thickets

BARK: brown, separating in long shaggy strips

TWIGS: stout, gray-brown with a velvety surface, producing an odor of onion when cut or bruised

PITH: large, pale tan, solid

BUDS: rounded, terminal bud larger with several overlapping bud scales

LEAVES: leaves 10–20 inches long, pinnately compound with 10–22 leaflets; edges slightly toothed to entire

FALL LEAF COLOR: yellow

STIPULES: none

LEAF SCARS: large, heart-shaped with 5 bundle scars

FLOWERS: small, white, in large drooping clusters, perfect, each with 5 petals and 5 stamens

FRUIT: a woody capsule about 1 inch long with spreading valves when open

SEEDS: small, winged, wind-dispersed

WOOD: reddish-brown, fine-grained, used in China for furniture and building interiors

CURRENT CHAMPION: Lebanon County, diameter 2 feet 8 inches, height 97 feet, spread 74 feet

Chinese-cedar— dormant twig

One way to distinguish Chinese-cedar from tree-of-heaven (*Ailanthus altissima*), which it resembles, is by the strong onion odor of its twigs and leaves. Chinese-cedar also has shaggy bark unlike the smooth trunks of tree-of-heaven.

Chinese-cedar is native to China, where it is a common component of the deciduous broad-leaved forest and mixed mesophytic forest types. Although introduced into cultivation in 1862, it has never been widely planted. Even so it has managed to escape and become naturalized in urban forest lands in the Philadelphia area. In China young shoots and leaves are cooked and eaten and are considered a delicacy.

Chinese-cedar—fruits

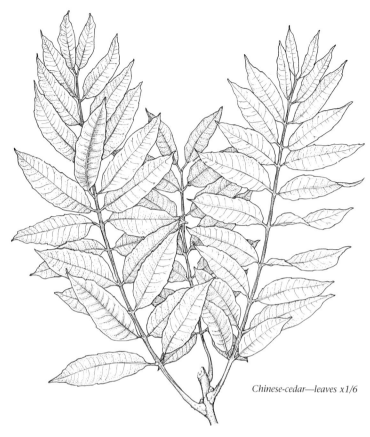

Chinese-cedar—leaves x1/6

Chinese-cedar—bark

Chinese-cedar— flowers

CHINQUAPIN—SEE CHESTNUT

COFFEETREE
GYMNOCLADUS LAM.
Caesalpinia Family—Caesalpiniaceae

Kentucky coffeetree   ***Gymnocladus dioica*** (L.) K. Koch

FORM: deciduous tree to 80 feet, crown rounded, taller than wide

BARK: dark gray to dark brown, irregularly fissured and curling away from the trunk along the edges of the scaly ridges

TWIGS: coarse and stout

PITH: large, pinkish-orange

BUDS: surrounded by a ring of bark, several buds present at each node, stacked above each other with the lowest in a depression on the upper surface of the leaf scar; a terminal bud is not present

LEAVES: alternate, twice pinnately compound, a single leaf may be 3 feet in length and almost 2 feet wide with numerous small elliptical leaflets each about 2 inches long

FALL LEAF COLOR: yellow

STIPULES: none

LEAF SCARS: broadly heart-shaped with 3–5 large, raised bundle scars

FLOWERS: greenish-white or purplish, in large terminal clusters, regular, unisexual or some perfect; each flower with a tubular hypanthium, 5 petals, 5 sepals, and 10 stamens; flowering in late May or early June after the leaves have expanded; this species is mostly dioecious

FRUIT: a thick, flat pod 4–8 inches long and 1–2 inches wide containing a few large seeds surrounded by pulp

SEEDS: several per pod, about ¾ inch in diameter

WOOD: heavy, strong, coarse-grained, light brown to reddish brown, of little commercial importance

CURRENT CHAMPION: Clinton County, diameter 3 feet, height 84 feet, spread 66 feet

Kentucky coffeetree—fruit

Kentucky coffeetree—seed

The delicate texture created by huge, twice pinnate leaves contrasts with the coarse, stubby winter appearance of the branches of this distinctive tree. In fact the genus name *Gymnocladus* means naked branches. The heavy pods, which often persist unopened on the tree through the winter, can also be helpful in identification.

The range of Kentucky coffeetree is mainly midwestern, New York to South Dakota and south to western Virginia, Tennessee, Arkansas, and Oklahoma. Nowhere is it abundant. Although Kentucky coffeetree is found in moist, rich woods and bottomlands scattered throughout the southern part of the state there is some question as to whether it is originally native to Pennsylvania. It has been widely planted, and most if not all of the populations, especially those in the eastern part of the state, are likely of naturalized origin.

The common name refers to the use of the roasted and ground seeds by Native Americans and early settlers to brew a coffee-like beverage. Medicinally, an infusion of the root of Kentucky coffeetree was used as a cure for constipation by several Native American tribes. Other widespread uses were as a tonic and as a

Kentucky coffeetree—bark

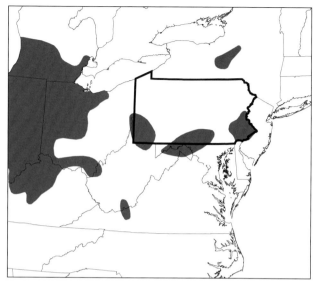

Kentucky coffeetree

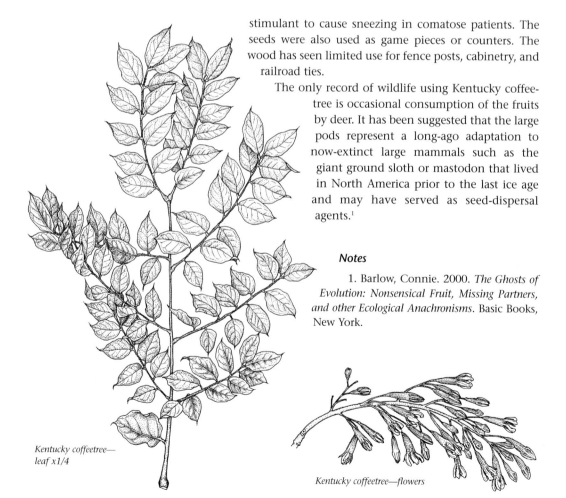

Kentucky coffeetree—
leaf x1/4

Kentucky coffeetree—flowers

stimulant to cause sneezing in comatose patients. The seeds were also used as game pieces or counters. The wood has seen limited use for fence posts, cabinetry, and railroad ties.

The only record of wildlife using Kentucky coffeetree is occasional consumption of the fruits by deer. It has been suggested that the large pods represent a long-ago adaptation to now-extinct large mammals such as the giant ground sloth or mastodon that lived in North America prior to the last ice age and may have served as seed-dispersal agents.[1]

Notes

1. Barlow, Connie. 2000. *The Ghosts of Evolution: Nonsensical Fruit, Missing Partners, and other Ecological Anachronisms*. Basic Books, New York.

CORKTREE
PHELLODENDRON RUPR.
Rue Family—Rutaceae

The corktrees are native to China, Korea, and Japan; several species are present in Pennsylvania and 2 or 3 have become naturalized to some extent. Japanese corktree and Lavalle corktree are described below; in addition another species (*Phellodendron sacchalinense*) is naturalized at a single site in Bucks County.

The corktrees are characterized by opposite, pinnately compound leaves and bright yellow inner bark. The absence of a terminal bud and lateral buds encircled by the base of the leaf stalk are characteristics that can be used to distinguish the corktrees from the very similar bee-bee tree (*Tetradium daniellii*), another naturalized member of the Rue family.

All three species are very similar in appearance, differing mainly in the degree of hairiness of the leaves and the corkiness of the bark. The largest specimens in Pennsylvania of both the species described below are located at the Morris Arboretum in Philadelphia.

Japanese corktree   ***Phellodendron japonicum* Maxim.**

FORM: deciduous trees, 30–60 feet, with upright branches; crown becoming rounded and spreading with age

BARK: thin and only slightly fissured, not strongly corky

TWIGS: stout, yellowish gray with prominent lenticels, inner bark bright yellow

PITH: large, light tan, continuous

BUDS: lateral buds completely hidden by the base of the leaf stalk; terminal buds not present

Japanese corktree   bark

Japanese corktree—fruit

Japanese corktree—flowers

*Japanese corktree—
flower detail x2*

LEAVES: opposite, 10–15 inches long, pinnately compound with 5–11 leaflets; leaflets have a rounded to almost heart-shaped base

FALL LEAF COLOR: yellow

STIPULES: none

LEAF SCARS: horseshoe-shaped with 3 clusters of bundle scars, completely surrounding the lateral buds

FLOWERS: yellowish-green, in clusters up to 3 inches wide, appearing in late May to early June, unisexual, insect-pollinated; plants dioecious;

FRUIT: clusters of fleshy black berries each about ½ inch long, ripening in October and persisting well into the winter

SEEDS: each fruit contains 5 small seeds dispersed by birds

CURRENT CHAMPION: Philadelphia County, diameter 3 feet, height 47 feet, spread 77 feet

Lavalle corktree   *Phellodendron lavallei* Dode

CURRENT CHAMPION: Philadelphia County, diameter 2 feet 8 inches, height 61 feet, spread 69 feet

Lavalle corktree differs from Japanese corktree by its thick, deeply fissured, corky bark and the tapered (rather than rounded) base of the leaflets. It is the most common corktree found in Pennsylvania and is spreading at an alarming rate, invading urban and suburban forest remnants in the southeast including Fort Washington State Park and the Wissahickon section of Philadelphia's Fairmount Park. Several Pittsburgh parks also contain naturalized populations.

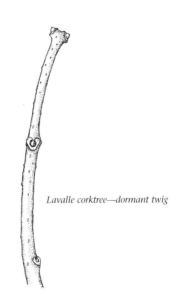

Lavalle corktree—dormant twig

Lavalle corktree—bark

COTTONWOOD—SEE POPLAR

CRABAPPLE
MALUS MEDIK.
Rose Family—Rosaceae

Wild crabapples occur throughout Pennsylvania; they are represented by one clearly distinguished native species and a highly variable complex of hybrids. Based on several nonnative, naturalized species including Siberian crabapple (*Malus baccata* [L.] Borkh.), Showy crabapple (*Malus floribunda* Siebold ex Van Houtte), and Chinese crabapple (*Malus prunifolia* [Willd.] Borkh.), members of this complex defy classification at the species level.

In southeastern Pennsylvania successional thickets dominated by hybrid crabapple trees are not uncommon. Within a single population flower color can range from pure white to deep rosy pink; fruit size ranges from ¼ to ⅝ inch in diameter with the color of the fruit varying from yellow to orange, or red. Typically the fruits do not retain their sepals at maturity, however, some do, suggesting that hybridization may also involve the native sweet crabapple, which is described below.

Crabapples are small trees to about 30 feet tall, but often less. They have alternate, simple, deciduous leaves that are toothed and sometimes somewhat lobed. Bark of the trunk and larger branches is gray and scaly. The flowers consist of 5 spreading petals, 5 sepals, numerous stamens, and 5 styles. The flowers are insect-pollinated, primarily by bees. The inferior ovary develops into a fruit that looks like a miniature apple but is usually very sour.

Flowering crabapples are very popular landscape ornamentals; many cultivars have been developed featuring attractive displays of spring flowers and autumn fruits plus resistance to several pests and diseases. Some crabapples are also used for jelly or preserves. Wild crabapples provide food for birds, deer, bear, and other wildlife.

Sweet crabapple   *Malus coronaria* (L.) Mill.

FORM: small tree to 30 feet with the trunk dividing into several spreading limbs and forming a broad, rounded crown

BARK: gray to reddish-brown, forming long, shaggy scales

TWIGS: red-brown and hairy at first, becoming smooth and light gray; many small branches along the main trunk ending abruptly in sharp thorns

PITH: white, homogeneous

BUDS: rounded at the tip, covered with 3–6 overlapping, red bud scales

LEAVES: simple, alternate, 1½–3 inches long with a pointed tip; margin coarsely toothed or even slightly lobed

FALL LEAF COLOR: yellow

STIPULES: present but not persistent

LEAF SCARS: raised, narrow with indistinct bundle scars

FLOWERS: in small clusters on short spur branches, white tinged with pink, fragrant, appearing after the leaves have expanded

FRUIT: yellowish-green, 1–1½ inches in diameter with persistent sepals, sour

SEEDS: dark brown, disseminated by birds and mammals that consume the fruit

Sweet crabapple—bark

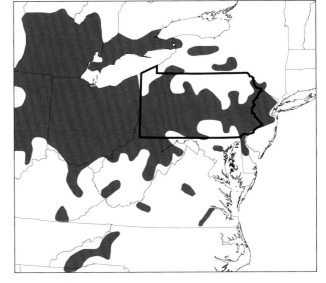

Sweet crabapple

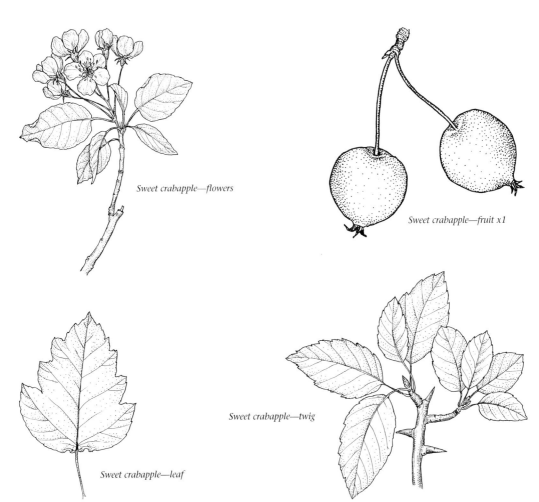

Sweet crabapple—flowers

Sweet crabapple—fruit x1

Sweet crabapple—leaf

Sweet crabapple—twig

WOOD: light red and heavy but not strong, close-grained, used for tool handles and other small items

CURRENT CHAMPION: Warren County, diameter 1 foot 1 inch, height 42 feet, spread 18 feet

Sweet crabapple is our only native crabapple. It is also sometimes cultivated for its attractive flowers; the fruit are used for jelly. In the wild it provides food for grosbeaks, grouse, mice, opossum, raccoon, deer, and bear.

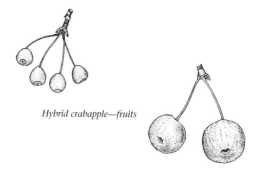

Hybrid crabapple—fruits

CUCUMBER-TREE—SEE MAGNOLIA

DOGWOOD
CORNUS L.
Dogwood Family—Cornaceae

The dogwoods are small understory trees with simple, entire leaves. A distinctive feature of the leaves is the lateral veins that curve to become more-or-less parallel with the leaf margins. Flowers are small but clustered in an umbel-like or head-like inflorescence. In some species the clusters of flowers are surrounded by 4 showy, white bracts. Each flower has 4 tiny sepals, 4 petal lobes, 4 stamens, and an inferior ovary; the fruit is a drupe.

Flowering dogwood   *Cornus florida* **L.**

FORM: understory tree to 30 feet with spreading branches and a flat-topped crown

BARK: light gray, broken into a pattern of small scaly squares on mature trees

TWIGS: reddish or sometimes greenish, smooth

PITH: tan, homogeneous

BUDS: lateral buds small, reddish, covered by 2 bud scales; terminal buds present, frequently they are larger, stalked, globose flower buds

LEAVES: opposite, elliptic, 3–5 inches long

FALL LEAF COLOR: red to purple

STIPULES: none

LEAF SCARS: raised, with 3 or more bundle scars, the two opposite leaf scars typically encircling the twig

FLOWERS: tiny, greenish-yellow, in a small cluster surrounded by 4 showy white or pinkish bracts, opening in late April or early May before the leaves

FRUIT: about ½ inch long, bright red, borne in small, stalked clusters of 2–5

SEEDS: dispersed by birds and small mammals

WOOD: very hard, reddish-brown to pinkish

CURRENT CHAMPION: Delaware County, diameter 1 foot 6 inches, height 38 feet, spread 59 feet

In the past 20–30 years the much beloved flowering dogwood has been attacked by a fungus disease, which first appeared in North America in the early 1970s.[1] Its origin is not known. The disease, dogwood anthracnose (causal agent: *Discula destructiva*), has killed cultivated and wild trees alike from Connecticut to Tennessee. While it does not appear that flowering dogwood will be eliminated from our forests, its prevalence and its use as an ornamental are declining because of the disease.

A prominent component of the forest understory in Pennsylvania, flowering dogwood is common throughout the state except in the northern tier of counties and at the highest elevations along the Allegheny

Flowering dogwood—flowers

Flowering dogwood—bark

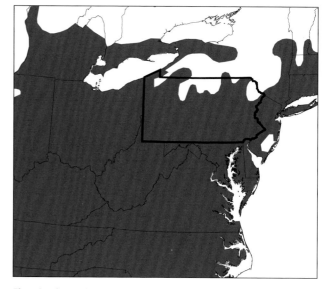
Flowering dogwood

Front. Its early spring blooms come at a time when the wildflower display in the eastern deciduous forest is at its maximum. Dogwood ranges from Maine, southern Ontario, and Michigan south to Florida and northeastern Mexico.

Flowering dogwood was used by Native Americans to treat children for worms and diarrhea, to counteract poisons, and as an antiseptic and astringent. The roots were also used as a tonic and the twigs were chewed as a sort of early toothbrush. The bark of dogwood roots was sold in apothecary shops in Philadelphia in the mid-1700s as a substitute for quinine for treating ague (malaria). Because of its extreme hardness, the wood was used to make bearings, tool handles, and wheel hubs. Native Americans are reported to have relied on the appearance of the flowers of dogwood to signal the time to plant corn.

The bright red dogwood fruits are eagerly eaten by songbirds, grouse, turkey, and small mammals such as squirrel, raccoon, and opossum. The flowers are a nectar source for spring azure and red-spotted purple butterflies.

Flowering dogwood—fruit

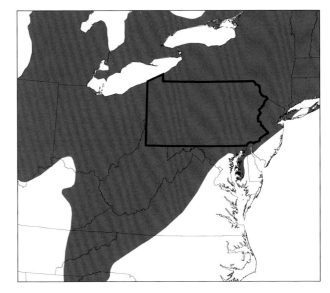

Alternate-leaf dogwood—bark   *Alternate-leaf dogwood*

Pagoda dogwood, alternate-leaf dogwood *Cornus alternifolia* L.f.

FORM: small deciduous tree to 18 feet with mostly horizontal branches and a broad, flat-topped crown

BARK: greenish streaked with white when young, roughened with shallow fissures when older

TWIGS: red with whitish lenticels

PITH: white

BUDS: oval, covered with 2–3 bud scales

LEAVES: alternate, but crowded toward the ends of the branches, 2–5 inches long

FALL LEAF COLOR: reddish-purple

STIPULES: not present

LEAF SCARS: raised, crescent-shaped with 3 bundle scars

FLOWERS: creamy white, in a dome-shaped cluster about 1½–2½ inches in diameter, appearing with the leaves

FRUIT: about ⅓ inch in diameter, blue-black on red stalks

SEEDS: dispersed by birds and small mammals

WOOD: very hard

CURRENT CHAMPION: none recorded

The horizontal branches of alternate-leaf dogwood create a tiered appearance, which is undoubtedly the reason for it also being known as pagoda dogwood. This plant is especially striking in fruit when the dark blue drupes contrast with the red stalks of the inflorescence. It is more cold tolerant than flowering dogwood, but lacks the showy white bracts around the flower clusters.

Alternate-leaf dogwood occurs throughout Pennsylvania in low, moist woods, along stream banks, and in shaded ravines. Its total range extends from Nova Scotia and Newfoundland west to Minnesota and south to Arkansas and Florida.

Alternate-leaf dogwood—flowers

Alternate-leaf dogwood—fruit

Alternate-leaf dogwood and other shrub dogwoods were virtually a one-stop drug store for Native Americans who used them to treat a wide variety of medical problems including childhood diseases such as worms and measles as well as diarrhea, laryngitis, cough, blisters, nausea associated with pregnancy, sore eyes, cancer, venereal disease, and piles.

Songbirds and small mammals eat the fruits of alternate-leaf dogwood. The branches are so intensively browsed by deer that this species is much less common than it used to be in the forests of northern Pennsylvania.

Notes

1. Daughtrey, Margery L., Craig R. Hibben, Kerry O. Britton, Mark T. Windham, and Scott C. Redlin. 1996. Dogwood anthracnose, understanding a disease new to North America. *Plant Disease* 80 (4): 349–58.

DOUGLAS-FIR
PSEUDOTSUGA CARRIÈRE
Pine Family—Pinaceae

Douglas-fir   *Pseudotsuga menziesii* **(Mirb.) Franco**

FORM: conical evergreen to 120–180 feet (in its native habitat)

BARK: smooth with resin blisters on young trees, becoming deeply furrowed in age

TWIGS: greenish- or grayish-brown, hairy

BUDS: slenderly conical, pointed

LEAVES: needle-like, bright green to sometimes bluish, ½–1⅓ inches long, flat with a prominent midvein

LEAF SCARS: slightly raised

CONES: 2–4 inches long, cylindrical with long tongue-like bracts extending beyond the cone scales, maturing in a single year

SEEDS: about ¼ inch with a longer wing

WOOD: a very valuable source of timber and pulpwood in the west

CURRENT CHAMPION: Chester County, diameter 2 feet 9 inches, height 92 feet, spread 34 feet

Douglas-fir—cone

The long, shaggy, 3-pronged bracts that extend beyond the cone scales make douglas-fir easy to identify if cones are present. Its slender, pointed buds are also distinctive. Douglas-fir is native to the western United States where it is a dominant tree in coniferous or mixed forests from New Mexico, Arizona, and California to British Columbia. In the east, it is planted in Christmas tree plantations or as an ornamental but does not achieve the massive size it does in its native habitat, where it is a major source of lumber.

Douglas-fir—twig

Douglas-fir—bark

ELM
Ulmus L.
Elm Family—Ulmaceae

The elms are large, deciduous trees with alternate, simple, pinnately veined leaves with singly or more commonly, doubly toothed margins. Two species are native to Pennsylvania; two others, from Asia, are planted and have occasionally become naturalized. All except Chinese elm bloom early in the spring before the leaves emerge, the perfect flowers are wind-pollinated. The disk-shaped, winged fruits mature within a few weeks and are dispersed by the wind.

American Elm   *Ulmus americana* L.

FORM: deciduous tree to 120 feet with a graceful vase-shape and drooping branches

BARK: light brown to gray, coarsely longitudinally fissured

TWIGS: slender, brownish

PITH: white, homogeneous

BUDS: approximately ⅜ inch long, curved inward toward the twig, pointed, and covered with 6–10 overlapping scales; terminal bud lacking; flower buds larger and rounded

LEAVES: alternate, simple, usually unequal at the base; upper surface smooth to the touch; margin sharply and doubly toothed

FALL LEAF COLOR: yellow

STIPULES: falling early and leaving a small triangular scar on each side of the base of the leaf stalk

LEAF SCARS: raised, semicircular, with 3 bundle scars

FLOWERS: perfect with a 7 to 9-lobed calyx and an equal number of stamens; stigmas 2; flowering before the leaves emerge

FRUIT: disk-shaped, approximately ½ inch in diameter, with a single seed surrounded by a winged margin that is notched at the tip, maturing in the late spring

SEEDS: wind-dispersed

WOOD: light-colored, hard and tough

CURRENT CHAMPION: Allegheny County, diameter 6 feet 8 inches, height 96 feet, spread 131 feet

American elm—leaf

Described as "the most magnificent vegetable in the temperate zone" by French botanist, Francois André Michaux,[1] American elm was a favorite shade tree in many areas because of its graceful form and fast growth. However, the accidental introduction of Dutch elm disease (caused by the fungus *Ceratocystis ulmi*) in the 1930s, has greatly limited its landscape use. First found on elms in Holland in 1921, Dutch elm disease appeared in Ohio and several eastern states in the 1930s. It is a very destructive disease that can kill large branches or entire trees within weeks or a year or two.

American elm—bark

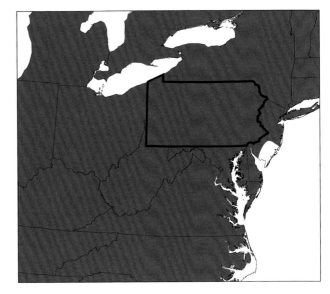

American elm

American elm grows naturally on river and stream banks, floodplains, and other moist lowland sites throughout Pennsylvania. Its total range extends from Nova Scotia to Montana and south to Florida and eastern Texas.

Native Americans made use of the bark for making canoes and containers for storing corn and other foods. Log sections were used to make mortars and pestles for grinding corn. Rope was made by pounding, and then twisting strips of the fibrous inner bark. Medicinal uses included the treatment of dysentery, coughs, colds, and bleeding. Early settlers split off long narrow strips of elm wood with which to weave chair seats and used the bark to prepare a dye for cloth.

The wood is light colored, hard, and strong. It was valued for such items as wagon and carriage wheels, agricultural implements, furniture, heavy-duty flooring, and sporting goods. The yoke that the Liberty Bell hangs from is American elm. However, Dutch elm disease and changing needs have relegated elm wood to minor commercial significance today.

Elm seeds are food for finches, bobwhite, grouse, squirrels, and opossums; they are said to have been a favored food of the now extinct passenger pigeon. Baltimore orioles frequently select the slender, drooping branches of American elm as a place to build their nest. American elm is a larval food source for several butterflies including the tiger swallowtail, painted lady, red-spotted purple, question mark, eastern comma, and mourning cloak. Caterpillars of polyphemus and several sphinx moths also feed on elm leaves.

American elm—fruit detail x1

American elm—fruit

Chinese elm, lacebark elm   *Ulmus parvifolia* Jacq.

FORM: deciduous tree to 50 feet tall with a broad, rounded crown

BARK: mottled brownish with orange patches

TWIGS: hairy when young but becoming smooth and grayish-brown

PITH: yellowish

BUDS: small, brown

LEAVES: alternate, simple, 1–2 inches long with an asymmetrical base, dark green, firm and somewhat leathery in texture; edge sharply and singly toothed

FALL LEAF COLOR: leaves remaining green very late then turning yellow or bronzy red

STIPULES: falling early and leaving a small scar on each side of the leaf base

LEAF SCARS: oval, raised with 3 small bundle scars

FLOWERS: perfect, opening in the fall, each with a 5- to 9-lobed calyx and 5–9 stamens

FRUIT: disk-shaped, approximately ½ inch in diameter with a single seed surrounded by a wing that is notched at the tip, maturing in the fall

SEEDS: wind-dispersed

WOOD: tough and strong

CURRENT CHAMPION: Philadelphia County, diameter 4 feet 6 inches (at 2 feet), height 64 feet, spread 74 feet

Native to northern and central China, Korea, and Japan, this tree is often planted for its attractive mottled bark and glossy, dark green leaves. Many cultivars have been described. Chinese elm's potential to become widely naturalized is evident in the large number of seedlings that frequently occur near planted specimens. In some suburban areas it has invaded remnant hedgerows and disturbed woodlots.

Unlike our native elms, Chinese elm blooms and produces its seeds in the fall. The largest known specimen in Pennsylvania is at the Morris Arboretum in Philadelphia.

Chinese elm—detail of fruit x2

Chinese elm—twig with fruit

Chinese elm—bark

Siberian elm   *Ulmus pumila* L.

FORM: deciduous tree to 60 feet with a widely spreading crown

BARK: gray, deeply furrowed in age

TWIGS: slender, green becoming grayish-brown, smooth

PITH: small, white, and homogeneous

BUDS: flower buds conspicuous, ⅛ inch in diameter and rounded with overlapping bud scales; leaf buds much smaller, almost black

LEAVES: to 3 inches long, singly toothed on the margins

FALL LEAF COLOR: drab

STIPULES: falling early and leaving a small triangular scar on each side of the base of the leaf stalk

LEAF SCARS: oval with 3 bundle scars

FLOWERS: produced in the spring

FRUIT: nearly circular, ½ inch across

SEEDS: wind-dispersed

WOOD: weak, easily broken

CURRENT CHAMPION: Montour County, diameter 5 feet 3 inches, height 88 feet, spread 102 feet.

Siberian elm—fruit x1

Native to Asia, Siberian elms have been widely planted for fast-growing windbreaks. It has naturalized at scattered locations across the southern half of Pennsylvania. The wood is brittle leading to frequent breakage of limbs in mature trees. Unlike most other elms the leaves are singly toothed. Flowers and fruits are produced in the spring.

Siberian elm—bark

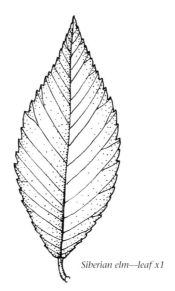

Siberian elm—leaf x1

Slippery elm   *Ulmus rubra* **Muhl.**

FORM: deciduous tree to 70 feet with a spreading, flat-topped crown

BARK: reddish-brown, deeply and irregularly furrowed

TWIGS: hairy when young but becoming smooth and grayish-brown

PITH: white, homogeneous

BUDS: reddish-brown, approximately ⅜ inch long, pointed, curved inward toward the twig, covered with 6–8 overlapping bud scales; terminal bud absent

LEAVES: alternate, simple with an asymmetrical base, doubly toothed, rough to the touch especially on the upper surface

FALL LEAF COLOR: yellow to brown

STIPULES: present but dropping early and leaving a small triangular scar on each side of the base of the leaf stalk

LEAF SCARS: oval, raised with 3 bundle scars

FLOWERS: perfect, opening before the leaves emerge; each flower with a 5 to 9-lobed calyx and 5–9 stamens

FRUIT: disk-shaped, approximately ½ inch in diameter with a single seed surrounded by a wing that is notched at the tip, surface hairy over the seed, maturing in the late spring

SEEDS: wind-dispersed

WOOD: tough and strong

CURRENT CHAMPION: Armstrong County, diameter 4 feet 9 inches, height 97 feet, spread 64 feet

Slippery elm—fruit x2

Slippery elm—leaf x1

Slippery elm is easily confused with American elm; it is most easily distinguished by the rough upper surface of the leaves. When fruits are present the hairy surface over the seed of slippery elm is also a good distinguishing characteristic; American elm fruits are smooth.

In Pennsylvania slippery elm grows in moist woods, stream banks, and floodplains throughout. Its total range extends from New Hampshire to Georgia and west to Minnesota and eastern Texas.

Native Americans used preparations made from the mucilaginous inner bark of slippery elm to treat many ailments including consumption, fevers, and diarrhea and to ease labor pains. The bark was also powered and used as a food, food supplement, or a food preservative. Poultices made from the dried bark of elm roots were used on wounds, bruises, ulcers, and burns. Early settlers adopted many of the same practices and in the mid to late 1800s, slippery elm bark could be purchased in drug stores in a dry powdered form.

Slippery elm— dormant twig

Slippery elm— flower detail x2

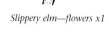

Slippery elm—flowers x1

Slippery elm—bark

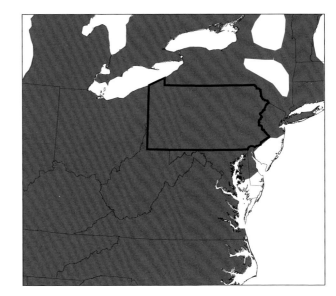

Slippery elm

The wood was useful too, as railroad ties, frameworks for small boats, and many of the same applications as American elm.

Notes

1. Michaux, F. Andrew. 1817. *The North American Sylva, or A Description of the Forest Trees of the United States, Canada, and Nova Scotia*, in 3 volumes. Thomas Dobson-Solomon Conrad, Philadelphia.

EMPRESS-TREE
PAULOWNIA SIEBERT & ZUCC.
Trumpet-creeper Family—Bignoniaceae

Empress-tree, princess-tree   *Paulownia tomentosa* **(Thunb.) Steud.**

FORM: deciduous, fast growing, upright tree to 60 feet with a rounded crown and spreading branches

BARK: dark brown, rough

TWIGS: coarse

PITH: thick, pinkish-orange

BUDS: flower buds hairy, brown, in erect clusters, very conspicuous all winter

LEAVES: opposite or whorled, simple, broadly ovate to slightly lobed, to 2 feet long, rounded or heart-shaped at the base and pointed at the tip, densely hairy on both sides; margin smooth or coarsely toothed

FALL LEAF COLOR: yellow to brown

STIPULES: none

LEAF SCARS: large, 3-lobed with 3 groups of bundle scars

FLOWERS: in large erect clusters, tubular, purple, appearing in May before the leaves, insect-pollinated

FRUITS: 1½ to 2- inch-long, egg-shaped capsules that split in half lengthwise

SEEDS: small, winged, wind-dispersed

WOOD: valuable, used in Asia to craft ceremonial items

CURRENT CHAMPION: Philadelphia County, diameter 4 feet 10 inches, height 91 feet, spread 22 feet

*Empress-tree—
seed x5*

Whether flowering, in leaf, in fruit, or dormant, this tree is hard to miss. In mid-May its bare branches support immense upright clusters of tubular purple flowers. The leaves are huge, more than 2 feet long on vigorous shoots; in the winter the fuzzy brown flower buds are very conspicuous. The egg-shaped capsules, which hang on through the winter are about 1½ inches long and contain many small winged seeds that are dispersed by the wind.

An early successional component of mixed mesophytic forests in China, Japan, and Korea, here empress-tree is very common in urban waste ground, along highways and railroad tracks, and in disturbed urban or suburban wood-lots.[1] Young shoots can grow as much as 8–10 feet in a single season. Although it occasionally naturalizes in forested sites, it appears to be limited to openings created by disturbances that leave gaps in the canopy over exposed mineral soil. Most of the documented occurrences are in southeastern Pennsylvania and the Pittsburgh vicinity, however empress-tree probably occurs elsewhere in the state also; its northern spread is limited by the vulnerability of the flower buds to winter injury.

Empress-tree was introduced from Asia in the 1840s as an ornamental. Today it is occasionally grown in plantations for its wood, which is valued in Japan for making ceremonial wedding chests and other specialty items. If you have an empress-tree with a straight, solid trunk you might want to keep a careful eye on

Empress-tree—bark

Empress-tree—flowers

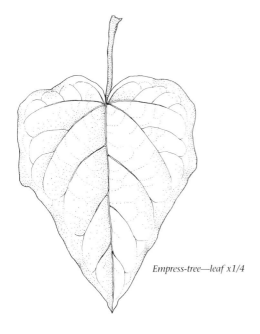

Empress-tree—leaf x1/4

Empress-tree—fruit

it. With a value of several thousand dollars each, the logs have been the target of thieves wielding chainsaws in more than one instance.

Notes

1. Williams, Charles E. 1993. The exotic empress tree, *Paulownia tomentosa*: an invasive pest of forests? *Natural Areas Journal* 13 (3): 221; Williams, Charles E. 1993. Age structure and importance of naturalized *Paulownia tomentosa* in a central Virginia streamside forest. *Castanea* 58 (4): 243–49.

FIR
ABIES MILL.
Pine Family—Pinaceae

Balsam fir   *Abies balsamea* (L.) Mill.

FORM: to 60 feet (in the wild), narrow with a pyramidal crown
BARK: smooth and grayish-brown with resin blisters, becoming scaly with age
TWIGS: smooth grayish-brown, sparsely hairy when young
BUDS: clustered at the ends of the twigs, ovoid or conic, resinous
LEAVES: evergreen, dark green and shiny, linear, flattened, ½–1 inch long, lacking a petiole
LEAF SCARS: round and flat
CONES: erect, oblong-cylindrical, 1½–3 inches long
SEEDS: up to ¼ inch long, winged
WOOD: light, soft, weak, white
CURRENT CHAMPION: Adams County, diameter 4 feet, height 104 feet, spread 48 feet

Balsam fir is a rare native species in Pennsylvania where it is found in cool swamps and bogs in peaty soil. It occurs in scattered locations from the Poconos west to Warren County with a southern outpost at Bear Meadows in Centre County where a recent study found it to be in decline, perhaps a result of global warming.[1] Red spruce and Canadian hemlock are frequent associates. The total range of balsam fir stretches from Newfoundland and Labrador across Canada to Alberta, and south to the mountains of West Virginia and Virginia.

Balsam fir was never commercially important in Pennsylvania because there was so little of it. Farther north it is used for lumber and paper pulp and is also a very popular Christmas tree. In recent years Fraser fir (*Abies fraseri*), a native of

Balsam fir—twig with cones x1

Balsam fir—bark

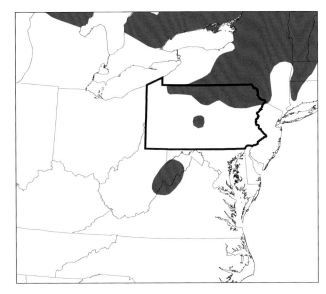

Balsam fir

the Blue Ridge Mountains from Virginia to North Carolina and Tennessee has achieved more popularity for the latter use here, because it can be grown more successfully in plantations in our state.

Medicinal uses of balsam gum, the resinous sap that oozes from beneath the bark of balsam fir trees, were recorded in the Icelandic sagas and many subsequent writings. They included promoting the healing of wounds and burns and use as a diuretic, cough suppressant, and stimulant. Several Native American groups applied the aromatic qualities of balsam gum via a sweat bath. Like spruce gum, balsam gum was also useful for caulking the seams in birch bark canoes. A more recent use was to prepare permanent microscope slides by sealing the specimen to be viewed in "Canadian balsam."

The seeds of balsam fir are eaten by a variety of birds and small mammals. Deer and moose (farther north) browse on the foliage, especially during the winter.

Notes

1. Abrams, M. D., C. A. Copenheaver, B. A. Black, and S. van de Gevel. 2001. Dendroecology and climate impacts for a relict, old-growth, bog forest in the Ridge and Valley Province of central Pennsylvania, U.S.A. *Canadian Journal of Botany* 79 (1): 58–69.

FRINGETREE
CHIONANTHUS L.
Olive Family—Oleaceae

White fringetree   *Chionanthus virginicus* **L.**

FORM: deciduous shrub or small tree to 25 feet

BARK: grayish, smooth

TWIGS: green to brown, square in cross section, hairy or smooth with prominent lenticels

PITH: white, homogeneous

BUDS: rounded at the base with a pointed tip, covered by 3 overlapping pairs of keeled bud scales; terminal bud similar

LEAVES: opposite, simple, 4–6 inches long, oblong; margin smooth

FALL LEAF COLOR: yellow

STIPULES: none produced

LEAF SCARS: raised, semicircular with a ring of bundle scars

FLOWERS: white, in large drooping clusters, unisexual, male and female flowers on separate plants (dioecious); both with 4 narrow petals about an inch long, male flowers with 2 stamens and somewhat longer petals, female flowers with a single ovary

FRUIT: dark blue, fleshy, about ¾ inch long

SEEDS: one per fruit, bird-dispersed

WOOD: light brown, hard, and heavy, but too small to be of commercial importance

CURRENT CHAMPION: Philadelphia County, diameter 8 inches, height 24 feet, spread 29 feet

The large drooping clusters of white flowers make this species conspicuous in flower. White fringetree occurs in moist, open woods at widely scattered sites in central and southern Pennsylvania. Because of its rarity here at the northern edge of its range, Pennsylvania Biological Survey has recommended that it be designated as a threatened species in the state. The range of the species extends from southern Pennsylvania to Florida and Texas.

Native Americans treated infected sores or wounds with poultices prepared from roots or bark of white fringetree. Today its main use is as a landscape specimen. The leaves are a food source for larvae of several sphinx moths.

White fringetree—bark

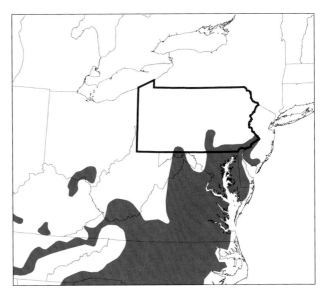

White fringetree

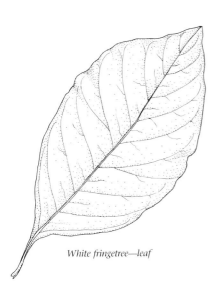

White fringetree—leaf

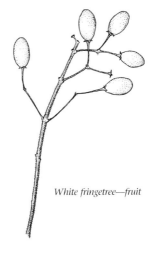

White fringetree—fruit

White fringetree—flowers

GINKGO
Ginkgo L.
Ginkgo Family—Ginkgoaceae

Ginkgo, maidenhair tree   *Ginkgo biloba* L.

FORM: deciduous tree with stiff, stout branches
BARK: light brown, irregularly fissured
TWIGS: stout, with short, crowded lateral shoots that bear the leaves and seeds
BUDS: ⅛ inch long, broadly conical with 6–8 overlapping bud scales
LEAVES: distinctly fan-shaped with a long petiole, bright green, 2–3 inches wide
FALL LEAF COLOR: yellow
LEAF SCARS: half moon shaped with 2 bundle scars
CONES: the seeds of ginkgo are not produced in cones, but rather are covered only by a fleshy seed coat
SEEDS: produced by female trees only, plum-like, light tan to pinkish-orange, about 1 inch long with a foul-smelling, fleshy outer layer; the inner hard-shelled kernel is edible when cooked
WOOD: light tan
CURRENT CHAMPION: Philadelphia County, diameter 5 feet 9 inches, height 146 feet, spread 101 feet

If you consider the fossil record, ginkgo has been in North America for 125 million years, since the Mesozoic.[1] However, it has been extinct in the wild here for about 50 million years; the trees we see today in Pennsylvania have been planted or have spread from planted sources. Despite its broad, flat leaves, deciduous habit, and plum-like seeds, ginkgo is an ancient member of the gymnosperms, a group that also includes the pines, spruces, and other conifers.

Ginkgo—leaves

The smelly outer covering of the seeds, the inner bony layer that surrounds the kernel, and the tendency for large numbers of seeds to drop to the ground en masse are thought to be adaptations that evolved in connection with seed dispersal by plant-eating dinosaurs.[2]

Ginkgo is native to the mountains of Anhwei Province in eastern China; it has been cultivated in China since the Sung dynasty, about A.D. 1000, for its edible seeds and as an ornamental. The first ginkgo to be grown in Pennsylvania in modern times was planted in 1784 at William Hamilton's estate, The Woodlands, now Woodlands Cemetery, in West Philadelphia. Another early specimen was located nearby at Bartram's Garden. Today ginkgo continues to be valued as a street tree due to its tolerance for urban conditions; however, only male trees are used to avoid the smelly seeds.

Ginkgo is thought to have medicinal properties, as a visit to a health food store will quickly reveal. It is promoted for uses ranging from improving blood

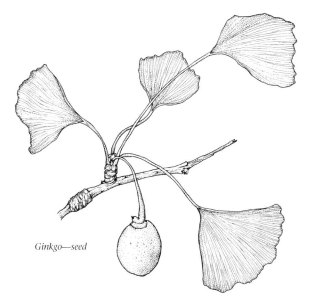

Ginkgo—seed

Ginkgo—bark

circulation to memory enhancement; there is no scientific evidence to support these claims, however.

Notes

1. Basinger, J. F., E. E. Mciver, and B. A. Lepage. 1988. The fossil forests of Axel Heiberg Island. *Musk-ox* 36: 50–55.

2. Wing, Scott L. and Hans-Dieter Sues. 1992. Mesozoic and early Cenozoic terrestrial ecosystems. Chapter 6 in A. K. Behrnesmeyer, J. D. Damuth, W. A. DiMichele, R. Potts, H.-D. Sues, and S. L. Wing (eds.), *Terrestrial Ecosystems Through Time: Evolutionary Paleoecology of Terrestrial Plants and Animals*, University of Chicago Press, Chicago.

Ginkgo—young female strobili

Ginkgo—male strobili (cones)

GOLDENRAIN TREE
KOELREUTERIA LAXM.
Soapberry Family—Sapindaceae

Goldenrain tree   *Koelreuteria paniculata* **Laxm.**

FORM: deciduous tree to 40 feet with a broad, rounded crown

BARK: light brown, furrowed

TWIGS: stout, light brown with prominent orange-brown lenticels

PITH: white, solid

BUDS: lateral buds broadly rounded, terminal bud absent

LEAVES: alternate, 6–18 inches long, pinnately compound with 7–15 coarsely and irregularly toothed leaflets

FALL LEAF COLOR: yellow

STIPULES: none

LEAF SCARS: large, raised, and shield-shaped

FLOWERS: yellow, about ½ inch long, in large, showy clusters at the ends of the branches in mid-summer, perfect, insect-pollinated

FRUIT: 3-lobed, papery capsules 1½–2 inches long and borne in large clusters at the ends of the branches, persisting well into the winter

SEEDS: black, about the size of a small pea

CURRENT CHAMPION: Lebanon County, diameter 1 foot 9 inches, height 61 feet, spread 48 feet

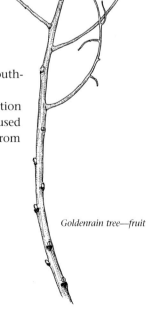

Goldenrain tree is native to China, Japan, and Korea; it was introduced into cultivation in 1763. Its tolerance for drought and salt has made it popular in urban areas. Scattered instances of naturalized plants have been noted in southeastern and southwestern Pennsylvania.

In traditional Chinese medicine a preparation made from the flowers of goldenrain tree was used to treat conjunctivitis. Yellow dye was made from the flowers and black dye from the leaves.

Goldenrain tree—fruit

Goldenrain tree—bark

Goldenrain tree—flowers

Goldenrain tree—leaf

HACKBERRY
CELTIS L.
Elm Family—Ulmaceae

Hackberry is a small to large deciduous tree with distinctive warty, ridged bark. Both unisexual and perfect flowers occur on the same tree; the flowers are wind-pollinated. In Pennsylvania there are two highly variable native species of hackberry, both in need of further taxonomic study.

The branches of hackberry frequently bear dense growths of twigs referred to as "witches' brooms." These galls are thought to be caused by a combination of a mite (*Eriophes celtis*) and a powdery mildew fungus (*Spherotheca phytoptophila*), which irritate the tree, causing a localized proliferation of buds. In addition hackberry leaves often sport wart-like growths on the lower surface, known as hackberry nipple gall, caused by an insect known as a psyllid (*Pachypsylla celtidismamma*).

The fruit is a small drupe with a thin fleshy layer that is an important winter food for many birds and small mammals. Hackberry leaves are the only food source for the hackberry emperor and tawny emperor butterflies. Other butterflies, including the question mark, red-spotted purple, and mourning cloak, also feed on hackberry.

The wood is heavy and dense and has been used for manufacturing agricultural implements, inexpensive furniture, crates, and boxes. However, hackberry, which tends to occur as scattered individual trees, has never been sufficiently abundant to have much commercial significance in Pennsylvania. Native Americans used extracts of the bark to treat menstrual problems and sore throat.

Hackberry, sugarberry   *Celtis occidentalis* L.

FORM: large, upright deciduous tree to 80 feet or more, but usually closer to 20–30 feet, or even smaller on dry rocky sites

BARK: gray, bearing irregular corky warts and ridges

TWIGS: slender, brownish

PITH: white, chambered

BUDS: ovate, sharp-pointed with 2–3 overlapping bud scales, hairy

LEAVES: yellow-green, 2–6 inches long, alternate, simple with an unequal base and long tapered tip, rough to the touch; edges toothed except at the base

FALL LEAF COLOR: yellow

STIPULES: present, but falling early

LEAF SCARS: oval or somewhat curved, with 3 bundle scars

FLOWERS: appearing with the leaves, unisexual with staminate and pistillate flowers on the same tree, and often a few perfect flowers too

FRUIT: a small drupe about ¼ inch in diameter with a thin, dryish, sweet, edible fleshy layer surrounding the large rounded seed, ripening in September, dark red to black

SEEDS: dispersed by birds

WOOD: heavy, coarse-grained, and yellowish in color

Hackberry—bark

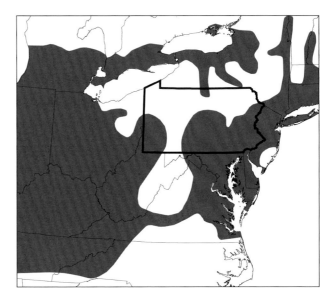

Hackberry

CURRENT CHAMPION: Montgomery County, diameter 4 feet 6 inches, height 106 feet, spread 81 feet

Hackberry reaches its greatest size on rich, moist soils along streams and rivers. However, this highly variable species also grows as stunted specimens on shale cliffs and other dry, rocky sites.

Hackberry occurs scattered across Pennsylvania, but is absent from the northern tier of counties and the highest elevations along the Allegheny Front. The total range of this species is from Connecticut to the Dakotas and eastern Colorado and south to Georgia, Mississippi, and Oklahoma.

Hackberry—flowers

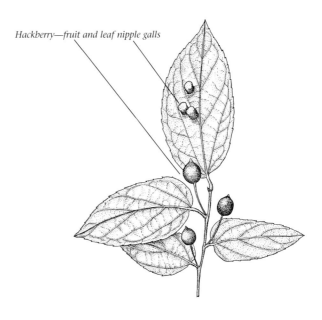

Hackberry—fruit and leaf nipple galls

Hackberry—witch's broom gall

Dwarf hackberry   *Celtis tenuifolia* Nuttall

FORM: small tree or large shrub, 15–25 feet

BARK: gray, ridged, and warty

TWIGS: slender, brownish

PITH: white, chambered

BUDS: ovate, sharp-pointed with 2–3 overlapping bud scales

LEAVES: yellow-green, 2–2½ inches long, alternate, simple, unequal at the base, tapering to the tip, rough to the touch; margins mostly smooth with only a few teeth toward the tip

FALL LEAF COLOR: yellow

STIPULES: present, but falling early

LEAF SCARS: oval or somewhat curved with 1–3 bundle scars

FLOWERS: appearing with the leaves, unisexual with staminate and pistillate flowers on the same tree, a few perfect flowers often present as well

FRUIT: a small drupe about ¼ inch in diameter with a thin, dryish, edible fleshy layer surrounding the seed, ripening in September, orange-brown to red

SEEDS: dispersed by birds

WOOD: of no commercial value

Dwarf hackberry

Dwarf hackberry—flowers x1

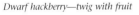

Dwarf hackberry—twig with fruit

CURRENT CHAMPION: none recorded

In Pennsylvania dwarf hackberry occurs almost entirely east of the Allegheny Front, in the Ridge and Valley, Piedmont, and Coastal Plain physiographic provinces. It grows on dry, shaly slopes and limestone cliffs. It is a variable species that extends from southern Pennsylvania, western Ohio, southern Michigan, and Illinois to eastern Kansas and south to eastern Texas, Louisiana, and Georgia.

HAWTHORN
CRATAEGUS L.
Rose Family—Rosaceae

The hawthorns are small trees generally not more than 25–30 feet tall, or some-times large shrubs. The branches of hawthorns, and sometimes also their trunks, bear sharp thorns; those on the branches are straight or slightly curved and very sharp; the thorns on the trunk are usually branched. Hawthorn bark is gray and scaly on the trunk and larger branches. Twigs occur as long shoots that bear leaves only and short lateral shoots on which flowers and fruits are produced. Hawthorn buds are rounded and reddish-brown.

The leaves of hawthorns are simple, alternate, and deciduous; they are con-spicuously and sharply toothed and sometimes also lobed. Leaf form often varies on a single tree, especially on the long shoots; for this reason only short shoot leaves should be used for determining species. Flowers are produced in small, flat-topped clusters; individual flowers are white and about ½–¾ inch across with 5 petals, 5 sepals, and 5–20 stamens. The trees bloom in early May to June dur-ing or after leaf expansion; flowers are insect-pollinated. Hawthorn fruits, which ripen in the fall, look like miniature apples up to ½ inch in diameter; they con-tain 1–5 nutlets surrounded by a dryish or juicy fleshy layer and are red or green-ish when ripe.

The hawthorns can be very challenging to identify to species, even for profes-sional botanists. Species distinctions are blurred by hybridization, polyploidy, and the ability to form seeds without sexual reproduction having occurred.[1] In Penn-sylvania alone, hundreds of species have been named over the years, many based on only a single tree. Hawthorns are trees of open woods, roadsides, hedgerows, pastures, and fields. The clearcutting of Pennsylvania's forests between 1890 and 1930 created extensive areas where hawthorns could and did proliferate.

We have chosen to simplify the treatment of this bewildering variability by grouping our tree hawthorns into 14 native species or species complexes. In addition to those listed, Brainerd's hawthorn (*Crataegus brainerdii*) has been listed for Pennsylvania, but its status is unclear. Two naturalized species, English hawthorn and Washington hawthorn, are included. One-flowered hawthorn (*C. uniflora*), our other native species, is not described here because it is not a tree.

Hawthorn fruits, sometimes referred to as "haws," were used by many Native American groups as food, either fresh or pressed into cakes and dried for the win-ter. A tea was made from the twigs of several species. Medicinal applications included the use of an infusion of hawthorn twigs to treat bladder troubles and an infusion of the shoots for the treatment of diarrhea in children. A compound decoction of the roots was employed to treat back pain and menstrual problems. The thorns were used as needles for a form of acupuncture and as tools for pierc-ing holes in items to be sewn together.

The hard, dense wood of hawthorn trees is good for carving and turning; but the trees are too small to have any commercial timber value. Some species,

---

1. Phipps, J. B. and M. Muniyamma. 1980. A taxonomic revision of *Crataegus* (Rosaceae) in Ontario. *Canadian Journal of Botany* 58: 1621–99.

including cockspur hawthorn and Washington hawthorn, are grown as ornamentals; several cultivars of each are common in the nursery trade.

The dense, thorny branches of hawthorns provide good cover for birds; cedar waxwings, fox sparrows, ruffed grouse, and other birds and small mammals eat the fruits, and disperse the seeds. Deer browse on the twigs. Tiger swallowtail, viceroy, red-spotted purple, and striped hairstreak butterflies utilize hawthorn as a larval food source. Caterpillars of several sphinx moths also feed on the leaves.

The hawthorns are arranged alphabetically by species because of the obscurity of most of the common names.

Pear hawthorn, black-thorn hawthorn
Crataegus calpodendron (Ehrh.) Medik.

FORM: multistemmed shrub or small tree, 15–18 feet

TWIGS: slender, gray, nearly thornless, hairy when young

THORNS: few, ½–1¼ inches long, stout and slightly curved

LEAVES: 2–4 inches long, elliptic to ovate, tapering at the base, coarsely toothed with 3–5 pairs of shallow lateral lobes, dull yellowish-green to dark green, hairy when young and remaining so beneath at maturity

FLOWERS: stalks, bases of the flowers, and sepals hairy; stamens about 20; anthers pink or white; sepals with glandular teeth

FRUIT: about ⅜ inch in diameter, somewhat pear-shaped, shiny orange-red; flesh thin and sweet, becoming juicy; nutlets 2–3

CURRENT CHAMPION: none recorded

The pear hawthorn is found mainly in the southeastern part of the state where it grows in woods, thickets, and low meadows. Its total range extends from southern Ontario west to Minnesota and south to Alabama and Texas.

Pear hawthorn—leaf

Pear hawthorn—flowers

Pear hawthorn—fruit

Round-leaf hawthorn complex *Crataegus chrysocarpa* Ashe

FORM: shrub or small tree to 18 feet tall

TWIGS: grayish-brown, smooth or hairy

THORNS: numerous, straight, 1½–2½ inches long, blackish

LEAVES: 1–2 inches long and up to 2 inches broad, tapered at the base, shallowly lobed, hairy above when young; leaf stalk and teeth usually glandular

FLOWERS: stalks smooth to hairy; stamens 10–20; anthers cream-colored; sepals toothed and glandular

FRUIT: about ⅜ inch in diameter, red, becoming soft and juicy; nutlets 3–4

CURRENT CHAMPION: none recorded

Round-leaved hawthorn is near its southern limit at scattered sites throughout the state; its total range extends from Newfoundland to British Columbia and south to New York, Pennsylvania, Virginia, and Missouri. (Includes *C. rotundifolia* Ashe.)

Round-leaf hawthorn—fruit

Round-leaf hawthorn—flowers

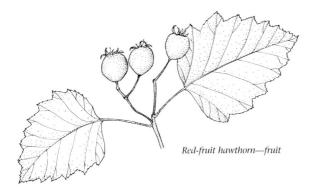

Red-fruit hawthorn—fruit

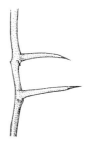

Red-fruit hawthorn—
thorns

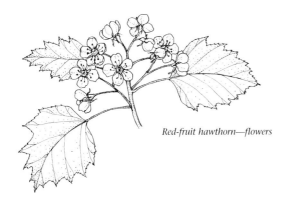

Red-fruit hawthorn—flowers

Red-fruit hawthorn complex   *Crataegus coccinea* L.

FORM: shrub or tree to 30 feet

TWIGS: smooth or hairy when young, light brown

THORNS: stout, curved, 1–2¼ inches long

LEAVES: 2–3 inches long, nearly round in outline, with 3–5 pairs of shallow lateral lobes, smooth or short-hairy above; edges sharply toothed

FLOWERS: stalks smooth or hairy; stamens about 10; anthers pink or red; sepals with glandular teeth

FRUIT: bright red, about ½ inch in diameter with juicy flesh and 3–5 nutlets

CURRENT CHAMPION: none recorded

Red-fruited hawthorn occurs throughout Pennsylvania with the exception of the northeastern corner. Its total range extends from New England and southeastern Canada to Minnesota and south to Delaware, West Virginia, Illinois, and Kentucky and in the mountains to North Carolina.

Cockspur hawthorn complex   *Crataegus crus-galli* L.

FORM: small tree, 18–20 feet with widely spreading, horizontal branches; trunk often covered with branched thorns

TWIGS: smooth and flexuous

THORNS: numerous, stout, 1½–2½ inches long, straight or slightly curved

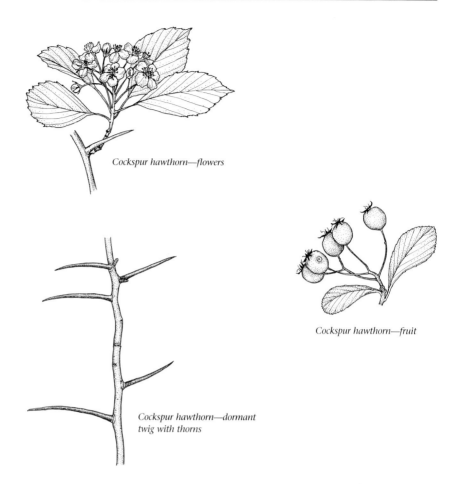

Cockspur hawthorn—flowers

Cockspur hawthorn—fruit

*Cockspur hawthorn—dormant
twig with thorns*

LEAVES: 1–2 inches long, dark green and glossy, broadest toward the tip, toothed but usually not lobed, tapering at the base to the short leaf stalk

FLOWERS: stalks smooth; stamens 10–20; anthers ivory-colored or pink

FRUIT: orange-red to green with thin, dry flesh, ¼–⅜ inches in diameter and slightly longer than wide, containing 1–2 nutlets

CURRENT CHAMPION: Philadelphia County, diameter 1 foot 10 inches, height 37 feet, spread 45 feet

The cockspur hawthorn is common across the southern half of Pennsylvania in woods, pastures, stream banks, and thickets. It can be recognized by its glossy, unlobed leaves and layered, horizontal branches. Its total range extends from Quebec to Minnesota and south to Florida and Texas.

Broad-leaf hawthorn   *Crataegus dilatata* Sarg.

FORM: shrub or small tree, 20–25 feet
TWIGS: slender, flexuous
THORNS: slender, about 2 inches long
LEAVES: broadly ovate or nearly triangular, heart-shaped at the base with 4–5 triangular lobes on each side, sparsely hairy when young, becoming smooth at maturity
FLOWERS: nearly an inch wide; stamens about 20; stalks smooth or with long hairs
FRUIT: about ½ inch thick, bright red, flesh thick and juicy, nutlets 5
CURRENT CHAMPION: none recorded

Broad-leaf hawthorn is known from only a small cluster of sites in Centre and Huntingdon Counties that are the southern limit for the species, and a single location in Erie County. It grows in pastures, thickets, and hillsides. The Pennsylvania Biological Survey has recommended a classification of undetermined pending further study of its status in the state. Outside Pennsylvania the range of broad-leaf hawthorn extends north to New York, New England, Quebec, and southern Ontario.

Broad-leaf hawthorn—flowers

Broad-leaf hawthorn—fruit

Dodge's hawthorn   *Crataegus dodgei* Ashe

FORM: shrub or small tree 12 feet
TWIGS: slender, smooth, gray, thorny
THORNS: about 1 inch long, straight or slightly curved, dark brown and shiny
LEAVES: broadly rounded in outline, 1–2 inches long and equally wide or wider, with 3–5 pairs of triangular lobes; base rounded to tapering to the somewhat winged leaf stalk
FLOWERS: stalks smooth; stamens about 10; anthers cream-colored
FRUIT: about ½ inch thick, yellowish-green with a red blush, flesh dry, nutlets 2–3
CURRENT CHAMPION: none recorded

This tree occurs in Ontario, Wisconsin, New York, and Pennsylvania. Here it is known from scattered sites across the central part of the state, where it grows in thickets and along forest edges.

Dodge's hawthorn—flowers

Dodge's hawthorn—fruit

Holmes' hawthorn   *Crataegus holmesiana* Ashe

FORM: small tree or large shrub to 18 feet

TWIGS: slender, smooth, and somewhat thorny

THORNS: moderately stout, slightly curved, about 1½ inches long

LEAVES: 2–3 inches long, broadly ovate, narrowed or tapered at the base, with 4–6 pairs of shallow lateral lobes; leaf margins sharply and deeply toothed

FLOWERS: stalks with a few long hairs; stamens 5–8; anthers pink or red; sepals toothed and glandular

FRUIT: bright red, about ⅜ inch in diameter and slightly longer than wide; flesh thin and firm; nutlets 3

CURRENT CHAMPION: none recorded

This hawthorn is notable for its early blooming time, the first week of May, and the distinctive appearance of the leaves caused by the pronounced teeth. It is known mainly from the southeastern and central parts of the state; however, its total range extends from Pennsylvania north to New England and southeastern Canada, and west to Minnesota.

Holmes' hawthorn—fruit

Holmes' hawthorn—twig with thorns

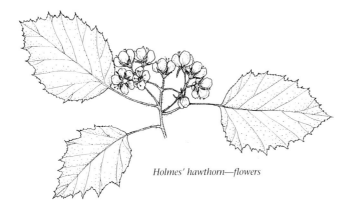

Holmes' hawthorn—flowers

Biltmore hawthorn complex   *Crataegus intricata* Lange

FORM: shrub or small tree to 9 feet

TWIGS: very thorny

THORNS: to 2 inches long, curved or straight, dark glossy brown to blackish

LEAVES: elliptic or egg-shaped with several pairs of lateral lobes, toothed to the base; leaf stalks glandular

FLOWERS: in a 5 to 10-flowered cluster containing numerous glandular bracts; stamens 5–10; anthers red to pink

FRUIT: ⅜–½ inch in diameter, red with hard, dry flesh and 3–5 nutlets

CURRENT CHAMPION: none recorded

Biltmore hawthorn grows across the southern half of Pennsylvania in woods, pastures, thickets, and barrens. Its total range extends from New England and southern Ontario west to Michigan and south to Alabama and Arkansas.

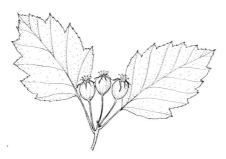

Biltmore hawthorn—fruit

Biltmore hawthorn—flowers

Biltmore hawthorn—twig with thorns

Large-seed hawthorn complex   *Crataegus macrosperma* Ashe

FORM: shrub or small tree to 18 feet

TWIGS: slender, smooth, brownish-gray

THORNS: moderately stout, straight to slightly curved, 1½–2 inches long

LEAVES: 1½–2 inches long, broadly egg-shaped in outline, with 4–5 sharply toothed, triangular lobes on each side; rounded to truncate at the base; leaf stalks grooved above

FLOWERS: stalks smooth or hairy, stamens 8–20; anthers ivory-colored or pink; sepals toothed and glandular to nearly entire

FRUIT: about ⅜ inch in diameter, orange-red to dark red; flesh thick, becoming soft and juicy; nutlets 3–5

CURRENT CHAMPION: none recorded

This group of hawthorns includes the most common species in Pennsylvania. Habitat includes open woods, fencerows, pastures, old fields, and roadsides throughout the entire state. Its total range extends from New England and southeastern Canada west to Minnesota and south to Georgia and Louisiana. (Includes the fanleaf hawthorn, *Crataegus flabellata* (Bosc) K. Koch.)

Large-seed hawthorn—bark

Large-seed hawthorn—flowers

Large-seed hawthorn—fruit

Downy hawthorn   *Crataegus mollis* (Torr. & A. Gray) Scheele

FORM: tree to 40 feet with widely spreading branches

TWIGS: stout, hairy when young, nearly thornless

THORNS: ¾–2¼ inches long, straight and slender

LEAVES: 1½–5 inches long, double toothed to shallowly or deeply lobed, very hairy when young, hairs present only on the lower surface at maturity

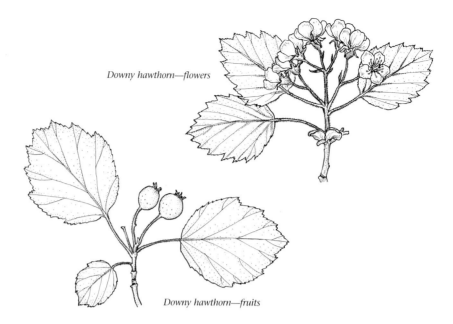

Downy hawthorn—flowers

Downy hawthorn—fruits

FLOWERS: almost an inch across, stalks hairy, stamens about 20; anthers ivory-colored

FRUIT: about ½–¾ inch in diameter, red with pale dots, hairy at least on the ends; flesh thick and juicy; nutlets usually 5

CURRENT CHAMPION: none recorded

Downy hawthorn is usually found on limestone soils, in Pennsylvania it is known from just a few sites in the northwestern part of the state. The Pennsylvania Natural Heritage Program has classified it as undetermined. Its total range extends from New England and southeastern Canada west to Minnesota, and south to Alabama and Oklahoma.

English hawthorn   *Crataegus monogyna* Jacq.

FORM: large shrub or tree to 40 feet

TWIGS: slender, thornless to very thorny

THORNS: ½–¾ inch long, straight, and stout

LEAVES: 1–2 inches long, wedge-shaped to truncate at the base, deeply 3- to 5-lobed with veins ending at the notches as well as the points of the lobes; conspicuous leafy stipules present on new growth

FLOWERS: stalks smooth; stamens 20; anthers reddish

FRUIT: about ¼ inch in diameter, red; flesh thin, containing a single nutlet

CURRENT CHAMPION: Delaware County, diameter 1 foot 7 inches, height 44 feet, spread 33 feet

English hawthorn is native to Europe and western Asia; it is cultivated and occasionally naturalized here, mostly in the southeastern and southwestern regions of the state.

English hawthorn—fruit

English hawthorn—flowers

Pennsylvania hawthorn   *Crataegus pennsylvanica* Ashe

FORM: tree to 30 feet with widely spreading branches

TWIGS: slender, thorny, densely hairy when young

THORNS: slender at first, becoming stout on older wood, about 1½ inches long

LEAVES: broadly egg-shaped to almost round, up to 3 inches long by 3 inches wide, sharply toothed with 4–6 pairs of shallow lateral lobes, thin, yellow-green, densely hairy on the undersides when young, more thinly so as they age, rough to the touch above; leaf stalks hairy, especially when young

FLOWERS: stalks and bases of the flowers densely hairy; stamens about 10; anthers ivory-colored; sepals with glandular teeth

FRUIT: about ½ inch in diameter; flesh thin and firm; nutlets 4–5

CURRENT CHAMPION: none recorded

Pennsylvania hawthorn—thorn

Pennsylvania hawthorn has a very limited global distribution that includes southern Ontario, New York, Pennsylvania, Delaware, and West Virginia. It has recently been found at a number of sites across southern Pennsylvania; the Pennsylvania Biological Survey has recommended a status of undetermined pending further study of its abundance.

Pennsylvania hawthorn—fruit

Pennsylvania hawthorn—flowers

Washington hawthorn   *Crataegus phaenopyrum* (L. f) Medik.

FORM: small tree to 40 feet with spreading branches
TWIGS: slender, thorny
THORNS: stout, 1–2 inches long
LEAVES: 1–2½ inches long, broadly triangular in outline with 3–5 well-defined lobes on each side, the lowest pair of lobes widely spreading; veins ending in the notches as well as the tips of the lobes
FLOWERS: small, on smooth stalks; stamens 20; anthers pale yellow
FRUIT: scarlet, less than ¼ inch in diameter; flesh dry; nutlets 3–5
CURRENT CHAMPION: Montour County, diameter 1 foot 1 inch, height 35 feet, spread 44 feet

Washington hawthorn is native from Pennsylvania to Florida and west to Missouri and Arkansas; it is also frequently planted as an ornamental and most populations probably represent escapes from cultivated sources. Pennsylvania sites are mainly in the southeast on roadsides and in hedgerows and open ground; a few additional locations are scattered across the southern half of the state.

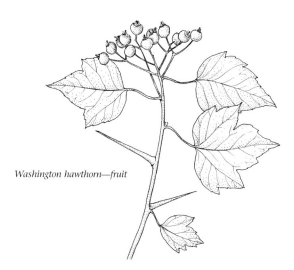

Washington hawthorn—fruit

Washington hawthorn—flowers

Frosted hawthorn complex

Crataegus pruinosa
(H. L. Wendl.) K. Koch

FORM: large shrub or small tree to 24 feet

TWIGS: slender, grayish or whitened when young, thorny

THORNS: straight, 1½–2 inches long, slender, whitened when young but becoming dark and shiny with age

LEAVES: 1–2½ inches long by ¾–1 inches wide, bluish-green and thick and firm, rounded at the base, with 3–5 pairs of shallow lobes, and a sharp tip

FLOWERS: stalks smooth; stamens 10–20; anthers ivory-colored

FRUIT: red or greenish with darker dots and a whitish waxy coating that give them a bluish appearance, calyx prominent and elevated; flesh thin and dry with 4–5 nutlets

CURRENT CHAMPION: none recorded

The name, frosted hawthorn, refers to the whitish waxy coating that is present on the young twigs and mature fruits of this species. It occurs in open woods and thickets scattered throughout Pennsylvania, with the exception of the northeastern corner. The total range of this species extends from Newfoundland to Wisconsin and south to North Carolina and Oklahoma.

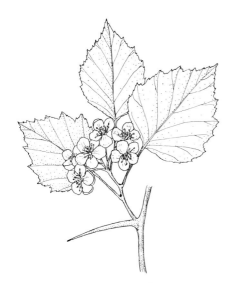

Frosted hawthorn—flowers

Frosted hawthorn—fruit

Dotted hawthorn, white hawthorn   *Crataegus punctata* Jacq.

FORM: small tree, 25–30 feet with horizontal, layered branches; trunk frequently covered with large, branched thorns

TWIGS: pale gray, stout

THORNS: stout, pale gray, to 2½ inches long, straight to somewhat curved

LEAVES: 1–2½ inches long, oblong-elliptic and tapering to a winged leaf stalk, mostly unlobed, but those of the nonflowering shoots sometimes shallowly lobed, dark green, thick and firm with indented veins

FLOWERS: stalks and base of the flowers finely hairy; stamens 20; anthers red, pink, or rarely white; blooming in mid to late May

FRUIT: about ½ inch in diameter, dull to bright red or yellow, conspicuously dotted; flesh thick and succulent, containing 2–4 nutlets

CURRENT CHAMPION: Warren County, diameter 1 foot 3 inches, height 32 feet, spread 40 feet

Named for the speckled appearance of the fruits, dotted hawthorn is very common in woods, pastures, and stream banks throughout Pennsylvania. Its total range extends from Newfoundland and Quebec west to Minnesota and south to Georgia, and Oklahoma.

Dotted hawthorn—flowers

Dotted hawthorn—fruit

Long-spine hawthorn, *Crataegus succulenta* Schrad. ex Link
fleshy hawthorn complex

FORM: shrub or small tree to 24 feet

TWIGS: slender and flexuous, smooth to slightly hairy when young, dark in color

THORNS: stout, to 3 inches or more in length, blackish

LEAVES: 2–3 inches long, elliptic to ovate, frequently shallowly lobed toward the tip, tapering at the base to the grooved and winged leaf stalks, dark green and glossy with short hairs present on the upper surface and sometimes also the lower

FLOWERS: stalks, base of the flower, and sepals finely hairy; stamens 10–20; anthers reddish; sepals with glandular teeth; blooming in mid-May

FRUITS: about ⅓–⅔ inch in diameter, deep red, juicy, containing 2–3 nutlets

CURRENT CHAMPION: none recorded

Long-spine hawthorn occurs at scattered sites in southern and western Pennsylvania in woods, thickets, fencerows, and pastures. Its total range extends from New England and southeastern Canada west to Manitoba, the Dakotas, and south in the mountains to North Carolina, Tennessee, and Missouri. (Includes *C. macracantha* Lodd.)

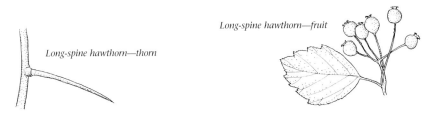

Long-spine hawthorn—thorn

Long-spine hawthorn—fruit

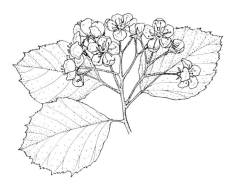

Long-spine hawthorn—flowers

HEMLOCK
Tsuga Carrière
Pine Family—Pinaceae

Canadian hemlock, eastern hemlock   *Tsuga canadensis* (L.) Carrière

FORM: crown broadly conic, to 140 feet; young trees have a graceful, drooping tip

BARK: reddish-brown, scaly and fissured

TWIGS: hairy, branches have a flattened appearance due to the mostly 2-ranked needles

BUDS: ovate

LEAVES: linear, ½–¾ inch long with a short stalk; the edges of the needles are minutely toothed and the tip is notched

LEAF SCARS: small, round, on raised projections on the bark

CONES: at the ends of twigs of the current year, ovoid, ⅗–1 inch long, maturing in a single year

SEEDS: light brown, about ¼ inch long including the wing

WOOD: light reddish-brown, coarse-grained, brittle

CURRENT CHAMPION: Clarion County, diameter 5 feet 1 inch, height 125 feet, spread 70 feet

Canadian hemlock, the state tree of Pennsylvania, is a prominent part of forests throughout the state. In southern counties it occurs mainly on steep, north- or east-facing slopes along streams. To the north it forms nearly pure stands in moist ravines, stream valleys, wooded swamps, and steep slopes. Not much light reaches the ground in these areas, a fact reflected in place names such as "Dark

Canadian hemlock—young cones

Canadian hemlock—bark

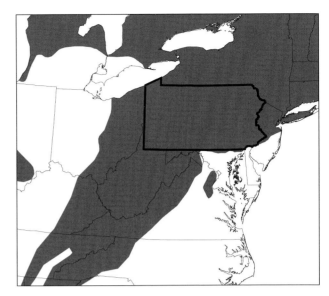

Canadian hemlock

Hollow" and "Shades of Death." Hemlock is also a component of the northern hardwood forest type and other mixed stands where it grows with white pine, beech, birch, maple, and sometimes oaks.

Hemlocks can live 300 to 400 years or more, reaching 3–4 feet in diameter and over 140 feet tall. The grandeur of hemlock forests can still be experienced in remnant stands of old growth remaining at Heart's Content and Tionesta in the Allegheny National Forest in northwestern Pennsylvania and at Cook Forest State Park in Clarion County. Smaller groves of big, old trees persist in a few state forests as well. The range of Canadian hemlock extends from Nova Scotia to Alabama and west to Minnesota.

Although hemlock seedlings and saplings are extremely shade tolerant and able to grow even in the shade of a dense grove of the mature trees, today hemlock is threatened by excessive numbers of deer that are preventing the growth of young trees in many areas because the evergreen foliage is sought out as winter browse. Another problem is damage caused by the hemlock woolly adelgid (*Adelges tsugae*), an insect first reported in eastern North America in the 1950s in Richmond, Virginia. The adelgid has spread north and west and is now present in many areas of Pennsylvania. Recent mild winters have permitted it to spread rapidly.

The hemlock woolly adelgid is not the first insect scourge this species has faced. The record of hemlock abundance provided by fossil pollen preserved in bogs reveals that hemlock declined drastically throughout its range approximately 5,000 years ago.[1] The sudden loss of 90 percent of the hemlock trees is believed to have been caused by an insect outbreak, probably in concert with a period when the climate was warmer and drier.[2] It took 2,000 years for the species to rebound.

Elongate hemlock scale (*Fiorinia externa*), another insect that punctures the needles and feeds on the sap of hemlock trees, is also widespread in the state. But despite its vulnerability, hemlock is still a popular landscape plant.

Canadian hemlock—with cones

Hemlock trees have played a major role in Pennsylvania's economic development. Massive amounts of hemlock bark were harvested for use in tanning leather in the eighteenth and nineteenth centuries. So much bark was required that it was more economical to haul the hides to tanneries established in or near the forests than to move the bark long distances. The peeled logs went to the sawmills.

Medicinal applications of hemlock by many Native American tribes included a plaster made by boiling and then pounding the tannin-rich inner bark, and an astringent used to stop blood flow from wounds and promote healing. Early European explorers and settlers in eastern North America learned to make hemlock tea from the young branch tips from the natives; the bark was used by settlers to make a reddish-brown dye for wool and cotton.

Dense stands of hemlock provide important protective winter cover for deer, ruffed grouse, wild turkey, and other wildlife. The seeds are a winter food source for birds such as juncos, pine siskins, and crossbills as well as small mammals.

Notes

1. Davis, Margaret Bryan. 1981. Outbreaks of forest pathogens in Quaternary history. IV International Palynological Conference, Lucknow (1976–1977) 3: 216–28.

2. Haas, Jean Nicolas and John H. McAndrews. 1999. The summer drought related hemlock (*Tsuga canadensis*) decline in eastern North America 5,700 to 5,100 years ago. 81–88 in *Proceedings: Symposium on Sustainable Management of Hemlock Ecosystems in Eastern North America*, U.S.D.A. Forest Service, Durham, N.H., June 22–24, 1999.

HERCULES'-CLUB—SEE ARALIA

HICKORY
CARYA NUTT.
Walnut Family—Juglandaceae

The hickories are truly American trees, showing their greatest diversity in eastern North America. The fossil record reveals that prior to the ice age the genus *Carya* was found in China, Japan, Siberia, and Europe as well as Colorado and Washington in North America. Today, however, with the exception of a few species that are found in eastern Asia, all species are North American. Of the twelve North American species, five are native to Pennsylvania.

The hickories have alternate compound leaves with 5–9 pinnately arranged leaflets, which turn a rich golden yellow in the autumn. The flowers are unisexual, but both staminate and pistillate flowers are present on each tree, making the species monoecious. Staminate flowers are in drooping catkins, which are usually in clusters of three. The pistillate flowers are in small spikes at the tips of the new growth. The fruit matures in a single season and consists of a hard-shelled nut surrounded by a husk that splits apart at maturity.

Hickory nuts are rich in fats and proteins and were an important food for Native Americans who used the nuts in many ways including pounding the nutmeats in water in a mortar to make a milky liquid that was added to other foods. Fragments of hickory shells have been found at many archeological sites throughout the mid-Atlantic, Northeast, and Midwest, indicating their widespread use.

Hickory was also used medicinally to treat intestinal worms, arthritis, and poliomyelitis pain. Small shoots were steamed to make an inhalant for headache. The astringent inner bark was used to dress cuts. Hickory lumber was, and still is, especially valued for tool handles and other applications where light but strong wood is needed, including the rims of snowshoes, bows and arrows, and barrel hoops. The inner bark was used in basketry. Reports by early travelers in Pennsylvania indicate that hickory trees were frequently abundant in the vicinity of native villages.

Many forms of wildlife rely on hickory nuts for a fall and winter food source. The seeds are stored, and dispersed, by squirrels. Hickory leaves are the food source for the larvae of the tiger swallowtail, hickory hairstreak, and banded hairstreak butterflies and the walnut sphinx, polyphemus, and luna moths.

Bitternut hickory *Carya cordiformis* **(Wang.) K. Koch**

FORM: upright tree to 75 feet with a rounded crown
BARK: light gray with shallow fissures and ridges
TWIGS: tan, smooth, but scaly near the tip
PITH: brown and angular
BUDS: yellow
LEAVES: alternate, 6–10 inches long with 7–11 lanceolate to lance-ovate leaflets; leaflets, sessile, hairy beneath, pointed at the tip, and toothed on the margin
FALL LEAF COLOR: yellow
STIPULES: none

Bitternut hickory—bark

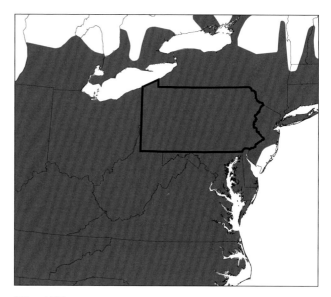

Bitternut hickory

LEAF SCARS: conspicuous, raised, heart-shaped with 3 clusters of bundle scars

FLOWERS: appearing in May with the leaves

FRUIT: ¾–1½ inches long with a thin husk that is winged along the sutures, maturing in October

SEEDS: bitter tasting, inedible

WOOD: lighter and more brittle than other hickories

CURRENT CHAMPION: Warren County, diameter 3 feet 7 inches, height 107 feet, spread 56 feet

Bitternut hickory—winter buds

Bitternut hickory occurs scattered throughout Pennsylvania except at the highest elevations along the Allegheny Front. It is a tree of the eastern United States from Vermont and New Hampshire to Minnesota and south to Georgia, Alabama and eastern Texas. Bitternut hickory is the easiest of the hickories to identify because of its distinctive yellow buds.

Bitternut hickory—fruit x1

Bitternut hickory—leaves x1/4

Mockernut hickory   *Carya tomentosa* (Lam. ex Poir.) Nutt.

FORM: a large tree to 75 feet with a narrow to broadly rounded crown

BARK: gray with a regular pattern of interlacing ridges and shallow furrows, not shaggy

TWIGS: very stout and hairy

PITH: angular

BUDS: terminal bud ⅖–⅗ inch long with overlapping scales

LEAVES: 8–12 inches long, with 7–9 leaflets; leaflets wider toward the tip, coarsely toothed; leaf stalk and lower surface of the leaflets very hairy

FALL LEAF COLOR: yellow

STIPULES: none

LEAF SCARS: heart-shaped with 3 clusters of bundle scars

FLOWERS: appearing in May when the leaves are half expanded

FRUIT: 1½–2½ inches long with a thick husk; nut ridged toward the tip

SEEDS: sweet and edible

WOOD: with a broad, white sapwood

CURRENT CHAMPION: Philadelphia County, diameter 2 feet 10 inches, height 82 feet, spread 64 feet

Mockernut hickory is found mainly in the southern half of Pennsylvania where it grows in moist open woods and slopes. It is a tree of the eastern United States

Mockernut hickory—bark

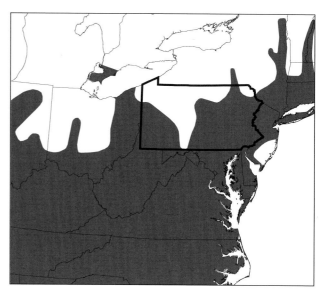

Mockernut hickory

extending from southern New England to northern Florida and west to eastern Texas, Oklahoma, and Iowa. The hairy leaf stalks and tight, but regularly ridged and furrowed, bark are good identification characteristics.

Mockernut hickory—leaf

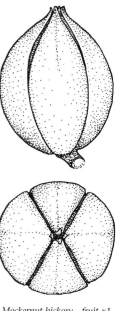

Mockernut hickory—fruit x1

Pignut hickory   *Carya glabra* **(Miller) Sweet**

FORM: upright tree to 90 feet with a narrow, oblong crown

BARK: dark gray, close with shallow fissures, or scaly and somewhat shaggy in age

TWIGS: slender and smooth

PITH: angular

BUDS: terminal bud ¼–½ inch long

LEAVES: 8–12 inches long with 5–7 leaflets; leaflets oblong or somewhat wider toward the tip, sharp-pointed at the tip and rounded or tapered at the base; margins finely toothed

FALL LEAF COLOR: yellow

STIPULES: none

LEAF SCARS: heart-shaped or oblong with bundle scars usually in three clusters

FLOWERS: opening in May when the leaves are half grown

FRUIT: 1–2 inches long with a husk that varies from thick to thin

SEEDS: sweet initially but turning bitter

WOOD: highly valued

CURRENT CHAMPION: Huntingdon County, diameter 3 feet, height 101 feet, spread 60 feet

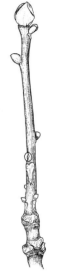

Pignut hickory— dormant twig

Pignut hickory occurs across the southern half of Pennsylvania in upland forests and elsewhere on dry ridge tops and slopes. Its total range extends from southern New England to central Florida and west to Illinois, Missouri, and Mississippi.

Pignut hickory is a very variable species; variants with scaly or shaggy bark, thick warty husks, and 7 leaflets have sometimes been called *Carya ovalis*, but we have chosen to lump them into *C. glabra* following the treatment in *The Flora of North America*, Vol. 3.

Pignut hickory—bark

Pignut hickory

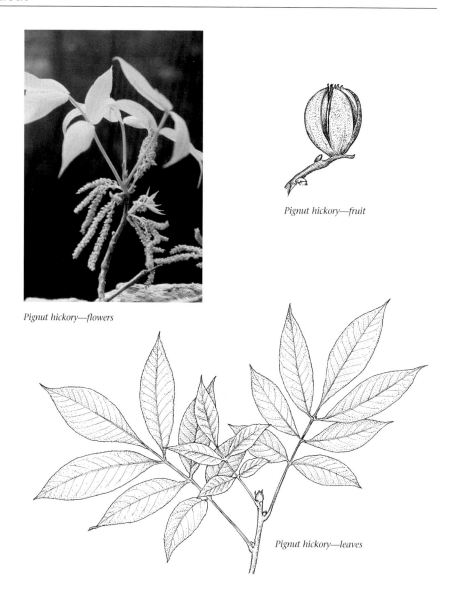

Pignut hickory—fruit

Pignut hickory—flowers

Pignut hickory—leaves

Shagbark hickory   *Carya ovata* (Mill.) K. Koch

FORM: upright tree to 100 feet with a narrow, cylindrical crown

BARK: light gray, peeling off in long shaggy strips

TWIGS: smooth to slightly hairy, reddish-brown to grayish

PITH: angular

BUDS: terminal buds ⅖–⅘ inch long

LEAVES: 8–14 inches long with 5 (or occasionally 7) leaflets; the terminal 3 leaflets much larger than the basal pair; margins toothed with a tuft of hairs at the base of each tooth

FALL LEAF COLOR: yellow

STIPULES: none

LEAF SCARS: heart-shaped or roughly triangular with 3 clusters of bundle scars

FLOWERS: appearing in May when the leaves are nearly fully expanded

Shagbark hickory—bark

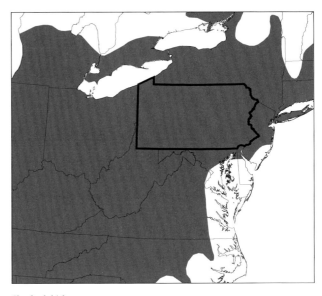

Shagbark hickory

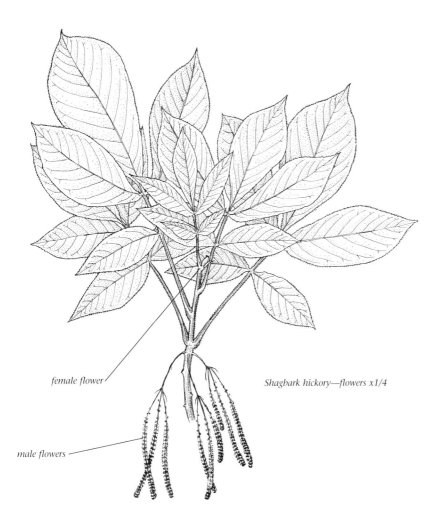

female flower

male flowers

Shagbark hickory—flowers x1/4

FRUIT: 1–2 inches long with a very thick husk; nut somewhat flattened and strongly angled

SEEDS: large, sweet, and edible

WOOD: heavy, hard, and strong

CURRENT CHAMPION: Schuylkill County, diameter 3 feet 9 inches, height 93 feet, spread 77 feet

Shagbark hickory—nut with husk

Shagbark hickory is common in moist to wet forests throughout most of Pennsylvania, except for the northernmost counties where it is only occasionally found. The shaggy bark, leaf with 5 leaflets, thick husk, and strongly angled nut are good characteristics for distinguishing shagbark from other hickories.

Its range extends from New Hampshire, Vermont, and southern Ontario south to northern Georgia and west to Iowa and eastern Texas.

Shellbark hickory   *Carya laciniosa* (F. Michaux) Loudon

FORM: upright tree to 100 feet with a narrow, cylindrical crown

BARK: dark gray and peeling off in long shaggy strips

TWIGS: stout

PITH: angular

BUDS: terminal bud ⅖–⅘ inch long

LEAVES: up to 22 inches long, with 7–9 leaflets; terminal 3 leaflets larger than the basal pairs

FALL LEAF COLOR: yellow

STIPULES: none

LEAF SCARS: heart-shaped or triangular with 3 clusters of bundle scars

FLOWERS: appearing when the leaves are nearly completely expanded

FRUIT: 1¾–2¼ inches; nut strongly flattened, pointed at both ends

SEEDS: sweet and edible

WOOD: very similar to shagbark hickory

CURRENT CHAMPION: Schuylkill County, diameter 4 feet, height 96 feet, spread 93 feet

Shellbark hickory—nut with husk

Shellbark hickory—nut

Shellbark hickory is the least common of the Pennsylvania hickories, it occurs in widely scattered sites across the southern counties and an isolated location along the Susquehanna River in Northumberland County. It is primarily a tree of moist, rich bottomlands and floodplains, often on limestone or diabase geology. Although its shaggy bark might be confused with that of shagbark hickory, shellbark has more leaflets (7–9) and the largest nuts of all our native hickories.

The total range of shellbark hickory extends irregularly from western New York to eastern Kansas and south to Alabama, Mississippi, and northern Georgia.

Shellbark hickory—bark

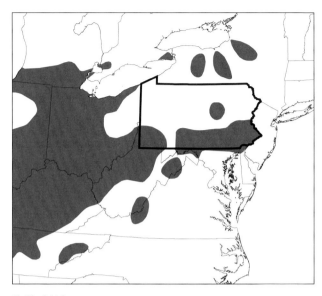

Shellbark hickory

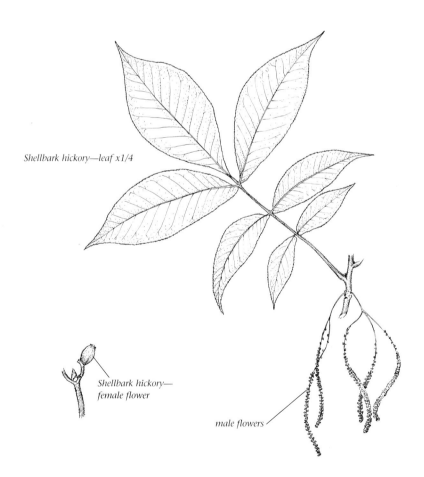

Shellbark hickory—leaf x1/4

*Shellbark hickory—
female flower*

male flowers

HOLLY
Ilex L.
Holly Family—Aquifoliaceae

The hollies are evergreen or deciduous trees or shrubs with alternate simple leaves. Flowers are unisexual, with male and female flowers on separate plants (dioecious). Male flowers have 4–5 each of sepals and petals and an equal number of stamens; pistillate flowers have sepals and petals, a single ovary, and nonfunctional stamens. Holly fruits are small red berries with 4–5 seeds. Only those species with a tree-like growth form are described here.

American holly   *Ilex opaca* **Aiton**

FORM: evergreen tree to 60 feet with horizontal branches and a narrow, conical crown
BARK: smooth, gray
TWIGS: pale brown, finely hairy
PITH: small, pale green
BUDS: green, rounded, covered with narrow overlapping bud scales
LEAVES: alternate, simple, evergreen, 2–3 inches long, stiff and shiny with 4–6 spines on each side
FALL LEAF COLOR: green
STIPULES: very small, dark, persistent
LEAF SCARS: circular with a single bundle scar
FLOWERS: as for other hollies see description above, 4-parted, blooming in the spring as the new shoots are expanding
FRUIT: red berry about ¼ inch in diameter
SEEDS: 3–4 per fruit, disseminated by birds
WOOD: dense, white, used for inlay work and fine furniture
CURRENT CHAMPION: York County, diameter 2 feet 2 inches, height 65 feet, spread 35 feet

American holly, the familiar Christmas holly, occurs in moist, sandy soil along the Atlantic coast from Massachusetts to Texas and inland in the south. In Pennsylvania native stands occur in bottomland sites on or near the coastal plain, in the lower Susquehanna River valley, and as far inland as the Ridge and Valley Physiographic Province. Because of its relative rarity in the state, American holly is classified as threatened by the Pennsylvania Natural Heritage Program.

Native Americans used a decoction of holly bark as an eye wash. A decoction of the leaves was employed to treat measles and skin sores. Another use involved chewing the berries to treat colic and dyspepsia. Squirrel, turkey, grouse, quail, robins, mockingbirds, catbirds, and other game birds and songbirds eat holly berries. American holly is a food plant for the woodland elfin butterfly.

American holly is also widely grown as a landscape ornamental and a source of cut greens at Christmas. Hundreds of ornamental cultivars have been developed, including yellow-berried forms. The frequent occurrence of young Amer-

American holly—bark

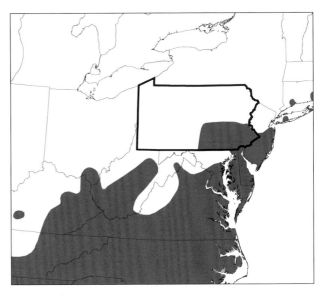

American holly

ican holly trees in urban and suburban forest remnants is often the result of seeding from landscape plants.

American holly—fruit

American holly—female flowers

American holly—male flowers

Mountain holly   *Ilex montana* (Torr. & A. Gray) A. Gray

FORM: deciduous, large, multistemmed shrub or small tree to 25 feet

BARK: light brown, warty

TWIGS: reddish-green to olive green; leaves and flowers borne on short lateral shoots after the first year

PITH: white, continuous

BUDS: rounded with overlapping light brown bud scales

LEAVES: alternate, simple, 2½–5 inches long with a sharply toothed edge

FALL LEAF COLOR: yellow

STIPULES: tiny, dark, persistent

LEAF SCARS: oval to somewhat 3-lobed, containing a single bundle scar

FLOWERS: as for other hollies, 4 to 5-parted, see description above

FRUIT: red, about ¼ inch in diameter with persistent sepals at the stem end

SEEDS: conspicuously ribbed or grooved, bird-dispersed

WOOD: hard, dense, nearly white, but too small to be of commercial significance

CURRENT CHAMPION: McKean County, diameter 5 inches, height 30 feet, spread 12 feet

Mountain holly is a plant of rocky mountain woods and slopes, it occurs in most regions of Pennsylvania except in the southeast and southwest. The very similar *Ilex beadlei* Ashe differs in having leaves less than twice as long as wide and densely hairy lower leaf surfaces; in addition the sepals are hairy.

Mountain holly—bark

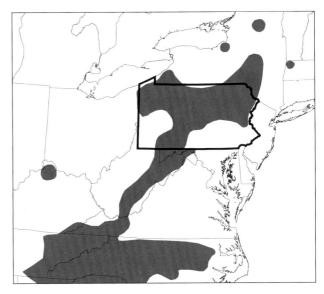

Mountain holly

Mountain holly—berries

Mountain holly—male flowers x1

HONEY-LOCUST
GLEDITSIA L.
Caesalpinia Family—Caesalpiniaceae

Honey-locust *Gleditsia triacanthos* **L.**

FORM: deciduous tree to 100 feet with large, branched thorns on the trunk and larger branches, branches spreading, forming a broad, open crown

BARK: dark grayish-brown to almost black with prominent raised lenticels

TWIGS: slender and spreading or even drooping, with short lateral spur branches that bear once-pinnate leaves and flowers

PITH: thick and white

BUDS: 3–5 at a node, one above another, the upper more conspicuous than the lower, terminal bud absent

LEAVES: alternate, pinnately compound (on short spur shoots) or bipinnate (on long shoots), leaflets ½–¾ inch long

FALL LEAF COLOR: yellow

STIPULES: present

LEAF SCARS: U-shaped with 3 bundle scars

FLOWERS: greenish-yellow, male and female flowers borne in separate inflorescences, some perfect flowers may also be present, flowers appearing with the leaves

FRUIT: dark reddish-brown, curving or somewhat twisted pods 10–18 inches long and 1–1½ inches wide containing seeds imbedded in a sweetish pulp

SEEDS: flat, oval, brown, about 1 inch in diameter

WOOD: hard, strong and heavy, reddish-brown with white sapwood, very durable when in contact with soil

CURRENT CHAMPION: Cumberland County, diameter 5 feet 2 inches, height 105 feet, spread 79 feet

Honey-locust— leaf scar x2

Scientists have suggested that honey-locust and several North American trees still show growth and fruit characteristics that evolved in response to large mammals that were driven to extinction about 13,000 years ago at the close of the last ice age.[1] An example is the formidable branched thorns on the trunks and larger branches of wild honey-locust trees that may have been effective in preventing ice age mammals, such as mastodons, from damaging the bark while trying to reach to the large seed pods. Although today animals such as deer, rabbits, squirrels, and quail eat the seeds and the soft pulp of the honey-locust seedpods, none are big enough to serve as effective seed dispersers by swallowing the seeds whole and depositing them elsewhere.

In Pennsylvania wild honey-locust is a tree of stream banks and moist floodplain soils across the southern two-thirds of the state. While some of the occurrences, especially in eastern counties, may be of naturalized origin, the southwestern corner of the state is clearly within the native range of the species. Abraham Steiner, who traveled with Moravian missionary John Heckewelder from Bethlehem to recently established Indian settlements in Ohio in April 1789, commented that on the Allegheny river bottoms in the vicinity of Pittsburgh, "one begins to see honey-locusts here, and from this point west they

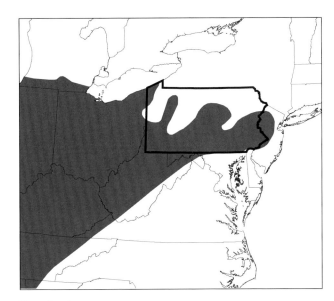

Honey-locust—trunk with thorns   *Honey-locust*

grow beside all streams and in all bottoms."[2] Honey-locust extends from Pennsylvania to Tennessee and northern Florida and west to Minnesota, North Dakota, and Texas.

Native Americans mixed bark of honey-locust with that of prickly-ash, wild cherry, and sassafras to make a tonic to purify the blood. The pods were considered helpful in treating many diseases of children, and the fleshy portion of the pods was used as a food or to prepare a beverage. The wood has been used mainly for fence posts and rails. Horticulturists have developed thornless and fruitless cultivars that have become very popular urban and suburban shade trees.

Honey-locust is a larval food plant for the silver-spotted skipper butterfly.

Notes

1. Barlow, Connie. 2000. *The Ghosts of Evolution: Nonsensical Fruit, Missing Partners, and Other Ecological Anachronisms.* Basic Books, New York.

2. Excerpts from the journal of Abraham Steiner, who accompanied Heckewelder on a journey from Bethlehem to Pettquotting on the Huron River near Lake Erie (in Ohio) in the spring of 1789. Quoted in Wallace, Paul A. W. (ed.). 1958. *Thirty Thousand Miles with John Heckewelder.* University of Pittsburgh Press, Pittsburgh.

Honey-locust—twig with thorn x1

Honey-locust—male flowers

Honey-locust—female flowers

Honey-locust—seed x1

Honey-locust—fruit

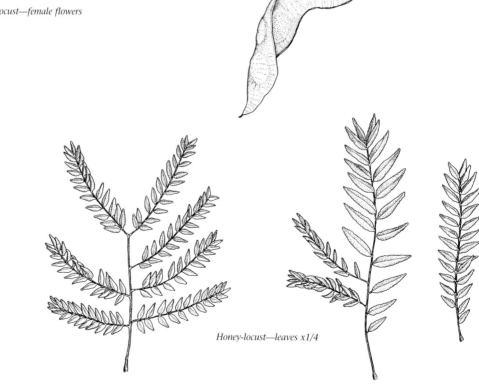

Honey-locust—leaves x1/4

HOP-HORNBEAM
OSTRYA SCOP.
Birch Family—Betulaceae

Hop-hornbeam   *Ostrya virginiana* **(Miller) K. Koch**

FORM: deciduous tree to 60 feet with widely spreading branches forming a broad crown

BARK: grayish-brown with a loose flaky surface

TWIGS: slender, reddish-brown, hairy at first becoming smooth

PITH: white, homogeneous

BUDS: ¼ inch long, sharp-pointed with numerous bud scales, angled away from the twig, terminal bud absent; dormant buds of the male flowers (catkins) conspicuous at the ends of the twigs through the winter

LEAVES: simple, alternate, 3–5 inches long, oblong with a sharply and doubly toothed margin

FALL LEAF COLOR: yellow

STIPULES: present but falling early

LEAF SCARS: small, curved with 3 bundle scars

FLOWERS: appearing in April with the leaves; male flowers in drooping catkins, female flowers in erect clusters, each flower enclosed in a papery bract

FRUIT: a drooping cone-like cluster of small, hard nutlets each enclosed in an inflated papery bract

SEEDS: dispersed by small mammals that store them for the winter

WOOD: strong, hard, and durable, light brown to white

CURRENT CHAMPION: Montour County, diameter 3 feet 4 inches, height 56 feet, spread 52 feet

Hop-hornbeam—bark

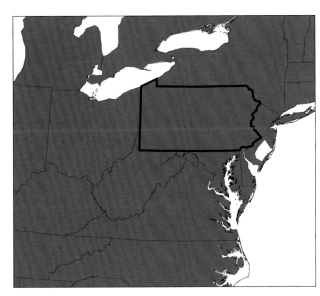

Hop-hornbeam

Hop-hornbeam is an understory tree of dry, rocky slopes and ridges, frequently on limestone or other calcareous soils. Its finely textured, flaky bark is a distinctive feature year round. Present throughout Pennsylvania, it is more common in the southern half of the state. Hop-hornbeam is rarely abundant, but rather occurs in mixed stands often with maple, beech, birch, elm, and hickories. The full range of hop-hornbeam extends from Nova Scotia to Manitoba and south to Florida and Texas.

Native Americans used a decoction of the heartwood of hop-hornbeam as a tonic and treatment for dyspepsia and kidney trouble. A treatment for rheumatism was made from a combination of hop-hornbeam, spruce, and ground-pine. Early settlers used a fluid extract of the inner bark of hop-hornbeam as a substitute for quassia to treat malaria. The hard, durable wood was used to make the runners on sleighs, handles for tools, wooden mallets, and other small articles where strength was important.

The seeds are eaten by wildlife including squirrels, mice, and some game birds. Cottontail rabbits chew on the bark and twigs, and deer browse it too. Hop-hornbeam is also a larval host plant for red-spotted purple, white admiral, and mourning cloak butterflies.

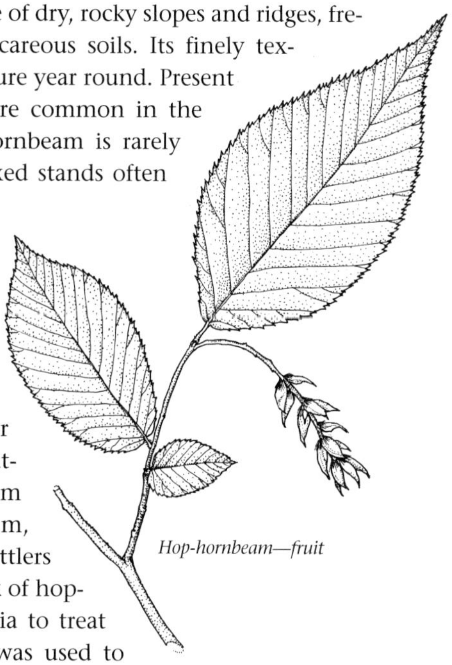

Hop-hornbeam—fruit

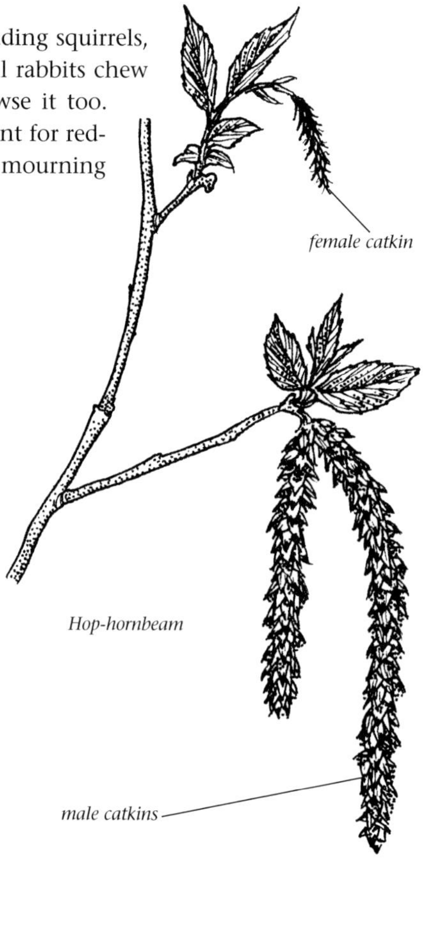

female catkin

Hop-hornbeam

male catkins

HOPTREE
PTELEA L.
Rue Family—Rutaceae

Hoptree, wafer-ash   *Ptelea trifoliata* L.

FORM: large deciduous shrub or small tree to 20 feet

BARK: brown, smooth with warty growths, becoming scaly with age

TWIGS: light brown and shiny with raised lenticels

PITH: large, white, and continuous

BUDS: small, rounded, hairy, terminal bud absent

LEAVES: alternate, compound with 3 leaflets, shiny above and often hairy on the lower surface

FALL LEAF COLOR: yellow

STIPULES: none

LEAF SCARS: U-shaped and encircling the buds, containing 3 bundle scars

FLOWERS: small, greenish-white, in clusters at the ends of branches, unisexual or perfect; male flowers containing 4–5 stamens; female flowers with a single pistil and abortive stamens; insect-pollinated

FRUIT: a flattened, disk-like samara about ¾–1 inch in diameter, with 2 seeds in the center surrounded by a broad, buff-colored wing

SEEDS: wind-dispersed

WOOD: yellowish, hard, heavy, and close-grained but too small to have any commercial significance

CURRENT CHAMPION: none reported

Hoptree gets its name from the fact that the seeds have been used as a substitute for hops to flavor beer. All parts of the plant, including the flowers have an unpleasant odor.

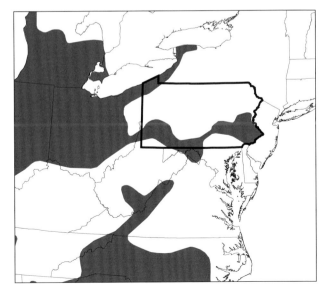

Hoptree—bark   *Hoptree*

Hoptree is a wide-ranging species that occurs in Mexico and the southwestern United States and ranges north and east to Kansas, Wisconsin, southern Ontario, New Jersey, and Florida. It grows on riverbanks and in other low moist ground. In Pennsylvania it is scattered across the southern half of the state and along Lake Erie in the northwestern corner. Because of its rarity in the state, it is classified by the Pennsylvania Natural Heritage Program as a threatened species.

Hoptree was used medicinally by several Native American tribes. The roots were considered a panacea or sacred medicine that could cure many ailments; they were also added to other cures to increase their potency. Giant swallowtail and tiger swallowtail butterflies feed on the leaves.

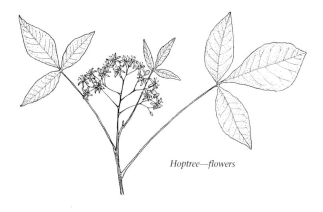

Hoptree—flowers

Hoptree—fruit

HORNBEAM
CARPINUS L.
Birch Family—Betulaceae

Hornbeam, ironwood, musclewood   *Carpinus caroliniana* **Walter**

FORM: deciduous tree to 30 feet with ascending branches and a spreading crown

BARK: smooth, bluish-gray, and muscular in appearance

TWIGS: slender, green and hairy at first, later smooth and reddish-brown with scattered lenticels

PITH: small, pale tan, solid

BUDS: ⅛ inch long with numerous overlapping bud scales, true terminal bud absent

LEAVES: oblong, 2–4 inches long, unlobed but sharply and doubly toothed on the margins

FALL LEAF COLOR: orange to red

STIPULES: present but falling early

LEAF SCARS: small, elliptical with 3 bundle scars

FLOWERS: appearing in April with the leaves; staminate flowers in drooping catkins; pistillate flowers in smaller catkins at the ends of the new shoots

FRUIT: produced in a terminal cluster consisting of 3-lobed, leafy bracts each containing a small nutlet at the base

SEEDS: stored (and dispersed) by squirrels

WOOD: heavy, hard, and strong

CURRENT CHAMPION: Chester County (1988), diameter 2 feet 6 inches, height 55 feet, spread 53 feet

Hornbeam—bark

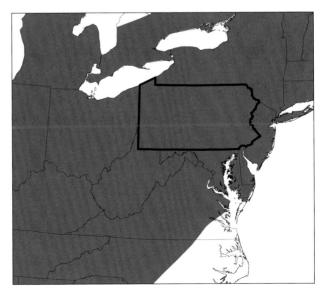

Hornbeam

Hornbeam is an understory tree of stream banks and floodplain forests that can easily be recognized by its smooth, tight, bluish-gray bark. The muscular appearance of the trunk and larger branches adds to the distinctive appearance and gives this tree one of its common names. It occurs throughout Pennsylvania and ranges from Nova Scotia and Minnesota south to Florida and Texas.

Native Americans used a decoction of hornbeam to treat diarrhea in infants; compound infusions including hornbeam combined with other species were employed in the treatment of urinary problems, gynecological ailments, and tuberculosis. The wood is tough, strong, and durable and was used for tool handles. However, the trees are too small to be of much commercial importance as a lumber source.

Squirrels, chipmunks, ruffed grouse, bobwhites, pheasants, and wild turkeys consume the nutlets. Hornbeam leaves are a larval food source for tiger swallowtail, red-spotted purple, white admiral, and striped hairstreak butterflies.

Hornbeam—fruit

Hornbeam—female and male catkins x1

HORSE-CHESTNUT
AESCULUS L.
Horse-chestnut Family—Hippocastanaceae

Horse-chestnut   *Aesculus hippocastanum* L.

FORM: deciduous tree to 100 feet with a broad, rounded crown

BARK: dark gray or brown, coarsely scaly or platy, inner bark orangey-brown

TWIGS: stout

PITH: large, tan, and homogeneous

BUDS: terminal buds ½–¾ inch long, covered with sticky resin

LEAVES: opposite, palmately compound with 5–7 leaflets, the longest to 10 inches

FALL LEAF COLOR: yellow

STIPULES: not present

LEAF SCARS: large, heart-shaped or triangular with 3 clusters of bundle scars

FLOWERS: in 12-inch-long clusters at the ends of the branches; perfect; petals 5, white with a red or yellow blotch

FRUIT: a spiny capsule splitting open to release a large, shiny brown seed, maturing in September–October

SEEDS: smooth, shiny brown about 1–1¼ inches in diameter

WOOD: soft and weak, used for carving

CURRENT CHAMPION: Lebanon County, diameter 5 feet 3 inches, height 79 feet, spread 72 feet

This tree, which is native to northern Greece and Albania, is a popular street and ornamental tree for parks and other urban sites in temperate regions worldwide. Since the late 1500s, when seeds were sent to Vienna, it has been enjoyed for its

Horse-chestnut—bark

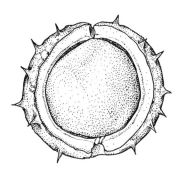

Horse-chestnut—fruit x3/4

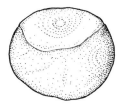

Horse-chestnut—seed x3/4

Horse-chestnut—inflorescence

striking flower display and dense shade. Over the years many cultivars have been selected with double flowers or varied leaf shapes or colors.

The importation of horse-chestnut to North America occurred in 1741 when Peter Collinson of London sent seeds to John Bartram. In 1763 Bartram wrote to Collinson that the trees he subsequently grew at his botanical garden in West Philadelphia had bloomed for the first time.

In recent years the use of horse-chestnut in the United States has declined as a result of a fungal leaf disease that causes leaves to appeared scorched by late summer, and a general trend toward smaller trees. In Pennsylvania horse-chestnut has naturalized at scattered locations across the southern part of the state.

As for other members of the genus *Aesculus*, the seeds and young shoots of horse-chestnut contain a toxin known as aesculin and are little used by wildlife.

IRONWOOD—SEE HORNBEAM

JUNEBERRY—SEE SHADBUSH

KATSURA
CERCIDIPHYLLUM SIEBOLD & ZUCC.
Katsura-tree Family—Cercidiphyllaceae

Katsura-tree   *Cercidiphyllum japonicum*
                          Siebold & Zucc. ex J. Hoffm. & Schult.

FORM: large tree to 70 feet with widely spreading branches; young trees have a more upright form

BARK: brown, slightly shaggy on older stems

TWIGS: slender, pale brown with prominent lenticels; leaves and flowers borne on short lateral shoots after the first year

PITH: small, greenish-yellow

BUDS: terminal bud not produced, lateral buds slender, curved, covered with red bud scales

LEAVES: opposite, simple, 2–4 inches long, heart-shaped, dark bluish-green; edge with rounded teeth

FALL LEAF COLOR: yellow

STIPULES: falling early

LEAF SCARS: slender, crescent-shaped with 3 bundle scars

FLOWERS: unisexual with male and female flowers on separate trees (dioecious); male flowers each with a tiny calyx and a cluster of 8–13 magenta stamens; female flowers, each consisting of a single ovary, are grouped in clusters of 4 surrounded by tiny sepal-like bracts

FRUIT: clusters of ¾-inch-long, banana-shaped pods that split open along one side

SEEDS: tiny, winged, and wind-dispersed

CURRENT CHAMPION: Philadelphia County, diameter 6 feet 5 inches (at 2 feet), height 67 feet, spread 86 feet

Katsura-tree—bark

A striking characteristic of katsura-tree is the heart-shaped leaves that line the branches far into the interior of the crown. In the fall when the leaves are turning they have a very noticeable sweet fragrance like that of cotton candy.

Katsura-tree is native to China and Japan. In China it occurs as part of the canopy of the deciduous broad-leaved forest and mixed mesophytic forest formations. It has been cultivated since 1865; horticultural selections include forms with yellow leaves or drooping branches. Katsura-tree grows readily from seed and occasionally has become naturalized in urban and suburban forest remnants. The largest known specimen in the state is at the Morris Arboretum in Philadelphia.

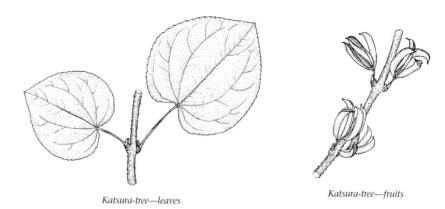

Katsura-tree—leaves

Katsura-tree—fruits

Katsura-tree—male and female flowers

LARCH
LARIX MILL.
Pine Family—Pinaceae

Unlike most conifers, the larches are deciduous, losing their needle-like leaves each fall like most of our broad-leaved trees. The needles are alternately arranged on long shoots and clustered or tufted on short lateral shoots. Young seed cones are magenta in color and appear at about the same time the pale green new needles are starting to emerge in the spring. The mature cones remain on the branches after the needles have dropped. Only one species of larch is native to Pennsylvania, but several others are grown here in forest plantations or as landscape ornamentals.

European larch   *Larix decidua* **Mill.**

FORM: crown narrowly conic, to 110 feet; branches dense, drooping with upturned tips

BARK: grayish-brown with irregular plates that are shed

TWIGS: smooth, light grayish-yellow at first, turning darker in the second and third years

BUDS: short and pointed with many brown scales

LEAVES: linear, about 1 inch long, blue-green

FALL LEAF COLOR: yellow

LEAF SCARS: triangular and forming a line that extends down along the stem, containing a single bundle scar

European larch—twig with cone x1

European larch—bark

CONES: ovate, 1–1½ inches long; cone scales straight or slightly incurved, finely hairy on the outside surface
SEEDS: winged, wind-dispersed
WOOD: dense, resinous; heartwood bright red or yellow; sapwood yellow
CURRENT CHAMPION: Warren County, diameter 3 feet 3 inches, height 111 feet, spread 44 feet

European larch is occasionally planted as a landscape ornamental or in forest plantations in Pennsylvania. This species is native to the mountains of central and eastern Europe. Several cultivars have been developed and hybrids with Japanese larch and tamarack are known.

Japanese larch   *Larix kaempferi* (Lamb.) Carr.

FORM: crown conic, to 90 feet tall
BARK: brown, with shallow fissures, forming narrow plates or strips that are shed
TWIGS: light yellow or light reddish-brown and hairy at first, becoming smooth and darker by the second year
BUDS: small, conical, resinous
LEAVES: linear, blue-green, about 1¼–1½ inches long, keeled below
FALL LEAF COLOR: yellow
LEAF SCARS: triangular and forming a line that extends down along the stem, containing a single bundle scar
CONES: ovoid, about 1 inch long; cone scales curved outward at the tip
SEEDS: winged, wind-dispersed
WOOD: resinous, hard, and durable; used mainly for construction; heartwood bright red
CURRENT CHAMPION: Chester County, diameter 2 feet 9 inches, height 71 feet, spread 77 feet

Japanese larch—bark

Japanese larch has been used extensively in reforestation plantings and has begun to naturalize at some sites. It grows to a height of 90 feet and is considered a desirable timber tree. This species is native to Japan where it grows at a 4,000 to 8,000 foot elevation on the slopes of volcanic mountains.

Japanese larch is distinguished by the strongly recurved tips of its cone scales. Both this species and European larch are usually found in more upland situations than the native tamarack, which always grows in or near sphagnum bogs.

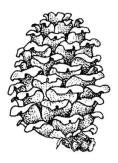

Japanese larch—cone x1

Tamarack, American larch *Larix laricina* (Du Roi) K. Koch

FORM: deciduous, to 60 feet but usually shorter, crown narrowly and often irregularly conical but becoming rounded with age

BARK: reddish-brown, scaly

TWIGS: slender, light orange-brown with numerous short lateral shoots

BUDS: rounded, dark red, slightly resinous

LEAVES: needle-like, about 1 inch long, keeled below, yellow-green to bluish

FALL LEAF COLOR: yellow

LEAF SCARS: triangular and forming a line that extends down along the stem, containing a single bundle scar

CONES: ovoid, ½ inch long with approximately 20 scales that are curved inward slightly at the tip

SEEDS: light brown, ⅔ inch long including the wing, wind-dispersed

WOOD: dense and resinous; heartwood yellowish or reddish-brown; sapwood whitish

CURRENT CHAMPION: Delaware County, diameter 2 feet 8 inches, height 81 feet, spread 48 feet

Tamarack—cone x1

Tamarack, our native larch, like black spruce with which it often grows, is a plant of sphagnum bogs in Pennsylvania. As such it is found primarily in the glaciated northeastern and northwestern parts of the state. Tamarack is a northern species extending to tree line in the arctic from Newfoundland west to Alaska. Pennsylvania, and a single site each in Maryland and the mountains of West Virginia, represent the southern limit of its range.

The delicate light green needles of tamarack emerge in May in tufts at the tips of short lateral shoots or singly on elongating branch tips. In the fall they turn a warm yellow before dropping. The cones offer the best way to distinguish the three species of larch; those of tamarack are only about ½ inch long. European larch and Japanese larch both have larger cones, 1–1½ inches long.

Tamarack—bark

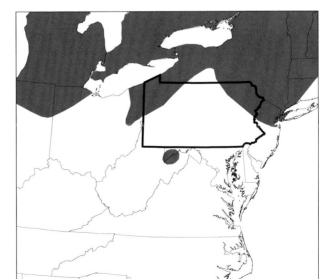

Tamarack

Tamarack—twig with cones

Tamarack was never abundant enough in Pennsylvania to be commercially important. However, the wood of this tree was formerly valued for ship construction due to its resinous qualities and durability. Native Americans made various medicinal preparations from the needles, bark, and the gum that exudes from the tree to treat burns, wounds, headache, and inflammation. Tamarack roots were used for weaving bags and other items and to stitch birch bark canoes. In addition the inner bark and new shoots were used as an emergency food.

Small mammals including red squirrels and mice, as well as birds such as ruffed grouse and crossbills, eat the seeds of tamarack. The caterpillars of several sphinx moths feed on the needles.

LINDEN—SEE BASSWOOD

LOCUST
ROBINIA L.
Bean Family—Fabaceae

Black locust   *Robinia pseudoacacia* L.

FORM: upright tree to 75 feet

BARK: brown, deeply furrowed

TWIGS: stout, brittle with a pair of spines at each node

PITH: white, angular

BUDS: small, imbedded in the leaf scar and nearly hidden by dense rusty hairs, frequently with 3–4 buds located immediately above each other; terminal bud absent

LEAVES: alternate, pinnately compound; leaflets 1–2 inches long, pale bluish-green

FALL LEAF COLOR: grayish-brown

STIPULES: modified as spines

LEAF SCARS: large and conspicuous, triangular with 3 bundle scars, surrounding the buds

FLOWERS: white, fragrant, about 1 inch long, in conspicuous drooping clusters, appearing in May as the leaves are expanding, insect pollinated

FRUIT: a dry, brown pod 2–4 inches long and ½ inch wide that splits open along both sides

SEEDS: 4–8 per pod, dark and mottled in appearance

WOOD: heavy, hard, and very durable, yellowish-brown in color

CURRENT CHAMPION: Susquehanna County, diameter 5 feet 10 inches, height 98 feet, spread 55 feet

Black locust—bark

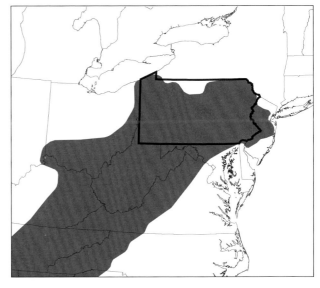

Black locust

Found throughout the state except in the north central region, black locust usually grows on floodplains or in open woods, waste ground, or fencerows. While it sometimes grows mixed with other hardwoods, it often forms nearly pure stands in old fields and other open sites in which it spreads rapidly by root sprouts. The range of black locust extends from Pennsylvania to southern Indiana and Oklahoma, and south to Georgia and Alabama. Although considered native only west of the Allegheny Mountains by some, written accounts of the flora in the Pocono region of Pennsylvania from the late 1700s and early 1800s, mention well-established stands of locust.[1] Seeds of black locust were sent to Europe in the early 1600s, and it is now widely naturalized there and in other parts of the world.

Native Americans used preparations of black locust as an emetic and to treat toothaches. The wood was used to make bows. Native Americans, early settlers, and later farmers all valued the rot resistant wood for fence posts and other uses requiring contact with soil. A grove of black locust on a farm was considered a valuable asset. The wood was also highly valued for ship building and was shipped to England during the 1800s for that purpose.

Black locust honey is held in high regard, and quail and squirrels eat the seeds, although cattle and horses have been poisoned by eating the inner bark or grazing on sprouts. On the other hand, young shoots of black locust are the preferred larval food of the silver-spotted skipper butterfly and are also used by the common sulfur, aspen duskywing, and dreamy duskywing.

Notes

1. Cook, Frederick. 1887. *Journals of the Military Expedition of Major General John Sullivan Against the Six Nations of Indians in 1779*, facsimile reprint, 2000. Heritage Books, Bowie, Md.; Pursh, Frederick. 1869. *Journal of a Botanical Excursion in the Northeastern Parts of the States of Pennsylvania and New York During the Year 1807*. Brinckloe & Marot, Printers, Philadelphia.

Black locust—flowers

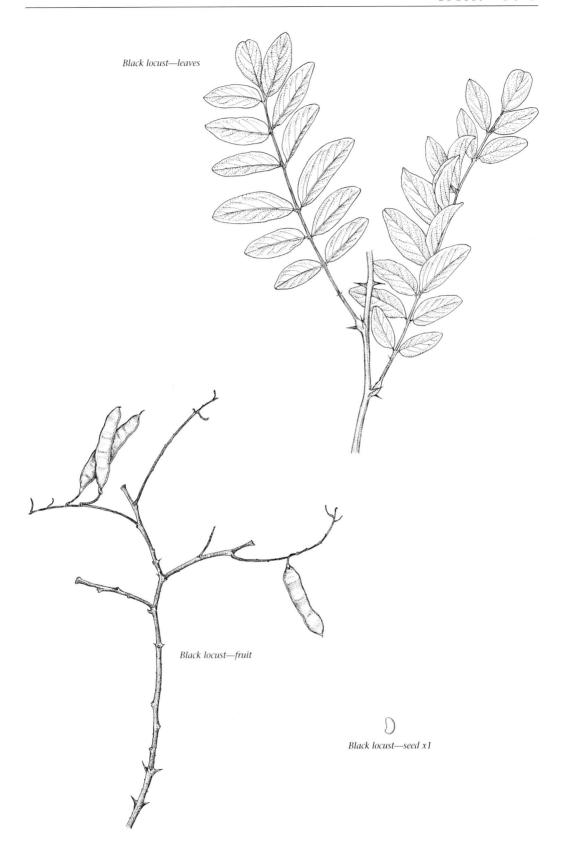

Black locust—leaves

Black locust—fruit

Black locust—seed x1

MAGNOLIA
MAGNOLIA L.
Magnolia Family—Magnoliaceae

Pennsylvania's forests include three native magnolias, in addition two Asian species are naturalized in the state. *Magnolia* is one of several genera of plants that occur naturally only in eastern Asia and eastern North America.[1] This curious widely separated distribution is believed to be due to the effects of the most recent glacial period when plants that were once more widespread were forced south into a few widely separated survival zones. Eastern North America boasts a total of eight magnolia species while the number of species in China is 30.

Our magnolias are deciduous or semievergreen trees with simple entire leaves, aromatic wood, and large, showy flowers produced in the spring or early summer. Magnolia flowers are insect-pollinated, mostly by beetles that visit the flowers to feed on the copious amounts of pollen they contain. The numerous stamens are surrounded by 9–15 creamy white, greenish, or pink petals. The fruit is a cone-like cluster of pods or follicles each containing a single seed that dangles on a slender thread when mature. A fleshy red, pink, or orange covering on the seeds, called an aril, makes them attractive (and nutritious) to birds that serve as the dispersal agents. Many magnolias, both native and introduced species, are popular landscape ornamentals.

Cucumber-tree   ***Magnolia acuminata*** (L.) L.

Cucumber-tree—fruit

FORM: erect tree to 90 feet, crown narrowly pyramidal
BARK: gray-brown with long furrows and loose scaly ridges
TWIGS: gray-brown or reddish, smooth to slightly hairy
PITH: tan, homogeneous
BUDS: ⅝ inch long, densely covered with short whitish hairs
LEAVES: alternate, 5–9 inches long, broadly ovate or oblong with an acuminate tip, margin entire
FALL LEAF COLOR: yellow
STIPULES: hairy on the back, falling early
LEAF SCARS: crescent- or U-shaped with an irregular line of bundle scars; stipule scars appearing as a line encircling the twig
FLOWERS: greenish-yellow, opening after the leaves have expanded
FRUIT: cylindrical, often knobby, to 3 inches long
SEEDS: covered with a reddish-orange aril
WOOD: light, soft, and brittle
CURRENT CHAMPION: Chester County, diameter 5 feet 6 inches, height 100 feet, spread 79 feet

Named for the supposed resemblance of the young fruit to a cucumber, this tree is the largest of our native magnolias. In Pennsylvania, cucumber-tree grows in rich stream valleys and forested lower slopes mainly in the central and western parts of the state. While it is a common canopy species in such areas, it was never abundant. Forty to fifty years of excessive deer browsing has drastically

Cucumber-tree—bark

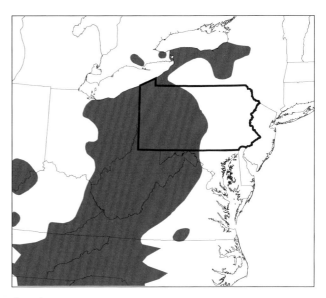

Cucumber-tree

reduced its occurrence in some areas. Cucumber-tree is the most northern of our native magnolia species. Its range extends from southern Canada to the Gulf Coast and west to Arkansas and Illinois.

Native Americans used preparations of the bark of this tree to treat stomachache, cramps, toothache, and venereal disease. F. A. Michaux, while traveling in the vicinity of Bedford Pennsylvania in 1802, noted in his journal, "The

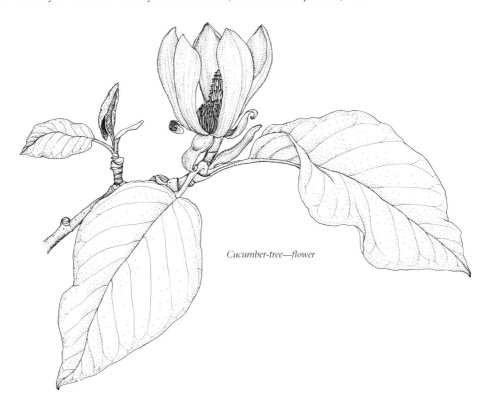

Cucumber-tree—flower

Magnolia acuminata is very common in the environs; it is known in the country by the name of the cucumber tree. The inhabitants of the remote parts of Pennsylvania, Virginia, and even the western countries, pick the cones when green to infuse whiskey, which gives it a pleasant bitter. This bitter is very much esteemed in the country as a preventive against intermittent fevers; but I have my doubts whether it would be so generally used if it had the same qualities when mixed with water."[2]

The wood of cucumber-tree is very similar to that of tuliptree for which it has been substituted.

Kobus magnolia   *Magnolia kobus* DC.

FORM: deciduous tree to 30 feet or sometimes more shrub-like

BARK: smooth, brownish-gray

TWIGS: dark reddish-brown, smooth

PITH: white, homogeneous

BUDS: flower buds densely covered with long silvery hairs, leaf buds blackish and only sparsely hairy

LEAVES: alternate, deciduous, broadly obovate, to 6 inches long, pointed at the tip and tapering at the base

FALL LEAF COLOR: yellow

STIPULES: present but not persistent

LEAF SCARS: U-shaped with a row of bundle scars; stipule scars appearing as a narrow line encircling the twigs

FLOWERS: creamy white, 4½ inches across with narrow, spreading petals

FRUIT: about 4 inches long, cylindrical or sometimes curved

SEEDS: covered with a red aril

CURRENT CHAMPION: Montgomery County, diameter 1 foot 10 inches, height 44 feet, spread 45 feet

Kobus magnolia—fruit

The kobus magnolia has been found naturalized in a number of locations in southeastern Pennsylvania. Its fragrant, white flowers appear in late March or early April, well before the leaves begin to expand. A native of Japan and South Korea, the kobus magnolia was introduced into cultivation in 1865. It is considered one of the hardiest of the Asian magnolias.

Kobus magnolia—bark

Kobus magnolia—flower

Saucer magnolia   *Magnolia soulangeana* Soul.-Bod.

FORM: deciduous tree to 30 feet with a rounded crown, sometimes shrubby

BARK: smooth, gray

TWIGS: reddish-brown, smooth with white lenticels

PITH: white, homogeneous

BUDS: densely covered with long silvery hairs

LEAVES: deciduous, elliptical

FALL LEAF COLOR: yellow to brown

STIPULES: present but not persistent

LEAF SCARS: V-shaped, with a row of bundle scars; the narrow stipule scars encircle the twig

FLOWERS: large, appearing before the leaves, petals purple on the outside and white within

FRUIT: cylindrical, to 4 inches long, pinkish-green eventually becoming dark red

SEEDS: covered by a red aril

CURRENT CHAMPION: Dauphin County, diameter 2 feet 3 inches, height 36 feet, spread 39 feet

Saucer magnolia, a chance hybrid of *M. denudata* and *M. liliflora*, both native to central China, was first discovered in a garden near Paris in 1820. It has become the most popular of the cultivated magnolias and has given rise to many cultivated forms. Only occasionally has it shown a tendency to naturalize in disturbed urban or suburban forests.

Saucer magnolia—dormant twig

Saucer magnolia—flower

Saucer magnolia—bark

Sweetbay magnolia   *Magnolia virginiana* L.

FORM: small tree to 30 feet, often multistemmed
BARK: smooth, gray
TWIGS: green, smooth with prominent lenticels
PITH: white with denser partitions developing
BUDS: densely covered with silky gray hairs, pointed
LEAVES: alternate, semievergreen, thick and leathery, whitish underneath, margins smooth
FALL LEAF COLOR: green
STIPULES: present but not persistent
LEAF SCARS: oval to crescent-shaped with a U-shaped line of bundle scars; stipule scars appear as a line encircling the twig
FLOWERS: creamy white, 2–3 inches across, intensely fragrant, appearing over several weeks from late May to late June
FRUIT: to 2 inches long
SEEDS: covered with a red aril
WOOD: white, soft, and brittle
CURRENT CHAMPION: none recorded

Sweetbay magnolia—fruit

Sweetbay magnolia is a rare native plant in Pennsylvania where it is confined to sandy, peaty swamps of the Coastal Plain and nearby areas of the Piedmont and Blue Ridge Provinces; it is classified as a threatened species by the Pennsylvania Natural Heritage Program. Its total range extends along the Atlantic and Gulf coasts from Massachusetts to Louisiana.

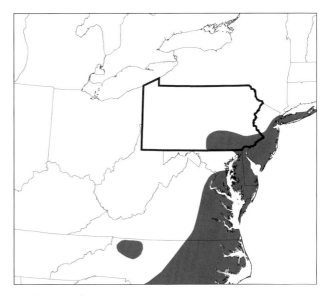

Sweetbay magnolia—bark

Sweetbay magnolia

If you have a sweetbay magnolia tree near your home you will notice that the fragrance of the flowers is greatest in the early evening, presumably to attract late day and evening pollinators such as moths. The flowers open a few at a time over a span of a month or more, extending the season of olfactory pleasure.

Because of its small size and slow growth rate sweetbay magnolia has no value as a timber species. However, it is a very popular landscape ornamental and has been shown to be tolerant, in cultivation, of drier and less acidic soils than it occurs on naturally. Sweetbay magnolia has long been grown as a landscape plant in Europe and the United States. Seed was first sent to the continent in 1688 from Virginia by missionary and plant collector John Bannister.

Native Americans used decoctions of leaves and twigs of sweetbay magnolia to warm the blood and to treat chills and colds.

*Sweetbay magnolia—
flower*

Umbrella-tree   *Magnolia tripetala* (L.) L.

FORM: deciduous tree to 36 feet, often multistemmed; crown round-topped

BARK: smooth, gray

TWIGS: stout, smooth, and brown

PITH: large, whitish, and homogeneous

BUDS: smooth, the terminal bud to 2 inches long and tapering to a long pointed tip

LEAVES: deciduous, to 18 inches long, crowded in a whorl-like cluster at the ends of the branches

FALL LEAF COLOR: yellow

STIPULES: present but not persistent

LEAF SCARS: clustered, oval with irregularly scattered bundle scars; stipule scars encircling the twigs

FLOWERS: appearing after the leaves have expanded, stiffly erect, with an unpleasant odor; petals creamy white

FRUIT: cylindrical, to 4 inches long

SEEDS: covered with a pink to red aril

WOOD: light, weak, and brittle, of no commercial value

CURRENT CHAMPION: Bucks County, diameter 3 feet 3 inches, height 50 feet, spread 51 feet

This species, with its huge leaves, is hard to miss in the forest understory where it creates a tropical look. The fact that the leaves are crowded at the branch tips adds to the umbrella-like appearance. The coarse branches and very large terminal buds are quite distinctive in the winter landscape also. Umbrella-tree is shade-tolerant, reproducing readily under a dense canopy of taller trees.

Umbrella-tree is clearly a native component of the rich ravine forests of the Lower Susquehanna River Valley and a few locations farther west in Pennsylva-

Umbrella-tree—bark

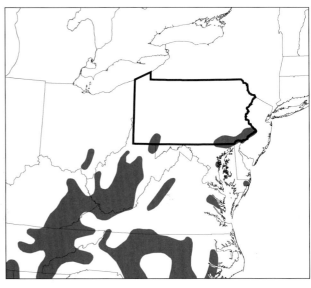

Umbrella-tree

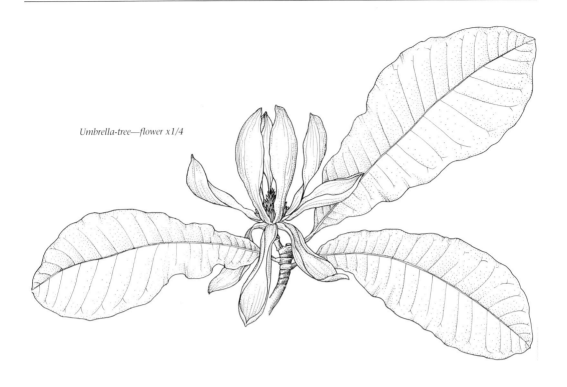

Umbrella-tree—flower x1/4

Umbrella-tree—fruit

nia. The Pennsylvania Biological Survey has recommended its classification as a rare species in the state.

In Philadelphia, Bucks, Montgomery, and Chester Counties, where it has appeared only in the past 70 to 80 years and increased rapidly, umbrella-tree seems more likely to have spread from cultivated sources.[3] It is known to have been grown in the late 1700s by Humphrey Marshall at his arboretum in Marshallton, Chester County,[4] and to have been one of the most commonly grown magnolias in the mid-1800s. While not as popular today as saucer magnolia or some of the other Asian species, umbrella-tree is still occasionally grown as a landscape specimen.

The range of umbrella-tree extends from southern Pennsylvania to Mississippi, mainly in the uplands, only rarely does it occur on the Coastal Plain. Its wood has no commercial value.

Notes

1. Li, Hui-Lin. 1971. *Floristic Relationships Between Eastern Asia and Eastern North America*, Morris Arboretum Monograph, Morris Arboretum of the University of Pennsylvania, Philadelphia.

2. Michaux, F. Andrew. 1805. *Travels to the West of the Allegheny Mountains in the States of Ohio, Kentucky, and Tennessee, and Back to Charleston by the Upper Carolines Undertaken in the Year 1802*, September 24, 1801–March 1, 1803, in Reuben Gold Thwaits (ed.) *Early Western Travels 1748–1846*, Vol. 3. AMS Press, New York.

3. Rhoads, Ann F. 1994. *Magnolia tripetala* in Pennsylvania. *Bartonia* 58: 75–77.

4. Gutowski, Robert R. 1988. Humphrey Marshall's Botanic Garden: Living Collections 1773–1813. Master's thesis, University of Delaware.

MAIDENHAIR-TREE—SEE GINKGO

MAPLE
ACER L.
Maple Family—Aceraceae

Our native maples include both canopy and understory trees. They have opposite leaves that are simple and palmately lobed except for one species with compound leaves, box-elder (*Acer negundo*). The fruit, described as a double samara, is perhaps the most distinctive feature of the maples overall. Flowering takes place in the spring before, with, or after leaf expansion. Flowers are perfect and/or unisexual with 4–6 petals and/or sepals, usually 8 stamens and a flattened, 2-lobed ovary.

Several maples serve as larval food sources for tiger swallowtail and mourning cloak butterflies.

The Pennsylvania flora includes 7 native maples and 5 naturalized species.

Amur maple   *Acer ginnala* **Maxim**

FORM: small deciduous tree to 20 feet with a dense, rounded crown, sometimes multistemmed and shrubby

BARK: grayish-brown and smooth with darker streaks

TWIGS: gray-brown and smooth, becoming streaked and roughened on older stems

PITH: small and inconspicuous

BUDS: reddish-brown, smooth, ⅛ inch long with overlapping bud scales

LEAVES: opposite, simple, 3–4 inches long, 3-lobed with the central lobe much longer than the other two, dark green; margin with large and small teeth alternating

FALL LEAF COLOR: yellow to red

Amur maple—bark

Amur maple—flowers

STIPULES: not present

LEAF SCARS: V-shaped with 3 bundle scars, each pair of leaf scars projecting out and joined around the twig by a narrow line

FLOWERS: yellowish-green, in small clusters appearing with the leaves, fragrant, insect-pollinated

FRUIT: double samara, wings nearly parallel, turning bright red in the summer while the leaves are still green; maturing September–October

SEEDS: wind-dispersed

WOOD: too small to be commercially significant

CURRENT CHAMPION: Delaware County, diameter 1 foot 6 inches, height 57 feet, spread 40 feet

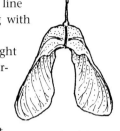

Amur maple—fruit x1

Native to northern China, Manchuria, and Japan, Amur maple was introduced into cultivation in 1860. A number of cultivars have been developed featuring intense fall color or exceptionally compact growth habit. Extensive naturalized populations of Amur maple can be found at Lackawanna State Park and in other locations in eastern Pennsylvania.

Black maple   *Acer nigrum* **Michx. f.**

FORM: deciduous tree to 85 feet with a rounded crown

BARK: dark grayish-brown becoming deeply furrowed with longitudinal ridges and plates

TWIGS: stout, reddish-brown

PITH: white, continuous

BUDS: ¼–½ inch long, sharp-pointed, conical, hairy at the tip with 8–16 overlapping bud scales

LEAVES: dark green, 4–5 inches long, 3 to 5-lobed with the edges of the lobes tending to curl under; margin with fewer teeth than sugar maple

FALL LEAF COLOR: orange or red

STIPULES: present, attached to the base of the leaf stalk and frequently breaking off leaving a ragged edge

LEAF SCARS: U- or V-shaped, with 3 bundle scars

FLOWERS: drooping on long slender stalks, produced in April or May before the leaves expand, wind-pollinated

FRUIT: a double samara with wings nearly parallel to curving inward toward each other, maturing late September–early October

SEEDS: wind-dispersed

WOOD: very similar to sugar maple and usually marketed as such

CURRENT CHAMPION: Wayne County, diameter 5 feet 10 inches, height 85 feet, spread 86 feet

Black maple is primarily a midwestern tree, ranging from Ontario to Wisconsin, Iowa, and Missouri. In Pennsylvania it occurs mainly west of the Allegheny Mountains, although the largest black maple known in the state is in a meadow near the Delaware River in Wayne County.

Black maple can be hard to distinguish from sugar maple. The mostly 3-lobed, dark green leaves with the edges curled under and the less divergent wings of the

Black maple—bark

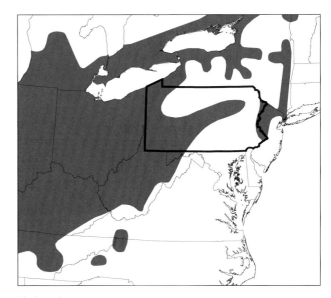

Black maple

samaras are the best characteristics for separating the two species. In addition, stipules are present on black maple but not on sugar maple.

Uses by both humans and wildlife are as described for sugar maple. Black maple has not always been considered a distinct species, some botanists have classified it as a subspecies of sugar maple (*Acer saccharum* ssp. *nigrum*).

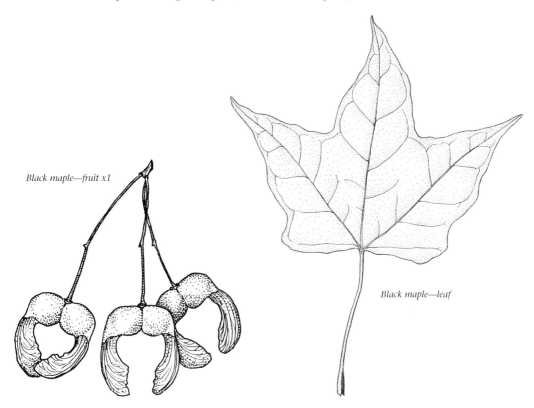

Black maple—fruit x1

Black maple—leaf

State champion black maple, Wayne County.

Box-elder, ash-leaved maple   *Acer negundo* L.

FORM: medium-sized deciduous tree to 60 feet

BARK: smooth and grayish-brown, becoming strongly ridged on older stems

TWIGS: stout, smooth, and green

PITH: large, tan

BUDS: ¼ inch long, pointed with orangey-brown bud scales covered with silky hairs

LEAVES: opposite, pinnately compound with 3–5 coarsely toothed leaflets, each to 4 inches long

FALL LEAF COLOR: yellow-green to tan

STIPULES: not present

LEAF SCARS: V-shaped with 3 bundle scars; each pair encircling the stem

FLOWERS: yellowish-green; on long, very slender, drooping stalks; unisexual with the staminate and pistillate flowers on separate plants (dioecious), wind-pollinated; blooming in late March or April before the leaves expand

FRUIT: a double samara with slightly divergent wings, maturing in September but often remaining on the trees into the winter

SEEDS: wind-dispersed

WOOD: light, soft, white

CURRENT CHAMPION: York County, diameter 5 feet, height 70 feet, spread 68 feet

Box-elder—bark

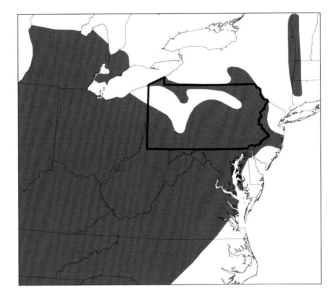

Box-elder

The green twigs and opposite compound leaves are distinctive features of this tree. Box-elder is a common tree of stream banks, floodplains, and other low, moist sites. It is most abundant in the southern half of Pennsylvania, with the exception of high elevation areas along the Allegheny Front.

Box-elder has a large native range extending from Canada to Mexico and west to Colorado and Texas; it continues at scattered lowland locations along streams and rivers all the way to California.

Native Americans burned the wood of box-elder for ceremonial purposes. In addition the sap and inner bark were boiled to make sugar and syrup. The seeds of box-elder are eaten by squirrels and birds

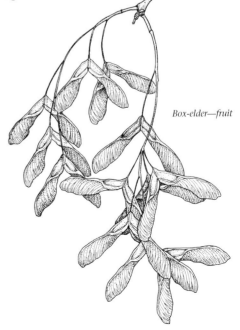

Box-elder—fruit

Box-elder bugs

Box-elder—leaf

Box-elder—female flowers

Box-elder—male flowers

including grosbeaks. Larvae of the banded hairstreak butterfly feed on the leaves of box-elder. The pistillate trees are host to the box-elder bug (*Boisea trivittatus*), an insect with vivid red and black markings, that has the sometimes annoying habit of congregating in large numbers to seek winter shelter in buildings.

Dozens of cultivars of box-elder with variegated leaves and other selected ornamental characteristics have been cultivated in Europe since it was introduced there in the late 1600s. It has also naturalized in many locations.

Hedge maple   *Acer campestre* L.

FORM: small, deciduous tree to 25 feet with a dense, rounded crown; twigs and leaves ooze milky sap when cut or torn

BARK: gray-brown with shallow furrows

TWIGS: light brown and smooth with lenticels, often developing corky fissures

PITH: solid, white

BUDS: terminal bud ⅛–¼ inch long, with overlapping bud scales; lateral buds smaller

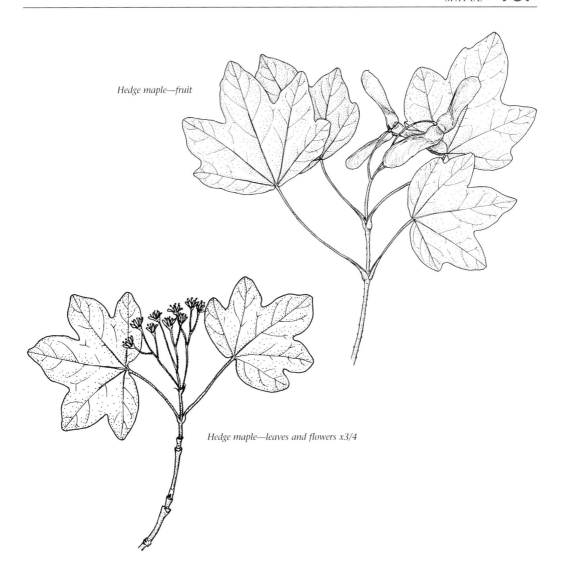

Hedge maple—fruit

Hedge maple—leaves and flowers x3/4

LEAVES: simple, 5-lobed, 2–4 inches long
FALL LEAF COLOR: yellowish
STIPULES: not present
LEAF SCARS: narrowly V-shaped, each pair nearly encircling the twigs
FLOWERS: yellow-green, in erect clusters, containing both petals and sepals, appearing with the leaves, insect-pollinated
FRUIT: a double samara with wings widely divergent to recurved
SEEDS: wind-dispersed
WOOD: too small to be of any commercial importance
CURRENT CHAMPION: Lebanon County, diameter 3 feet 2 inches at 3 feet, height 35 feet, spread 30 feet

This small, almost shrubby maple is occasionally cultivated here. In Europe it is common in hedgerows and as a plant for formal hedges. Native to Europe, the Near East, and northern Africa, it has escaped from cultivation at scattered sites across southern Pennsylvania.

Japanese maple

Acer palmatum **Thunb.**

FORM: deciduous tree to 30 feet with a rounded crown

BARK: dark gray, smooth, developing a few shallow fissures in age

TWIGS: green or reddish-purple, smooth

PITH: tan, small and inconspicuous

BUDS: small, red or green, hidden by the bases of the leaf stalks

LEAVES: green to red, 2–5 inches long with 5–9 lobes; margins sharply toothed

FALL LEAF COLOR: scarlet

STIPULES: not present

LEAF SCARS: semicircular with a single bundle scar, each pair of leaf scars joining to form a line around the twig,

FLOWERS: red or purple, in small stalked clusters, appearing with the leaves

FRUIT: a double samara with widely divergent (180°) wings, ripening in September or October

SEEDS: wind-dispersed

WOOD: dense and hard, but too small to be of any commercial importance

CURRENT CHAMPION: Lebanon County, diameter 3 feet 4 inches, height 40 feet, spread 58 feet

*Japanese maple—
fruit x1*

This slow-growing and very ornamental tree, which is native to Japan, Taiwan, and eastern China, has yielded close to 400 named cultivars. Unfortunately it has also established itself in the understory of urban and suburban forests.

Japanese maple—bark

Japanese maple—leaves and flowers

Moosewood, striped maple   *Acer pensylvanicum* L.

FORM: small deciduous understory tree to 40 feet with a short trunk and a deep, broad crown

BARK: smooth with conspicuous green and white longitudinal streaks

TWIGS: greenish becoming red

PITH: brown

BUDS: terminal bud ⅗ inch long, tapering, covered by 2 red bud scales; lateral buds smaller

LEAVES: opposite, simple, 3-lobed at the top with a finely toothed margin

FALL LEAF COLOR: yellow

STIPULES: not present

LEAF SCARS: broadly U-shaped, nearly encircling the stem with 3 bundle scars

FLOWERS: yellowish, in a drooping raceme, unisexual with staminate and pistillate inflorescences on the same or different trees (monoecious or dioecious); blooming in late May or June after the leaves have expanded, insect-pollinated

FRUIT: a double samara with widely diverging wings, in drooping clusters, maturing in late spring

SEEDS: wind-dispersed

WOOD: soft, light brown

CURRENT CHAMPION: Lycoming County, diameter 1 foot 2 inches, height 49 feet, spread 20 feet

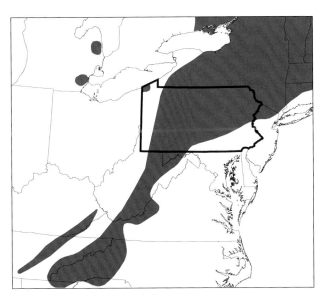

Moosewood—fruit x1

Moosewood is a common tree of moist, shaded mountain slopes and plateau areas in northern and central Pennsylvania. It has become the only tree in the forest understory in vast areas long overbrowsed by deer that seem to eat almost anything else in preference to this maple. Moosewood also occurs infrequently in the southeastern region of the state. Its total range extends from Nova Scotia to Michigan, New York, Pennsylvania, and south in the mountains to North Carolina, Tennessee, and Georgia.

Moosewood   bark

Moosewood

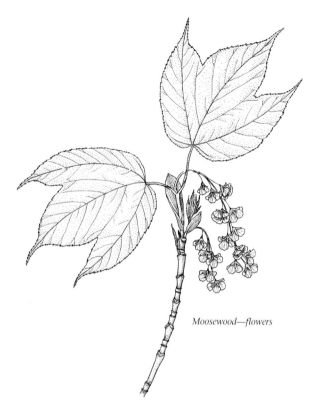

Moosewood—flowers

Native Americans used the wood or bark of moosewood to treat colds, coughs, kidney trouble, and gonorrhea. Poultices of the bark were also employed to treat swollen or paralyzed limbs. Arrows were made from the wood. Grouse, rodents, and songbirds eat the fruits.

Mountain maple   *Acer spicatum* Lam.

FORM: small deciduous understory tree to 30 feet with slender, upright branches and an irregular crown; sometimes more shrub-like; monoecious

BARK: brown or grayish-brown with mottled blotches

TWIGS: reddish-purple at first changing to grayish-brown

PITH: brown

BUDS: about ¼ inch long with 1 or 2 pairs of grayish or greenish scales that just meet at the edges

LEAVES: opposite, simple, 3 to 5-lobed with coarsely toothed margin, smooth on the upper surface and hairy on the underside

FALL LEAF COLOR: yellow, orange, and red

STIPULES: not present

LEAF SCARS: narrowly crescent-shaped with 3 bundle scars

FLOWERS: small, greenish-yellow, in narrow, erect clusters that appear in June after the leaves have expanded; each cluster contains one female and several male flowers; insect- pollinated

FRUIT: a double samara with only slightly divergent wings, maturing in September or October

SEEDS: wind-dispersed

Mountain maple—bark

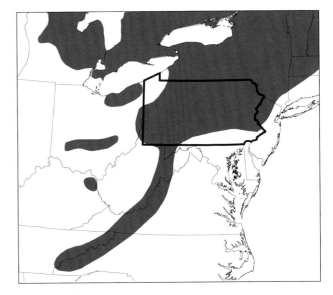

Mountain maple

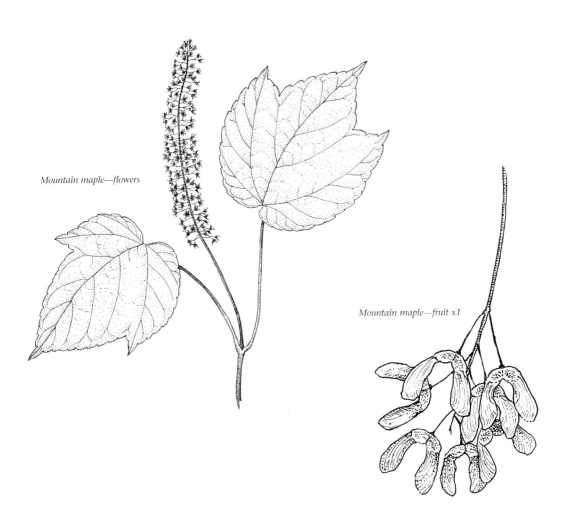

Mountain maple—flowers

Mountain maple—fruit x1

WOOD: soft, light brown
CURRENT CHAMPION: none recorded

Mountain maple is a small tree of the forest understory; it occurs on moist rocky hillsides and in ravines in the shade of sugar maple, yellow birch, beech, white pine, and hemlock. A northern tree, it extends from Labrador to Saskatchewan and south to Wisconsin and Pennsylvania and in the mountains to northern Georgia. In Pennsylvania it is found primarily in northern areas, at higher elevations in the Ridge and Valley physiographic province, and along the Allegheny Front.

Infusions of the bark of mountain maple were widely employed by Native Americans to treat sore eyes. Other medicinal uses included treatment of intestinal disorders and internal hemorrhaging. Arrows were made from the wood, and the leaf shape was a favorite motif for beadwork. Mountain maple is very susceptible to browsing by deer and appears to have declined in parts of Pennsylvania for that reason. Rabbits, beaver, and ruffed grouse also feed on the leaves, twigs, or fruits. In addition, it is a larval food source for the spring azure butterfly.

Norway maple   *Acer platanoides* L.

FORM: deciduous tree to 60 feet with a broad, rounded crown; leaves and twigs oozing milky sap when cut or torn
BARK: smooth, gray-brown
TWIGS: stout, brown, roughened by the many small lenticels
PITH: solid, white
BUDS: green, terminal bud ¼–⅜ inch long with overlapping bud scales; lateral buds smaller with 2 bud scales
LEAVES: dark green, about 6 inches wide and 4–5 inches long, with 5–7 lobes
FALL LEAF COLOR: leaves remaining green until early November then turning bright yellow
STIPULES: none
LEAF SCARS: crescent-shaped with 3 bundle scars, the pairs of leaf scars meet around the stem to form a sharp angle
FLOWERS: yellowish-green, in stalked clusters, appearing in late April with the leaves, insect-pollinated
FRUIT: a double samara with wings diverging at nearly 180°, maturing in September
SEEDS: wind-dispersed
WOOD: hard, pale in color
CURRENT CHAMPION: Lebanon County, diameter 7 feet 8 inches, height 65 feet, spread 74 feet

Norway maple is the most widespread maple in Europe and Asia where it occurs from Norway and Sweden to the Caucasus Mountains, Turkey, and northern Iran.[1] It was originally introduced into North America by John Bartram of Philadelphia who received seedlings from Philip Miller of London in 1756. Soon after, Bartram began offering the plant through his nursery business operated in West Philadelphia. George Washington received two Norway maples from the Bartrams in 1792 for his garden at Mount Vernon.[2] Norway maple subsequently

Norway maple—bark

Norway maple—leaves and fruits

Norway maple—flower detail x3

Norway maple—flowers x1

became one of the most popular trees for city plantings. Many cultivars have been developed including purple-leaved and columnar forms.

Like many potentially invasive, non-native plants, Norway maple did not emerge as a problem until many years after its initial introduction. It was not until the early 1900s that plant identification manuals began to include it with the notation "occasionally escaped." Today Norway maple is a frequent invader of urban and suburban forests. Its extreme shade tolerance, especially when young, has allowed it to become established beneath an intact forest canopy. Research has recently shown that forests that have been invaded by Norway maple suffer losses in diversity of native forest wildflowers compared with forests in which the canopy is dominated by native species.[3]

Red maple, swamp maple, soft maple   *Acer rubrum* L.

FORM: deciduous tree to 80–100 feet with ascending branches and a rounded crown

BARK: light gray, smooth becoming roughened with age

TWIGS: slender, red or grayish-brown

PITH: white, solid

BUDS: red or green, lateral buds blunt, terminal bud larger and pointed with several overlapping pairs of bud scales; flower buds nearly spherical arranged in clusters at the nodes

LEAVES: opposite, simple, 3- to 5-lobed with irregularly toothed margins, whitish beneath

FALL LEAF COLOR: yellow, orange, red, or purplish

STIPULES: not present

LEAF SCARS: V-shaped with 3 bundle scars, the pairs of leaf scars are joined around the twig by a small bark ridge

FLOWERS: red, appearing in early spring before the leaves, unisexual and perfect flowers occur on the same or different trees; wind-pollinated

FRUIT: a double samara with only slightly divergent wings, maturing in late spring

SEEDS: wind-dispersed

WOOD: soft, close-grained, light brown

CURRENT CHAMPION: York County, diameter 6 feet 10 inches, height 80 feet, spread 76 feet

Red maple is the most abundant forest tree in Pennsylvania today. It is common in all parts of the state and grows in a variety of habitats including early successional old fields, swamps, bogs, and numerous forest types on wet to dry sites.

It was not always so, in the early 1900s Joseph Illick, Chief of Research for the Pennsylvania Forest Commission, described chestnut and sugar maple as the most abundant forest species. However, red maple has been very successful in dominating second- and third-growth forests in many parts of Pennsylvania, in part due to its ability to sprout prolifically after cutting. It has been further favored by chestnut blight, overbrowsing by deer, gypsy moth infestations, and suppression of naturally occurring fires, all of which have caused other species to decline in importance.

Red maple—fruit x1

Red maple is also wide-ranging outside the state occurring throughout eastern North America from Nova Scotia to southern Florida.

Medicinal uses of red maple by Native Americans included use of infusions of the bark to treat sore eyes, hives, gynecological problems, and dysentery. The sap was boiled to make sugar and the wood was used for basketry and carving. The wood of red maple is not as desirable as that of sugar maple, but is used for furniture manufacture. Red maple is also grown as a landscape tree and several cultivars with exceptionally brilliant autumn foliage have been developed.

Red maple—bark

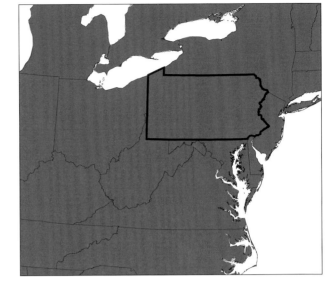

Red maple

Red maple—female flowers

Red maple—male flowers

Red maple—leaves

Silver maple   *Acer saccharinum* **Marshall**

FORM: deciduous tree to 100 feet or more, the trunk usually dividing into several large upright limbs that create a spreading crown, the smaller branches tend to droop with upturned ends

BARK: gray-brown, very flaky with long shaggy strips separating from the trunk at both ends

TWIGS: slender, green becoming chestnut-brown

PITH: solid, white

BUDS: about ¼ inch, red, somewhat pointed with 6–8 overlapping bud scales; flower buds, which are in dense clusters, are more rounded

LEAVES: opposite, simple, deeply 5-lobed, silvery beneath; margins coarsely toothed

FALL LEAF COLOR: drab yellow

STIPULES: none

LEAF SCARS: U- to V-shaped with 3 bundle scars, not encircling the twigs

FLOWERS: in dense clusters along the twigs, brownish, blooming in late February to early April, wind-pollinated

FRUIT: a double samara with the wings diverging at about 90°, often with one side malformed, maturing in May

SEEDS: wind-dispersed

WOOD: hard, brittle, close-grained, white or pale brown

Silver maple—bark

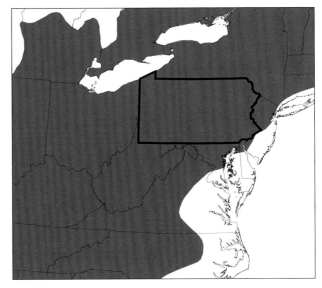

Silver maple

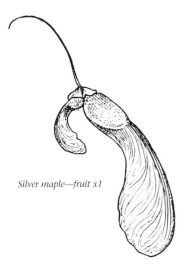

Silver maple—fruit x1

*Silver maple—
flower detail x3*

CURRENT CHAMPION: Lancaster County, diameter 7 feet 2 inches, height 100 feet, spread 113 feet

Silver maple attains its greatest size in the rich, deep soils of floodplains; it occurs along larger streams and rivers throughout Pennsylvania. This wide-ranging species grows from southern Canada to Mississippi and west to eastern Nebraska, Kansas, and Oklahoma.

As is true for several other maple species, the sap of silver maple was boiled by Native Americans and early settlers to make syrup and sugar. Medicinal uses of silver maple included an infusion of bark taken for cramps, dysentery, or hives. Bark and twigs were used to make a black dye used to color leather and the wood was used to make arrows and baskets.

Silver maple—flowers x1

Silver maple—leaf

Silver maple leaves frequently bear galls caused by infestations of eriophyid mites. Maple bladder galls (caused by *Vasates quadripedes*) are small spherical growths on the upper surface of the leaves, erinum gall (caused by *Aceria elongatus*) is a red felt-like growth on the lower leaf surface. Silver maple fruits are eaten by foxes, squirrels, and grosbeaks. Trunk cavities, which are frequent in this species, provide dens for raccoons, squirrels, and cavity nesting birds.

Sugar maple, rock maple, hard maple — *Acer saccharum* Marshall

FORM: deciduous tree to 90 feet, branches erect-spreading, crown upright and rounded at the top

BARK: brownish-gray, deeply furrowed and separating into longitudinally oriented plates or flakes

TWIGS: smooth, reddish-brown or orangey-brown

PITH: white, continuous

BUDS: ¼–½ inch long, sharp-pointed, conical, hairy at the tip with 8–16 overlapping bud scales

LEAVES: opposite, simple, 5-lobed and palmately veined, 3–5 inches long; margin with a few coarse teeth

FALL LEAF COLOR: brilliant orange to red

STIPULES: none

LEAF SCARS: V- or U-shaped, with 3 bundle scars, each pair encircling the twig

FLOWERS: pale green, in clusters on slender, drooping stalks, staminate and pistillate on the same tree (monoecious); flowering in April or May as the leaves are beginning to expand, wind-pollinated

FRUIT: a double samara with wings at right angles, maturing in September

SEEDS: wind-dispersed

WOOD: heavy, hard and close-grained, light brown
CURRENT CHAMPION: Erie County, diameter 6 feet 2 inches, height 69 feet, spread 74 feet

It is hard to say which is the most valuable product of sugar maple—maple syrup, fine lumber, or the spectacular display of autumn leaf color. Present throughout the state, it is an important component of the northern hardwood forest type in combination with beech, birch, white pine, and hemlock. In the western part of the state sugar maple teams up with basswood and to form the sugar maple—basswood forest type more common in the Great Lakes region. To the south it grows with tuliptree, red oak, beech, and many other species in the highly diverse mixed mesophytic forest association. Sugar maple is very shade tolerant, which allows it to continue to reproduce under a mature forest canopy.

Sugar maple decline, caused at least in part by acid rain,[4] and high levels of deer browse are causing a decrease in sugar maple in northwestern Pennsylvania. In parts of southeastern Pennsylvania, sugar maple seems to be increasing in abundance as a result of differential browsing by deer on more preferred species such as oak, ash, and tuliptree.

The range of sugar maple extends from Nova Scotia and the Great Lakes region south to Tennessee and western North Carolina.

The earliest European settlers quickly learned from Native Americans how to make maple sugar and syrup and did so in sufficient quantity to supply their everyday need for sweeteners. Michaux estimated an annual production of 10 million pounds of maple sugar in the United States in the early 1800s. At that time white sugar was an imported luxury. The wood of sugar maple was valued for making such items as canoe paddles and furniture, and remains a valuable commodity today.

Sugar maple seeds are eaten by birds and small mammals, and the twigs and bark are winter food for rabbits, deer, and porcupines.

Sugar maple—bark

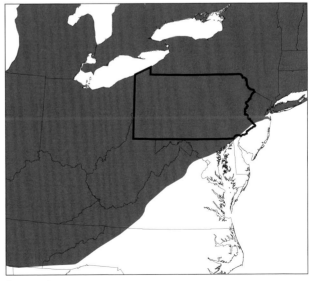

Sugar maple

Sugar maple—flowers

Sugar maples in autumn

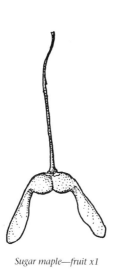

Sugar maple—fruit x1

Sugar maple—leaf

Sycamore maple   *Acer pseudoplatanus* L.

FORM: deciduous tree to 60 feet with a broad, spreading crown

BARK: grayish-brown, rough, and platy; inner bark orangey-brown

TWIGS: gray-brown, dull, with lenticels

PITH: solid, white

BUDS: terminal bud greenish, ¼–⅓ inch with several overlapping bud scales; lateral buds smaller

LEAVES: up to 7 inches wide by 4–5 inches long, 5-lobed, with coarsely toothed margins, dark green, greenish-white beneath

FALL LEAF COLOR: brown or slightly yellowish

STIPULES: not present

LEAF SCARS: broadly V-shaped with 3 bundle scars, not encircling the twigs

FLOWERS: appearing with the leaves, greenish-yellow, in a slender, drooping panicle containing some perfect and some staminate flowers, insect pollinated

FRUIT: a double samara with wings diverging at less than 90°, maturing September to October

SEEDS: wind-dispersed

CURRENT CHAMPION: Philadelphia County, diameter 4 feet 5 inches, height 56 feet, spread 75 feet

Native to Europe and western Asia, sycamore maple is found in disturbed urban and suburban forests, waste ground, and along railroad tracks in and near towns and cities scattered across the southern part of Pennsylvania. The earliest record of sycamore maple occurring as a naturalized tree in Pennsylvania forests is from Lehigh County in 1908.

Sycamore maple has a long history of cultivation in Europe, it was introduced very early here, but has never achieved the same level of popularity as a landscape plant as Norway maple.

Sycamore maple—bark

Sycamore maple—flowers

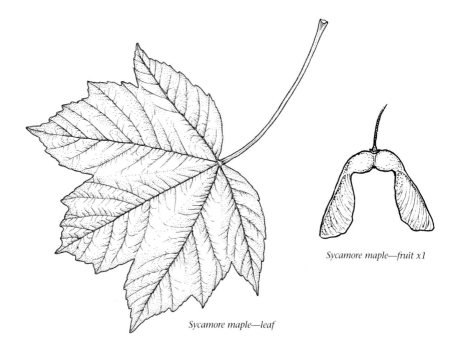

Sycamore maple—fruit x1

Sycamore maple—leaf

Notes

1. Nowak, David J. and Rowan A. Rowntree. 1990. History and range of the Norway maple. *Journal of Arboriculture* 16 (11): 291–96.

2. List of Plants from John Bartram's Nursery, March 1792 and letters from George Augustine Washington to George Washington of April 8–9, 1792 and April 15–16, 1792, in Washington, George. 2002. *The Papers of George Washington,* Vol. 2, *March–August 1792.* Ed. Robert F. Haggard and Mark A. Mastromarino. University of Virginia Press, Charlottesville.

3. Webb, Sara L. and Christina Kalafus Kaunzinger. 1993. Biological invasion of the Drew University (New Jersey) forest preserve by Norway maple (*Acer platanoides* L.). *Bulletin of the Torrey Botanical Club* 120 (3): 343–49; Wyckoff, Peter H., and Sara L. Webb. 1996. Understory influence of the invasive Norway maple (*Acer platanoides*). *Bulletin of the Torrey Botanical Club* 123 (3): 197–205; Webb, Sara L., Marc Dwyer, Christina K. Kaunzinger, and Peter H. Wyckoff. 2000. The myth of the resilient forest: Case study of the invasive Norway maple (*Acer platanoides*). *Rhodora* 102 (911): 332–54.

4. Driscoll, Charles T., Gregory B. Lawrence, Arthur J. Bulger, Thomas J. Butler, Christopher A. Cronan, Christopher Eagar, Kathleen F. Lambert, Gene E. Likens, John L. Stoddard, and Kathleen C. Weathers. 2001. Acidic deposition in the Northeastern United States: sources and inputs, ecosystem effects, and management strategies. *BioScience* 51 (3): 180–98.

MIMOSA
ALBIZZIA DURAZZ.
Mimosa Family—Mimosaceae

Mimosa, silktree   *Albizia julibrissin* **Durazz.**

FORM: deciduous tree to 35 feet with widely spreading branches and a broad, low, flat-topped crown

BARK: smooth, gray-brown

TWIGS: green with numerous, conspicuous, light-colored lenticels

PITH: white and homogeneous

BUDS: small, rounded, brownish with 2–3 scales; terminal bud absent

LEAVES: alternate, 8–20 inches long, twice compound with numerous small leaflets about ¼–½ inch long with the midrib close to one edge, leaflets fold in toward the leaf stalk when disturbed or at night

FALL LEAF COLOR: foliage turns brown after frost

STIPULES: present, but not persistent

LEAF SCARS: semicircular with 3 bundle scars

FLOWERS: pink, borne in fluffy, radiating heads in midsummer, insect-pollinated; the numerous stamens extend well beyond the corolla and form the most conspicuous part

FRUIT: a flat pod 5–7 inches long and about 1 inch wide, dry and papery when mature

SEEDS: several per pod, flat, brown, oval, about ¼ inch long

Mimosa—flowers x1

Mimosa—flowers

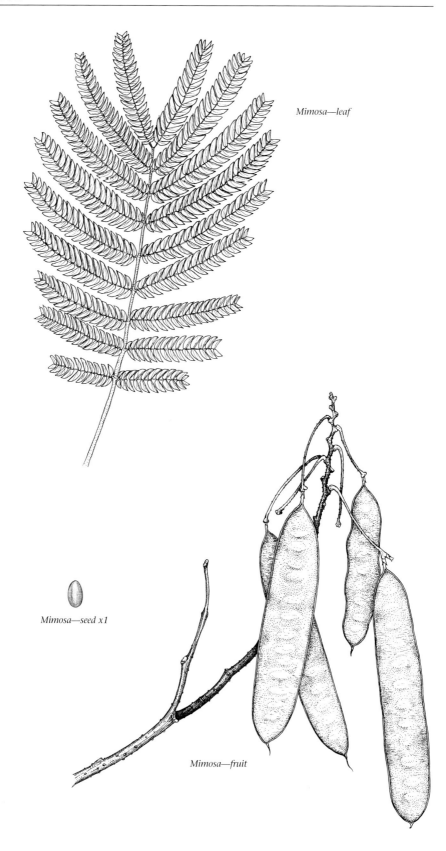

Mimosa—leaf

Mimosa—seed x1

Mimosa—fruit

Mimosa—bark

WOOD: not commercially significant
CURRENT CHAMPION: Philadelphia County, diameter 2 feet 1 inch, height 60
   feet, spread 77 feet

This tropical-looking Asian native is widely cultivated and occasionally naturalized especially along roadsides and forest edges. Its native habitat is the understory of the mixed mesophytic forests of central China, one of the most diverse
temperate ecosystems known.

Mimosa is highly tolerant of drought and salt. It is late to leaf out, often
remaining leafless until late May or early June. Its fluffy pink flowers serve as a
midsummer nectar source for the eastern tiger swallowtail butterfly. A single
enlarged flower in each cluster produces nectar, and attracts pollinators that
contact the extending brush-like stamens and stigmas of the remaining flowers
in each cluster.

MOOSEWOOD—SEE MAPLE

MOUNTAIN-ASH
SORBUS L.
Rose Family—Rosaceae

The mountain-ashes are not at all related to the true ash trees, which are in the genus *Fraxinus* in the Olive Family. Perhaps it was the pinnately compound leaves that *Sorbus* and *Fraxinus* have in common that led to the name. Our two native species of mountain-ash are trees of moist forests, rocky slopes, bogs, and swamps across the northern counties of Pennsylvania. Their clusters of brilliant orange-red fruits make them conspicuous in late summer and fall.

The alternate, deciduous leaves of mountain-ash have up to 17 small, toothed leaflets. The small white flowers, which appear in May after the leaves have expanded, are in flat-topped clusters 3–6 inches across.

The bark of mountain-ash has a bitter almond smell like some of the cherries, and has been used medicinally to treat malarial fevers. The fruits were eaten to prevent scurvy, and an infusion of the inner bark was used to treat colds. Bears frequently break the lower branches in their efforts to reach the clusters of berries; other wildlife also consume the fruits.

American mountain-ash   *Sorbus americana* Marshall

FORM: deciduous tree to 50 feet, or sometimes more shrubby
BARK: smooth, dark gray
TWIGS: stout, deep red to greenish-brown, smooth with conspicuous lenticels
PITH: large, pale tan or orangey-brown, homogeneous
BUDS: red, sticky
LEAVES: alternate, pinnately compound, 6–10 inches long with 11–17 toothed leaflets; leaflets 3–5 times as long as wide with soft white hairs on the lower surface, and a long tapered point
FALL LEAF COLOR: orange-yellow to red-purple
STIPULES: small, fringed, falling early and leaving a small scar on each side of the base of the leaf stalk
LEAF SCARS: large, raised, U-shaped with 3–5 bundle scars
FLOWERS: small, white, in large flat-topped clusters, perfect, insect-pollinated
FRUIT: red-orange, about ¼ inch in diameter
SEEDS: brownish-yellow, flat and about ⅛ inch long
WOOD: fine-grained, soft, light brown
CURRENT CHAMPION: Erie County, diameter 1 foot 7 inches, height 59 feet, spread 39 feet

American mountain-ash is found in northern Pennsylvania and at high elevations along the Allegheny Front to Somerset and Fayette Counties. Its total range extends from Newfoundland to Minnesota. It reaches its southern limits in northern Illinois and Pennsylvania, except for scattered sites in the mountains to Georgia.

American mountain-ash—bark

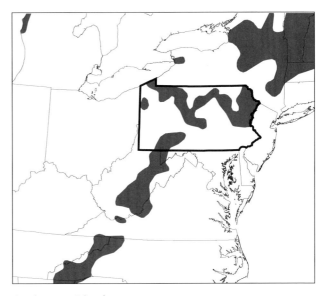

American mountain-ash

American mountain-ash—flowers

American mountain-ash—fruit

European mountain-ash   *Sorbus acuparia* L.

current champion: Clarion County, diameter 1 foot 6 inches, height 51 feet, spread 40 feet.

European mountain-ash, which is grown as an ornamental and only occasionally escapes, differs from American mountain-ash in having shorter leaflets, twigs and lower leaf surfaces that are densely white-hairy when young, and winter buds that are not sticky.

European mountain-ash—bark

European mountain-ash—fruit

Showy mountain-ash   *Sorbus decora* (Sarg.) Schneid

Showy mountain-ash is very similar to American mountain-ash and is distinguished mainly by its more abruptly pointed leaflets and slightly larger (⅜ inch diameter) fruits. It grows only at a few sites on rocky slopes or swampy woods in northeastern and northwestern Pennsylvania, and is classified as endangered by the Pennsylvania Natural Heritage Program. The total range of showy mountain-ash extends from Labrador to Minnesota and south to Pennsylvania and northern parts of Ohio, Indiana, and Iowa.

Decoctions of the inner bark and of peeled sticks of showy mountain-ash were used by Native Americans to treat rheumatism and back pain respectively.

Showy mountain-ash—leaf

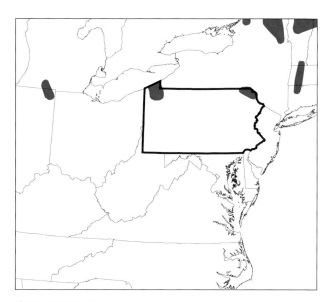

Showy mountain-ash

MULBERRY
Morus L.
Mulberry Family—Moraceae

The mulberries are deciduous trees with milky sap. The leaves are alternate, simple, variously lobed or unlobed, more-or-less palmately veined, and coarsely toothed.

Mulberry flowers are unisexual, borne in cylindrical catkins with male and female inflorescences borne on the same (monoecious) or different (dioecious) trees. Male flowers have 4–5 sepals and 4 stamens; female flowers have 4 sepals and a superior ovary with a 2-branched stigma. The fruit is a multiple structure comprising many small drupelets, the product of an entire catkin of individual flowers.

Both the red and the white mulberry are highly variable and often confused; hybridization may also be a factor.

Red mulberry   *Morus rubra* L.

FORM: tree to 50–60 feet, with a rounded crown
BARK: grayish, becoming deeply furrowed with age
TWIGS: green becoming orange-brown
PITH: white, continuous
BUDS: sharp-pointed with 3–9 bud scales, terminal bud absent
LEAVES: unlobed or variously 3- to 5-lobed, coarsely toothed
FALL LEAF COLOR: pale greenish-yellow
STIPULES: linear, falling early
LEAF SCARS: nearly circular with a ring of bundle scars

Red mulberry—bark

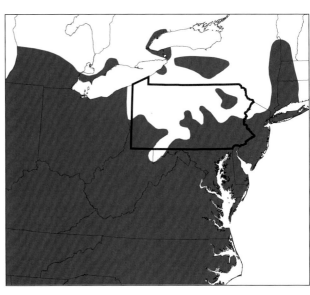

Red mulberry

FLOWERS: male and female flowers on different plants (species dioecious), wind-pollinated
FRUIT: maturing in July, dark purple, edible
SEEDS: bird- and mammal-dispersed
WOOD: yellow to yellowish-brown with white sapwood, very durable
CURRENT CHAMPION: Erie County, diameter 4 feet 1 inch, height 49 feet, spread 63 feet

Red mulberry is a native tree that grows in mixed stands on rich, moist soils; it extends across the southern half of the state except at high elevations on the Allegheny Front. It appears to have declined greatly in abundance in the past 200 years. Its total range includes most of the eastern United States with the exception of northern New England.

Mulberry was an important plant to Native Americans and early settlers alike. The fruits were eaten and made into preserves and beverages. Native Americans used infusions of the bark as a laxative or a purgative and to treat dysentery. Preparations of the roots were used to treat urinary problems and the milky sap was applied directly to treat ringworm. The inner bark yielded fibers that were twisted into rope or woven into a coarse cloth. The durable, rot-resistant wood was used by Colonial era ship-builders and by farmers for fence posts. In addition the fruits are eaten by more than 20 species of birds as well as squirrels, skunks, and raccoons.

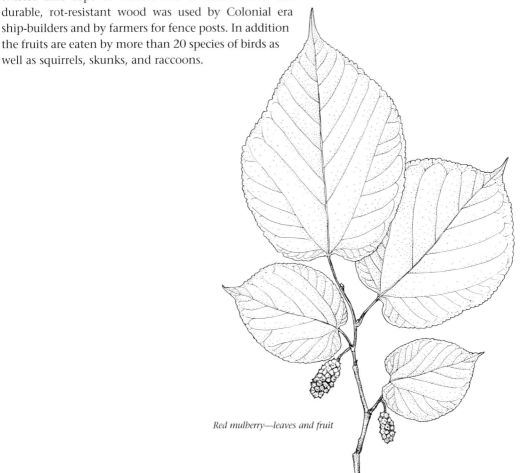

Red mulberry—leaves and fruit

White mulberry   *Morus alba* L.

FORM: small tree to 45 feet
BARK: brown, furrowed, exposing orange inner layers
TWIGS: reddish-brown or orange
PITH: white, continuous
BUDS: acute to rounded with yellow-brown bud scales
LEAVES: variously lobed or unlobed, coarsely toothed; palmately veined when lobed
FALL LEAF COLOR: mostly turning from green to brown when touched by frost, sometimes slight yellowing occurs
STIPULES: ovate to lanceolate
LEAF SCARS: rounded with a circle of bundle scars
FLOWERS: appearing with the leaves; staminate and pistillate flowers on the same or different trees, wind-pollinated
FRUIT: white to pink or occasionally purple, maturing late June through July, edible
SEEDS: bird- and mammal-dispersed
WOOD: light yellowish-brown, soft and coarse-grained, used for carving and fence posts
CURRENT CHAMPION: Philadelphia County, diameter 6 feet, height 55 feet, spread 16 feet

This tree from Asia was introduced in the late 1700s and early 1800s in the expectation of supplying a native silk industry with food for the silkworms. Leaves of the native red mulberry were considered to be too hairy for the purpose. Although commercial silk moth culture was short-lived here, white mulberry rapidly took hold and spread to fencerows, disturbed woods, and waste ground throughout the eastern United States. In Pennsylvania it is mainly found in the southern half of the state.

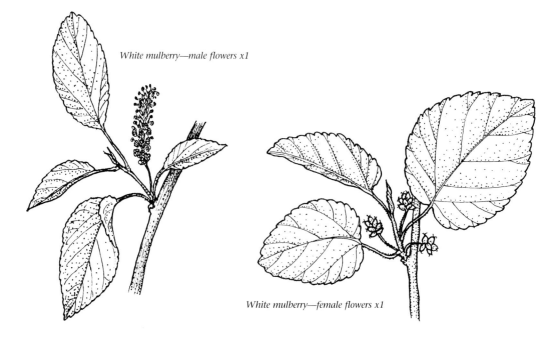

White mulberry—male flowers x1

White mulberry—female flowers x1

White mulberry—bark

White mulberry—leaves

MUSCLEWOOD—SEE HORNBEAM

OAK
QUERCUS L.
Beech Family—Fagaceae

The oaks are one of our best-known groups of trees, as indicated by the many literary references to their strength and longevity. Like hickory, oak is primarily a North American genus. Although oaks also occur in Europe and Asia, their area of greatest diversity is in the mountains of Mexico. Seventeen native oaks and one naturalized species occur in Pennsylvania; in addition, hybrids are not unusual.

Two local species, scrub oak and dwarf chestnut oak, are often more shrub-like than tree-like; however, they are included here. All species of oak that occur in Pennsylvania are deciduous; however, evergreen oaks are found farther south. The dead leaves of some species, most notably pin oak, remain attached through the winter on young trees or on the central part of the crown, which represents the juvenile portion of older trees.

The oaks have simple, alternate leaves that are mostly pinnately lobed or toothed, but two species, willow oak and shingle oak, have unlobed leaves with a smooth edge. Many oaks have short, spreading, star-shaped hairs on the lower leaf surface. Stipules are present but inconspicuous and drop early on all but bur oak where those of the upper leaves often persist among the buds on dormant twigs. Leaf scars are raised, concave above and rounded below with numerous scattered bundle scars. The twigs have a true terminal bud surrounded by a cluster of associated buds. Below the tip, buds are alternately arranged on the twigs. A feature that the oaks share with other members of the Beech Family is pith that is star-shaped in cross section.

Oak flowers are unisexual, with both male and female types occurring on the same tree (monoecious). Male flowers are arranged in drooping catkins that fall off once the pollen is shed. Female flowers are inconspicuous bud-like structures in the axils of newly expanding leaves; only the protruding stigmas provide external evidence that flowers lie within. Flowering occurs as the new growth is beginning to expand. The abundant, wind-dispersed pollen causes an allergic reaction in some people. The characteristic fruit of all oaks is the acorn, a thin-shelled nut with a scaly cap at the stem end. Acorns of the white oak group mature in a single season, those of the black oak group mostly require 2 years to reach maturity.

Acorns are the most important constituent of mast, a term that refers to the crop of nuts and seeds that provide food for forest animals such as deer, bear, raccoon, squirrels, rodents, wild turkey, wood duck, and others. Acorns have been found to make up 20 percent or more of the diet of Virginia white-tail deer in the fall and winter seasons. Most oak species produce a heavy crop of seeds only once every 2–5 years. Seed dispersal is provided by squirrels and other small mammals that store the acorns.

Oak leaves are the food source for the larval stages of numerous butterflies including duskywings, hairstreaks, viceroy, red-spotted purple, and white admiral. Caterpillars of polyphemus and cecropia moths also feed on the leaves of various oak species. The gypsy moth, accidentally introduced from Europe in

1869, has fed extensively on oaks throughout the northeastern states and killed many through repeated defoliation.

Other insects, mostly tiny wasps known as gall makers, cause deformities on oak leaves or twigs by inducing the tree to produce a growth that provides the insect with a brood chamber. Oak "apples" are leaf galls about the size of a golf ball. They are pale green when fresh and light brown and hollow after they dry out. Woolsower galls are similar in size and shape but composed of a white cottony mass of tissue. Smaller hairy hedgehog galls form along the midvein of the leaves of white oak. Several common galls that form on twigs include horned oak gall and gouty oak gall, both are especially common on pin oaks. Overall more than 700 different kinds of galls have been described on oaks worldwide. Generally they are more of a curiosity than a health threat to the trees, however, large numbers of twig galls can be disfiguring.

Acorns were an important food for Native Americans. The nuts were peeled and dried for winter use, then pounded to make flour from which bread was made, or boiled to make soup or porridge. Acorns of the black oak group had to be soaked or boiled in several changes of water or lye to remove the tannins that gave them a bitter taste. Oak bark was used to cover dwellings, in addition its high tannin content made it useful for tanning leather and as a dye. Certain types of oak galls were used to make black ink.

Medicinally, the powdered bark of white oak was used against dysentery. Boiled preparations of the roots or bark of several species served to treat wounds, sore throat, and soreness of the eyes. The recognized astringent properties of oaks led to their use to counteract hemorrhaging, fluxes, and other similar conditions. Oak bark was chewed for mouth sores.

Oak lumber remains one of the most valuable products of Pennsylvania's forests today. However, the abundance of oak has decreased, apparently due to a combination of factors including overbrowsing by deer, which destroys seedling and sapling trees and removes acorns before they can sprout. Fire suppression[1] and gypsy moth damage are other factors believed to have contributed to the reduction in oaks in the state.

The oaks form two groups, the white oaks that have rounded leaf lobes and acorns that mature in a single season and the black oaks with pointed or bristle-tipped lobes and acorns that take two years to mature. Of the 19 oak species that occur in Pennsylvania, 8 belong to the white oak group and 11 are of the black oak group. Hybridization is a well-known phenomenon within the both the white oak and black oak groups. Hybrids usually have characteristics intermediate between the parental species; among those identified in Pennsylvania are the following:

Bartram oak (*Quercus* x *heterophylla* Michx., *Q. phellos* x *rubra*)
Bebb oak (*Quercus* x *bebbiana* Schneid., *Q. alba* x *macrocarpa*)
Bender oak (*Quercus* x *benderi* Baenitz, *Q. coccinea* x *rubra*)
Lea oak (*Quercus* x *leana* Nutt., *Q. imbricaria* x *velutina*)
Rehder oak (*Quercus* x *rehderi* Trel., *Q. ilicifolia* x *velutina*)
Saul oak (*Quercus* x *saulii* Schneid, *Q. alba* x *montana*)
Saw-toothed oak (*Quercus* x *runcinata* (DC.) Engelm., *Q. imbricaria* x *rubra*)

WHITE OAK GROUP

Bur oak, mossycup oak, overcup oak   *Quercus macrocarpa* Michx.

FORM: large tree to 80 feet or more with broadly spreading branches and a rounded crown

BARK: thick, gray-brown, becoming deeply ridged and furrowed

TWIGS: stout, yellowish-brown, hairy at first becoming smooth, developing corky ridges

PITH: star-shaped in cross section

BUDS: reddish-brown, ¼ inch long, obtuse to acute

LEAVES: 6–12 inches long, with a large terminal lobe and 2–3 additional lobes on each side of the midrib toward the base; all lobes with rounded tips; leaf blades pale green and covered with small, star-shaped hairs beneath

FALL LEAF COLOR: yellow to yellow-brown

STIPULES: those of the upper leaves often persist among the buds on dormant twigs after the leaves have fallen

LEAF SCARS: as for other oaks, see above

FLOWERS: as for other oaks, see above

FRUIT: acorns maturing in a single season, usually stalked, the nut ⅘–1 inch long, one-half to nearly completely covered by a thick fringed cap

SEEDS: animal- and bird-dispersed

WOOD: light to dark brown, heavy, hard, and strong, marketed as white oak

CURRENT CHAMPION: Lancaster County, diameter 5 feet 8 inches, height 100 feet, spread 102 feet

Bur oak—acorns x3/4

Bur oak is a midwestern tree that ranges from Quebec, Ontario, and Manitoba south to Texas in moist woods and alluvial floodplains. In Pennsylvania it occurs

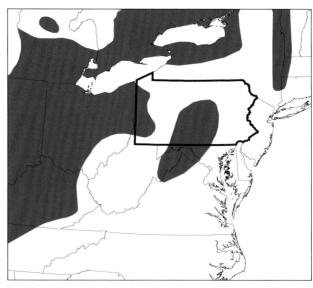

Bur oak—bark

Bur oak

Bur oak—tree

Bur oak—flowers

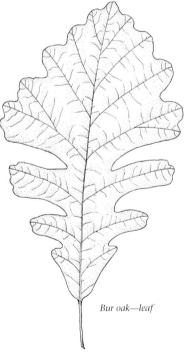

Bur oak—leaf

at scattered sites in central and southwestern counties, mainly on dry limestone ridges, slopes, and bottomlands. Bur oak is one of the most drought resistant oaks. Its seeds germinate soon after falling and establish an extensive root system before a shoot develops. The trees can live 400 years or more.

Chestnut oak   *Quercus montana* Willd.

FORM: upright tree to 70 feet or more with a broad, open crown

BARK: thick, with deep V-shaped fissures between the solid ridges, brown to black with reddish tones underneath, contains more tannin than any other oak

TWIGS: greenish-purple at first becoming orangey-brown, smooth and somewhat angled

PITH: star-shaped in cross section

BUDS: ¼–½ inch long, rounded, occasionally with a sharp tip, light brown, hairy

LEAVES: 5–9 inches long with coarse, rounded teeth; the lower surface covered with short, star-shaped hairs and longer straight hairs along the veins

FALL LEAF COLOR: yellow to brown

STIPULES: inconspicuous and falling soon after the leaves expand

LEAF SCARS: as for other oaks, see above

FLOWERS: as for other oaks, see above

FRUIT: acorns maturing in a single season, short stalked, 1–1½ inches long with the cup covering one-third of the nut

SEEDS: animal- and bird-dispersed

WOOD: heavy, strong, and durable, used for railroad ties and construction, usually marketed as white oak

CURRENT CHAMPION: York County, diameter 5 feet, height 115 feet, spread 72 feet

Chestnut oak—acorn x1

Chestnut oak is common on dry, rocky slopes and ridges throughout most of Pennsylvania, but is less abundant in northern counties and at high elevations along the Allegheny Front. Chestnut oak has largely replaced the blight-devastated American chestnut, which occupied similar habitats. Its total range extends along the Appalachian Mountains from Maine to northern Georgia and east to the coast from New Jersey to Virginia.

Seeds of chestnut oak germinate soon after falling, forming a root in the fall, however, the shoot does not grow until the following spring. Because of their large size, the acorns of chestnut oak are a favorite food of deer, gray squirrels, and wild turkeys.

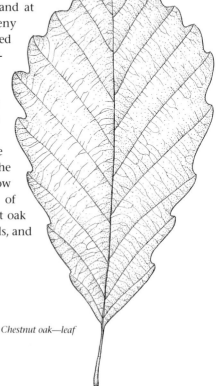

Chestnut oak—leaf

Chestnut oak—bark

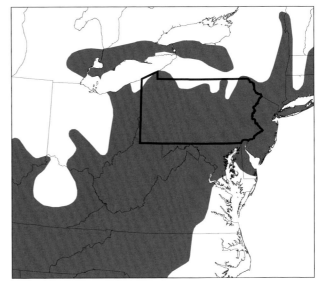

Chestnut oak—bark

Dwarf chestnut oak, dwarf chinquapin oak

Quercus prinoides **Willd.**

FORM: low, clump-forming shrub, 2–5 feet, or occasionally more tree-like and reaching a height of 18 feet

BARK: thin and light brown with gray blotches, smooth at first, becoming rough with age

TWIGS: slender, hairy at first, becoming reddish-brown and smooth

PITH: star-shaped in cross section

BUDS: light brown, rounded, with thin overlapping scales

LEAVES: 3–6 inches long with 3–6 rounded teeth on each side of the midrib; lower surface whitish with numerous or scattered, tiny star-shaped hairs

FALL LEAF COLOR: yellow-brown to brown

STIPULES: inconspicuous and falling soon after the leaves expand

LEAF SCARS: as for other oaks, see above

FLOWERS: as for other oaks, see above

FRUIT: maturing in a single season, ½–1 inch long, stalkless or with a short stalk, the cup covering about one-half of the nut

SEEDS: animal- and bird-dispersed

WOOD: of no commercial significance due to its small size

CURRENT CHAMPION: none recorded

Dwarf chestnut oak—acorn x1

Dwarf chestnut oak is a plant of dry rocky or sandy soils, barrens, and ridge tops throughout Pennsylvania. It is frequently confused with shrubby forms of yellow chestnut oak (*Q. muehlenbergii*), which it closely resembles; however, yellow chestnut oak occurs on limestone soils, unlike dwarf chestnut oak. Dwarf chestnut oak ranges from Massachusetts to North Carolina and west to Michigan, Indiana, and Oklahoma.

Dwarf chestnut oak—bark

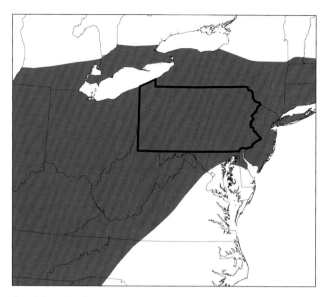

Dwarf chestnut oak

Dwarf chestnut oak—branch with acorns

Post oak   *Quercus stellata* **Wangenh.**

FORM: medium-sized tree to 50–60 feet with a rounded crown, sometimes shrubby

BARK: light gray and scaly

TWIGS: stout, light orange and hairy at first, later becoming dark brown

PITH: star-shaped in cross section

BUDS: reddish-brown, ⅛ inch long and often equally broad, sparsely hairy

LEAVES: 4–7 inches long with 3 rounded lobes on each side of the midrib, the middle one much larger than the others; lower leaf surface densely covered with glandular hairs and tiny star-shaped hairs

FALL LEAF COLOR: orangey- or reddish-brown

STIPULES: inconspicuous and falling soon after the leaves expand

LEAF SCARS: as for other oaks, see above

FLOWERS: as for other oaks, see above

FRUIT: acorn maturing in a single season, ¾–1 inch long with ⅓–½ its length enclosed by the cup

SEEDS: animal- and bird-dispersed

WOOD: heavy, hard and very durable, marketed as white oak

CURRENT CHAMPION: Montgomery County, diameter 3 feet 5 inches, height 113 feet, spread 68 feet

Post oak—acorn x1

Post oak is near the northern limit of its range in Pennsylvania where it occurs at scattered sites in the southeast and a few south central counties. It grows in dry upland woods and barrens in rocky or sandy soil. The total range of the species extends from southeastern New York to Ohio, Indiana, and southern Iowa and south to Florida and Texas.

Post oak—bark

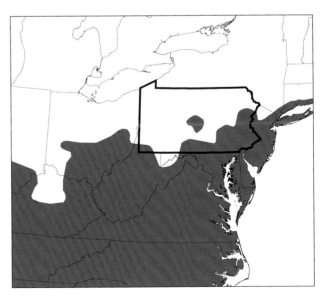

Post oak

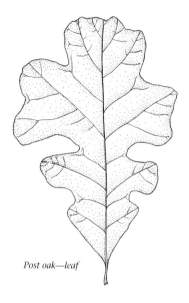

Post oak—leaf

Swamp white oak   *Quercus bicolor* **Willd.**

FORM: upright tree to 80 feet, in the open developing a broad, rounded crown with the upper branches ascending and the lower often drooping

BARK: dark grayish-brown with broad, flat ridges and peeling scales on the trunk, also scaly and peeling on branches

TWIGS: stout, light brown or tan, smooth

PITH: star-shaped in cross section

BUDS: ⅛–¼ inch long, rounded at the tip, brown

LEAVES: 5–6 inches long with very shallow rounded lobes or coarse teeth; lower surface whitish with tiny star-shaped hairs and longer straight and branched hairs

FALL LEAF COLOR: yellow-brown to reddish-purple

STIPULES: inconspicuous and falling soon after the leaves expand

LEAF SCARS: as for other oaks, see above

FLOWERS: as for other oaks, see above

FRUIT: acorn about 1 inch long with the cap enclosing ⅓ of the nut, borne singly or in pairs on a long stalk, maturing in a single season

SEEDS: animal- and bird-dispersed

WOOD: similar to that of white oak with which it is marketed

CURRENT CHAMPION: Luzerne County, diameter 6 feet 10 inches, height 65 feet, spread 80 feet

Swamp white oak—acorn x3/4

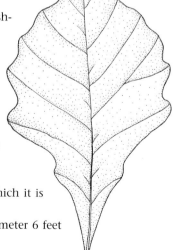

Swamp white oak—leaf

Swamp white oak is a tree of low, moist forests and forested swamps across the southern and extreme western portions

Swamp white oak—bark

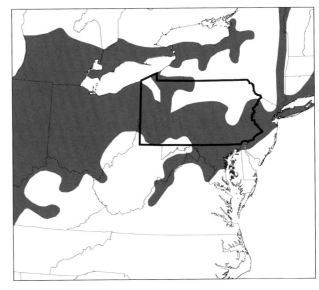

Swamp white oak

of Pennsylvania. It resembles white oak, but the bark is more shaggy and the leaves less deeply lobed. The stalked acorns are another distinguishing characteristic. The total range of swamp white oak extends from southern Maine and Quebec to Minnesota and south to North Carolina, Tennessee, and Arkansas.

White oak   *Quercus alba* L.

FORM: large tree to 100 feet or more, when grown in the open it develops a broad, spreading crown

BARK: light gray and separating in irregular scales or strips

TWIGS: light green tinged with red at first, becoming reddish to gray

PITH: star-shaped in cross section

BUDS: reddish-brown, blunt, ⅛–¼ inch long

LEAVES: 5–9 inches long, pinnately lobed with 3–4 rounded lobes on each side of the midrib, bluish-green

FALL LEAF COLOR: deep purplish-red

STIPULES: inconspicuous and falling soon after the leaves expand

LEAF SCARS: as for other oaks, see above

FLOWERS: as for other oaks, see above

FRUIT: ¾–1 inch long, stalkless or with a short stalk, nut enclosed by the cap for about ¼ of its length, maturing in a single season

SEEDS: animal- and bird-dispersed

WOOD: heavy, hard, and close grained

CURRENT CHAMPION: Adams County, diameter 6 feet 2 inches, height 115 feet, spread 122 feet

White oak—acorn x1

White oaks can live to be 400 years old or more and constitute some of the largest and oldest trees in the state. Of the 181 trees 250 years and older documented in the book, *Penn's Woods 1682–1982*, more than one-third were white oaks.[2] White oak is abundant throughout Pennsylvania in dry oak-heath, dry

White oak—bark

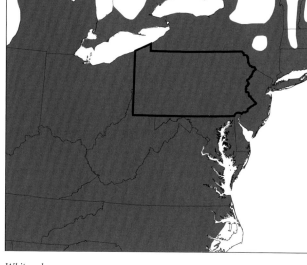

White oak

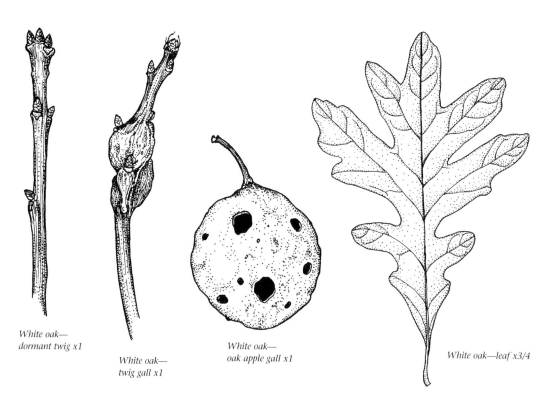

White oak—
dormant twig x1

White oak—
twig gall x1

White oak—
oak apple gall x1

White oak—leaf x3/4

oak-mixed hardwood, red oak-mixed hardwood, and sweetgum-oak coastal plain forest types. Its total range extends from Maine to Minnesota and south to northern Florida and eastern Texas.

White oak wood was highly valued for furniture, interior finishing, flooring, roof shingles, wine and whiskey casks, and ship building. In recent years it has been largely replaced in commerce by red oak, which is faster growing.

Yellow oak, chinquapin oak *Quercus muehlenbergii* Engelm.

FORM: medium-sized tree 60–100 feet, with a round-topped crown

BARK: light gray, scaly, flakier than white oak

TWIGS: slender, reddish to yellowish-brown, smooth

PITH: star-shaped in cross section

BUDS: ⅙ inch long, chestnut brown, broadly rounded, sharp-pointed at the tip

LEAVES: dark, shiny green, 4–7 inches long, ⅓ to ½ times as wide as long, with coarse, rounded teeth each with a tiny callous tip; leaves whitish beneath with spreading, star-shaped hairs

FALL LEAF COLOR: yellow to orangey-brown or dark red

STIPULES: inconspicuous and falling soon after the leaves expand

LEAF SCARS: as for other oaks, see above

FLOWERS: as for other oaks, see above

FRUIT: acorn maturing in a single season, stalkless, ¾–1 inch long, cup enclosing about ½ of the nut

SEEDS: animal- and bird-dispersed

WOOD: heavy, hard, strong, and durable, but nowhere abundant enough to be of commercial significance

CURRENT CHAMPION: Berks County, diameter 6 feet 6 inches, height 84 feet, spread 120 feet

Yellow oak—acorn x1

This limestone-loving oak is found at scattered sites across the southern half of Pennsylvania, always on calcareous soils. Yellow oak occurs from Vermont to western Nebraska and south to northern Florida, Alabama, and Texas.

The exceptionally durable wood of yellow oak was once valued for split rail fences and railroad ties. It is also good fuel.

Yellow oak—leaf x3/4

Yellow oak—bark

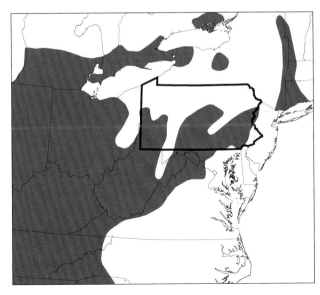

Yellow oak

BLACK OAK GROUP

Black oak   *Quercus velutina* Lam.

FORM: large tree to 100 feet or more with ascending branches above and spreading branches below, crown oblong or rounded in outline

BARK: rough, black, divided by vertical and horizontal fissures into small plates; inner bark yellow

TWIGS: stout, reddish-brown, hairy when young but becoming smooth

PITH: tan, star-shaped in cross section

BUDS: ⅓–½ inch long, sharp-pointed, angled, covered with grayish hairs

LEAVES: 4–10 inches long with 3–4 sharp-pointed and bristle-tipped lobes on each side of the midrib, leaf blades with rusty colored hairs covering the lower surface when young and persisting in the angles of the veins beneath, highly variable as to the depth of the sinuses between the lobes

FALL LEAF COLOR: yellow-brown or reddish

STIPULES: inconspicuous and falling soon after the leaves expand

LEAF SCARS: as for other oaks, see above

FLOWERS: as for other oaks, see above

FRUIT: acorn maturing the second year, ½–¾ inch long, cap covering about ½ of the nut

WOOD: hard, heavy, strong, light brown with lighter sapwood

CURRENT CHAMPION: Franklin County, diameter 6 feet 1 inch, height 107 feet, spread 130 feet

Black oak—acorn x1

Black oak is a prominent forest tree of upland sites in moist to dry soils, in all but the northernmost counties of Pennsylvania. Its total range extends from Maine to Minnesota and south to Florida and Texas.

Black oak—bark

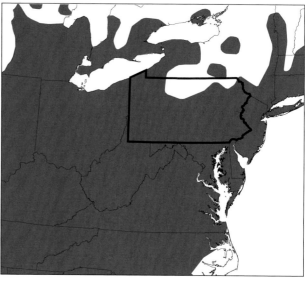

Black oak

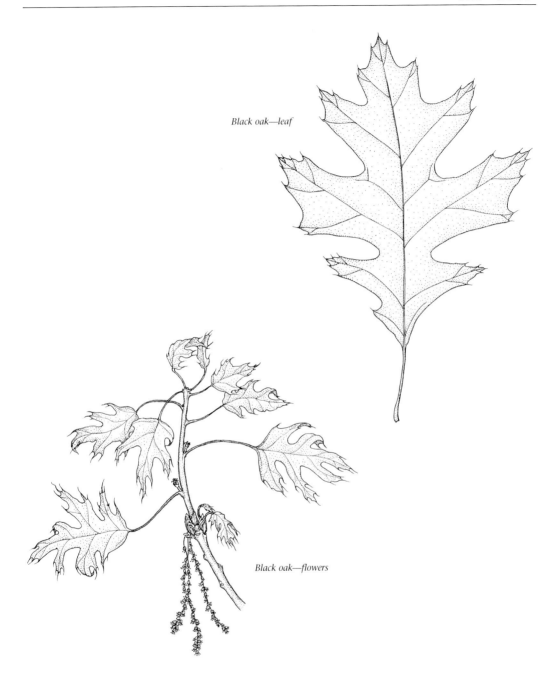

Black oak—leaf

Black oak—flowers

The leaf form of black oaks is extremely variable. Those of young trees and shade leaves of larger trees are frequently very shallowly indented between the lobes.

The inner bark of black oak, known as quercitron, was the source of a yellow dye used for coloring silk and wool until synthetic dyes took its place. In Philadelphia in 1808 quercitron brought $40 per ton for export to Europe.[3]

Blackjack oak

Quercus marilandica **Münchh.**

FORM: small tree to 40 feet, with a dense rounded crown; sometimes more shrubby

BARK: dark brown to nearly black, rough with scaly plates; inner bark orange

TWIGS: stout, dark brown to gray, hairy at first but becoming smooth

PITH: star-shaped in cross section

BUDS: ¼ inch long, reddish-brown with rusty brown hairs, sharp-pointed, angled

LEAVES: 4–8 inches long, variable, but usually nearly triangular with 3 shallow lobes at the wide end and tapering to a narrow base; leaf blades thick and leathery, with brown hairs beneath

FALL LEAF COLOR: orangey- or reddish-brown

STIPULES: inconspicuous and falling soon after the leaves expand

LEAF SCARS: as in other oaks, see above

FLOWERS: as in other oaks, see above

FRUIT: acorn maturing at the end of the second season, ¾–1 inch long, the cap covering ½ of the nut

SEEDS: animal- and bird-dispersed

WOOD: heavy, hard, and strong but too small to be of much economic importance except for charcoal and firewood

CURRENT CHAMPION: Delaware County, diameter 1 foot 5 inches, height 55 feet, spread 49 feet

Blackjack oak—acorn x1

Blackjack oak doesn't grow much farther north than southeastern Pennsylvania where it occurs on dry sterile soils and serpentine barrens. Its total range extends from Florida and Texas to southern Iowa and north along the coast to southeastern Pennsylvania, southern New Jersey, and Long Island.

Blackjack oak—bark

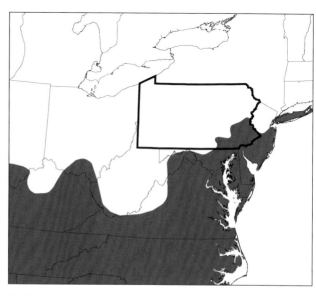

Blackjack oak

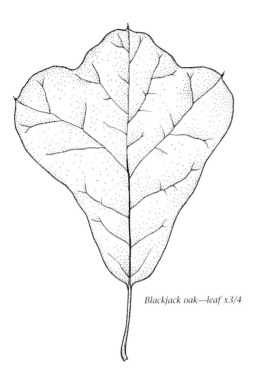

Blackjack oak—leaf x3/4

Pin oak   *Quercus palustris* **Müenchh.**

FORM: upright tree to 80 feet or more with a straight, continuous trunk and cylindrical crown; the lower lateral branches are short and drooping and eventually die and curl downward toward the trunk or break off leaving short stubs (pins)

BARK: gray-brown, smooth at first developing shallow furrows and broad ridges

TWIGS: slender, dark red to grayish brown, hairy at first becoming smooth

PITH: star-shaped in cross section

BUDS: ⅛–¼ inch long, sharp pointed, gray-brown to chestnut brown, smooth

LEAVES: 4–6 inches long, with 2–4 sharp, bristle-tipped lobes on each side of the midrib; sinuses deep, U-shaped; leaf blades smooth beneath

FALL LEAF COLOR: yellow or reddish-brown

STIPULES: inconspicuous and falling soon after the leaves expand

LEAF SCARS: as for other oaks, see above

FLOWERS: as for other oaks, see above

FRUIT: acorn maturing the second season, about ½ inch long, cap covering about ⅔ of the nut

WOOD: heavy, strong, and hard but of limited value due to its tendency to warp

CURRENT CHAMPION: Montgomery County, diameter 4 feet 2 inches, height 105 feet, spread 87 feet

Pin oak—acorn x1

Pin oak is found in seasonally wet woods and swamps in southeastern, south central, and western Pennsylvania. It can withstand inundation of the root system for weeks at a time, but is intolerant of alkaline soils. The natural range of the species is from Vermont to North Carolina and west to Iowa and Kansas. Pin oak is also planted extensively as a street tree and landscape specimen.

Pin oak—trunk and dead lower branches

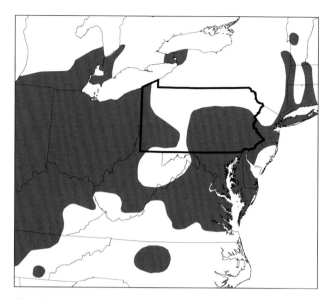

Pin oak

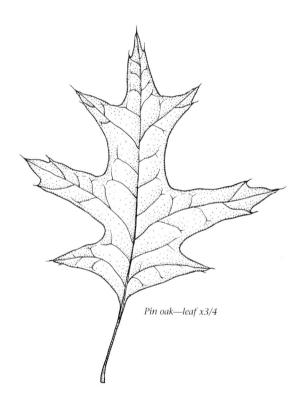

Pin oak—leaf x3/4

Red oak   *Quercus rubra* **L.**

FORM: a large tree to 100 feet or more, developing a broad symmetrical crown when grown in the open

BARK: dark gray-brown, fissured, marked by long, smooth gray streaks or "ski tracks" especially on the upper trunk

TWIGS: slender, smooth, greenish-brown to dark brown

PITH: star-shaped in cross section

BUDS: ¼–⅓ inches long, pointed; bud scales brown, smooth, or only slightly hairy on the edges

LEAVES: 5–9 inches long with 3–4 sharp, bristle-tipped lobes on each side of the midrib, pale green and smooth beneath with tufts of hairs in the angles of the veins

FALL LEAF COLOR: red or sometimes brown

STIPULES: inconspicuous and falling soon after the leaves expand

LEAF SCARS: as for other oaks, see above

FLOWERS: as for other oaks, see above

FRUIT: acorn maturing at the end of the second year, ¼–1¼ inches long with the cup covering only the base of the nut

SEEDS: animal- and bird-dispersed

WOOD: heavy, hard and strong, reddish-brown

CURRENT CHAMPION: Erie County, diameter 7 feet, height 108 feet, spread 74 feet

Red oak—acorn x1

Red oak is common and abundant in forests throughout most of Pennsylvania. The northernmost of our oaks, it ranges from Maine and southern Canada to Missouri and northern Georgia. Because it is one of the fastest growing oak species, red oak is also frequently cultivated as a shade tree or street tree.

Red oak—bark

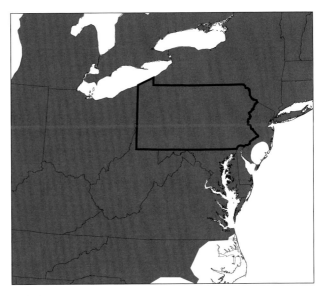

Red oak

Red oak—leaves in autumn

Red oak—branch with acorns

Sawtooth oak   *Quercus acutissima* Carruth.

FORM: medium-sized tree to 60 feet with a broadly spreading crown

BARK: deeply ridged and furrowed, almost corky

TWIGS: gray-brown, smooth

PITH: star-shaped in cross section

BUDS: ¼–⅜ inch long, gray-brown and hairy with numerous overlapping bud scales

LEAVES: 4–7 inches long, oblong with a long pointed tip, not lobed but with coarse, bristle-tipped teeth

FALL LEAF COLOR: yellow to golden-brown

STIPULES: inconspicuous and falling soon after the leaves expand

LEAF SCARS: as for other oaks, see above

FLOWERS: as for other oaks, see above

FRUIT: about 1 inch long, the nut nearly covered by the shaggy cap, maturing at the end of the second season

CURRENT CHAMPION: Philadelphia County, 2 feet 1 inch, height 78 feet, spread 56 feet

*Sawtooth oak—
acorn x3/4*

The leaves of sawtooth oak are very similar in appearance to those of chestnut. A native of Japan, Korea, China, and the Himalayas, it is planted by the Pennsylvania Game Commission as a source of mast for wildlife due to its frequent

Sawtooth oak—bark

Sawtooth oak—leaf

heavy acorn crops. It has occasionally naturalized in old fields. The largest specimen known in the state is at the Morris Arboretum in Philadelphia.

Scarlet oak   *Quercus coccinea* **Münchh.**

FORM: erect tree to 80 feet or more, lateral branches ascending above, horizontal in the middle, and drooping below; the lower branches usually dying from shading

BARK: dark with irregular deep fissures and intervening scaly ridges, inner bark orangey-pink

TWIGS: slender, reddish- or grayish-brown, smooth

PITH: star-shaped in cross section

BUDS: ¼–⅜ inch long, dark reddish-brown, angled, covered with gray-white hairs toward the tip, smooth below

LEAVES: 3–6 inches long with 3–4 sharp, bristle-tipped lobes on each side of the midrib; sinuses between the lobes C-shaped; leaf blades smooth beneath

FALL LEAF COLOR: brilliant scarlet

STIPULES: inconspicuous and falling soon after the leaves expand

LEAF SCARS: as for other oaks, see above

FLOWERS: as for other oaks, see above

FRUIT: acorn stalkless or short-stalked, ⅔ to ⅘ inch long, with the cap covering about ½ of the nut

WOOD: strong, heavy with a coarse texture, of little economic value other than for firewood

CURRENT CHAMPION: Chester County, diameter 3 feet 8 inches, height 110 feet, spread 105 feet

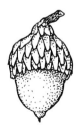

Scarlet oak—acorn x1

Scarlet oak and pin oak are similar in growth form and appearance, leaf shape is perhaps the best clue to distinguish them. The sinuses between the lobes of scarlet oak leaves are C-shaped whereas those of pin oak are U-shaped. The hairy tip

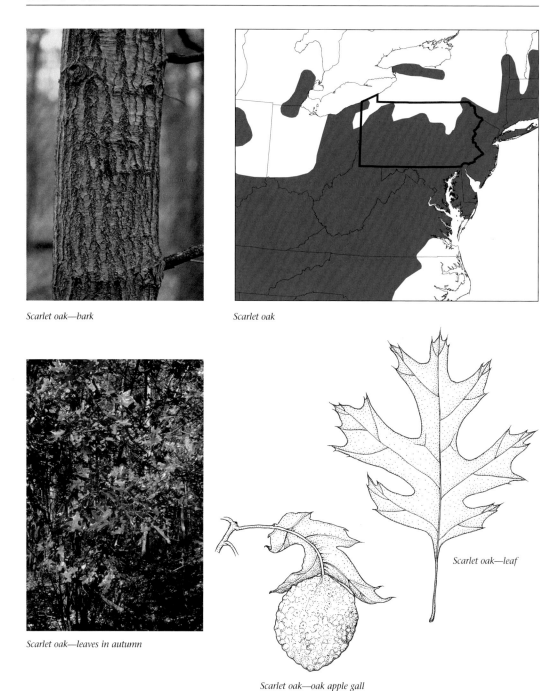

Scarlet oak—bark

Scarlet oak

Scarlet oak—leaves in autumn

Scarlet oak—leaf

Scarlet oak—oak apple gall

of scarlet oak buds is another good identification character as is habitat difference. Scarlet oak is a tree of dry upper slopes and ridges whereas pin oak is a tree of low, wet sites.

Scarlet oak occurs throughout the southern two-thirds of Pennsylvania, it is not present in areas of highest elevation. Overall it is a tree of the Appalachians from southern Maine to Georgia and irregularly west to Michigan, Missouri, and Mississippi.

Scrub oak, bear oak   *Quercus ilicifolia* Wangenh.

FORM: large shrub or small tree reaching a maximum height of 20 feet, usually multistemmed

BARK: gray to dark brown, thin and smooth or scaly on older stems

TWIGS: slender, brown or yellowish-brown, hairy at first becoming smooth

PITH: star-shaped in cross section

BUDS: ⅛ inch long, blunt, with numerous overlapping bud scales

LEAVES: 2–5 inches long, with 2–3 mostly triangular, bristle-tipped lobes on each side of the midrib, lower surface grayish-hairy

FALL LEAF COLOR: orangey-brown

STIPULES: inconspicuous and falling soon after the leaves expand

LEAF SCARS: as for other oaks, see above

FLOWERS: as for other oaks, see above

FRUIT: acorn maturing at the end of the second season, ½ inch long and about ⅓ enclosed by the cap

SEEDS: animal- and bird-dispersed

WOOD: strong, hard, and tough but too small to be of commercial significance other than for firewood

CURRENT CHAMPION: none recorded

Scrub oak—acorn x1

Scrub oak is highly fire tolerant due to its ability to sprout repeatedly from the base; it forms extensive thickets in areas where there are frequent forest fires. It is not shade tolerant, however.

Scrub oak—leaf x3/4

Scrub oak—bark

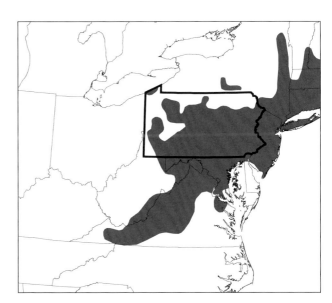

Scrub oak

Scrub oak is found in eastern and central Pennsylvania on dry ridge tops, barrens, and other areas of sterile, sandy soils. Pennsylvania is at the center of the native range of scrub oak, which extends from southern Maine to the border of West Virginia and North Carolina.

Scorned by the foresters because of its small size, scrub oak is ecologically very important to wildlife for both food and cover. Several rare moths and numerous other insects are associated with scrub oak.[4]

Shingle oak, laurel oak   *Quercus imbricaria* Michx.

FORM: tree to 100 feet with an open crown
BARK: gray-brown, developing shallow fissures alternating with scaly ridges
TWIGS: slender, dark green initially becoming brown, smooth and shiny
PITH: star-shaped in cross section
BUDS: light chestnut brown, ⅛ inch long, sharp-pointed, angled, covered with many overlapping bud scales, slightly hairy
LEAVES: 4–6 inches long, oblong with a smooth, rolled under edge, hairy beneath
FALL LEAF COLOR: yellow or reddish-brown
STIPULES: inconspicuous and falling soon after the leaves expand
LEAF SCARS: as in other oaks, see above
FLOWERS: as in other oaks, see above
FRUIT: acorn maturing at the end of the second season, stalked, nut about ⅝ inch long, enclosed for half its length by the cap
WOOD: hard, coarse-grained, reddish-brown, used for fuel, charcoal, and shingles
CURRENT CHAMPION: Greene County, diameter 4 feet 6 inches, height 103 feet, spread 75 feet

Shingle oak—acorn x1

Shingle oak—bark

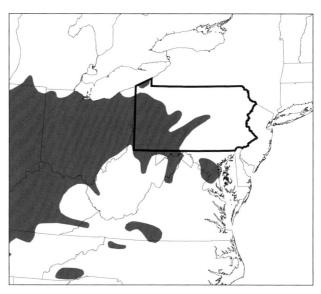

Shingle oak

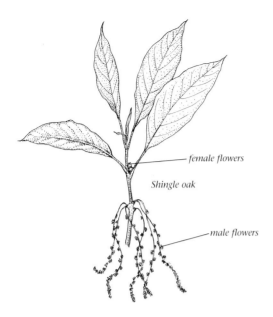

female flowers

Shingle oak

male flowers

Shingle oak is primarily a midwestern species, in Pennsylvania it occurs only west of the Alleghenies in rich, moist bottomlands of the southwestern counties. The total range of the species extends from Pennsylvania to Georgia and west to Nebraska and Arkansas. The common name of this tree refers to its use for making shingles.

Shumard oak   *Quercus shumardii* **Buckley**

FORM: tree to 80 feet with a broad, open crown

BARK: dark gray to black, smooth at first but developing broad, flat ridges with age

TWIGS: stout, gray-brown, smooth, and shiny

PITH: star-shaped in cross section

BUDS: about ¼ inch long, grayish-brown, sharp-pointed, angled, smooth or rarely finely hairy

LEAVES: 4–7 inches long, with 3–4 bristle-tipped lobes on each side of the midrib; sinuses extending more than half way to the midrib, sometimes described as thumb-shaped; leaf blade smooth, shiny green above, smooth beneath except for tufts of reddish hairs in the angles of the veins

FALL LEAF COLOR: orangey-yellow to dark red

STIPULES: inconspicuous and falling soon after the leaves expand

LEAF SCARS: as for other oaks, see above

FLOWERS: as for other oaks, see above

FRUIT: acorn ¾–1¼ inches long, with a shallow cap

SEEDS: animal- and bird-dispersed

WOOD: light brown, strong and durable

CURRENT CHAMPION: Chester County, diameter 3 feet 6 inches, height 93 feet, spread 97 feet

Shumard oak—acorn x1

Shumard oak is known from only a few sites in Bedford and Franklin Counties in Pennsylvania where it grows on stream banks and bottomlands. Because of its

Shumard oak—bark

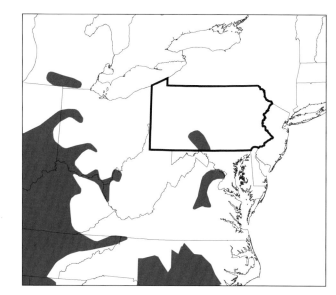

Shumard oak

limited occurrence it is classified as endangered by the Pennsylvania Natural Heritage Program. The total range of this primarily midwestern species extends from Ontario and western New York to Florida and Texas.

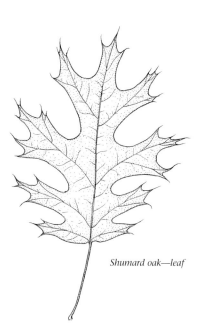

Shumard oak—leaf

Southern red oak, Spanish oak   *Quercus falcata* Michx.

FORM: tree to 80 or 100 feet tall with an open, round-topped crown

BARK: brown with low scaly ridges separated by fissures, inner bark orange

TWIGS: stout, reddish-brown to gray, hairy at first but becoming smooth

PITH: star-shaped in cross section

BUDS: red, sharp-pointed, hairy; terminal bud ¼ inch long; lateral buds ⅛ inch long

LEAVES: 6–7 inches long with a prominent central lobe that is often long and somewhat curved (falcate means sickle-shaped) and 2–4 pointed and bristle-tipped lateral lobes on each side of the midrib, base rounded; leaf blade with dense grayish hairs beneath

FALL LEAF COLOR: brown, sometimes with a tinge of red

STIPULES: inconspicuous and falling soon after the leaves expand

LEAF SCARS: as for other oaks, see above

FLOWERS: as for other oaks, see above

FRUIT: acorn maturing in the second year, ½ inch long, the cap covering ⅓–½ of the nut

SEEDS: animal- and bird-dispersed

WOOD: hard and strong but not durable, of limited commercial value due to its tendency to warp and check

CURRENT CHAMPION: Montgomery County, diameter 3 feet 11 inches, height 91 feet, spread 61 feet

Southern red oak—acorn x1

Southern red oak is classified as an endangered species in Pennsylvania where it is limited to dry or moist forests on or near the coastal plain. A prominent tree of the southeastern region from Florida and eastern Texas to southern Illinois, it extends north along the coast as far as Long Island, New York.

The shape of individual leaves of southern red oak is quite variable, but the prominent central lobe is a fairly consistent feature, as is the rounded base. On

Southern red oak—bark

Southern red oak

*Southern red oak—twig
with immature acorns x3/4*

*Southern red oak—
dormant twig x1*

the tree the leaves tend to have a droopy appearance that, combined with the long terminal lobe, gives the foliage the characteristic look of dangling swords.

Willow oak   *Quercus phellos* L.

FORM: tree to 80 feet with a straight trunk and rounded and somewhat open crown

BARK: gray-brown, shallowly fissured and scaly on old trees

TWIGS: reddish-brown to dark brown, smooth and shining

PITH: star-shaped in cross section

BUDS: ⅛–¼ inch long, strongly angled, sharp-pointed, covered with chestnut brown bud scales

LEAVES: 3–5 inches long, narrowly elliptical, with a smooth edge

FALL LEAF COLOR: yellow-brown to russet-red

STIPULES: inconspicuous and falling soon after the leaves expand

LEAF SCARS: as in other oaks, see above

FLOWERS: as in other oaks, see above

FRUIT: acorn maturing at the end of the second season, nut nearly spherical, ½ inch in diameter, with only the base enclosed by the cap

SEEDS: animal- and bird-dispersed

WOOD: strong, coarse-grained, but rather soft, light brown, used for fuel and general construction

CURRENT CHAMPION: Montgomery County, diameter 5 feet 5 inches, height 108 feet, spread 95 feet

Willow oak—acorn x1

The finely textured leaves of this tree do not immediately suggest an oak, but a close inspection will reveal the presence of acorns on the branches, a clear indication of its membership in the genus *Quercus*. Native to the southeastern states, willow oak is near the northern limit of its natural range in southeastern Pennsylvania. Because of its restricted occurrence in the state, willow oak is classified

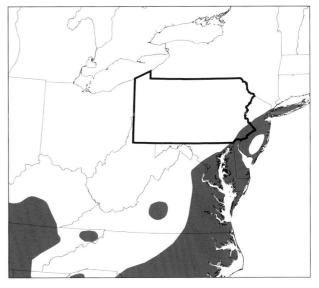

Willow oak—bark   *Willow oak*

Willow oak—foliage

Willow oak—leaf x1

as an endangered species by the Pennsylvania Natural Heritage Program. Its range extends from Florida and Texas north to southern Illinois and along the coast to Long Island, New York.

Willow oak is a tree of bottomlands and floodplains that withstands inundation of the roots for weeks at a time. It is also frequently planted as a street tree, but is intolerant of alkaline soils.

Notes

1. Abrams, M. D. 1986. Distribution, historical development and ecophysiological attributes of oak species in the eastern United States. *Annals de Sciences Forestières* 53: 487–512.

2. Wertz, Halfred A. and M. Joy Callender. 1981. *Penn's Woods 1682–1982*. Green Valleys Association, Birchrunville, Pa.

3. Michaux, F. Andrew. 1817. *The North American Sylva, or A Description of the Forest Trees of the United States, Canada, and Nova Scotia*, in 3 volumes. Thomas Dobson-Solomon Conrad, Philadelphia.

4. Wheeler, A. G., Jr. 1991. Plant bugs of *Quercus ilicifolia*: Myriads of myrids (Heteroptera) in pitch pine-scrub oak barrens. *Journal New York Entomological Society* 99 (3): 405–40.

OSAGE-ORANGE
MORUS L.
Mulberry Family—Moraceae

Osage-orange, hedge-apple   ***Maclura pomifera* (Raf.) C.K. Schneid.**

FORM: deciduous tree to 60 feet, with milky sap; stout thorns are present on the twigs in the juvenile stage

BARK: orange-brown, with long, flat ridges

TWIGS: greenish to orangey-brown

PITH: white, homogeneous

BUDS: broadly rounded, approximately ⅛ inch wide with 5–7 dark brown bud scales, terminal bud absent

LEAVES: shiny, dark green, alternate, simple, 2–6 inches long, egg-shaped with a pointed tip and a smooth edge

FALL LEAF COLOR: yellow

STIPULES: linear, falling early and leaving a narrow scar on each side of the base of the leaf stalk

LEAF SCARS: half-round with a ring of bundle scars

FLOWERS: unisexual, in spherical heads, male and female on separate plants (dioecious), opening in late May or early June after the leaves have expanded; the male flowers with 4 sepals and 4 stamens; the female flowers with 4 sepals and a superior ovary

FRUIT: green, spherical, 4–5 inches in diameter with a convoluted surface

SEEDS: egg-shaped, about ¼ inch long, gray

Osage-orange—flowers x1   *Osage-orange—bark*

WOOD: bright orange with yellow sapwood, heavy, strong and very durable, but hard to work

CURRENT CHAMPION: Montgomery County, diameter 5 feet 4 inches, height 83 feet, spread 72 feet

Osage-orange is a plant of hedgerows and roadside thickets across southern Pennsylvania where its green, grapefruit-sized fruits are conspicuous in the fall. Native to Texas, Oklahoma, and Arkansas, it was extensively planted for hedges at one time and now is widely naturalized in the eastern United States.

The wood was used to make bows by Native Americans, and served as a source of yellow dye. Medicinal uses included a decoction of the roots that was used as eyewash. The wood of osage-orange was highly prized for fence posts because of its durability. In recent years thornless cultivars have been developed for ornamental use.

Although squirrels occasionally dissect frost-softened osage-orange fruits in order to eat the seeds, the large fruits seem poorly adapted for consumption by animals alive today that might effectively disseminate the seeds. Some researchers suspect that the fruits were eaten by wild horses or other large ice age era mammals that became extinct approximately 13,000 years ago.[1] Once much larger, the range of osage-orange had become restricted to a few river valleys in eastern Texas and adjacent areas of Arkansas and Oklahoma by the time European settlers arrived.

Notes

1. Barlow, Connie. 2000. *The Ghosts of Evolution: Nonsensical Fruit, Missing Partners, and Other Ecological Anachronisms.* Basic Books, New York.

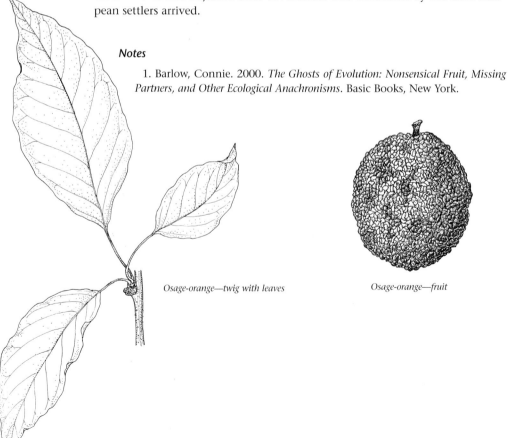

Osage-orange—twig with leaves   *Osage-orange—fruit*

PAGODA-TREE
SOPHORA L.
Bean Family—Fabaceae

Japanese pagoda-tree, scholar-tree   *Sophora japonica* L.

FORM: deciduous tree to 60 feet with spreading branches and a rounded crown

BARK: pale grayish- or yellowish-brown, shallowly furrowed

TWIGS: green with prominent, raised, tan-colored lenticels

PITH: white or greenish, homogeneous

BUDS: blackish, hairy, covered by the petiole base; terminal bud lacking

LEAVES: alternate, 7–9 inches long, pinnately compound with 7–17, 1- to 2-inch-long, egg-shaped leaflets

FALL LEAF COLOR: yellow or brownish

STIPULES: narrow, about ¼ inch long, dropping early and leaving a small triangular scar on each side of the base of the leaf stalk

LEAF SCARS: triangular, surrounding the lateral bud

FLOWERS: creamy white, in loose terminal clusters that are about 15 inches long, blooming in July or early August

FRUIT: a greenish, fleshy pod, 3–8 inches long and narrowed between the seeds

SEEDS: 3–6 per pod, black

WOOD: light-colored with a coarse grain

CURRENT CHAMPION: Montgomery County, diameter 5 feet 7 inches, height 88 feet, spread 91 feet

Fine-textured foliage and showy midsummer blooms have made Japanese pagoda-tree a popular street and yard tree in many areas. Several cultivated forms have been developed. Recently, this tree, which is native to China, has begun to appear as scattered naturalized plants in urban parks and suburban woodlands.

In its native habitat, Japanese pagoda-tree is a component of the vast temperate deciduous broad-leaved forest of eastern Asia. It occurs on lower slopes in oak-dominated forests with paper-mulberry, empress-tree, goldenrain tree, Chinese elm, Chinese chestnut, and persimmon among others. The flowers are used to make a yellow dye and various medicinal preparations were derived from the fruits, seeds, twigs, and bark.[1]

Notes

1. Stuart, G. A. 1979. *Chinese Materia Medica.* Southern Materials Center, Taipei, China.

Japanese pagoda-tree—bark

Japanese pagoda-tree—flowers x1/4

Japanese pagoda-tree—fruit x1

PAPER-MULBERRY
BROUSSONETIA L'HÉR.
Mulberry Family—Moraceae

Paper-mulberry **Broussonetia papyrifera (L.) Vent.**

FORM: broadly spreading deciduous tree to 45 feet with milky sap; spreads by root shoots to form thickets

BARK: light brown to gray, smooth or slightly furrowed

TWIGS: gray-green to gray-brown, hairy with conspicuous orange lenticels

PITH: large, white with a green partition at each node

BUDS: conical, outer bud scale grayish-brown and striped; terminal bud absent

LEAVES: alternate or sometimes nearly opposite on fast-growing branches, simple, variously lobed or unlobed, with toothed margins, softly gray-hairy beneath, rough above; venation palmate

FALL LEAF COLOR: yellow-green

STIPULES: linear, falling early

LEAF SCARS: nearly circular, elevated

FLOWERS: unisexual, staminate and pistillate on separate plants (dioecious); staminate flowers in drooping catkins, flowers with 4 sepals and 4 stamens; pistillate flowers in dense spherical heads, each flower with 4 fused sepals and a stalked ovary with a long, slender style

FRUIT: spherical, orange-red, about ¾ inch in diameter, consisting of the fused fruits of an entire inflorescence (a syncarp)

SEEDS: slightly flattened and about ⅛ inch long

Paper-mulberry—fruit x1

Paper-mulberry—leaves

Paper-mulberry—bark

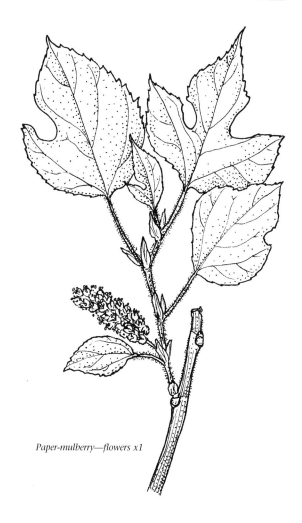

Paper-mulberry—flowers x1

WOOD: light in color and weight

CURRENT CHAMPION: Philadelphia County, diameter 2 feet 6 inches, height 45 feet, spread 50 feet

Paper-mulberry is often found in urban areas, where it colonizes roadsides, railroad rights-of-way, and vacant lots. Native to China and Japan, it was formerly cultivated as a shade tree and has become widely naturalized in the eastern United States. Weedy tendencies have discouraged its further use as an ornamental.

In Japan paper is made from the fibrous bark, and in Polynesia, the bark is used to make tapa cloth. In the American southwest, Native Americans used the plant as a source of a narcotic substance; in addition the seeds were strung to make ceremonial necklaces.

PAWPAW
ASIMINA ADANSON
Custard-Apple Family—Annonaceae

Pawpaw   *Asimina triloba* **(L.) Dunal**

FORM: small tree to 30 feet, forming colonies in the forest understory

BARK: smooth, becoming shallowly furrowed in older trees

TWIGS: brown, hairy at first, becoming smooth

PITH: small, white, with occasional denser green partitions in the 2-year-old twigs

BUDS: densely covered with dark brown hairs, but lacking bud scales (naked)

LEAVES: alternate, simple, 4–12 inches long, broadest near the tip, tapered to a short petiole, dark green; margins entire; the young expanding leaves droop characteristically at the tips of the twigs

FALL LEAF COLOR: yellow

STIPULES: none

LEAF SCARS: broadly U-shaped and nearly surrounding the bud; bundle scars 5

FLOWERS: green turning to dark red-purple, nodding, opening early in the spring before the leaves

FRUITS: yellow-green turning blackish, irregularly cylindrical, to 3 inches long

SEEDS: 3–6 per fruit, flattened, up to 1 inch in diameter

WOOD: too small to be commercially important

CURRENT CHAMPION: Cumberland County, diameter 1 foot 9 inches, height 33 feet, spread 31 feet

Pawpaw—seed x1

The opportunity to be "way down yonder in the pawpaw patch," as in the old folksong, exists across the southern half of Pennsylvania where this small tree

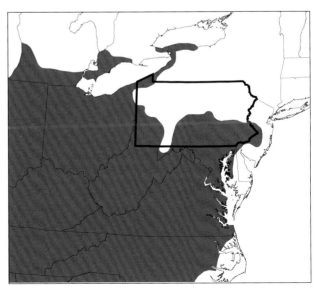

Pawpaw—bark   *Pawpaw*

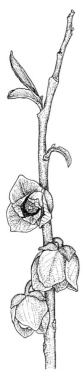

Pawpaw—flowers

forms dense clonal colonies in the understory of moist, rich deciduous forests. It is frequently found in floodplain forests along streams and rivers. Pawpaw's relatively large leaves make it conspicuous in the summer and autumn woods. Its dark red-purple flowers are followed by edible fruits that look something like small, lumpy bananas and ripen in September or early October. Pawpaw grows from Pennsylvania west to Kansas and south to Georgia and Louisiana. It is the hardiest species in the mostly tropical or subtropical Custard-Apple Family.

While pawpaw trees are too small to have any value as a wood source, chemicals extracted from the twigs and seeds have recently been shown to have promising anticancer and pesticidal properties.[1] The leaves and twigs have a petroleum-like odor when bruised. Deer do not eat pawpaw foliage, but raccoons, box turtles, and other wildlife eagerly consume the pulp of the fruits. The seeds are too big to be dispersed by small mammals and it has been suggested that larger ice-age mammals, such as mastodons, that became extinct about 13,000 years ago, may have been the original seed dispersal agents.[2]

Pawpaw leaves are the food source for the zebra swallowtail butterfly, the adults of which are often seen in the vicinity of colonies of the trees. The caterpillars of several sphinx moths also feed on pawpaw leaves.

Native Americans made dried cakes of the raw or cooked fruit pulp for use as food and extracted fibers from the inner bark to make string and rope. Efforts are currently underway to develop pawpaw as a commercial fruit crop.

Notes

1. Haribel, Meena, Paul Feeny, and Cathy C. Lester. 1998. A caffeoglyclohexane-1-carboxylic acid derivative from *Asimina triloba*. *Phytochemistry* 49 (1): 103–8; Woo, Mi-Hee, Dal Hwan Kim, and Jerry L. McLaughlin. 1999. Asitrilobins A and B: cytotoxic mono-THF annonaceous acetogenins from seeds of *Asimina triloba*. *Phytochemistry* 50 (6): 1033–40.

2. Barlow, Connie. 2000. *The Ghosts of Evolution: Nonsensical Fruit, Missing Partners, and Other Ecological Anachronisms*. Basic Books, New York.

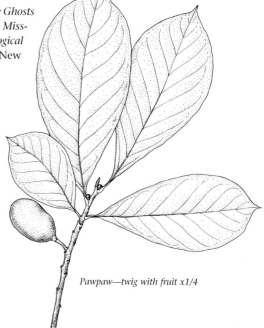

Pawpaw—twig with fruit x1/4

PEAR
Pyrus L.
Rose Family—Rosaceae

Pears are very similar to apples, differing mainly by their smooth, glossy leaves, and fruits that contain gritty stone cells scattered throughout the flesh. Flowers are white, ½–1 inch in diameter, consist of 5 separate petals, 5 sepals, numerous stamens, and a single style ending in 2–5 stigmas. Pears bloom early, before the leaves have expanded. The fruit, which develops from the inferior ovary, is technically a pome. Pears and apples are sometimes grouped together in the same genus.

Callery pear   *Pyrus calleryana* **Decne.**

FORM: deciduous tree to 50 feet with dense, upright branches; crown strongly pyramidal, especially when young

BARK: grayish-brown, becoming blocky with age

TWIGS: brownish, hairy when young, becoming smooth with prominent lenticels; short lateral spur branches are also present and in some cases end in thorns

PITH: green, homogeneous

BUDS: ½ inch long, gray-brown, densely hairy, with 7–8 overlapping bud scales

LEAVES: alternate, simple, shiny dark green, thick and leathery, about 3 inches long, broadly egg-shaped; leaf margin with small, rounded teeth

FALL LEAF COLOR: glossy purplish-red sometimes tinged with yellow, color not developing until mid-November

Callery pear—flowers

Callery pear—bark

Callery pear—fruit

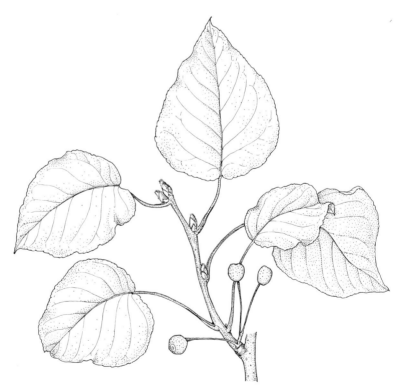

Callery pear—twig with leaves and fruit

STIPULES: small, triangular and falling early, but leaving two little nubs near the base of the petiole

LEAF SCARS: elongate, slightly 3-lobed with 3 bundle scars

FLOWERS: white, about ½ inch across, appearing in late March or early April before the leaves

FRUIT: a small, hard, apple-shaped fruit ⅜ inch in diameter with a brown speckled surface

SEEDS: about ³⁄₁₆ inch long, distributed by birds and small mammals that eat the fruit

CURRENT CHAMPION: none recorded

Callery pear is a native of China and Korea. It was originally introduced in 1918 for use in pear breeding programs. A single non-spiny seedling that was selected from a large batch of seedlings grown at the U.S. Department of Agriculture Plant Introduction Station at Glenn Dale, Maryland, was the origin of the popular "Bradford" cultivar. Introduced into the nursery trade in 1950, it became enormously popular and was planted extensively in urban and suburban areas, where its neat, tidy habit, attractive flowers, and pest-free foliage made it attractive for use along streets and in parking lots and commercial landscapes.

Among pears, a single cultivar is not self-pollinating; thus initially "Bradford" did not produce fruits or seeds. But as its popularity grew and additional callery pear cultivars joined the ranks, cross-pollination among them stimulated the production of large crops of tiny fruits containing numerous highly viable seeds. In recent years callery pear has spread and become naturalized in old fields, hedgerows, and roadsides in southeastern Pennsylvania and south to Washington, D.C. Some of the naturalized populations exhibit the very thorny characteristics of the ancestral species.

Common pear   *Pyrus communis* L.

FORM: deciduous tree to 50 feet, branches stout and stiffly upright forming a narrow crown

BARK: grayish-brown, becoming fissured and scaly with age

TWIGS: smooth and yellowish-green with numerous short, lateral spur branches sometimes ending in thorns

PITH: white, continuous

BUDS: broadly triangular with 4–5 overlapping bud scales, blunt at the tip

LEAVES: alternate or crowded on spur branches, simple, oval, 2–4 inches long, smooth and glossy with rounded teeth on the edge

FALL LEAF COLOR: red to maroon

STIPULES: small, but falling early

LEAF SCARS: elongate with 3 bundle scars

FLOWERS: white, 1 inch wide, 4–12 in a cluster with a common, branching stalk

FRUIT: yellowish-green or russet, 2–4 inches long, narrower at the stem end, flesh firm but juicy with small gritty stone cells scattered throughout

SEEDS: about ⅛ inch long, black, distributed by mammals that consume the fruits

WOOD: fine-grained and reddish in color, used for carving and small tools such as rulers

CURRENT CHAMPION: Montgomery County, diameter 2 feet 3 inches, height 65 feet, spread 41 feet

Common pear, which is widely cultivated, is often found growing wild in hedgerows, successional woodlands, and abandoned farmsteads. In the wild it grows larger than cultivated trees that are constantly pruned and shaped to maximize fruit production. Pear is originally native to Europe and western Asia; numerous commercial cultivars have been developed. It is a larval food source for viceroy, red-spotted purple, white admiral, and mourning cloak butterflies.

Common pear—bark

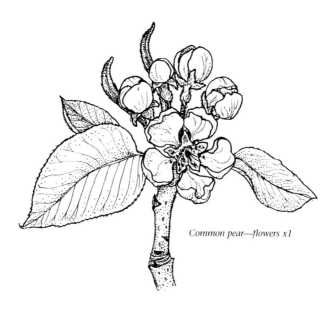

Common pear—flowers x1

PERSIMMON
DIOSPYROS L.
Ebony Family—Ebenaceae

Persimmon   *Diospyros virginiana* L.

FORM: deciduous tree to 60 feet with spreading and sometimes drooping branches, frequently forming colonial thickets through root sprouts

BARK: dark gray-brown, deeply furrowed longitudinally and vertically into square blocks about an inch wide

TWIGS: grayish-brown, covered with short downy hairs

PITH: pale green or tan

BUDS: about ⅛ inch long with overlapping, dark red-brown bud scales

LEAVES: alternate, simple, oval, 4–6 inches long; margin entire

FALL LEAF COLOR: brown or blackish

STIPULES: none

LEAF SCARS: raised, semicircular, with a curved line of bundle scars

FLOWERS: greenish-yellow, unisexual (the species dioecious), appearing with the leaves; corolla bell-shaped, about ½–¾ inch long; staminate flowers occurring in small clusters, each with 16 stamens; pistillate flowers solitary and slightly larger, containing a superior ovary and frequently with 8 nonfunctional stamens

FRUIT: a globe-shaped, fleshy berry about 1–1¼ inches in diameter with a persistent 4-lobed calyx, orange turning soft and blackish when ripe

SEEDS: 0–8, disk-shaped, about ½ inch across

WOOD: dark brown to nearly black, heavy and strong

CURRENT CHAMPION: Dauphin County, diameter 2 feet 1 inch, height 86 feet, spread 50 feet

Persimmon—bark

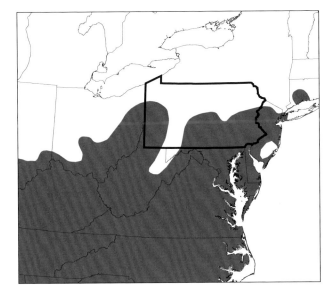

Persimmon

The globe-shaped orange fruits of persimmon are conspicuous on the female trees after the leaves have fallen, sometimes weighing the branches down by their abundance. Although sweet and delicious when fully ripe, the tannin-laden fruits have a well-deserved reputation for puckering the mouth of the impatient consumer. Wait to try them until after frost has mellowed and softened the pulp.

In Pennsylvania, persimmon trees are found mainly in the southeast in habitats that include open woods, floodplains, old fields, hedgerows, and edges. Primarily a southern plant, overall the species ranges from Connecticut and southern New York to Florida and eastern Texas.

Persimmon fruits were gathered and eaten fresh or dried for later use by many Native American tribes; in addition various parts of the tree were used medicinally. The bark was chewed to alleviate heartburn, and infusions of the bark were used to treat fever and sore throat. Toothache and venereal disease were other complaints treated with preparations made from persimmon. Commercial persimmons are derived from larger-fruited Asian species of *Diospyros*.

Persimmons are a valuable food for wildlife including deer, raccoon, fox, and skunk, however, most of these animals are too small to effectively disperse the seeds, rather they eat around them or spit them out leaving piles of seeds beneath the parent tree. It has been suggested that persimmon fruits, like those of pawpaw, honey-locust, and osage-orange, may be relics from an earlier period when large ice age mammals roamed the forests of North America. It is hypothesized that the many large animals, including mastodon, giant ground sloth, elephant, rhino, and horse, that became extinct in North America 13,000 years ago consumed the fruits in their entirety and scattered the seeds as they moved from place to place.[1]

Notes

1. Barlow, Connie. 2000. *The Ghosts of Evolution: Nonsensical Fruit, Missing Partners, and Other Ecological Anachronisms*. Basic Books, New York.

Persimmon—fruit

Persimmon—twig with flowers

PHOTINIA
PHOTINIA LINDL.
Rose Family—Rosaceae

Oriental photinia　　　　　　　　　*Photinia villosa* **(Thunb.) DC.**

FORM: small tree or large shrub to 15 feet

BARK: gray

TWIGS: slender with large lenticels

PITH: small, continuous

BUDS: egg-shaped with a sharp tip, covered by 4 sharp-tipped bud scales

LEAVES: alternate, simple, 1½–3½ inches long, widest toward the tip, dark green above, hairy beneath; edge with fine gland-tipped teeth; leaf stalk less than ⅛ inch long

FALL LEAF COLOR: orange or red

STIPULES: produced, but not persistent

LEAF SCARS: crescent-shaped with 3 bundle scars

FLOWERS: white, about ⅓ inch across, in small clusters at the ends of short lateral branches, blooming late May into June

FRUIT: red, ⅓-inch-long miniature "apples"

SEEDS: dispersed by birds or small mammals

CURRENT CHAMPION: none reported

This plant is occasionally grown as an ornamental and has become naturalized in urban and suburban forest remnants in southeastern counties. Several cultivars are available in the nursery trade that feature heavier flower production, larger fruits, and brighter fall color.

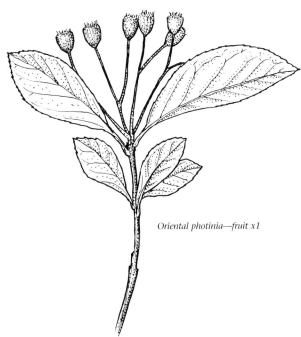

Oriental photinia—fruit x1

Oriental photinia—bark

Oriental photinia—flowers x1

PINE
Pinus L.
Pine Family—Pinaceae

With their evergreen needles in bundles of 2 to 5, the pines are a distinctive group within the conifers. Like other gymnosperms, the pines produce seeds but not flowers. Separate male (pollen), and female (seed) cones are produced on each tree. Male cones fall off after the pollen is shed, but the more substantial female cones remain on the tree. It takes 2 years for the seeds of pines to mature.

On all species except white pine, each cone scale has a thickened portion (umbo) at its tip, and on some, the umbo in turn bears a spine. Pennsylvania provides habitat for six native species of pine; in addition, 3 non-native species are frequently planted and occasionally become naturalized.

Pines have yielded a variety of useful products in addition to lumber; however, early accounts frequently did not distinguish the species utilized. Native Americans and later settlers, extracted resin, tar, and turpentine, which had many medicinal uses, some of which European settlers brought knowledge of from the Old World. The inner bark of white pine was pounded and applied as a poultice to wounds and used in a dry form as a cough suppressant by many Native American tribes. Pine sap or gum was applied to boils or abscesses to relieve pain. Pine gum was also used for waterproofing birch bark canoes and other containers.

Wild turkey, ruffed grouse, quail, songbirds, and small mammals eat pine seeds. The larval stages of several large moths including polyphemus, imperial, and northern pine sphinx moth feed on pine needles as do the eastern pine elfin and gray hairstreak butterflies.

When early English explorers made their way to the coast of North America the abundance of pine immediately caught their attention. The British navy needed vast amounts of "naval stores" in the form of pitch, tar, resin, and lumber for masts. As settlement proceeded, edicts from the king reserving the pine trees for the exclusive use of the crown helped to fuel the movement toward independence.

Austrian Pine *Pinus nigra* **Arnold**

FORM: to 90 feet, crown broadly conical, with regular whorls of branches, becoming umbrella-shaped in age as lower branches die

BARK: dark brown, deeply furrowed

TWIGS: stout, glabrous

BUDS: ½ inch long, tapering to a sharp pointed tip, covered by numerous overlapping bud scales, resinous

LEAVES: in bundles of 2, 3–6 inches long, straight and stiff (not breaking in half cleanly as do the needles of red pine), dark green

LEAF SCARS: rounded

CONES: ovoid, 2–3 inches long; scales with a small prickle

SEEDS: about ¼ inch with a papery wing, wind-dispersed

WOOD: coarse and full of knots, not commercially useful

Austrian pine—cone

Austrian pine—
needle cluster

Austrian pine—bark

Austrian pine—twig

CURRENT CHAMPION: Bucks County, diameter 3 feet 4 inches, height 60 feet, spread 60 feet

Austrian pine is native to southern Europe. It is frequently planted in forest plantations and as an ornamental, although its susceptibility to Diplodia tip blight (causal fungus: *Diplodia pineae*), which causes the lower branches to die, is a problem.

Eastern white pine   *Pinus strobus* L.

FORM: conical when young, irregular and flat-topped in age; branches become brittle and frequently break under the weight of ice and snow

BARK: thin and smooth on twigs and younger branches, becoming scaly with age

TWIGS: slightly roughened by raised leaf bases

BUDS: ¼–⅜ inch long with a very sharp tip, clustered at the ends of the branches, occurring singly on lateral branchlets

LEAVES: in clusters of 5, bluish-green, 2–5 inches long, slender and flexible

LEAF SCARS: on a persistent, slightly raised base

CONES: nearly cylindrical, 4–7 inches long and slightly curved, drooping on the branches

SEEDS: winged, wind-dispersed

WOOD: resinous, straight-grained, white or light brown, very desirable for many uses

White pine—bark

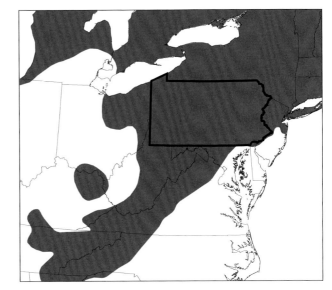

White pine

CURRENT CHAMPION: Warren County, diameter 4 feet 2 inches, height 167 feet, spread 33 feet, it is part of a small remnant of native old growth forest at Hearts Content in the Allegheny National Forest.

Tall, straight, and suitable for ships' masts, eastern white pine was the first large-scale target of waves of loggers who assaulted Pennsylvania's forests. Beginning in the 1760s white pine logs 120 feet long and 4 feet in diameter (or larger) were cut in the hills of northeastern Pennsylvania, fastened together in huge rafts, and floated down the Delaware River to Philadelphia to provide masts for British ships. The town of Masthope, at the mouth of the Lackawaxen River, recalls the period. Disputes arising over claims of ownership of all large white pines by the crown helped to fuel the desire for independence. Rafting ceased during the revolutionary war, but resumed afterward when domestic ship building began on a large scale.

In addition to its use for masts, white pine was the first tree species to be extensively harvested for lumber in the state. Light, strong, and durable, it found many uses from bridge construction to fine interior finishing and furniture making. In 1875, at a time when Pennsylvania led the nation in wood production, 10 times as much white pine as hemlock was being harvested. By 1900 white pine was in decline from over harvesting and loggers had turned to hemlock to provide the bulk of Pennsylvania's timber harvest. In 1902 only 94 million board feet of white pine was produced compared to 937 million board feet of hemlock.[1]

Eastern white pine is the only 5-needle pine that occurs naturally east of the Mississippi River. Its graceful needles and long slender cones are also distinctive. The range of white pine extends from Newfoundland to the western Great Lakes region and south in the mountains to northern Georgia. In Pennsylvania it is most abundant in the northern half of the state but occurs throughout.

Although strongly conical when young, white pines develop an irregular, flat-

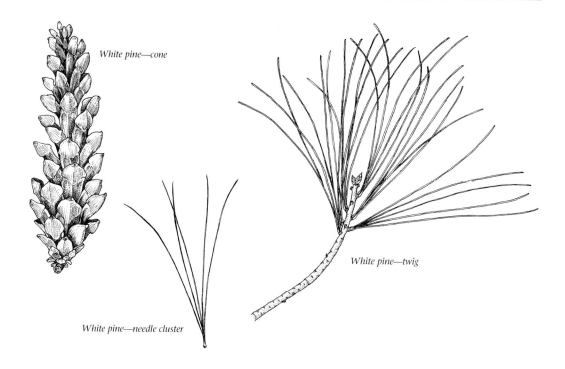

White pine—cone

White pine—twig

White pine—needle cluster

topped form with age. They frequently overtop other species with which they grow in the white pine-hemlock-northern hardwood forest. White pine grows to more than 170 feet tall and 3–4 feet in diameter. The branches occur in whorls of 3–7, each whorl representing a year's growth. Big white pines can be seen in Cook Forest State Park in Clarion County.

Today white pine is a popular landscape plant because of its relatively rapid growth and attractive soft green foliage.

Jack pine   *Pinus banksiana* Lamb.

FORM: to 80 feet, crown rounded, becoming flattened and spreading in age
BARK: orange- to red-brown, scaly
TWIGS: slender, orange or red-brown
BUDS: about ½ inch long and encrusted with resin
LEAVES: 2 per cluster, ½–1 inch long, twisted, yellow-green
LEAF SCARS: hidden under a resinous bract
CONES: 1–2 inches long, ovoid when open, narrow and often curved when closed; scales lacking prickles
SEEDS: ⅛ inch in diameter with a papery wing, wind-dispersed
WOOD: light brown, moderately hard and heavy, but weak; used for wood pulp, pilings, mine timbers, and other general construction
CURRENT CHAMPION: none recorded

Jack pine—cone x1

Jack pine is not now considered to be native to Pennsylvania, although it probably did grow here during the immediate postglacial period 10,000–18,000 years ago. Today it is found farther north where it extends across Canada from New Brunswick to the Northwest Territories. Around the Great Lakes it serves as a pio-

Jack pine—bark

Jack pine—twig

Jack pine—needle cluster x1

neer species on low-nutrient sandy soils and provides habitat for the federally endangered Kirtland's Warbler. In Pennsylvania, jack pine is occasionally planted in forest plantations.

The slender, curved cones of jack pine frequently persist on the twigs unopened until scorched by fire.

Pitch pine   *Pinus rigida* P. Mill.

FORM: wide pyramidal, to 50–60 feet, becoming irregular with age, the trunk frequently covered with short leafy shoots

BARK: coarse flaky plates separated by deep furrows

TWIGS: stout and rough from the persistent leaf bases

BUDS: clustered at the branch tip, slender and cylindrical, ¼–⅝ inch long, resinous

LEAVES: in clusters of 3, mostly 2–5 inches long

LEAF SCARS: on persistent raised leaf bases

CONES: frequently remaining on the branches for several years after reaching maturity, broadly ovoid with a nearly flat base when open, 2–3 inches long; scales with a slender, sharp, down-curved spine at the tip

SEEDS: black, sometimes with gray or red dots, winged, wind-dispersed

WOOD: resinous, brownish-red with lighter sapwood, durable, used for railroad ties, charcoal, and mine props.

CURRENT CHAMPION: Susquehanna County, diameter 1 foot 11 inches, height 120 feet, spread 28 feet

Pitch pine—cone

Pitch pine is our only native pine with its needles consistently in clusters of 3; the persistent cones and leafy shoots along the trunk are also useful identification features.

Pitch pine is noted for its tolerance for fire; it is frequently found in barrens,

Pitch pine—bark

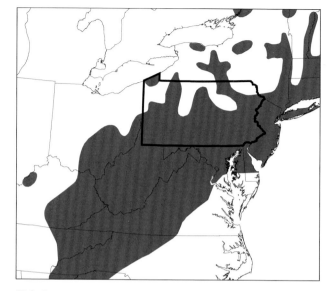

Pitch pine

Pitch pine—branch with male cones

Pitch pine—branch with young female cones

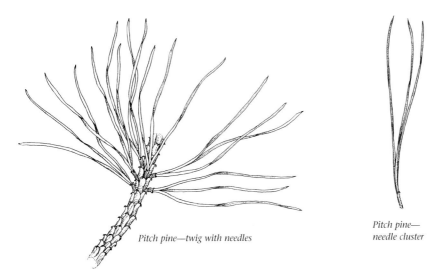

Pitch pine—twig with needles

Pitch pine—
needle cluster

dry ridge tops, and other fire-prone environments, forming pure stands or mixed with hardwoods. It is a dominant species on portions of many serpentine barrens and the Pocono till barrens. Pitch pine occurs throughout most of Pennsylvania. Its total range extends from Maine to western North Carolina and eastern Tennessee.

The exceptionally durable wood of pitch pine was valued for waterwheels, aqueduct pipes, sills of houses and barns, railroad ties, and mine props. It has also been widely used as a fuel for kilns and ovens, and to make charcoal. Tar and turpentine made from pitch pine were used to treat a wide variety of medical problems well into the 1800s.

The seeds, which are released gradually during the winter, provide a food source for birds and small mammals such as red squirrels.

Red pine   *Pinus resinosa* Aiton

FORM: crown narrowly rounded, to 110 feet, a single whorl of branches is produced each year
BARK: reddish-brown, thick with broad, flat ridges divided by shallow furrows
TWIGS: stout, rough from the persistent leaf bases, lacking hairs
BUDS: rounded at the base and tapering to a point, approximately ¾ inch long
LEAVES: dark green, 4–6 inches long, in clusters of 2
LEAF SCARS: rounded and raised on young twigs, becoming indistinct on older branches
CONES: broadly ovoid to globose, 1–2 inches long, lacking spines, dropping soon after releasing seed
SEEDS: winged, wind-dispersed
WOOD: resinous, hard, pale red with a whitish sapwood
CURRENT CHAMPION: Erie County, diameter 3 feet 11 inches, height 71 feet, spread 54 feet

In Pennsylvania red pine grows on mountain tops and other dry gravelly or sandy soils in the northern part of the state. It occurs in mixed stands with deciduous species and other conifers. It has also been extensively planted in for-

Red pine—bark

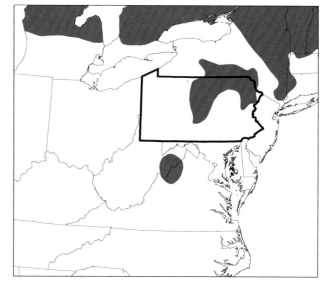

Red pine

Red pine—branch

Red pine—cone x1

Red pine—needle cluster

est plantations, many of which date from the Civilian Conservation Corps efforts of the 1930s. The overall range of red pine is from Nova Scotia to Minnesota and south to Pennsylvania making our state and a few isolated spots in West Virginia the southern limit of this species today.

The brittleness of fresh needles (they will snap cleanly if bent in half) provides a reliable check on the identification of this species.

The seeds of red pine (and white pine) were gathered by many Native American groups and cooked with meat. Preparations of the leaves and bark were used as a stimulant and to treat headache and backache. Red pine is also a valuable timber species with many uses ranging from heavy construction to pulpwood.

Scots pine   *Pinus sylvestris* L.

FORM: to 90 feet, conical when young, becoming rounded or flat-topped

BARK: distinctly orange-red in the upper part of the tree

TWIGS: greenish-brown, blunt-tipped, and lacking hairs

BUDS: slender, cylindrical, often with buds of male cones clustered around the base, the entire stem tip encased in dried resin

LEAVES: in clusters of 2, strongly twisted, 1–2½ inches long, bluish-green

LEAF SCARS: small, rounded with a bract just below each scar on the young twigs, scars oval and raised on older wood

CONES: narrowly ovoid, 1–2½ inches long, symmetrical, falling soon after the seeds are shed

SEEDS: about ¼ inch with a papery wing, wind-dispersed

WOOD: light reddish brown

CURRENT CHAMPION: Warren County, diameter 3 feet 4 inches at 1 foot, height 66 feet, spread 21 feet

*Scots pine—
needle cluster x1*

Scots pine is a Eurasian species that is widely planted and occasionally naturalized here. Native across northern Europe and Asia, it grows to 140 feet and is widely used for lumber. Here it is generally a smaller tree and is grown mainly for pulpwood and Christmas trees.

Scots pine—bark

Scots pine—twig

Scots pine—cone x1

Short-leaf pine, yellow pine
Pinus echinata **P. Mill.**

FORM: to 120 feet tall and 4 feet in diameter with a rounded or conic crown

BARK: red-brown and scaly

TWIGS: glaucous at first, later reddish-brown

BUDS: slender, cylindrical, and ½–¾ inch long, often with buds of male cones clustered around the base

LEAVES: mostly 2 per cluster (occasionally 3), 2½–4½ inches long, stiff and yellowish-green

LEAF SCARS: small, oval, raised

CONES: ovoid-conic, 1½–3 inches long, cone scales with a sharp prickle

SEEDS: about ¼ inch with a papery wing, wind-dispersed

WOOD: yellowish or dark brown, hard and strong, very desirable lumber for many uses

CURRENT CHAMPION: Franklin County, diameter 2 feet 8 inches, height 75 feet, spread 56 feet

Short-leaf pine is not common in Pennsylvania, occurring mostly in the south central counties, where it is usually found mixed with hardwoods in dry upland forests. Short-leaf pine is classified as undetermined by the Pennsylvania Natural Heritage Program. Its total range extends from southern New York to Florida and west to Kansas and Texas.

Although the source of very desirable lumber farther south, short-leaf pine has never been abundant enough in Pennsylvania to be economically important here.

Short-leaf pine—bark

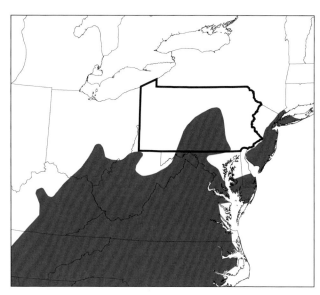

Short-leaf pine

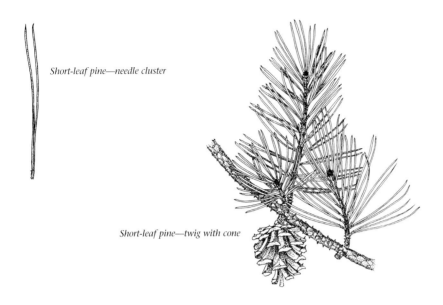

Short-leaf pine—needle cluster

Short-leaf pine—twig with cone

Table Mountain pine

Pinus pungens Lamb.

FORM: to 36 feet, with a broad, open crown
BARK: dark reddish-brown with shallow fissures
TWIGS: stout, roughened
BUDS: cylindrical, ½–¾ inch long, resinous
LEAVES: dark green, 1–3 inches long, twisted, in clusters of 2
LEAF SCARS: hidden by an overlapping bract on young twigs, small and oval and somewhat raised on older twigs
CONES: broadly ovoid, 2½–4 inches long, often asymmetrical at the base, long persistent; cone scales with a stout, spreading or upwardly curved spine
SEEDS: ¾–1 inch long including the wing
WOOD: resinous, coarse-grained
CURRENT CHAMPION: Franklin County, diameter 2 feet 1 inch, height 78 feet, spread 39 feet

Table Mountain pine is a small to medium-size, slow-growing tree of dry rocky or gravelly slopes

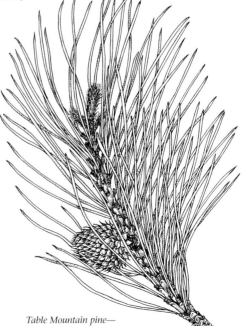

Table Mountain pine—cone

Table Mountain pine— needle cluster

Table Mountain pine— twig with immature seed cone

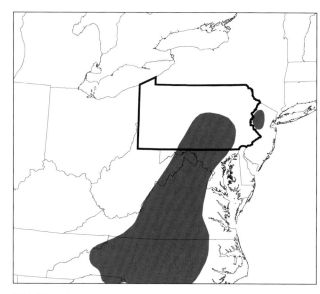

Table Mountain pine—bark   *Table Mountain pine*

and ridges. Its most distinctive characteristic is the large cone with stout, curved spines. In Pennsylvania it occurs mainly in the south central region. The total range of the species extends through the Appalachians from southern Pennsylvania to northern Georgia and Tennessee. Table Mountain pine is a pioneer species that usually grows in pure stands, but occasionally occurs mixed with other species.

It is rarely used for lumber due to its small stature and densely branched habit.

Virginia pine   *Pinus virginiana* **P.Mill.**

FORM: to 55 feet (occasionally more), crown irregularly rounded or flattened on top
BARK: gray-brown with scaly plated ridges
TWIGS: slender, red or purple tinged, frequently glaucous
BUDS: slender, cylindrical, approximately ¼ inch long, resinous
LEAVES: in clusters of 2, approximately 2 inches long, twisted, yellow-green, sharp-pointed
LEAF SCARS: small, oval, projecting out from the surface of the twig
CONES: lance-ovoid, 1–2¾ inches long, persisting on the branches after seeds are shed; scales with a slender, stiff prickle
SEEDS: about ¼ inch with a papery wing
WOOD: light, soft, brittle; used for railroad ties, mine props, or fuel
CURRENT CHAMPION: Allegheny County, diameter 2 feet 2 inches, height 92 feet, spread 44 feet

Virginia pine—
seed x1

Virginia pine is a small, irregularly shaped tree with dense branches. It is never strongly conical or symmetrical, even when young. It usually grows in pure stands and is not shade tolerant.

The usual habitat of Virginia pine is dry, sterile, or sandy soils of shale barrens, serpentine barrens, ridge tops, or other rocky areas. In Pennsylvania it occurs mostly in the Ridge and Valley and the Piedmont, and only rarely across the

Virginia pine—bark

Virginia pine

Virginia pine—twig x1/4

*Virginia pine—
needle cluster x1*

Virginia pine—cone x1

northern tier of counties. Unlike pitch pine, which occurs in similar situations, Virginia pine is not fire tolerant. The total range of the species extends from Pennsylvania and Ohio through the Appalachians to Tennessee and Georgia.

Virginia pine has been used for pulpwood and is valued for its ability to grow in areas with dry or low nutrient soils including abandoned agricultural lands and strip mines.

Virginia pine is the preferred larval food plant of the eastern pine elfin butterfly; however, the caterpillars will also feed on pitch pine and short-leaf pine.

Notes

1. DeCoster, Lester A. 1995. *The Legacy of Penn's Woods: A History of the Pennsylvania Bureau of Forestry*. Pennsylvania Historical and Museum Commission, Harrisburg.

PLANETREE—SEE SYCAMORE

PLUM
PRUNUS L.
Rose Family—Rosaceae

The plums are deciduous trees with alternate simple leaves that are generally elliptical, pointed at the tip, and toothed on the edges. Plum flowers have 5 white petals, 5 sepal lobes, and 15–30 stamens attached to a cup-like hypanthium that surrounds the superior ovary with its single style and stigma. All species are bee-pollinated. The fruit is a drupe characterized by a fleshy outer layer and a bony inner layer (stone), which surrounds the actual seed. The stone is flattened with a prominent ridge. The seeds are dispersed by fruit-eating birds and mammals.

The fruits of wild plums were an important food for Native Americans; they were eaten fresh and dried in large quantities for winter use. The twigs were bound together to make brooms, and the inner bark was used to prepare a yellow or red dye. Medicinal uses included a compound decoction of the inner bark that was used as a disinfectant, as well as treatments for asthma, mouth cankers, and diarrhea. Early settlers used wild plum fruits in pies, jellies, and preserves.

Wild plums are also an important food source for wildlife. Grouse, quail, pheasant, many songbirds, bear, deer, raccoon, and small mammals consume the fruit and several butterflies and moths rely on the leaves as a larval food.

Another member of the genus *Prunus*, the cultivated peach [*Prunus persica* (L.) Batsch] was a common feature of Native American villages when the first European settlers arrived in what is now the eastern United States, apparently the result of early contact with Spanish explorers. William Penn mentioned peaches in listing the fruits of his province of Pennsylvania.[1] Other early travelers also mentioned the prevalence of peach trees. Although peaches are still widely grown in the eastern United States, there is no evidence that they have ever become naturalized.

Allegheny plum   *Prunus alleghaniensis* Porter

FORM: straggling shrub or small tree to 12 feet with a rounded crown

BARK: dark, roughened with age

TWIGS: slender, dark reddish-brown to black, hairy when young, sometimes bearing short spine-like side shoots

PITH: homogeneous

BUDS: reddish, 1/10 inch long, tapering to a pointed tip, covered with overlapping red scales; terminal bud absent

LEAVES: alternate, simple, 2–3 inches long, narrowly elliptic, tapering to a pointed tip, glands present at the base, dark green above, paler and often hairy beneath; edges sharply toothed

FALL LEAF COLOR: drab brown

STIPULES: narrow, falling early

LEAF SCARS: small, elliptical, with 3 bundle scars

FLOWERS: white or pinkish, about 1/2 inch wide, covering the branches before the leaves have expanded

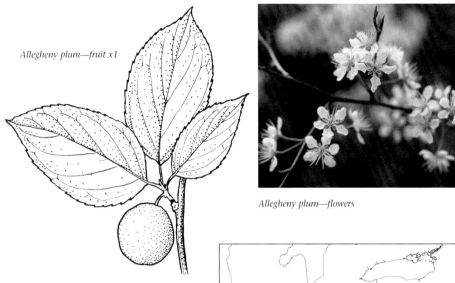

Allegheny plum—fruit x1

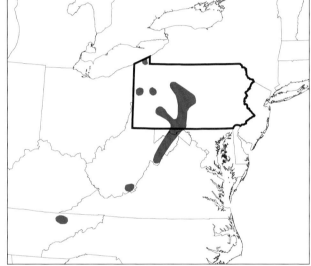

Allegheny plum—flowers

FRUIT: dark purple, often with a white waxy coating that give them a bluish hue, about ½ inch in diameter, edible

SEEDS: flattened, about ⅖ inch long

WOOD: reddish-brown, hard and close-grained but not commercially important due to its small size

CURRENT CHAMPION: none recorded

Allegheny plum is a rare plant of dry rocky slopes and shale barrens in south central Pennsylvania, Maryland, West Virginia, and eastern Tennessee. Its rarity is reflected by its recommended status as a threatened species by the Pennsylvania Natural Heritage Program.

Allegheny plum

American plum, wild plum *Prunus americana* Marshall

FORM: small tree to 30 feet with a broad, spreading crown, often forming thickets

BARK: dark grayish-brown, becoming scaly with age

TWIGS: green at first, becoming reddish with conspicuous lenticels, in the second year developing short, spine-like side shoots

PITH: yellow to brown, homogeneous

BUDS: less than ⅛ inch long, triangular, covered with numerous overlapping chestnut brown bud scales that have a hairy edge, flower buds clustered; terminal bud absent

LEAVES: 2–4 inches long, rounded at the base, tip pointed, edge with large and

American plum—bark

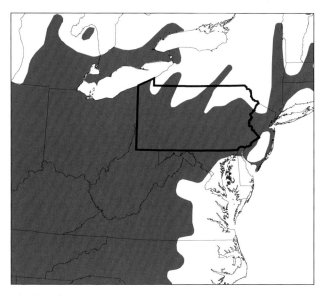

American plum

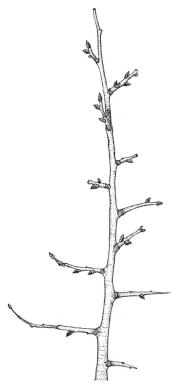

American plum—dormant twig

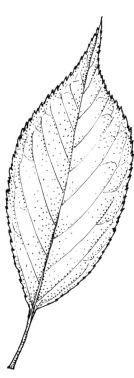

American plum—leaf x1

small teeth alternating; leaf stalk and base of the leaf blade with several tiny glands

FALL LEAF COLOR: drab brown

STIPULES: falling early but leaving a narrow scar on each side of the leaf base

LEAF SCARS: oval with 3 bundle scars

FLOWERS: white, 1 inch wide, numerous, covering the branches when the leaves are just beginning to expand; stalks and sepals smooth

FRUIT: about 1 inch in diameter, yellow or red, ripening in late summer

SEEDS: animal-dispersed

WOOD: reddish-brown, heavy, hard, and strong but too small to be commercially useful

CURRENT CHAMPION: none recorded

American plum—flowers

Look for this small tree in hedgerows, forest edges, and roadside banks in late April or early May when it is covered with white flowers. The rest of the year it is inconspicuous and can be hard to find even if you know where it is growing.

American plum grows throughout Pennsylvania except in areas of highest elevations in the northeast and north central regions. Its total range extends from New Hampshire to Manitoba and south to Oklahoma and Florida.

Tiger swallowtail, coral hairstreak, and woodland elfin butterflies feed on the leaves of this species in their larval stages.

Beach plum   *Prunus maritima* Marshall

FORM: small tree to 10 feet with a rounded, spreading crown

BARK: dark, roughened with age

TWIGS: hairy at first, becoming dark and smooth with some short lateral branches ending in thorns

PITH: tan to white, homogeneous

BUDS: leaf buds less than ⅛ inch long, pointed and covered with 6–8 overlapping bud scales; flower buds clustered

LEAVES: alternate, simple, 1½–2½ inches long, upper surface rough and veiny, lower surface hairy; edge finely toothed

FALL LEAF COLOR: drab brown

STIPULES: narrow, deeply fringed, falling early

LEAF SCARS: small, crescent-shaped with 3 bundle scars

FLOWERS: white, about ¾ inch in diameter, covering the branches in late April before the leaves have expanded, stalks and sepals densely covered with short hairs

FRUIT: purplish-black or sometimes red or yellow, with a waxy white coating, about ¾ inch long

SEEDS: flattened, animal-dispersed

WOOD: dark red in color but too small to be commercially valuable

CURRENT CHAMPION: none recorded

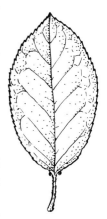

Beach plum—leaf x1

While primarily a tree of coastal sand dunes from New Brunswick, Canada to

Beach plum—bark

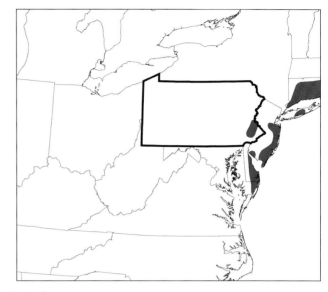

Beach plum

Beach plum—
flower detail x2

Beach plum—flowers

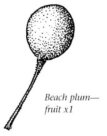

Beach plum—
fruit x1

Maryland, beach plum grows at several sites on the red shale of the Brunswick Formation in Bucks and Montgomery Counties, Pennsylvania, far from the salty sea breezes. Because of its limited occurrence in the state it is classified as endangered by the Pennsylvania Natural Heritage Program. Like our other native plums, beach plum is a small tree that is most conspicuous when in flower. It is distinguished from American plum by the presence of short hairs on the flower stalks and sepals.

Chickasaw plum

Prunus angustifolia Marshall

FORM: small tree to 15 feet, densely branched and thorny, often forming thickets

BARK: dark reddish brown, shallowly furrowed with curling papery scales

TWIGS: reddish becoming dark brown, short lateral branches ending in spines; lenticels prominent

PITH: white, continuous

BUDS: small, pointed, red brown, clustered at the ends of the twigs

LEAVES: 1–2 inches long, elliptic, often folded lengthwise and curved along the midrib; edge with glandular teeth

FALL LEAF COLOR: yellow

STIPULES: present but falling early

LEAF SCARS: small, elliptic, with 3 bundle scars

FLOWERS: white, about ⅜ inch wide, opening when the leaves are very tiny in early to mid-April, sepals smooth on the outer surface, hairy on the inner side

FRUIT: red or yellow, rounded with a slight crease on one side, about ¾ inch in diameter, edible

SEEDS: flattened with rounded surfaces, animal-dispersed

WOOD: hard, red brown with lighter sapwood, too small to be of commercial significance

CURRENT CHAMPION: none recorded

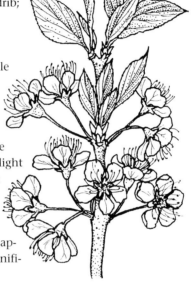

Chickasaw plum—flowers x1

Chickasaw plum—bark

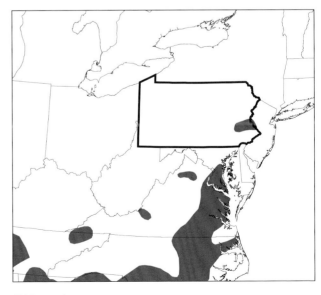

Chickasaw plum

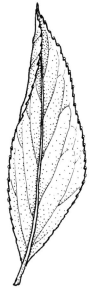

Chickasaw plum—
leaf x3

Pennsylvania is at the northern edge of the natural range of chickasaw plum, and the species is known from only three sites in the state, all in the southeast. It grows in hedgerows or old fields. Chickasaw plum occurs from Virginia to Florida and west to Kansas and Texas, but it ranges north irregularly to New Jersey, Pennsylvania, Ohio, and Nebraska.

Very similar to American plum, it is distinguished by its narrow leaves with glandular teeth.

Notes

1. Penn, William. 1683. Letter to the Committee of the Free Traders. In Myers, Albert Cook. 1912. *Narratives of Early Pennsylvania, West New Jersey and Delaware 1630–1707*. Charles Scribner's Sons, New York.

POPLAR
POPULUS L.
Willow Family—Salicaceae

The poplars are deciduous trees with alternate, simple leaves. Small glands are present at the base of the leaf blade in most species. The twigs have true terminal buds, which are often large and covered with sticky, glistening, often aromatic resin. Flowers are unisexual with staminate and pistillate flowers on separate trees (dioecious). The individual flowers are small and clustered in elongate, drooping catkins that expand before the leaves. Male flowers have 5–40 stamens. Female flowers contain a single pistil, which becomes a capsule containing numerous seeds covered with fine, white hairs. The flowers are wind-pollinated and the seeds wind-dispersed.

The leaves of several poplar species are a larval food source for mourning cloak, red-spotted purple, white admiral, viceroy, aspen duskywing, and dreamy duskywing butterflies. Several sphinx moths and the cecropia moth also feed on poplar in the larval stage.

Poplars are fast growing, but generally short-lived. Most species are early successional trees or species of disturbed habitats. Hybrid poplars have been widely used when rapid tree cover is desired and for generating biomass quickly. Most of those currently available in the nursery trade are crosses between eastern cottonwood (*P. deltoides*) and black poplar (*P. trichocarpa*), which grows in the Pacific Northwest and adjacent areas of Canada.

Balsam poplar, tacamahac　　　　　*Populus balsamifera* L.

FORM: tree to 100 feet, with a narrow, open crown; colonial by means of root suckers

BARK: developing deep furrows between the thick, gray ridges

TWIGS: stout, smooth, light brown tinged with red; lenticels bright orange

PITH: tan, angular in cross section

BUDS: about 1 inch long, pointed, sticky and resin-coated, terminal bud present

LEAVES: 3–6 inches long, ovate with a rounded or slightly heart-shaped base and a long pointed tip, dark green above and lighter beneath with orangey-brown resin blotches; edges toothed; stalk round, often with glands at the base of the blade

FALL LEAF COLOR: brown

STIPULES: present but falling early

LEAF SCARS: narrow with 3 bundle scars

FLOWERS: catkins 4–5 inches long; male flowers with 20–30 stamens, wind-pollinated

FRUIT: capsule about ⅓ inch long, 2-valved

SEEDS: wind-dispersed, germinating immediately

WOOD: light reddish-brown

CURRENT CHAMPION: Philadelphia County, diameter 3 feet, height 89 feet, spread 57 feet

Balsam poplar— twig x1

Balsam poplar—bark

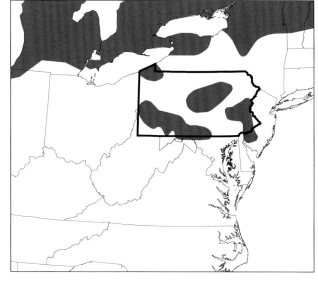

Balsam poplar

Balsam poplar is a northern tree that ranges from Newfoundland to Alaska and grows north to treeline. It occurs at scattered sites in Pennsylvania, usually on wet soils, and is classified by the Pennsylvania Natural Heritage Program as an endangered species.

Records of the use of the aromatic, resin-covered buds of balsam poplar to make a healing salve go back to the Icelandic manuscripts. Native Americans also applied a poultice of fresh leaves to sores to draw out infection. Decoctions of buds were used to treat colds and cough. In addition to its medicinal uses, resin from the buds was used as an insect repellent.

Balsam poplar provides food for deer, beaver, porcupine, grouse, and several songbirds. The wood is used for boxes, crates, and paper pulp, although in Pennsylvania the species is too rare to ever have had commercial significance.

Balsam poplar—leaf

Balm-of-Gilead (*Populus* x *jackii* Sarg.) is believed to be a hybrid of *Populus balsamifera* and *P. deltoides*. It is cultivated widely and occasionally naturalized. It was first introduced in 1900.

Big-tooth aspen   *Populus grandidentata* Michx.

FORM: erect tree to 50–70 feet, crown becoming open and irregular

BARK: light grayish-green when young with diamond-shaped patterns, becoming rough and furrowed in age

TWIGS: slender, yellowish-brown with a woolly surface

PITH: white, angular or star-shaped in cross section

BUDS: ¼–½ inch long, pointed, covered with 6–7 light chestnut-brown scales, hairy toward the tip

Big-tooth aspen—male catkins

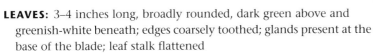

*Big-tooth aspen—
female catkins x1*

LEAVES: 3–4 inches long, broadly rounded, dark green above and greenish-white beneath; edges coarsely toothed; glands present at the base of the blade; leaf stalk flattened

FALL LEAF COLOR: yellow to brown

STIPULES: present but falling early

LEAF SCARS: crescent-shaped with 3 bundle scars

FLOWERS: wind-pollinated; male flowers with 5–12 stamens

FRUIT: a 2-valved capsule

SEEDS: tiny, dark brown with copious white hairs, wind-dispersed

WOOD: light and weak, used for paper pulp and miscellaneous small items

CURRENT CHAMPION: Erie County, diameter 3 feet 10 inches, height 79 feet, spread 75 feet

Big-tooth aspen is a frequent component of early successional forests throughout Pennsylvania; it is eventually replaced by more shade-tolerant species. Its total range extends from Nova Scotia and Minnesota south to North Carolina,

Big-tooth aspen—bark

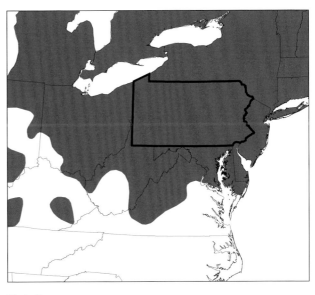

Big-tooth aspen

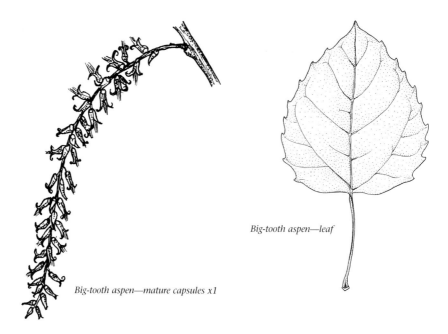

Big-tooth aspen—leaf

Big-tooth aspen—mature capsules x1

Kentucky, and Iowa. It is best recognized by its coarsely toothed leaves and light grayish-green bark with diamond-shaped markings.

Native Americans used an infusion of the bark of big-tooth aspen to treat menstrual problems. In addition the cambium layer was scraped, boiled, and eaten. Ruffed grouse, quail and several songbirds feed on the buds and catkins; deer, beaver, and rabbits eat the bark, buds, branchlets, and leaves. The wood is used for paper pulp.

Eastern cottonwood *Populus deltoides* **Marsh.**

FORM: fast growing tree to 100 feet with a rounded crown and spreading branches

BARK: thin, smooth, and greenish-yellow on young trees, becoming deeply furrowed and gray-brown with age

TWIGS: stout, smooth, yellowish brown with prominent lenticels

PITH: white, angular or star-shaped in cross section

BUDS: ½–¾ inch long, smooth, chestnut brown with a sticky, aromatic coating

LEAVES: broadly rounded-triangular, 3–5 inches long, with 2–5 glands at the base of the blade where it joins the stalk, bright green above and beneath, smooth and leathery; edges with rounded teeth; leaf stalk strongly flattened

FALL LEAF COLOR: yellow

STIPULES: present but falling early leaving conspicuous scars

LEAF SCARS: oval to somewhat triangular with 3 bundle scars

FLOWERS: wind-pollinated; male flowers with 6 to many stamens,

FRUIT: a 3- to 4-valved capsule

SEEDS: small, covered with long white hairs, wind-dispersed

WOOD: soft, white; used for boxes, crates, and paper pulp

CURRENT CHAMPION: Dauphin County, diameter 8 feet 9 inches, height 124 feet, spread 105 feet

Eastern cottonwood—bark

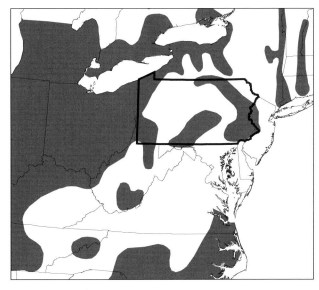

Eastern cottonwood

*Eastern cottonwood—
male catkins*

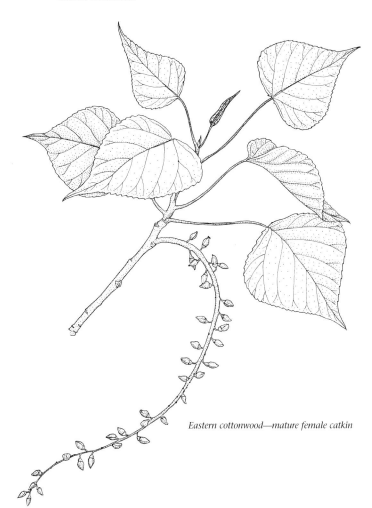

Eastern cottonwood—mature female catkin

The white hairs that serve as the seed dispersal mechanism of eastern cotton-wood accumulate on the ground like drifts of snow in early summer hence the name cottonwood. A tree of floodplains and swamps, eastern cottonwood forms tall gallery forests along the tidal regions of the lower Delaware River in south-eastern Pennsylvania, even on some very disturbed sites. Eastern cottonwood also grows in southwestern Pennsylvania and at other scattered sites, mainly on floodplains. It ranges from Quebec and New England to Florida and Texas and west to Kansas and the Dakotas. The eastern cottonwood is *P. deltoides* var. *deltoides*. A closely related variety, *P. deltoides* var. *occidentalis*, is the common tree of stream courses in the Great Plains.

The bark of eastern cottonwood, in combination with that of blackhaw and wild plum, was used by Native Americans to treat weakness and debility in women. A decoction of the bark was used to treat intestinal worms and steam from a decoction of stems, bark, and leaves was used to treat snakebite. Cotton-wood twigs are a good source of winter browse for deer and other animals.

Carolina poplar (*Populus* x *canadensis* Moench) includes a group of hybrids of eastern cottonwood and Lombardy poplar with erect branches and spreading by root shoots. These trees tend to have the leaves and habit of eastern cottonwood and buds and twigs more like Lombardy poplar. It is cultivated and occasionally escaped.

Lombardy poplar, black poplar   *Populus nigra* L.

FORM: erect and narrow to 100 feet, with numerous upright branches

BARK: thick, ridged, and furrowed

TWIGS: smooth, olive-green becoming gray; 3 ridges extend down the twig from the base of each leaf stalk

PITH: white, angular or 5-sided in cross section

BUDS: ⅓ inch long, reddish-brown, sticky and glistening

LEAVES: nearly triangular, 2–4 inches long, bright green above and paler beneath, edge with small, rounded teeth; leaf stalk flattened

FALL LEAF COLOR: brown

STIPULES: present initially but falling early

LEAF SCARS: oval with 3 bundle scars

FLOWERS: only male flowers are known for Lombardy poplar

FRUIT: none formed

SEEDS: none

WOOD: soft and light

CURRENT CHAMPION: Luzerne County, diameter 1 foot 8 inches, height 74 feet, spread 16 feet

Lombardy poplar—bark

This species is native to Western Europe, North Africa, and Russia. The narrow, erect form known as the cultivar "Italica" originated near Lombardy in Italy and

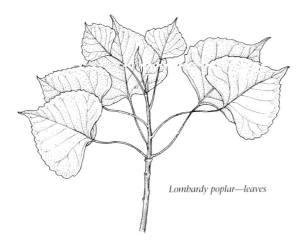

Lombardy poplar—leaves

has been in cultivation since the early 1700s as Lombardy poplar. Like many poplars it tends to be colonial from root shoots.

Swamp cottonwood *Populus heterophylla* L

FORM: erect, 70–90 feet with a narrow crown

BARK: thick, brown, strongly longitudinally ridged and furrowed

TWIGS: stout, gray-brown, covered with fine white hairs

PITH: orange, angular or 5-sided in cross section

BUDS: terminal buds ½–¾ inch long, reddish brown, somewhat resinous

LEAVES: up to 6 inches long, rounded to heart-shaped at the base with a rounded tip, dark green above and whitened and hairy beneath; leaf stalk rounded

FALL LEAF COLOR: pale yellow to brown

STIPULES: present initially but falling early

LEAF SCARS: triangular with 3 bundle scars

FLOWERS: unisexual, in 1- to 3-inch-long dangling catkins, wind-pollinated

FRUIT: capsules about ½ inch long with a long stalk, well spaced on the 4- to 6-inch-long fruiting catkins

SEEDS: released in the spring, wind-dispersed

WOOD: soft and light, pale brown, harvested in the south for the manufacture of boxes and crates

CURRENT CHAMPION: none recorded

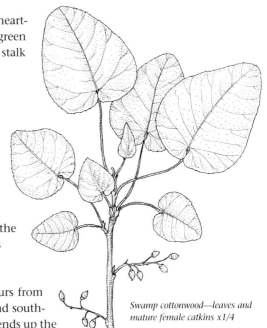

Swamp cottonwood—leaves and mature female catkins x1/4

Swamp cottonwood is a southern tree that occurs from Florida and Louisiana to southern New Jersey and southeastern Connecticut on the east coast; it also extends up the Mississippi Valley to southern Illinois. The only evidence that swamp cottonwood ever grew naturally in Pennsylvania is a herbarium specimen from 1828 collected in moist woods in East Marlborough, Chester County by the noted local botanist William

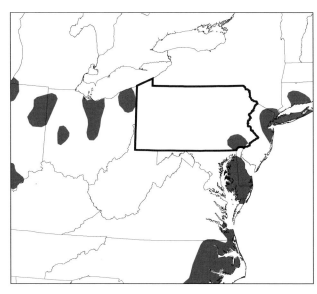

Swamp cottonwood

Darlington. It is classified as extirpated in the state by the Pennsylvania Natural Heritage Program.

Trembling aspen, quaking aspen   *Populus tremuloides* Michx.

FORM: a small, colony-forming tree usually 30–40 feet but occasionally to 60 feet with a narrow crown

BARK: smooth and light gray to white when young, becoming deeply fissured and almost black on older trees

TWIGS: slender, reddish-brown, glossy

PITH: white, angled, or star-shaped in cross section

BUDS: sharp-pointed, smooth and shiny, covered by 6–7 reddish-brown bud scales

LEAVES: rounded-triangular to nearly round, 1½–2 inches long, with a pointed tip, dark green above and pale green beneath; leaf stalk strongly flattened; edges with low rounded teeth

FALL LEAF COLOR: yellow

STIPULES: present but falling early leaving linear scars

LEAF SCARS: egg-shaped, with 3 bundle scars

FLOWERS: wind-pollinated; male flowers with 6–12 stamens

FRUIT: a 2-valved capsule

SEEDS: rarely produced

WOOD: light brown to white with dark brown heartwood, used for paper pulp, dishes and boxes

CURRENT CHAMPION: Cameron County, diameter 2 feet 7 inches, height 102 feet, spread 53 feet

*Trembling aspen—
dormant twig x1*

Trembling aspen is named for the movement of the leaves, whose flattened leaf stalks cause the leaves to flutter with the slightest breeze. A colonial tree that spreads by root shoots, trembling aspen often forms large uniform patches.

Trembling aspen is our widest ranging native tree species, it grows from New-

Trembling aspen—bark

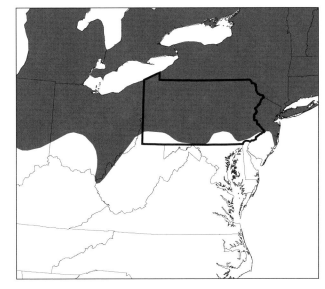

Trembling aspen

Trembling aspen—female catkins

Trembling aspen—leaf

foundland to Alaska and south to California, Mexico, and Kentucky. It occurs throughout most of Pennsylvania, where it is an early successional tree that is especially abundant in cutover or burned areas.

Native Americans employed an infusion of the bark of trembling aspen medicinally to treat intestinal worms and heartburn. A poultice of shredded roots was applied externally to joints for rheumatism. Shredded leaves were applied to bee stings and mouth abscesses. Other uses included treatment of colds, coughs, and venereal disease.

Trembling aspen is the favorite food of beaver; deer browse it and many birds feed on the buds, catkins, and seeds. In addition to the butterflies listed at the beginning of this section, tiger swallowtail, green comma, common tortoise shell, and striped hairstreak larvae also feed on the leaves of trembling aspen.

The wood is used to make boxes and crates and for paper pulp.

White poplar, silver-leaf poplar   *Populus alba* L.

FORM: tree to 75 feet with widely spreading branches and an irregularly rounded crown, colonial by root shoots

BARK: whitish-gray, becoming shallowly furrowed and dark gray to black toward the base of the trunk

TWIGS: white-woolly

PITH: brown, star-shaped in cross section

BUDS: ¼–⅓ inch long; hairy, especially toward the base

LEAVES: 2–4 inches long and prominently 5-lobed on long shoots, 1–2 inches long and unlobed on short shoots, dark green above and densely white-hairy beneath

FALL LEAF COLOR: brown, or sometimes yellowish or reddish

STIPULES: present but falling early

LEAF SCARS: with 3 bundle scars

FLOWERS: wind-pollinated; male flowers with 6–10 stamens

FRUIT: a 2-valved capsule

White poplar—bark

SEEDS: wind-dispersed, germinating immediately upon dispersal

WOOD: pale brown, soft, of no commercial value

CURRENT CHAMPION: none recorded

Dark bluish-green leaves with conspicuous white-woolly undersides make this species distinctive; it is also the only poplar with lobed leaves in our range. White poplar is native from central and southern Europe to western Siberia and Central Asia. It occasionally persists or spreads from cultivated sources. Several cultivars selected for growth form or leaf color have been marketed.

Gray poplar (*Populus* x *canescens* (Aiton) Sm.) is a hybrid of *P. alba* and *P. tremuloides* with coarsely toothed but not lobed leaves.

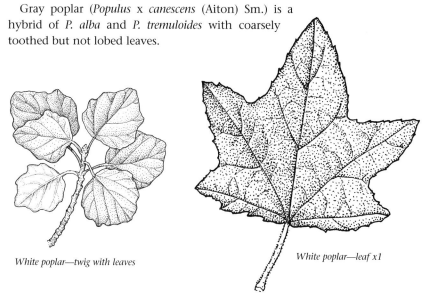

White poplar—twig with leaves

White poplar—leaf x1

PRICKLY-ASH
ZANTHOXYLUM L.
Rue Family—Rutaceae

Prickly-ash, toothache-tree   *Zanthoxylum americanum* Miller

FORM: small tree or large shrub to 25 feet with spiny stems, frequently forming thickets

BARK: thin and smooth, becoming furrowed with age, bearing very stout spines

TWIGS: slender, dark brown and smooth, developing lighter striations, spiny

PITH: white, solid

BUDS: small, rounded, covered with wooly red hairs, terminal bud present

LEAVES: alternate, 6–8 inches long, pinnately compound with 5–11 leaflets, aromatic when bruised

FALL LEAF COLOR: yellow

STIPULES: none, however the paired spines may represent modified stipules

LEAF SCARS: rounded or triangular, slightly raised with 3 bundle scars

FLOWERS: unisexual, male and female flowers on separate trees (dioecious), appearing before the leaves expand, greenish-yellow, insect-pollinated; male flowers containing 5–6 petals and as many stamens; the female flowers with 2–5 pistils

FRUIT: orangey-brown, fleshy, about ⅜ inch in diameter, with an odor of citrus, splitting open to expose 1–2 seeds

SEEDS: black

WOOD: hard, light brown, too small to be of commercial importance

CURRENT CHAMPION: none recorded

Prickly-ash—bark

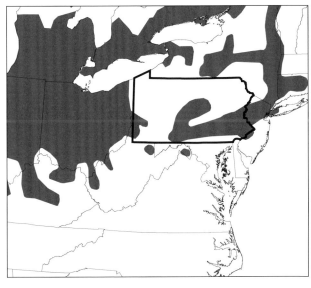

Prickly-ash

The bark and roots of prickly-ash have long been used medicinally to treat toothaches, giving this plant one of its common names. Chewing on the fruits or twigs causes a localized numbing effect in the mouth. In Pennsylvania this small, spiny tree grows in limestone or diabase soils on wet to dry sites mostly in the southern half of the state. Its total range extends from southern Quebec to Georgia and west to eastern Kansas.

In addition to treating toothaches, Native Americans had many other uses for prickly-ash. An infusion of the inner bark was used for heart trouble and bark or pulverized roots were used to relieve the pain of rheumatism. Other preparations were used to treat colds, coughs, pulmonary problems, burns, sore throat, and back pain.

Giant swallowtail and tiger swallowtail butterflies use prickly-ash as a larval food plant.

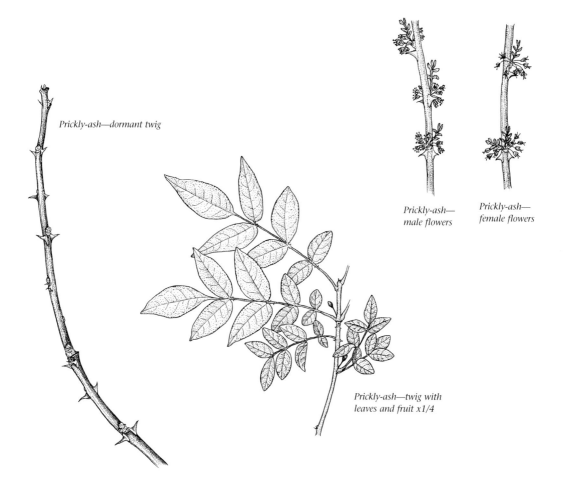

Prickly-ash—dormant twig

*Prickly-ash—
male flowers*

*Prickly-ash—
female flowers*

*Prickly-ash—twig with
leaves and fruit x1/4*

PRINCESS-TREE—SEE EMPRESS-TREE

REDBUD
Cercis L.
Caesalpinia Family—Caesalpiniaceae

Eastern redbud, Judas-tree   *Cercis canadensis* **L.**

FORM: deciduous tree to 36 feet with a short trunk and upright-spreading branches

BARK: dark brown to brownish-black, smooth to shallowly fissured

TWIGS: slender, smooth, light brown, somewhat zigzag

PITH: occasionally with reddish streaks

BUDS: blunt-tipped, with 2–3 visible bud scales, sometimes with several buds above each other at a node; flower buds larger and clustered at the nodes; terminal bud absent

LEAVES: alternate, simple, broadly heart-shaped, 3–5 inches long and equally wide; leaf edge smooth

FALL LEAF COLOR: yellow

STIPULES: present but falling early

LEAF SCARS: triangular to heart-shaped with 3 bundle scars

FLOWERS: magenta-pink, appearing early in the spring before the leaves, in clusters of 4–8 borne directly on the older branches and even the trunk, perfect

FRUIT: a flat pod about 3 inches long and ½ inch wide, frequently persisting on the tree through the winter

SEEDS: several per pod, about ¼ inch long

WOOD: heavy, hard, but not strong, of no commercial significance

CURRENT CHAMPION: Cumberland County, diameter 2 feet 8 inches, height 31 feet, spread 36 feet

Eastern redbud—bark

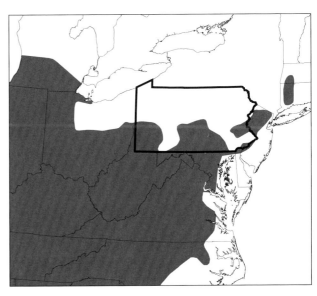

Eastern redbud

There is no mistaking redbud with its small magenta-pink, pea-like flowers arrayed along the major branches and even the trunk before the leaves appear. This tree of limestone and diabase soils is abundant across much of the southern half of the state. Driving through central Pennsylvania about the first week of May you can't miss the wonderful magenta-pink haze it creates in the forest understory. It often occurs with flowering dogwood or shadbush, which bloom at the same time. The range of eastern redbud extends from Connecticut and southern New York west to Nebraska and south to Florida and northern Mexico.

Native Americans used preparations made from the bark of redbud to treat vomiting, fever, and pulmonary congestion. Today redbud is widely grown as a landscape ornamental. It is the primary larval food plant for Henry's elfin butterfly. The flowers also serve as a spring nectar source for Henry's elfin, eastern pine elfin, spring azure, duskywings, and several other early butterflies.

Eastern redbud—flower x1

Eastern redbud—flowers

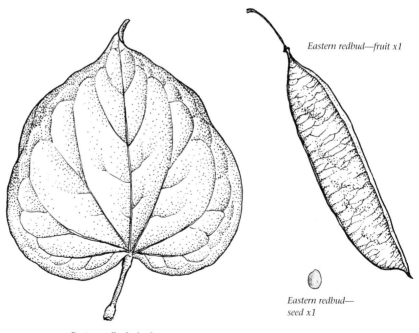

Eastern redbud—fruit x1

*Eastern redbud—
seed x1*

Eastern redbud—leaf

RED-CEDAR
JUNIPERUS L.
Cypress Family—Cupressaceae

Eastern red-cedar   *Juniperus virginiana* **L.**

FORM: 24–36 feet, crown narrowly upright to conic
BARK: reddish-brown, separating in long thin strips
TWIGS: 4-sided
BUDS: inconspicuous
LEAVES: evergreen, of 2 types; in its juvenile stage eastern red-cedar has short, sharp needles that diverge from the twig, the later growth has tiny opposite, scale-like leaves that clasp the twigs tightly. The foliage is bluish-green but often becomes reddish or bronze in the winter.
LEAF SCARS: inconspicuous
CONES: blue, fleshy and berry-like, globose, about ¼ inch long, pollen cones and seed cones are produced on separate trees making this a dioecious species
SEEDS: 1–4 per cone, less than ¼ inch long, brown
WOOD: very durable and rot-resistant, sapwood white, heartwood red
CURRENT CHAMPION: Delaware County, diameter 2 feet 6 inches, height 73 feet, spread 7 feet

Eastern red-cedar—cone x2

Eastern red-cedar is a common tree of old fields, serpentine barrens, diabase glades, rocky ledges, and cliffs in wet to very dry soils. On infertile sites it grows very slowly reaching an age of 200–300 years. Although it occurs at scattered locations throughout the state, it is most common in the southeastern and south central regions. The range of eastern red-cedar extends from Maine to Georgia and Louisiana and west to the edge of the prairie region.

Eastern red-cedar—bark

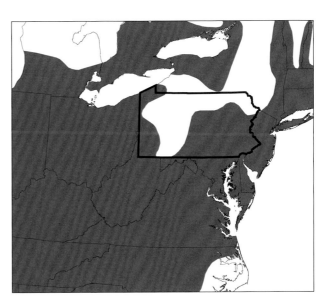

Eastern red-cedar

Eastern red-cedar—cones

Eastern red-cedar is one of the first woody species to invade abandoned agricultural fields or other cleared land, beginning the process of secondary succession through which forest cover is reestablished. It is not unusual in some areas of the state to see dense stands ranging from solid red-cedar to older groves in which deciduous trees are beginning to overtop the pioneers. Birds that eat the fleshy cones disperse the seeds. Dense stands of young red-cedars are often seen under isolated trees in which birds frequently perch.

Eastern red-cedar is often attacked by cedar-apple rust, a fungus disease that causes bright orange galls 1½–2 inches in diameter to form on the twigs. This disease, most conspicuous in the early spring, requires an apple tree as a second host to complete its life cycle.

Peter Kalm, who visited Pennsylvania in 1748–51, reported that the best canoes were made of a single piece of eastern red-cedar "because they last far longer than any other and are very light."[1] We rarely see trees of such large size today. The wood was formerly prized for the making of pencils and is still valued for its aromatic qualities useful for lining closets and chests to protect stored woolens from moths.

Medicinally, eastern red-cedar was found by the colonists to have many applications, as had the European species (*Juniperus sabina*) known as savin, which it resembled. It was taken to induce abortions, apparently sometimes with fatal results to the woman. Other uses included treatments for intestinal worms and venereal disease.

Eastern red-cedar provides food and cover for numerous songbirds and game birds including turkey, pheasant, bobwhite quail, mourning dove, and cedar waxwing. Opossums are also known to eat the cones of this species, and the fre-

Eastern red-cedar—cedar-apple rust gall

Eastern red-cedar—juvenile and adult leaves x1

quency with which a browse line is seen suggests that deer find the foliage to be an acceptable winter food. Eastern red-cedar is a larval food plant for the juniper hairstreak butterfly.

Notes

1. Kalm, Peter. (1772) 1972. *Travels into North America.* Translated by J. R. Forser. Imprint Society, Barre, Mass.

SAPPHIRE-BERRY
SYMPLOCOS JACQ.
Sweetleaf Family—Symplocaceae

Sapphire-berry, Asiatic sweetleaf *Symplocos paniculata*
(Thunb.) Miq.

FORM: small tree to 20 feet with a spreading crown, or sometimes more shrub-like

BARK: gray, becoming shaggy with age

TWIGS: stout, gray

PITH: brown and spongy, homogeneous

BUDS: small, rounded, less than ⅛ inch long

LEAVES: alternate, simple, 1½–3½ inches long, widest toward the tip, dark green and veiny above, hairy on the veins beneath; edge shallowly toothed; leaf stalk hairy, ⅛–⅓ inch long

FALL LEAF COLOR: brown

STIPULES: not present

LEAF SCARS: crescent-shaped with a single raised bundle scar

FLOWERS: white, fragrant, about ½ inch across with 5 petals and numerous stamens, produced in small clusters at the ends of terminal and lateral branches, blooming late May into June

FRUIT: brilliant turquoise-blue, oblong, ⅓ inch long, maturing September-October

SEEDS: dispersed by birds

CURRENT CHAMPION: none reported

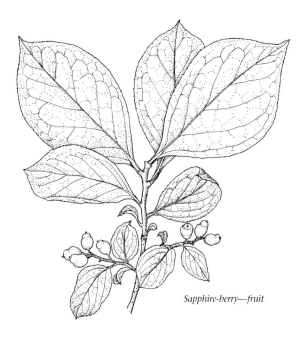

Sapphire-berry—fruit

Sapphire-berry—flowers

Sapphire-berry—bark

Sapphire-berry is occasionally grown as an ornamental and has spread to stream-side locations in urban and suburban forest remnants in southeastern counties. It is native from India to China and Japan where it occurs in mixed forests at 2,500–7,500-foot elevation.

SASSAFRAS

Sassafras Nees

Laurel Family—Lauraceae

Sassafras   *Sassafras albidum* **(Nuttall) Nees**

FORM: erect, medium-sized tree to 60 feet but usually less, with a rounded crown

BARK: reddish-brown, deeply furrowed, aromatic; inner bark mucilaginous when chewed

TWIGS: green, usually curved upward at the tips

PITH: large, white

BUDS: green; terminal bud ovate, sharp-pointed, about ½ inch long

LEAVES: alternate, variable on a single tree or branch, simple, unlobed or with 2–3 rounded lobes, bright green; margins smooth

FALL LEAF COLOR: yellow, orange, or red

STIPULES: none

LEAF SCARS: semicircular with a single bundle scar

FLOWERS: yellow-green, fragrant, opening before or with the leaves, unisexual, the male and female flowers on different plants (dioecious), insect-pollinated

FRUITS: blue, about ⅓ inch long, with a red cup-like calyx at the base

SEEDS: dispersed by birds

WOOD: soft and brittle, aromatic, rot resistant

CURRENT CHAMPION: Delaware County, diameter 4 feet 8 inches, height 68 feet, spread 57 feet

Known to children as the "mitten tree" for its 2- or 3-lobed leaves, sassafras is common throughout all but the most northern counties of Pennsylvania. It is a thicket-forming species of forest edges, fencerows, and old fields, which spreads through its prolific ability to form root shoots. Horizontal branches with up-curved ends give it a candelabra-like form most noticeable in the winter. The pale yellow flowers, which emerge just before the leaves expand, are fragrant but not conspicuous. In the autumn the leaves take on brilliant red, orange, and yellow hues, which contrast with the dark blue fruits. All parts of the plant have a spicy aromatic odor.

The native range of sassafras extends from Vermont and New Hampshire to northern Florida and west to Missouri and eastern Texas.

Native Americans had many uses for sassafras; medicinal applications reported by the earliest European visitors to North America included treatment of scurvy, syphilis, dropsy, and rheumatism. Word of its wonderful curative powers was sent back to Europe, along with samples, as early as 1574. Several subsequent voyages to the New World (in 1602 and 1603) were made with the express purpose of obtaining sassafras bark to satisfy the growing demand in Europe, where it was widely sought after for its reputed panacea-like effects.[1] Sassafras was one of the first exports from the Jamestown settlement in Virginia; however, it was not long before sassafras began to lose its luster as it failed to live up to the extravagant claims.

Additional uses included sassafras tea made from the flowers, which became a

Sassafras—bark

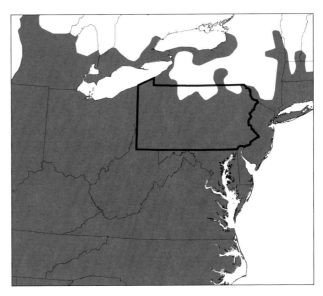

Sassafras

Sassafras—male flowers

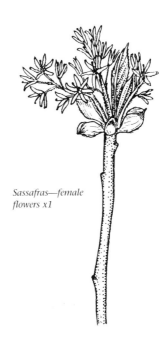

Sassafras—female
flowers x1

Sassafras—male flower detail x2

Sassafras—female flower detail x2

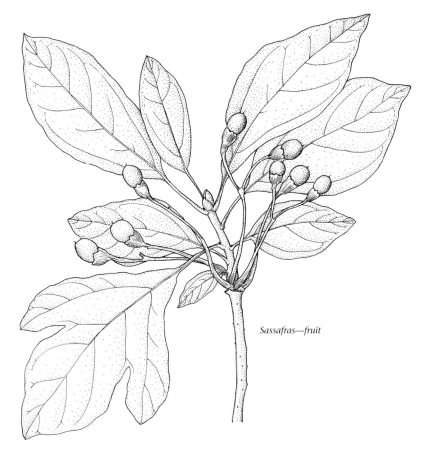

Sassafras—fruit

favorite drink of the colonists. An orange dye for wool was made from the bark, and chips of aromatic sassafras wood were placed in chests and closets to repel clothes moths. In modern times oil of sassafras was used to flavor root beer, until the discovery of carcinogenic properties caused it to be banned by the U.S. Food and Drug Administration in the 1960s.

The fleshy blue fruits are a valuable food for birds, which disperse the seeds. Larvae of tiger swallowtail and spicebush swallowtail butterflies and the promethea moth feed on the leaves.

Notes

1. The Voyage of Martin Pring, 1603, in Burrage, Henry S., D.D. (ed.) 1932. *Early English and French Voyages 1534–1608, Chiefly from Hakluyt.* Charles Scribner's Sons, New York.

SCHOLAR-TREE—SEE PAGODA-TREE

SHADBUSH
AMELANCHIER MEDIK.
Rose Family—Rosaceae

The shadbushes are deciduous shrubs or small trees with alternate simple leaves. Their white flowers are visible in forests and hedgerows in the early spring where they are one of the first native woody plants to flower. The name shadbush reflects the fact that the flowers appear about the time the shad are migrating upstream to spawn in the Delaware and Susquehanna Rivers. The alternate name serviceberry derives from the fact that these trees were blooming about the time traveling preachers of the early frontier were able to get around in the spring to conduct burial services for those who had died during the previous winter. "Sarvis-tree," another name that is sometimes applied, is a corruption of "service."

Shadbush flowers have 5 sepals, 5 white petals, 20 stamens, and a single, inferior ovary; they are insect-pollinated. The flowers are followed by small (⅓–½ inch in diameter) red to purple, apple-like fruits that ripen in June and are a prime food source for wildlife ranging from birds to black bears. Humans find them quite tasty too! The fruits of shadbush were widely used by Native Americans. They were eaten fresh and dried for winter use; many tribes, reportedly, preferred them to blueberries.

Leaves of shadbush are food for the larvae of tiger swallowtail, viceroy, red-spotted purple, white admiral, and striped hairstreak butterflies.

Hybridization, polyploidy, and other forms of irregular reproductive behavior can make shadbush plants difficult to identify to species. Only the tree-like species are included here; the Pennsylvania flora also includes six shrubby *Amelanchiers*.

Downy shadbush, downy serviceberry, downy Juneberry　　　　*Amelanchier arborea* (F. Michaux) Fernald

FORM: erect deciduous shrub or small tree to 45 feet with a narrow crown
BARK: smooth, gray with darker stripes or fissures developing with age
TWIGS: slender, green to purplish-brown
PITH: small, greenish, and angular
BUDS: slender, pointed, ¼–½ inches long, covered with several overlapping bud scales, greenish-yellow or brown, slightly curved toward the twig
LEAVES: folded along the midrib when they first emerge, 3–4 inches long when fully expanded with 11–17 pairs of lateral veins and half as many teeth per side, remaining hairy beneath throughout the season at least on the midrib; leaf base heart-shaped
FALL LEAF COLOR: yellow or red
STIPULES: linear, falling early
LEAF SCARS: small, linear with 3 bundle scars
FLOWERS: white, appearing mid-April to early May
FRUIT: maturing in June or July, red to purplish, about ¼ inch in diameter, dryish; sepals reflexed from the base

Downy shadbush—bark

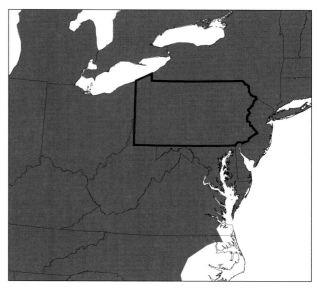

Downy shadbush

Downy shadbush—flowers

SEEDS: animal- or bird-dispersed

WOOD: dark brown streaked with red, heavy, hard, and strong

CURRENT CHAMPION: Susquehanna County, diameter 3 feet, height 53 feet, spread 38 feet

This small understory tree is the common shadbush found in low, wet woods to dry upland forests throughout Pennsylvania. It blooms in late April to mid-May, often combining with redbud to create a spectacular spring display. The fruits of downy shadbush are smaller and drier than those of smooth shadbush, and not as tasty.

Downy shadbush was used by Native Americans as a component of infusions taken to combat intestinal worms and diarrhea. An infusion of the bark was used to treat gonorrhea. The wood has been used for charcoal, mine props, and tool handles.

Downy shadbush—fruit

Smooth shadbush, smooth serviceberry   *Amelanchier laevis* **Wiegand**

FORM: erect shrub or tree to 40 feet
BARK: smooth, gray, becoming fissured with age
TWIGS: dark reddish-brown, smooth
PITH: pale greenish-white, continuous
BUDS: ⅜–⅝ inch long, green tinged with red
LEAVES: elliptic to oblong, 1½–2½ inches long, finely toothed with more than 20 teeth per side, bronzy-red when they first emerge, lower surface smooth
FALL LEAF COLOR: yellow to red
STIPULES: linear, falling early
LEAF SCARS: small, linear with 3 bundle scars
FLOWERS: white, in more or less drooping clusters, appearing mid-April to mid-May when the leaves are half expanded
FRUIT: dark purple-red, ⅓–½ inch in diameter, sweet and juicy
SEEDS: animal- or bird-dispersed
WOOD: heavy, hard, and close-grained
CURRENT CHAMPION: none reported

The sweet, juicy fruits of this species are the best eating of all the *Amelanchier* species. Smooth shadbush is easily distinguished from other species by its half expanded, bronzy red leaves present at flowering time. Additional distinguishing characteristics include the 9–17 pairs of lateral veins, which divide to form an interlacing network prior to reaching the leaf margin.

Smooth shadbush is found throughout Pennsylvania in rocky forests, thickets, and roadsides. Its total range extends from Newfoundland and Ontario to Minnesota, south to Iowa and Indiana, and in the mountains to Georgia.

Native Americans also prepared a tea from the bark that was taken by expectant mothers.

Smooth shadbush—bark

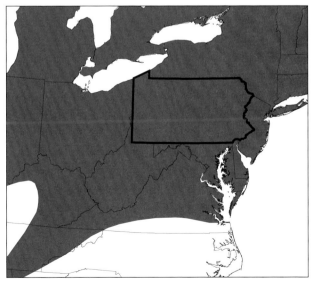

Smooth shadbush

Smooth shadbush—flowers

Smooth shadbush—fruit

SILVERBELL
HALESIA J.ELLIS EX L.
Storax Family—Styracaceae

Carolina silverbell   *Halesia carolina* L.

FORM: small tree to 40 feet with a rounded crown, or sometimes more shrubby

BARK: gray to brown, developing flat ridges with scaly plates

TWIGS: slender, brown, hairy or smooth with finely shredding bark

PITH: white, chambered

BUDS: ⅛–¼ inch long, pointed with dark brown to reddish bud scales; terminal bud absent

LEAVES: alternate, simple, 2–5 inches long, elliptic with smooth to somewhat toothed edges, dark green, smooth above and densely covered with branching hairs beneath

FALL LEAF COLOR: yellow to yellow-green

STIPULES: none

LEAF SCARS: semicircular with 1 bundle scar

FLOWERS: white, to 1 inch long, bell-shaped with 4 petals, perfect, appearing just before the leaves

FRUIT: dry, dangling, brown and woody, 1–1½ inches long with 4 equally spaced, longitudinal wings

SEEDS: 2–3 per fruit

WOOD: soft, close-grained, brown, not commercially important

CURRENT CHAMPION: Allegheny County, diameter 3 feet 3 inches, height 60 feet, spread 66 feet

Carolina silverbell—flowers

Carolina silverbell is a tree of the southern Appalachians from West Virginia to northern Florida and west to Oklahoma. It has become naturalized in Pennsylvania at several locations, but no native stands are known in the state. In its native range it inhabits moist wooded slopes in the Piedmont and the mountains.

Native Americans in the southeast used the wood of Carolina silverbell for construction. Today the tree is grown as an ornamental for its showy spring blooms and handsome reddish-brown, winged fruits.

Carolina silverbell—bark

Carolina silverbell—leaf

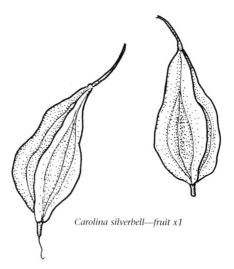

Carolina silverbell—fruit x1

SNOWBELL
Styrax L.
Storax Family—Styracaceae

Japanese snowbell   *Styrax japonicus* Siebold & Zucc.

FORM: deciduous tree to 30 feet with horizontally spreading branches

BARK: smooth, dark gray-brown

TWIGS: slender, light brown, hairy at first, becoming smooth with finely shredding or peeling bark

PITH: small, green, and solid

BUDS: small, brownish without bud scales (naked); terminal bud present

LEAVES: alternate, simple, 1–3 inches long, broadly elliptical with pointed tip and base and shallow rounded teeth, dark green and smooth above, hairy beneath when young, some tufts of branched hairs persisting in the angles of the veins; leaf stalk about ⅓ inch long

FALL LEAF COLOR: yellowish or reddish

STIPULES: none

LEAF SCARS: semicircular with a single bundle scar

FLOWERS: white, bell-shaped, in clusters of 3–6 from short lateral shoots, perfect with 5 petals and 10 stamens; ovary superior with a single style

FRUIT: a dry, fuzzy, gray capsule about ½ inch long that eventually splits open to release the seed

SEEDS: a single large brown seed per fruit

WOOD: not commercially significant

CURRENT CHAMPION: Bucks County, diameter 3 feet 1 inch, height 40 feet, spread 50 feet

Japanese snowbell—bark

Japanese snowbell—flowers

Japanese snowbell is native to China, Korea, Japan, the Philippines, and Taiwan. In China it is a component of the forest understory in mixed mesophytic and evergreen oak forest types. It has been in cultivation in the west since 1862; many cultivars have been selected including double- and pink-flowered forms. In Pennsylvania Japanese snowbell has become naturalized in urban and suburban forest remnants, mainly in the southeast.

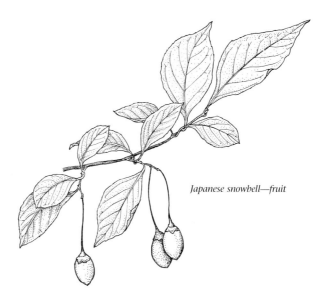

Japanese snowbell—fruit

SOURGUM—SEE BLACKGUM

SOURWOOD
OXYDENDRUM DC.
Heath Family—Ericaceae

Sourwood, sorrel-tree,   ***Oxydendrum arboreum* (L.) DC.**
lily-of-the-valley tree

FORM: deciduous tree to 60 feet with a narrow, erect crown
BARK: gray-brown, deeply furrowed with scaly intersecting ridges
TWIGS: slender, yellowish-green at first, becoming red-brown
PITH: white, homogeneous
BUDS: ⅛ inch long, dark red with overlapping scales; terminal bud lacking
LEAVES: alternate, simple, elliptic, 5–7 inches long; margins finely toothed
AUTUMN LEAF COLOR: orange, scarlet, or purple
STIPULES: none
LEAF SCARS: nearly triangular with a single curved bundle scar
FLOWERS: white, bell-shaped, about ⅓ inch long, perfect; borne in slender, clustered racemes at the ends of the branches; flowering in midsummer; pollinated by bees for whom it is an excellent nectar source
FRUIT: a small dry capsule with 5 segments
SEEDS: wind-dispersed
WOOD: hard and heavy, of little commercial importance
CURRENT CHAMPION: Delaware County, diameter 1 foot 1 inch, height 35 feet, spread 28 feet

Sourwood is a handsome tree, either in flower or in its fall shades of scarlet to purple, a fact attested to by its frequent cultivation as an ornamental. The distinctive midsummer flowers of sourwood, borne in large spreading clusters at

Sourwood—bark

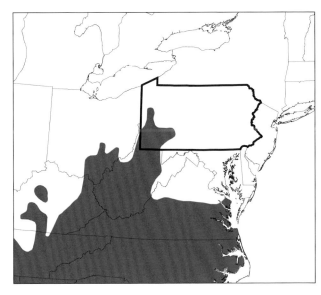

Sourwood

the ends of the branches, make this an easy tree to recognize. As a part of our native flora it is restricted to rocky, wooded slopes in the extreme southwestern corner of Pennsylvania, and has been recommended for listing as a threatened species by the Pennsylvania Biological Survey. The full range of the species extends from Pennsylvania and southern Indiana to northern Florida and Louisiana.

Native Americans used preparations of sourwood to treat diarrhea, dyspepsia, mouth ulcers, lung disease, and asthma. The wood was used to make arrow shafts.

Sourwood is the larval food source for a sphinx moth, and a nectar source for the white M hairstreak butterfly. It is also the source of nectar used by bees to make the highly regarded sourwood honey. The twigs and leaves are heavily browsed by deer; songbirds and mice feed on the seeds.

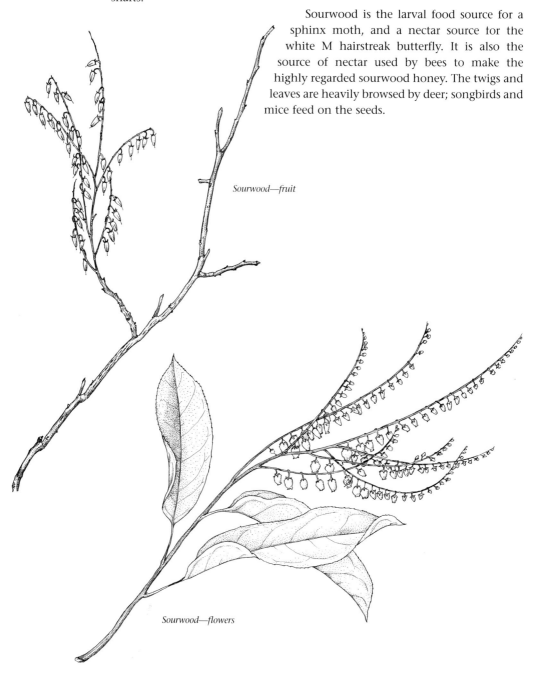

Sourwood—fruit

Sourwood—flowers

SPRUCE
PICEA A.DIETR.
Pine Family—Pinaceae

The spruces are evergreen conifers with needle-like leaves in a spiral arrangement on the twigs. The needles are attached to raised peg-like projections at the base that persist after the needles drop giving the twigs a roughened appearance. Rolling a needle between two fingers will reveal its 4-sided shape. The seed cones of spruce range from less than 1 inch in black spruce to 5–7 inches long in Norway spruce. The cone scales are thin and the winged seeds are wind-dispersed.

We have two native spruces in Pennsylvania, black spruce and red spruce, but they are a relatively minor part of our forests overall. Three additional species are planted and occasionally become naturalized.

Black spruce   *Picea mariana*
(Mill.) Britton, Sterns & Poggenb.

FORM: small tree to 30 feet with a narrow, irregular, pyramidal crown
BARK: rough, scaly, grayish-brown
TWIGS: hairy, roughened with raised leaf bases (sterigmata)
BUDS: ovoid, pointed
LEAVES: ¼–¾ inch long, 4-sided, bluish-green, blunt at the tip
LEAF SCARS: on woody projections along the twigs
CONES: ½–1 inch long; cone scales fan-shaped with an irregularly toothed margin
SEEDS: less than ¼ inch, dark brown, winged, wind-dispersed
WOOD: light, soft, pale yellowish-white
CURRENT CHAMPION: none recorded

Black spruce—cone x1

Black spruce—cone scale x1

Black spruce—seed x1

In Pennsylvania black spruce grows naturally only in sphagnum bogs, usually in the company of tamarack. Although found primarily in the glaciated northeastern part of the state, it grows as far south as Bear Meadows in Centre County. Pennsylvania is the southern limit of range for black spruce. It occurs with increasing abundance to the north where it can be found all the way to the limit of tree growth in the arctic from Newfoundland and Labrador west to Alaska.

Black spruce is a slow growing tree with a narrow, somewhat irregular, spire-like shape with age. In Pennsylvania, red spruce, our other native member of the genus *Picea*, is frequently found in wooded swamps and uplands in close proximity to the glacial wetlands where black spruce grows. The two species are quite similar, differing by the shorter, blunt needles of black spruce that have a bluish-green hue. Black spruce cones are smaller, and the cone scales have an irregularly toothed margin. Black spruce is known to hybridize with red spruce in some parts of its range; however, no hybrids have been identified in Pennsylvania.

Black spruce is frequently host to dwarf mistletoe (*Arceuthobium pusillum*), a tiny parasitic plant that appears as short, branched or unbranched projections growing out of the spruce twigs. Dwarf mistletoe, which is not the same as the

Black spruce—bark

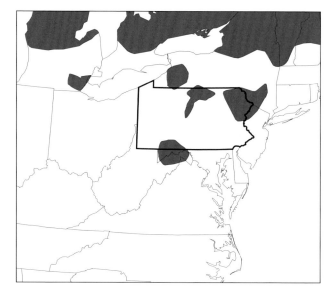

Black spruce

Black spruce—bog habitat

Black spruce—twig

well-known Christmas mistletoe, is classified as a threatened plant by the Pennsylvania Natural Heritage Program.

Black spruce has no commercial value in our state but farther north it is harvested for paper pulp and lumber. Native Americans used the roots to stitch together birch bark to make canoes; spruce gum was used as caulking. The seeds provide food for wildlife including red squirrels.

Black spruce—branch infected with dwarf mistletoe

Blue spruce   *Picea pungens* Sarg.

FORM: to 60 feet, crown broadly conical
BARK: gray-brown, scaly
TWIGS: yellow-brown, glabrous, stiffly horizontal
BUDS: dark orange-brown, rounded to acute
LEAVES: blue-green, ¾–1¼ inch long, rigid, ending in a narrow, pointed tip
LEAF SCARS: on raised sterigmata, with a single bundle scar
CONES: 2½–4½ inches long; cone scales diamond-shaped, widest in the middle
SEEDS: less than ¼ inch, dark brown with a wedge-shaped wing, wind-dispersed
WOOD: light, soft, pale in color
CURRENT CHAMPION: Luzerne County, diameter 3 feet, height 90 feet, spread 40 feet

Blue spruce is a popular landscape ornamental that is native to the Rocky Mountains of western North America. In Pennsylvania it occasionally persists at abandoned home sites, old Christmas tree plantations, or in conservation plantings. The blue color if its needles, caused by a thick layer of wax on the surface, and stiff horizontal branches are distinctive characteristics of this species.

Blue spruce—bark

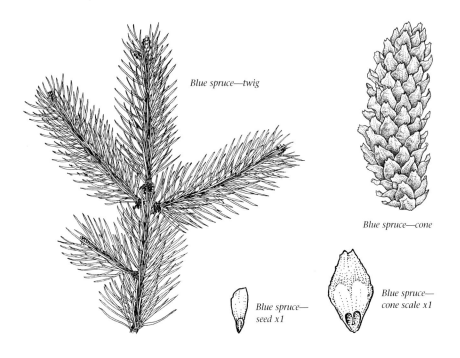

Blue spruce—twig

Blue spruce—cone

*Blue spruce—
seed x1*

*Blue spruce—
cone scale x1*

Norway spruce   *Picea abies* (L.) H. Karst

FORM: to 120 feet, crown conical; secondary branches hanging straight down

BARK: gray-brown, scaly

TWIGS: roughened by raised needle bases (sterigmata), young twigs lacking hairs

BUDS: ovoid, sharp-pointed with reddish scales

LEAVES: linear, 4-sided, ½–1 inch long, dark green, blunt-tipped

LEAF SCARS: on raised sterigmata, with a single bundle scar

CONES: 5–7 inches long, cylindrical; cone scales diamond-shaped, widest at the middle

SEEDS: winged, wind-dispersed

WOOD: light colored, used for construction grade lumber and paper pulp

CURRENT CHAMPION: Susquehanna County, diameter 4 feet 5 inches, height 116 feet, spread 55 feet

Norway spruce—twig

Norway spruce, a native of northern and central Europe, is the most commonly planted spruce in our area; many cultivated forms have been developed. It frequently persists at old or abandoned home sites and has also been used extensively in forest plantations. Norway spruce is also popular for Christmas tree plantings. The large cones, dark green needles, and the distinctive drooping secondary branches of mature trees make it easy to recognize.

Norway spruce—bark

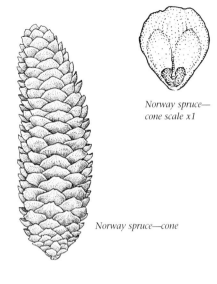

Norway spruce—
cone scale x1

Norway spruce—cone

Red spruce   *Picea rubens* Sargent

FORM: to 90 feet, crown narrowly conical; branches with upturned tips
BARK: reddish-brown, scaly
TWIGS: young twigs hairy
BUDS: ovoid, sharp-pointed with reddish scales
LEAVES: linear, 4-sided, ½–1 inch long, yellowish-green with a pointed tip
LEAF SCARS: on raised sterigmata, with a single bundle scar
CONES: 1–2 inches long; cone scales fan-shaped with an entire or irregularly toothed margin
WOOD: light, soft, pale in color
SEEDS: less than ¼ inch, dark brown, with a broad wing about twice as long as the seed
CURRENT CHAMPION: Wayne County, diameter 3 feet, height 74 feet, spread 29 feet

Red spruce—cone x1

Red spruce is a native tree of moist, cool northern forests and forested swamps in Pennsylvania. This evergreen conifer has a broadly conical form when young, becoming proportionally narrower with age. Needles are yellowish-green, sharp-pointed and ½–1 inch long. Cones are 1–2 inches long, with generally smooth-margined cone scales. The very similar black spruce has smaller cones with irregularly toothed cone scales and shorter, blunt-tipped needles.

Red spruce—
cone scale x2

Red spruce occurs only in northeastern North America, where it ranges from the mountains of North Carolina and Tennessee north to Nova Scotia, Newfoundland, and eastern Ontario. It reaches its greatest abundance in New England and the maritime provinces of eastern Canada. In Pennsylvania red spruce occurs mostly in the Poconos, scattered sites in the north central region, and at high elevations along the Allegheny Front. It sometimes forms dense groves in low swampy areas, or may occur with other components of the northern hard-

Red spruce—seed x2

Red spruce—bark

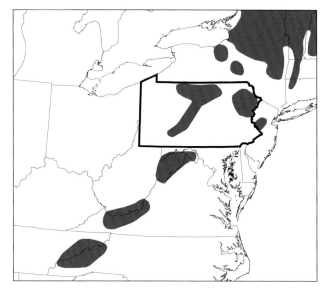

Red spruce

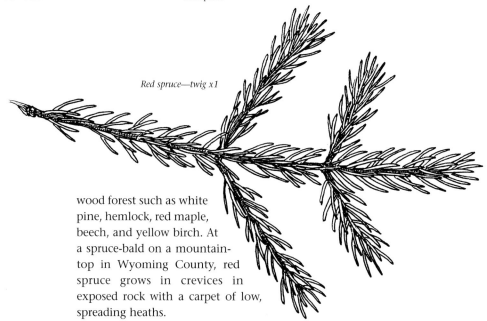

Red spruce—twig x1

wood forest such as white pine, hemlock, red maple, beech, and yellow birch. At a spruce-bald on a mountain-top in Wyoming County, red spruce grows in crevices in exposed rock with a carpet of low, spreading heaths.

Stands of red spruce were harvested in Pennsylvania in the late 1800s and early 1900s with little regard for their sustainability. Today the wood of red spruce is valued for use in making fine musical instruments; however, commercial harvesting of the wood is based farther north.

Native Americans extracted the fibrous inner bark from roots to use for lashing or sewing such items as canoes, snowshoes, and baskets. The resinous gum of spruce trees was chewed prior to the introduction of chicle-based chewing gum. Native Americans made a drink that was effective in preventing scurvy by boiling spruce twigs with maple syrup. Spruce beer, which was brewed by early settlers, had similar benefits.

Red squirrels and other wildlife eat the seeds. Young trees provide winter browse and shelter for deer and rabbits.

White spruce   *Picea glauca* **(Moench) Voss**

FORM: to 120 feet, crown broadly conical when young; secondary branches not drooping

BARK: gray-brown, scaly

TWIGS: pinkish-brown, smooth

BUDS: about ¼ inch, orange-brown, rounded at the tip

LEAVES: linear, 4-sided, ½–¾ inches long, bluish-green with a pointed tip

LEAF SCARS: on raised sterigmata, with a single bundle scar

CONES: 1–2½ inches long; cone scales fan-shaped, usually with an entire margin

SEEDS: winged, wind-dispersed

WOOD: light, soft, pale in color

CURRENT CHAMPION: Cumberland County, diameter 1 foot 11 inches, height 98 feet, spread 24 feet

*White spruce—
cone scale x1*

*White spruce—
seed x1*

White spruce is a native North American species that undoubtedly grew in Pennsylvania during the most recent glacial period that ended approximately 13,000 years ago. Today its range is farther north where it is the dominant tree in interior forests of Canada and Alaska. In Pennsylvania, it is limited to forest plantations and other cultivated sites.

In Canada, white spruce is extensively harvested for wood pulp and lumber. As a species it is extremely variable in form and habitat. It is a larval food plant for the eastern pine elfin butterfly.

White spruce—bark

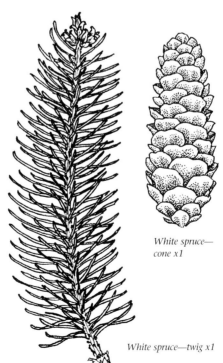

*White spruce—
cone x1*

White spruce—twig x1

SUMAC
RHUS L. AND *TOXICODENDRON* MILL.
Cashew Family—Anacardiaceae

The sumacs are small trees with few branches and alternate, pinnately compound leaves. The twigs are stout and exude milky sap when cut or broken. Staghorn sumac is primarily a plant of dry, open sites, and frequently occurs on roadside banks where it spreads by root suckers to form colonies. It is particularly conspicuous in the fall when its leaves turn brilliant red. Poison sumac, on the other hand, is a wetland plant.

Flowers are perfect or unisexual; they have 5 stamens and/or a single ovary with 3 styles, and are insect-pollinated. Sumac fruits, small berries that are produced in erect or drooping clusters, are eaten by grouse, pheasant, turkey, quail, many songbirds, and small mammals, all of which serve as seed-dispersal agents.

Poison sumac   ***Toxicodendron vernix* (L.) Kuntze**

FORM: small deciduous tree to 20 feet, frequently multistemmed from the base
BARK: smooth, light gray
TWIGS: slender, dark green, and finely hairy when very young, becoming grayish-brown and smooth
PITH: brownish, solid
BUDS: pointed, covered with dark purple overlapping bud scales; terminal bud present
LEAVES: alternate, pinnately compound, to 14 inches long, with 7–13 leaflets; leaflets dark green with red stalks, edges smooth
FALL LEAF COLOR: red
STIPULES: none
LEAF SCARS: large, broadly triangular or rounded with numerous bundle scars
FLOWERS: small, yellowish, regular, unisexual, male and female flowers usually on separate plants (dioecious), in large, branched clusters in the axils of the upper leaves, blooming in early summer after the leaves have expanded; male flowers with 5 sepals, 5 petals, and 5 stamens; female flowers with 1 pistil
FRUIT: small grayish-white drupes about ⅕ inch in diameter, borne in 4–8 inch long drooping clusters, ripening in the early fall
SEEDS: pale yellow, bird-dispersed
WOOD: contains resin channels containing the toxin urusiol; not used commercially
CURRENT CHAMPION: Monroe County, diameter 4 inches, height 26 feet, spread 14 feet

Like its close relative, poison ivy, poison sumac can cause a severe skin rash in sensitive people. However, you are unlikely to encounter it unless you venture deep into swamps. Unlike the more common staghorn sumac, which is a species of dry ground, poison sumac is a plant of wetland habitats. Its drooping clusters of grayish-white fruits are also distinctive.

Poison sumac occurs from southern Quebec to central Florida and west to

Poison sumac—bark

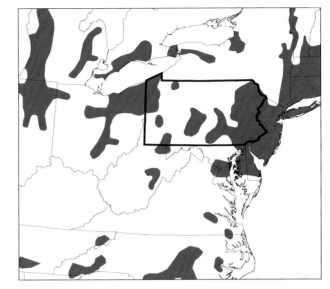

Poison sumac

Poison sumac—fruit x1/4

Texas. In Pennsylvania it is found in swamps, fens, and marshes mainly in the eastern and the western parts of the state.

Native Americans recognized its poisonous qualities and used preparations of poison sumac to treat some forms of ulcers, fever, and ague.

Poison sumac—flowers

Staghorn sumac   *Rhus typhina* L.

FORM: small tree usually not exceeding 30 feet, branches few, upright

BARK: smooth, thin, and papery with numerous lenticels

TWIGS: stout, densely covered with short hairs

PITH: large, orangey-brown, solid

BUDS: terminal bud absent, lateral buds conic, densely covered with rusty hairs

LEAVES: alternate, 16–24 inches long with 11–31 toothed leaflets, central stalk hairy

FALL LEAF COLOR: red

STIPULES: none

LEAF SCARS: large, U-shaped to nearly circular and almost encircling the bud; bundle scars in several clusters

FLOWERS: yellowish-green, about ⅛ inch across, in branched clusters at the ends of the stems in May or June after the leaves have expanded, mostly perfect but some unisexual; insect-pollinated

FRUIT: hairy red drupes produced in dense, upright, cone-like clusters at the ends of the branches

SEEDS: dispersed by birds and small mammals

WOOD: soft, light, golden-brown, formerly used to make small household items

CURRENT CHAMPION: Luzerne County, diameter 11 inches, height 43 feet, spread 27 feet

Staghorn sumac is a common sight on roadside banks, old fields, and forest edges. It turns brilliant red in the fall and the red fruit clusters often persist well into the winter providing a food source for wildlife. It occurs throughout most of Pennsylvania, north to Nova Scotia and Minnesota, south to West Virginia, and at scattered sites to Georgia and Iowa.

Staghorn sumac—bark

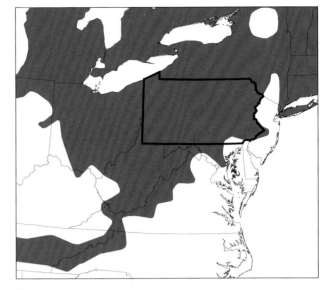

Staghorn sumac

Native Americans had many uses for staghorn sumac, all parts of which are very astringent due to high levels of tannin. The berries were eaten to control vomiting. An infusion of sumac, choke cherry, yellow birch, and dogwood was used to treat rheumatism and a decoction of the flowers was used for stomach pains and as a mouthwash for teething babies. A compound preparation including sumac root was used to treat venereal disease. A gargle for sore throats was prepared from the berries. Gum from the twigs was used to dull toothache pain. The berries have been used for food, fresh or dried, and steeped to make a lemonade-like drink. Red and black dyes were prepared from various parts of the plants. Sumac was also used as a tanning agent for fine leathers.

Staghorn sumac is a nectar source for the striped hairstreak and spring azure butterflies; red-banded hairstreak caterpillars feed on the leaves.

Staghorn sumac—fruit

Staghorn sumac—leaf x1/4

SWEETGUM
LIQUIDAMBAR L.
Witch-hazel Family—Hamamelidaceae

Sweetgum *Liquidambar styraciflua* L.

FORM: deciduous, to 100 feet; crown strongly pyramidal when young, becoming flat-topped to rounded later

BARK: gray-brown, longitudinally furrowed

TWIGS: stout, olive-green the first year, sometimes developing prominent corky wings on the bark

PITH: white, homogeneous

BUDS: pointed, with several overlapping bud scales

LEAVES: alternate, simple, palmate with 5 pointed lobes and a toothed edge

FALL LEAF COLOR: yellow to red and purple

STIPULES: linear-lanceolate, falling early

LEAF SCARS: oval to kidney-shaped with 3 bundle scars

FLOWERS: unisexual, with both sexes present on a single plant (monoecious), wind-pollinated; male flowers in an upright, pyramidal, branched cluster with a single head of female flowers on a long stalk at the base

FRUIT: a prickly, woody capsule 1–1½ inches in diameter

SEEDS: about ¼ inch, winged, wind-dispersed; the capsules also contain many aborted seeds that are smaller and lack wings

WOOD: dark reddish-brown and heavy

CURRENT CHAMPION: Montour County, diameter 4 feet 5 inches, height 100 feet, spread 84 feet

Sweetgum—fruit

Prickly seed capsules covering the ground are a year-round reminder of the presence of sweetgum trees, and a reason why this species is not welcome in some landscape situations. However, its star-shaped leaves with their 5 pointed lobes are distinctive and especially beautiful in the fall when they take on shades of dark purple grading to red and yellow.

Sweetgum is a native tree of the Atlantic Coastal Plain and the lower Mississippi Valley from coastal Connecticut to northern Florida; it extends west to Texas and up to southern Illinois. It also grows naturally in parts of Mexico and Central America. In Pennsylvania sweetgum is currently confined to the narrow strip of coastal plain in southern Bucks, Philadelphia, and Delaware counties with only a few scattered sites remaining where sizeable natural populations still exist. However, pollen identified in sediments at the Sheep Rock Shelter archaeological site in central Pennsylvania indicates that sweetgum occurred there in the past.[1] The genus *Liquidambar* is represented in the Americas by a single species, two others occur in Asia.

Sweetgum prefers low, seasonally wet forests on acidic, sandy, peaty soils; it frequently grows with other coastal plain species such as willow oak and sweetbay magnolia. It is characteristic of two coastal plain forest types: the sweetgum-oak coastal plain forest and the red maple-magnolia coastal plain palustrine forest.

The common name of this tree refers to the aromatic gum known as storax

Sweetgum—bark

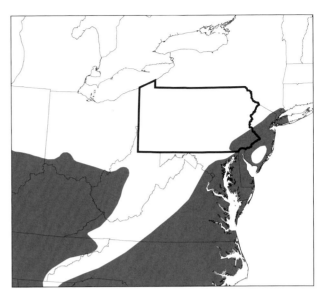

Sweetgum

*Sweetgum—twig
with corky wings*

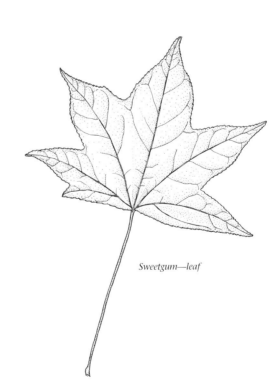

Sweetgum—leaf

Sweetgum—flowers

Sweetgum—fall leaf color

that it exudes when wounded. Storax is used as a natural chewing gum, to flavor tobacco, to perfume soaps and cosmetics, and medicinally to treat coughs, wounds, and dysentery. Sweetgum wood is commercially valuable for furniture and plywood manufacture. Although there was never much of it in Pennsylvania, it is extensively harvested in the southeastern states. Goldfinches, purple finches, squirrels, and chipmunks eat the seeds. Luna and promethea moth caterpillars feed on the leaves.

Notes

1. Michels, Joseph W. and James S. Dutt. 1968. A Preliminary Report of Archaeological Investigations of the Sheep Rock Shelter Site, Huntingdon, Pennsylvania. Occasional Papers in Anthropology No. 5. Department of Anthropology, The Pennsylvania State University, University Park.

SYCAMORE
PLATANUS L.
Planetree family—Platanaceae

Sycamore, planetree, buttonwood   *Platanus occidentalis* **L.**

FORM: deciduous, upright tree to 120 feet with spreading branches

BARK: mottled white and brownish on the trunk and larger limbs, the outer layer flaking off in irregular patches to expose a chalky white surface beneath, chalky white on branches; mature trees develop a brown scaly bark on the trunk.

TWIGS: angular, zigzag

PITH: large, white, homogeneous

BUDS: covered by the expanded, hollow base of the leaf petiole

LEAVES: simple, palmately 3- to 7-lobed, alternate; margins entire to coarsely toothed

FALL LEAF COLOR: yellowish to brown

STIPULES: present but not persistent

LEAF SCARS: ring-like, completely surrounding the bud

FLOWERS: unisexual, in dense spherical heads containing either male or female flowers, wind-pollinated; female flowers with 3–4 distinct pistils and 3–4 sepals plus staminodes; male flowers with 3–6 sepals, an equal number of stamens, and tiny petals.

FRUITS: densely packed in a spherical head about 1 inch in diameter

SEEDS: each fruitlet a 1-seeded achene bearing a tuft of hairs from the base, wind-dispersed

WOOD: light in color, hard, difficult to split

CURRENT CHAMPION: Franklin County, diameter 9 feet 11 inches at 1 foot, height 102 feet, spread 122 feet

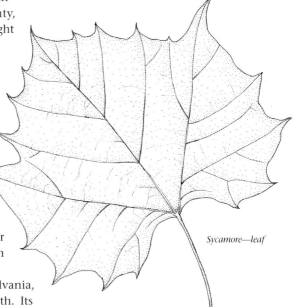

Sycamore—leaf

The chalky white branches of sycamore trees are very conspicuous in the winter landscape marking the courses of streams and rivers or signaling the extent of their floodplains. In addition to the white branches, the mottled white and greenish-tan exfoliating bark of the trunk and larger limbs is also very distinctive. For a few weeks in late July the ground beneath sycamores is littered with irregular pieces of the outer bark, which is shed from the upper branches each year.

Sycamore occurs throughout Pennsylvania, although it is more common in the south. Its total range extends from southwestern Maine to southern Michigan south to Florida and Texas.

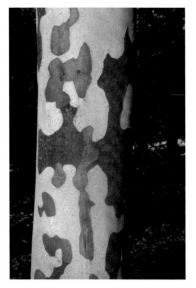

Sycamore—bark of young tree

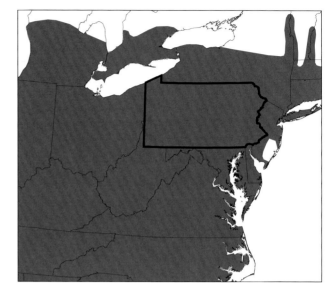

Sycamore

Sycamore—bark of mature tree

Sycamore—fruiting head

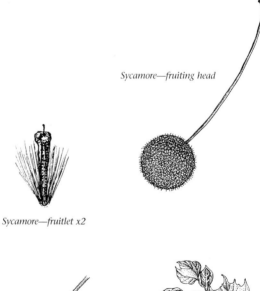

Sycamore—fruitlet x2

Sycamore—bud and
leaf base

Sycamore—flowering
heads

Sycamores are the result of long evolutionary development in the Platanoid lineage, of which the fossil record reaches back to the early Cretaceous, 110 million years ago.

The lobed leaves are late to expand and early to drop, giving the tree popularity as a dooryard specimen on early farmsteads, where it was valued for its shade in the summer but appreciated for allowing the sun to penetrate in the spring and fall. However, some people find the hairs that are shed as the leaves expand irritating.

The flowers appear in spring as the leaves are beginning to emerge. They, and later the fruits, are borne in spherical heads that dangle from the branches on long stalks. The fruiting heads shatter in the late winter and the individual fruitlets, which bear a tuft of hairs, are wind-dispersed.

Native Americans used sycamore to make various medicinal preparations with which they treated colds, coughs, sore throat, and other ills. In addition sycamore trunks were sometimes used for making canoes. More recently the wood has been used for butcher blocks, handles, interior trim, crates, and boxes. Purple finches, juncos, chickadees, and fox squirrels eat the seeds and many animals use the frequent trunk cavities for shelter.

Few other native trees equal the sycamore in size. The journals of François André Michaux, who explored the flora of Pennsylvania for the king of France in the early 1800s, contain descriptions of trees 15–16 feet in diameter along the Ohio River in southwestern Pennsylvania and Ohio.[1]

London planetree   *Platanus x acerifolia* Willd.

CURRENT CHAMPION: Delaware County, diameter 5 feet 8 inches, height 87 feet, spread 93 feet.

London planetree, a frequent urban street tree, is a hybrid between the American sycamore (*Platanus occidentalis*) and the Oriental sycamore (*P. orientalis*). Its bark is yellowish-green mottled with darker greenish-brown patches; the spherical fruiting heads occur 2–3 to a stalk compared to one, or occasionally 2, in the American sycamore. Back crosses with native sycamores apparently occur in urban areas, as trees with intermediate characteristics can be seen along riverbanks and other alluvial areas in cities.

London planetree—bark

Notes

1. Michaux, F. Andrew. 1805. *Travels to the West of the Allegheny Mountains in the States of Ohio, Kentucky, and Tennessee, and Back to Charleston by the Upper Carolines Undertaken in the Year 1802*, September 24, 1801–March 1, 1803 in Reuben Gold Thwaits, (ed.) *Early Western Travels 1748-1846*, Vol. III. Reprint AMS Press, New York.

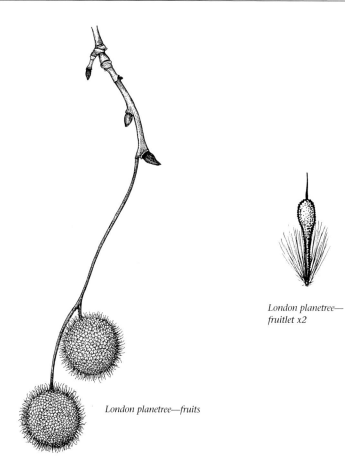

London planetree—
fruitlet x2

London planetree—fruits

TAMARACK—SEE LARCH

TREE-OF-HEAVEN
AILANTHUS DESF.
Quassia Family—Simaroubaceae

Tree-of-heaven   *Ailanthus altissima* **L.**

FORM: to 100 feet with stout branches and few branchlets

BARK: smooth, light gray, old trunks becoming somewhat fissured

TWIGS: stout, yellowish-green to reddish-brown, covered with fine short hairs

PITH: large, light brown

BUDS: lateral buds ⅛–⅙ inch long, located in the notch of the leaf scar; true terminal bud absent

LEAVES: 18–36 inches long, compound with 11–41 pinnately arranged leaflets that have a few coarse teeth near the base that often bear tiny glands

FALL LEAF COLOR: yellowish-green to brown

STIPULES: none

LEAF SCARS: large, heart-shaped with 8–14 bundle scars arranged in a V-shaped line

FLOWERS: unisexual with male and female flowers produced on separate plants (dioecious), appearing in June after the leaves have fully expanded

FRUIT: a samara with the seed in the center and a wing extending on each side

SEEDS: wind-dispersed

WOOD: white to pale yellow, light, soft, and weak

CURRENT CHAMPION: Bucks County, diameter 4 feet 9 inches, height 80 feet, spread 50 feet

Tree-of-heaven—fruit x1

Popularized by Betty Smith in her 1943 classic, *A Tree Grows in Brooklyn*, tree-of-heaven also grows throughout Pennsylvania. This tree, which is native to China,

Tree-of-heaven—bark

Tree-of-heaven—leaves and fruits

Tree-of-heaven—flowers x1/4

was first planted in Philadelphia and New York City in the 1700s. Since that time it has become an aggressive invader of disturbed areas, especially in urban areas and along roadsides throughout the southern and central parts of the state. The tree's prolific seed production and its ability to spread by root sprouts[1] both contribute to its success. In China, tree-of-heaven is a minor component of the canopy of the highly diverse mixed mesophytic forests of the Yangtze Valley.

Tree-of-heaven produces large clusters of greenish-yellow, unisexual flowers at the ends of the branches. Male flowers consist of 10 stamens and have an unpleasant odor. Female flowers have 2–5 ovaries united at the base only. The fruits are produced in large, showy clusters on the female trees, they are reddish at first, fading to dull tan or light brown.

Tree-of-heaven has been shown to produce a chemical (ailanthone) that inhibits the growth of many other plants under experimental conditions and may contribute to its ability to form large pure stands.[2] The use of ailanthone as an herbicide is also being investigated. Other plants in the Quassia family are known to produce chemicals that are fungicidal or insecticidal; activity against viruses and cancer cells has also been documented.

Notes

1. Kowarik, Ingo. 1995. Clonal growth in *Ailanthus altissima* on a natural site in West Virginia. *Journal of Vegetation Science* 6: 853–56.

2. Heisey, Rod M. 1996. Identification of an allelopathic compound from *Ailanthus altissima* (Simaroubaceae) and characterization of its herbicidal activity. *American Journal of Botany* 83 (2): 192–200.

TULIPTREE
LIRIODENDRON L.
Magnolia Family—Magnoliaceae

Tuliptree, yellow-poplar *Liriodendron tulipifera* L.

FORM: deciduous, tall and straight, to 140 feet, with a narrow crown

BARK: light grayish-brown, marked with a regular network of ridges and fissures, becoming more deeply fissured and irregularly platy with age

TWIGS: green when young, becoming reddish- or yellowish-brown, smooth, aromatic when broken or scraped

PITH: white with pale green cross partitions

BUDS: large, flattened, smooth with 2 bud scales that just meet at the edges

LEAVES: alternate, deciduous, bright green, squared-off at the tip with 2 lobes on each side, surface smooth and somewhat glossy, edges smooth

FALL LEAF COLOR: yellow

STIPULES: leafy, but soon falling

LEAF SCARS: nearly round with numerous bundle scars, stipule scars forming a line around the twig

FLOWERS: appearing in May after the leaves have expanded, tulip-shaped, yellow-green with orange blotches, insect-pollinated (mainly by pollen-eating beetles)

FRUIT: a cone-like cluster of samaras

SEEDS: the single-seeded samaras fall separately and are wind-dispersed

WOOD: soft, light, yellowish, easily worked; used for construction, furniture, and interior finishing

CURRENT CHAMPION: Perry County, diameter 6 feet 5 inches, height 133 feet, spread 80 feet

Tuliptree—fruit

Tuliptree—bark

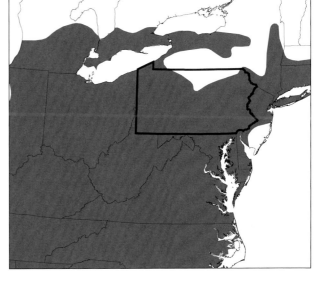

Tuliptree

Tuliptree—flowers

Tuliptrees are the tallest and straightest trees in the forest, their trunks rising to 120 feet or more. In a forest setting the trunks are usually free of branches for most of their length. The flowers are often so high in the canopy that they are rarely noticed unless one falls to the ground. In addition to the tall straight trunks, the presence of upright, candelabra-like remains of the fruit clusters on the ends of the branches can aid in wintertime recognition. Tuliptrees are relatively fast growing, but can live to be 200–300 years old.

Although tuliptree is not shade tolerant, saplings persist in the understory waiting for an opening in the canopy and their chance to grow. Ecologically, tuliptree, which contains a substance that deters feeding by gypsy moth caterpillars, has been the beneficiary where repeated outbreaks of the moth have caused high oak mortality. Deer, however, find seedlings and saplings of tuliptree very tasty and have interfered with its ability to regenerate.

Tuliptree can be a pioneer species on rich, moist, but well-drained soils, and often dominates early successional forests on such sites. In more mature forest associations it occurs in mixed stands with hemlock, oaks, and other hardwoods. While it is present throughout most of the state, it is more abundant in the southern part. The range of tuliptree extends from southern Vermont to northern Florida and west to the Mississippi Valley. The only other member of the genus *Liriodendron* is an eastern Asian species (*L. chinense*).

The light, easily worked wood of tuliptree is highly valued for many uses. Using fire and stone or shell scrapers, Native Americans hollowed out the straight trunks of tuliptrees to make canoes; early European explorers described boats big enough to carry 20 men plus baggage. Today the wood is used for furniture, interior finishing, and construction. Infusions of the bark or of root bark have been used medicinally as a heart stimulant and to treat a variety of ailments including cough, fever, pinworms, rheumatism, hysteria, and snakebite. Tuliptree is sometimes grown as a shade tree or ornamental.

Cardinals, purple finches, squirrels, and other small mammals eat the seeds of tuliptree. The leaves are a larval food plant for tiger swallowtail and spicebush swallowtail butterflies.

Tuliptree—young emerging leaves

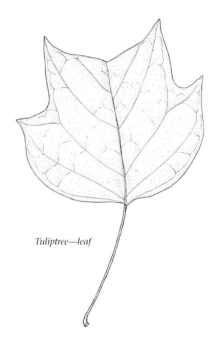

Tuliptree—leaf

TUPELO—SEE BLACKGUM

UMBRELLA-TREE—SEE MAGNOLIA

WALNUT
JUGLANS L.
Walnut Family—Juglandaceae

Black walnut   *Juglans nigra* L.

FORM: large, deciduous, 80–100 feet with a rounded crown

BARK: dark brown to grayish-black, fissured and broken into blocky squares

TWIGS: stout

PITH: tan with numerous cross partitions separating the pith into a series of hollow spaces or chambers

BUDS: rounded, densely covered with short gray hairs, sometimes with several buds located immediately above each other; terminal bud present

LEAVES: alternate, pinnately compound with 13–23 leaflets each 2–5 inches long, asymmetrical at the base, smooth on the upper surface, velvety beneath, and sharply toothed around the edge; the leaves (and other parts also) have a distinctive aroma when crushed

FALL LEAF COLOR: drab yellow or brown

STIPULES: none

LEAF SCARS: large, 3-lobed or heart-shaped with 3 U-shaped clusters of bundle scars

FLOWERS: unisexual, appearing as the leaves are emerging, wind-pollinated; male flowers in drooping catkins; female flowers bud-like in appearance and located on the new shoots; both sexes occur on each tree making the species monoecious

FRUIT: spherical, green, 2–3 inches in diameter, a hard-shelled, woody nut enclosed in a fibrous husk that does not split open along predetermined seams, maturing and dropping to the ground in September or October

SEED: nut with a rough, sculptured surface

WOOD: dark brown, very hard and durable

CURRENT CHAMPION: Chester County, diameter 5 feet 7 inches, height 93 feet, spread 109 feet

Black walnut— nut x3/4

Black walnut is the most valuable native timber species in the northeastern states. Its wood, usually in the form of veneer, is used for fine furniture, interior woodwork, and other specialty products including gunstocks. Black walnut planks were an early export from the colonies to England. The edible nuts are also commercially significant.

As landscape specimens, black walnut trees have some drawbacks. They are late to leaf out in the spring and early to drop their leaves in the fall. Black walnut trees are not good neighbors to some other plants, such as rhododendron, white pine, white birch, apple, tomatoes, and potatoes. The problem arises from a form of chemical warfare known as allelopathy.[1] The trees produce a chemical compound in their leaves, fruits, and roots (juglone) that inhibits the growth of many other nearby plants, causing wilting and even death; the effect is to reduce the competition for soil nutrients and water.

Black walnut occurs throughout the southern two-thirds of Pennsylvania except at the highest elevations. Primarily a tree of floodplains, open riparian

Black walnut—bark

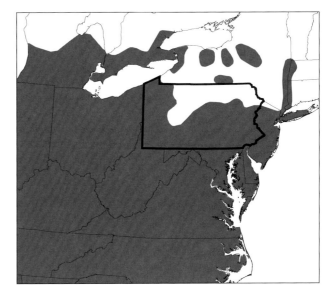

Black walnut

forests, and bottomlands, its total range extends from New Jersey to southern Minnesota and south to eastern Kansas, Oklahoma, Texas, and Georgia.

Native Americans tapped the sap of black walnut and boiled it to make syrup. The nutmeats were eaten plain, mixed with honey, or pulverized and made into a soup. Medicinal uses were many and varied. Juice from the green fruits was used to treat ringworm, a decoction of the bark was used as a laxative, and bark was chewed to relieve toothaches. In addition oil from the nutmeats was mixed with bear grease and used as insect repellent; dried and pulverized leaves were used in dwellings to suppress fleas. Oil extracted from the nuts was used for cooking fuel for oil lamps, and as a base for certain paints. Unripe fruits were pickled or preserved in syrup by the colonists. The husks have been used to prepare a brown or black dye for wool and other cloth; just handling the nuts will result in stained fingers.

The nuts are dispersed (stored) and eaten by squirrels. The leaves of black walnut are a larval food source for banded hairstreak and hickory hairstreak butterflies and the walnut sphinx moth.

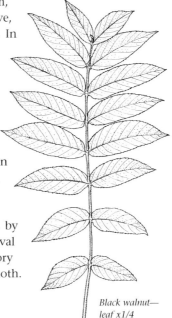

Black walnut— leaf x1/4

Notes

1. Rice, Elroy L. 1984. *Allelopathy*. Academic Press, New York.

Black walnut—male flowers

Black walnut—female flowers

Black walnut—pith

Black walnut—fruit

WHITE-CEDAR
CHAMAECYPARIS SPACH
Cypress Family—Cupressaceae

Atlantic white-cedar
           Chamaecyparis thyoides (L.)
            Britton, Stearns and Poggenb.

FORM: to 60 feet, narrowly erect, evergreen

BARK: reddish-brown, fibrous, separating in long, flat strips

TWIGS: mostly covered with the scale-like leaves, forming flattened sprays

BUDS: inconspicuous

LEAVES: bluish-green, tiny, and scale-like with a glandular dot on the back, clasping the twigs tightly, or in the juvenile phase, sharp-pointed and spreading

LEAF SCARS: inconspicuous

CONES: spherical, about ¼ inch in diameter, maturing in 1 year

SEEDS: ⅛ inch with 2 narrow wings, wind-dispersed

WOOD: very decay resistant, heartwood reddish

CURRENT CHAMPION: Montour County, diameter 3 feet 2 inches, height 89 feet, spread 38 feet

Atlantic white-cedar—cone x2

Direct evidence that Atlantic white-cedar grew naturally in Pennsylvania is limited to a preserved log extracted from buried sediments unearthed during excavation of a railroad cut near the Schuylkill River in Philadelphia in the late 1800s.[1] According to Illick, the species occurred at Tinicum Marsh (now John Heinz National Wildlife Refuge) in Delaware County and in swamps at Bristol, Bucks County, "at an early date." Although there are no herbarium specimens of Atlantic white-cedar from Pennsylvania, other remnants of Coastal Plain vege-

Atlantic white-cedar—bark
        Atlantic white-cedar

Atlantic white-cedar—branchlets x3

tation have persisted in both areas. The demand for white-cedar wood for shingles may have led to local extirpation early in the development of Philadelphia.

In New Jersey, where Atlantic white-cedar was once abundant in the cedar swamps of the Pine Barrens, the wood has long been valued for outdoor items such as fence posts and shingles due to its decay-resistant qualities. There, too, demand for the wood has led to a decline in its abundance.

The native range of Atlantic white-cedar extends from Maine to Georgia and Mississippi on the Coastal Plain and Gulf Coast. Atlantic white-cedar has been introduced at several sites in Pennsylvania and has naturalized in a disturbed bog on Laurel Mountain in Westmoreland County. It is also grown as a landscape ornamental; numerous cultivars have been developed.

Atlantic white-cedar is the primary host for caterpillars of the white-cedar hairstreak butterfly.

Notes

1. Smith, Aubrey H. 1886. *Proceedings of the Academy of Natural Sciences of Philadelphia* 38: 253–54.

WILLOW
SALIX L.
Willow Family—Salicaceae

Twenty-five species of willow grow in Pennsylvania of which eight are trees or sometimes tree-like. Four of those are native and four are non-native. Almost all willows are plants of wet places.

All the species included here have alternate, simple leaves with a prominent midvein and numerous pinnately arranged lateral veins. The edges of the leaf blades are finely to coarsely toothed, smooth, or rolled under. Tiny glands are often present on the leaf teeth and/or at the base of the blade. Willows frequently have conspicuous stipules, especially on juvenile shoots, but stipules may drop off early or be absent on some species.

The winter buds of most willow species are covered by a characteristic, cap-like fused bud scale. A few species have a single wrap-around bud scale with the edges overlapping on the side adjacent to the twig. Willows lack a true terminal bud.

The flowers of willows are borne in catkins that appear before, with, or after the leaves. Each catkin contains dozens of tiny unisexual flowers crowded together, each consisting of an ovary or 2–9 stamens, a gland, and a bract. Willows are dioecious, the male and female flowers are produced on separate plants; they are primarily wind-pollinated but nectar glands are present and their pollen may also serve as an early spring food source for bees.[1] The male catkins fall once pollen is released, but the female flowers remain on the plant to produce capsules that eventually split open to release tiny seeds covered with fine white hairs. Willow seeds are dispersed by the wind. Intolerant of drying, they germinate quickly on reaching a moist surface.

In addition to seed propagation, willows also spread naturally when broken twigs become lodged in the mud and sprout roots forming erosion reducing thickets along stream banks. For that reason, they are frequently employed in stream bank and riparian restoration plantings.

Willows are important ecologically, especially in wetland habitats where they provide cover for waterfowl and food for beaver, deer, snowshoe hare, rabbit, and grouse. Butterfly larvae including green comma, gray comma, mourning cloak, common tortoiseshell, tiger swallowtail, red-spotted purple, white admiral, viceroy, northern willow hairstreak, striped hairstreak, hairy duskywing, and aspen duskywing feed on willow leaves. The caterpillars of several sphinx moths, cecropia moth, and luna moth also eat willow leaves.

Several gall-making insects also occur on willow. Willow cone gall, which occurs on several species, is caused by a midge (*Rhabdophaga strobiloides*) that deposits an egg in the terminal bud as it is beginning to swell. Instead of opening normally, the bud enlarges until it is about an inch long and looks like a miniature pinecone. The larva remains within the gall until the following spring when it pupates and emerges as an adult. Other gall-making insects cause swellings or abnormal growths on the leaves and stems of various willows.

Humans too, have found uses for willows. Icelandic manuscripts from the fifteenth century recorded the recommendation that juice from willow dripped in the nostrils was good for headache; use as a contraceptive was also mentioned. Early colonists used willow bark as a substitute for quinine to treat fever. By 1875 salicin or salicylic acid, obtained from the bark of willow (*Salix*), was being used medicinally to treat fever, inflammation, and other conditions. Manufactured acetylsalicylic acid, or aspirin, remains a standard treatment for many of the above ailments.

Willow also provided Native Americans with the raw materials for making bows, snowshoes, and baskets. The flexible branches were woven into fish weirs, traps, fences, and cages. Bark was twisted into cords and fashioned into nets, rugs, and mats. The wood was used to make fire drills and cooking tools. Their weak, light wood and small size prevent most willows from having much value as lumber, however, they have occasionally been a source of fuel and charcoal. Because of the high tannin content, the bark of some willow species was also useful for tanning leather.

Black willow   *Salix nigra* Marshall

FORM: tree to 60 feet with a broad, round-topped crown
BARK: blackish-brown, thick with deep furrows and wide ridges
TWIGS: light grayish-brown and hairy at first, becoming smooth and reddish- or yellowish-brown, brittle
PITH: small, white with darker streaks, solid
BUDS: about ⅛ inch long, sharp-pointed and covered by a single wrap-around bud scale with overlapping edges
LEAVES: alternate, 3–5 inches long, narrow, tapering to a long slender tip, smooth on both sides or with sparse hairs, upper surface bright yellow-green, the lower surface paler but still green; edge finely toothed
FALL LEAF COLOR: yellow
STIPULES: broadly rounded, varying in size
LEAF SCARS: narrow with 3 bundle scars
FLOWERS: appearing with the leaves; male flowers with 4–6 stamens
FRUIT: capsules smooth, about ⅛ inch long
SEEDS: as for other willows, see above
WOOD: weak, light reddish-brown with white sapwood, used for packing cases, fuel, wood pulp, or charcoal
CURRENT CHAMPION: Crawford County, diameter 8 feet 10 inches, height 75 feet, spread 80 feet

Black willow is the largest of our native willows. It is a common tree of floodplains, riverbanks, pond margins, and other moist sites throughout Pennsylvania. It has a large native range that extends from southern Ontario to Wisconsin and south to northern Florida and Texas; but reaches its best development in the Mississippi River valley. It is the only large willow species in the state that has bright green leaves and erect twigs. Another distinguishing feature is the pointed winter buds with a single wrap-around bud scale.

Because of its large size, black willow has been used as a timber tree. The wood, which is flexible and does not warp or splinter, is useful for making wicker furniture, boxes, crates, toys, and coffins. Black willow was also employed to make a pinkish-tan dye for wool.

Black willow—bark

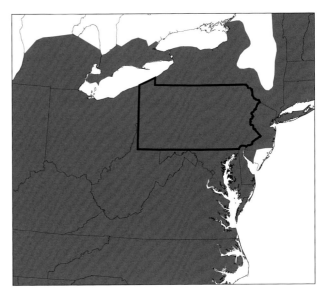

Black willow

Black willow—male catkins

Black willow—bud scale
(back side) x5

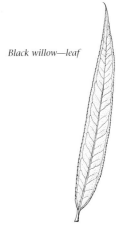

Black willow—leaf

Carolina willow   *Salix caroliniana* Michx.

FORM: tree to 30 feet
BARK: dark to light brown
TWIGS: yellowish becoming reddish-brown, smooth or somewhat hairy, not breaking readily
PITH: small, white, and continuous
BUDS: reddish-brown, smooth to hairy, sharp-pointed with a single bud scale with overlapping edges

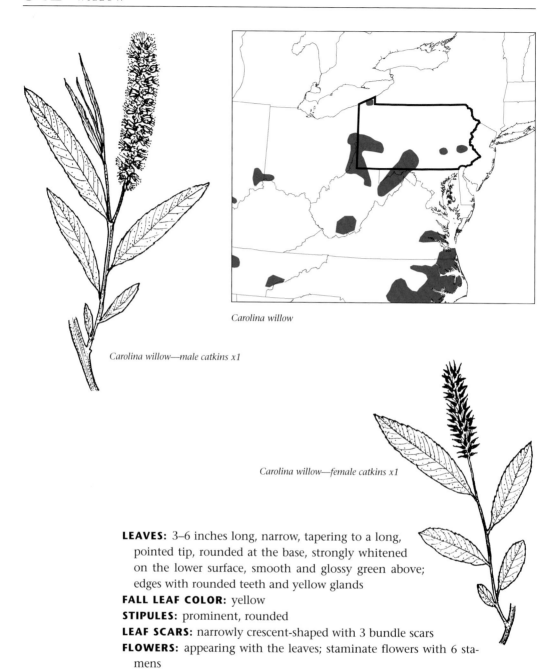

Carolina willow

Carolina willow—male catkins x1

Carolina willow—female catkins x1

LEAVES: 3–6 inches long, narrow, tapering to a long, pointed tip, rounded at the base, strongly whitened on the lower surface, smooth and glossy green above; edges with rounded teeth and yellow glands

FALL LEAF COLOR: yellow

STIPULES: prominent, rounded

LEAF SCARS: narrowly crescent-shaped with 3 bundle scars

FLOWERS: appearing with the leaves; staminate flowers with 6 stamens

FRUIT: as for other willows, see above

SEEDS: as for other willows, see above

WOOD: too rare to be commercially important

CURRENT CHAMPION: none recorded

Carolina willow is a southern species that occurs in southwestern Pennsylvania and a few scattered sites across the south central and southeastern counties. Its range extends from Pennsylvania to Florida and west to Oklahoma and eastern Kansas. It also grows in Cuba and Guatemala. In Pennsylvania it is a plant of river and stream banks, riparian forests, and swamps primarily on limestone or other calcareous soils. It has been recommended for designation as an endangered species in the state by the Pennsylvania Biological Survey.

Carolina willow is very similar to black willow, although it does not grow as large; it is most readily distinguished by the presence of whitened lower leaf surfaces.

Crack willow   *Salix fragilis* L.

FORM: tree 30–70 feet with a broad rounded crown
BARK: gray, rough, and furrowed
TWIGS: yellowish-brown, smooth or with a few sparse hairs, very brittle and easily broken off at the base
PITH: white or tan streaked with orange
BUDS: yellowish-green, smooth with a blunt tip and a single cap-like bud scale
LEAVES: leaves 4–5½ inches long, tapering to the somewhat rounded or broadly wedge-shaped base and long, tapering tip, shiny dark grayish-green above and whitened beneath; edges with coarse teeth
FALL LEAF COLOR: drab gray-brown
STIPULES: falling early
LEAF SCARS: narrowly crescent-shaped with 3 bundle scars
FLOWERS: appearing with the leaves; male flowers with 2 stamens
FRUIT: smooth, less than ¼ inch long
SEEDS: as for other willows, see above
WOOD: distinctive due to its unusual salmon color and durability, used in Europe for boat building, fence posts, and tool handles; also used for charcoal manufacture
CURRENT CHAMPION: Cambria County, diameter 6 feet 9 inches, height 80 feet, spread 70 feet

Crack willow is one of four large willows that occur in Pennsylvania. It frequently grows with black willow along stream banks; the two can easily be dis-

Crack willow—bark

Crack willow—female catkin in fruit

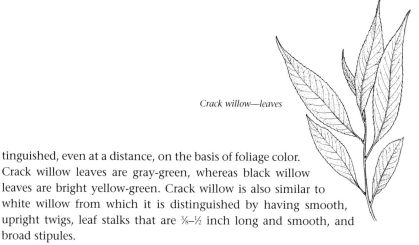

Crack willow—leaves

tinguished, even at a distance, on the basis of foliage color. Crack willow leaves are gray-green, whereas black willow leaves are bright yellow-green. Crack willow is also similar to white willow from which it is distinguished by having smooth, upright twigs, leaf stalks that are ⅜–½ inch long and smooth, and broad stipules.

Crack willow is native to Asia Minor (Russia, Turkey, Iran, and Iraq) and widely naturalized throughout Pennsylvania and the northeast. It was introduced during colonial times and grown in southeastern Pennsylvania and Delaware for the production of charcoal used in gunpowder manufacture.

The wood of crack willow, which is distinctively salmon-colored and more durable than that of other species, was also used for fence posts, tool handles and house construction. In Scotland it was highly favored for building small boats.

Goat willow   *Salix caprea* L.

FORM: large shrub or tree to 45 feet
BARK: gray, fissured
TWIGS: stout, yellow-green or reddish-brown, hairy
PITH: white streaked with tan, solid
BUDS: reddish-brown, hairy to nearly smooth, covered by a single cap-like bud scale
LEAVES: alternate, 2–5 inches long, elliptic with the edges slightly toothed to smooth and rolled under; densely white-hairy beneath when young
FALL LEAF COLOR: yellow
STIPULES: to ½ inch long, usually rounded
LEAF SCARS: crescent-shaped, conspicuously raised, with 3 bundle scars
FLOWERS: appearing before the leaves, male flowers with 2 stamens
FRUIT: capsules about ¼ inch long and densely hairy
SEEDS: as for other willows, see above
WOOD: too small and light to be of any significance
CURRENT CHAMPION: none recorded

Goat willow is a Eurasian species that is occasionally cultivated as a "pussy willow" for the attractive silky appearance of the male catkins as they swell in the spring. It is often confused with *Salix cinerea*, the most common cultivated pussy willow, or the native pussy willow, *Salix discolor,* both of which are shrubbier in their growth habit. Naturalized populations of goat willow are clustered in the southeastern counties and scattered elsewhere.

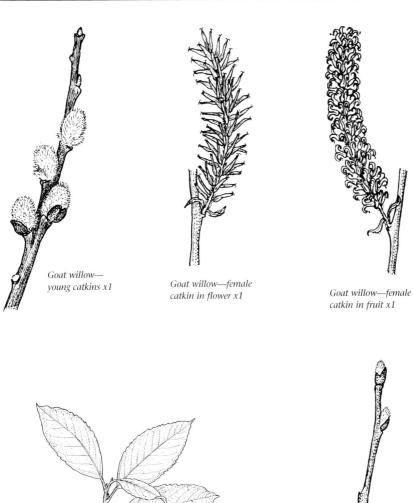

Goat willow—
young catkins x1

Goat willow—female
catkin in flower x1

Goat willow—female
catkin in fruit x1

Goat willow—leaves

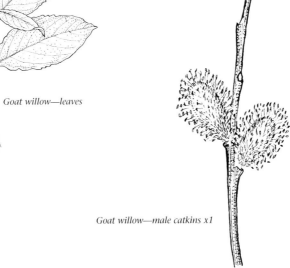

Goat willow—male catkins x1

Peach-leaf willow   *Salix amygdaloides* Andersson

FORM: tree 12–40 feet, frequently with several trunks

BARK: reddish-brown, deeply furrowed with wide scaly ridges

TWIGS: slender, yellowish-brown to reddish-brown, smooth, not brittle

PITH: small, white, and continuous

BUDS: yellowish, sharp-pointed with a single bud scale with overlapping edges, smooth

LEAVES: alternate, 2–5 inches long, tapering at the base and the tip, glossy yellow-green to dark green above, whitened beneath with few to no hairs; leaf edge with gland-tipped teeth

FALL LEAF COLOR: yellow

STIPULES: small and falling early except on sprouts where they are larger and kidney-shaped

LEAF SCARS: raised, crescent-shaped with 3 bundle scars

FLOWERS: appearing with the leaves; male flowers with 3–7 stamens; pistils of the female flowers borne on a long stalk

FRUIT: smooth, pear-shaped, less than ⅛ inch long

SEEDS: as for other willows, see above

WOOD: occasionally used for firewood or charcoal

CURRENT CHAMPION: none recorded

Peach-leaf willow is characterized by yellowish twigs and long tapering leaves that are whitened beneath. The presence of a single wrap-around bud scale on the overwintering buds is another good distinguishing character shared by only 2 other species in the state. Peach-leaf willow grows in swamps, bogs, and wet shores of northwestern Pennsylvania and scattered sites in the north central region. Primarily a plant of the Great Plains region of the United States and Canada, peach-leaved willow ranges from western New York to Washington and British Columbia and south to western Texas and New Mexico.

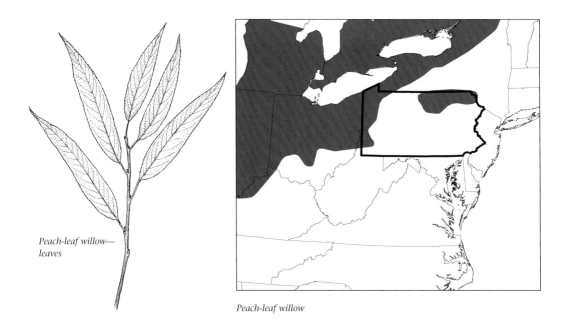

*Peach-leaf willow—
leaves*

Peach-leaf willow

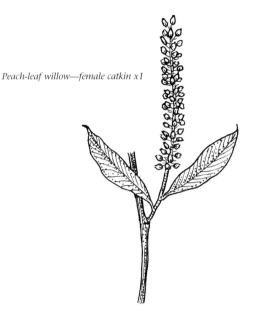

Peach-leaf willow—female catkin x1

Peach-leaf willow—male catkin x1

Shining willow   *Salix lucida* Muhl.

FORM: a small tree to 25 feet or often shrub-like

BARK: smooth and thin, brown to reddish-brown

TWIGS: yellowish-brown becoming darker brown, smooth and shiny or sometimes with white or rusty hairs

PITH: white with tan streaks, continuous

BUDS: about ¼ inch long, blunt-tipped, covered with a single cap-like fused bud scale

LEAVES: alternate, 1½–5½ inches long, broad at the base and tapering to a slender pointed tip, tapering or somewhat rounded at the base, glossy green above with a yellow midrib, lighter green beneath; leaf edge finely toothed

FALL LEAF COLOR: yellow

STIPULES: semicircular, glandular, and usually persisting through the summer

LEAF SCARS: narrowly crescent-shaped, with 3 bundle scars

FLOWERS: appearing before the leaves; male flowers with 3–6 stamens

FRUIT: shiny, about ⅓ inch long

SEEDS: as for other willows, see above

WOOD: too small and light to be of value except for occasional use as fuel

CURRENT CHAMPION: none recorded

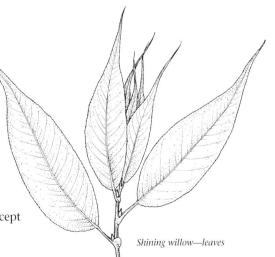

Shining willow—leaves

Shining willow is primarily a northern species; it extends from Newfoundland to Manitoba and south to Iowa and West Virginia.

Shining willow—male catkin x1

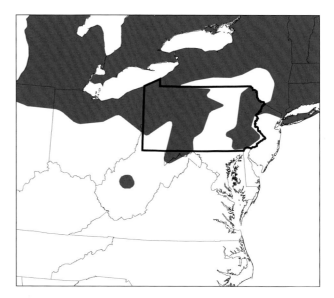

Shining willow

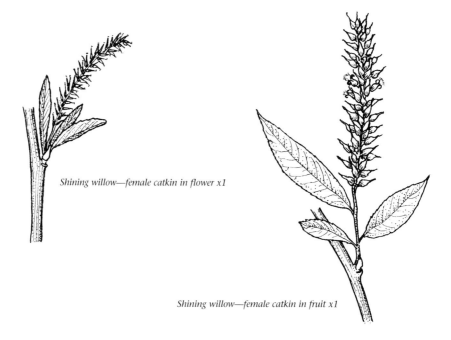

Shining willow—female catkin in flower x1

Shining willow—female catkin in fruit x1

In Pennsylvania, which is near the southern limit of its range, it grows in swamps and wet edges of lakes and streams scattered throughout the eastern, central, and northwestern regions of the state. It is easily recognized because of its glossy green leaves that taper to a slender point.

Weeping willow   *Salix babylonica* **L.**

FORM: a large tree to 40 feet with long drooping branches that hang straight down, usually reaching the ground at their tips

BARK: rough and brownish-gray on mature trees

TWIGS: yellowish-green to brown, slender, drooping

PITH: small, white, and continuous

BUDS: yellowish, sparsely hairy, blunt-tipped, covered by a single cap-like bud scale

LEAVES: alternate, 3–6 inches long, narrow and tapering to a long slender tip, smooth with a coarsely toothed edge; leaf stalk often hairy, especially when young

FALL LEAF COLOR: golden yellow

STIPULES: narrow with a pointed tip, glandular, falling early

LEAF SCARS: narrow, crescent-shaped with 3 bundle scars

FLOWERS: appearing with the leaves

FRUIT: as for other willows, see above

SEEDS: as for other willows, see above

WOOD: light-colored, weak

CURRENT CHAMPION: Schuylkill County, diameter 7 feet 2 inches, height 63 feet, spread 46 feet

Weeping willow is perhaps the most easily recognized tree in Pennsylvania due to its vertical hanging branchlets that often touch the ground. The origin of the

Weeping willow—Embroidered mourning scene with weeping willows, courtesy of Nora Vizzachero.

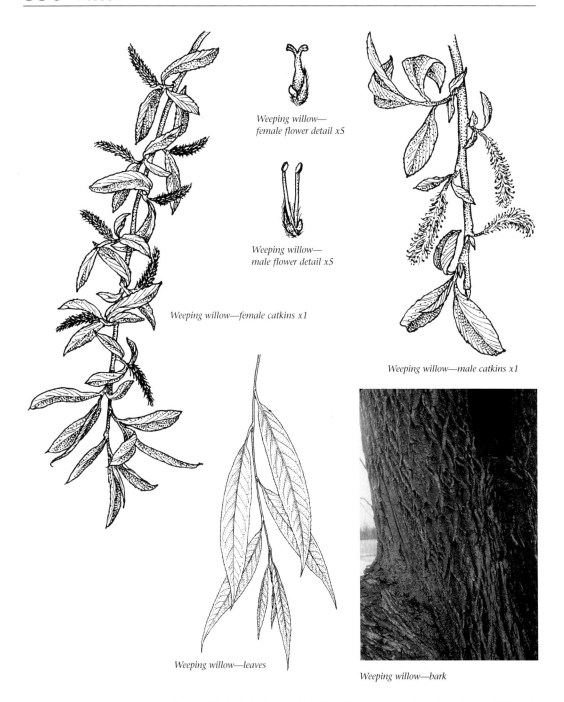

Weeping willow—female flower detail x5

Weeping willow—male flower detail x5

Weeping willow—female catkins x1

Weeping willow—male catkins x1

Weeping willow—leaves

Weeping willow—bark

weeping form of *S. babylonica*, which is native to central and northern China, is said to have been a female clone that was introduced into cultivation in 1730. Many additional ornamental forms have been developed over the years. Today, what is most often seen is a series of hybrids between weeping willow and crack willow or a pendulous variety of white willow (see below). In Pennsylvania weeping willow has naturalized at scattered sites, mostly in the southeast.

Weeping willows appear as a symbol of mourning in American folk art depicting funeral scenes.

White willow   *Salix alba* L.

FORM: tree to 75–100 feet with a narrow, upright crown; variety *vitellina* has weeping branchlets

BARK: yellowish-brown to brown with corky ridges and furrows

TWIGS: yellowish-green to reddish-brown, often drooping, hairy at first becoming smooth and shiny

PITH: small, white, and continuous

BUDS: about ¼ inch long, yellowish-brown, hairy with a blunt tip and a single fused, cap-like bud scale

LEAVES: 2½–5 inches long, narrow, tapered to the base and the long slender tip, grayish-green, whitened beneath and with long silvery hairs, especially when young; edges very finely toothed; leaf stalk about ¼ inch long, hairy

FALL LEAF COLOR: yellow

STIPULES: narrow, falling early

LEAF SCARS: narrowly crescent-shaped with 3 bundle scars

FLOWERS: appearing with the leaves; male flowers with 2 stamens

FRUIT: pear-shaped, about ⅛ inch long, yellowish-brown, and smooth

SEEDS: as for other willows, see above

WOOD: used for baskets and sports equipment

CURRENT CHAMPION: Schuylkill County, diameter 6 feet 4 inches, height 78 feet, spread 79 feet

White willow is a Eurasian species that is native from central Europe to western Siberia and Central Asia. Many cultivars have been developed including forms with yellow or silvery leaves and others with twigs ranging from red to yellow. It was introduced to North America in colonial times and has naturalized throughout the northeastern states. In Pennsylvania it occurs mainly across the southern half of the state in low ground along stream banks.

White willow and crack willow are quite similar and to make matters worse, they hybridize (producing *Salix* x *rubens* Schrank); both also hybridize with

White willow—bark   *White willow—leaves*

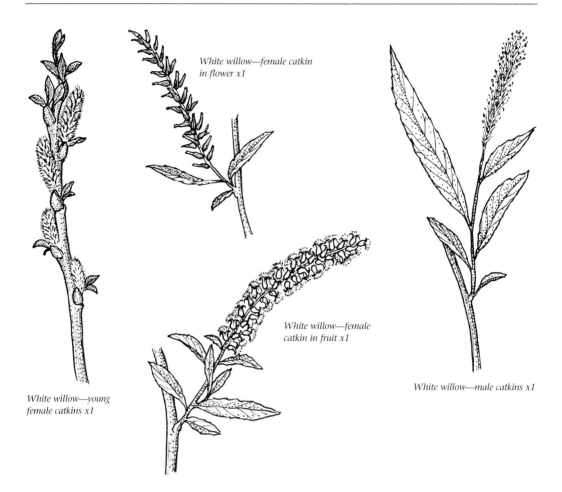

White willow—female catkin
in flower x1

White willow—female
catkin in fruit x1

White willow—young
female catkins x1

White willow—male catkins x1

weeping willow. *Salix alba* var. *vitellina* is often mistaken for weeping willow; white willow, however, has gray-green leaves as opposed to the bright yellowish-green leaves of true weeping willow. White willow is best distinguished from crack willow by its hairy twigs, leaf stalks that are about ¼ inch long and hairy, and narrow stipules. In addition white willow often has drooping twigs, whereas the branchlets of crack willow are upright.

The wood of white willow was used for construction, for the production of charcoal, and for making baskets and wicker furniture. The leaves have been used for forage for cattle and other domestic animals.

Notes

1. Argus, George W. 1986. The Genus *Salix* in the Southeastern United States. *Systematic Botany Monographs* 9: 1–170.

WITCH-HAZEL
HAMAMELIS L.
Witch-hazel Family—Hamamelidaceae

Witch-hazel   *Hamamelis virginiana* L.

FORM: large deciduous shrub or small tree to 25 feet, usually multistemmed

BARK: smooth when young, dark and scaly on older stems

TWIGS: light brown, zigzag

PITH: small, light green

BUDS: often curved, naked (lacking bud scales), hairy

LEAVES: alternate, simple, 3–6 inches long and 2–4 inches wide, pinnately veined; leaf edge with coarse, rounded teeth

FALL LEAF COLOR: yellow

STIPULES: not present

LEAF SCARS: semicircular with 3 or more bundle scars

FLOWERS: perfect, containing 4 yellow petals, each about 1 inch long, narrow and strap-shaped; blooming in the fall, fragrant, insect-pollinated

FRUITS: a 2-seeded, explosive capsule

SEEDS: black, glossy, ¼–⅜ inch long, mechanically dispersed when the capsules burst open

WOOD: of no commercial value

CURRENT CHAMPION: Potter County, diameter 5 inches, height 42 feet, spread 28 feet

Witch-hazel is the last of our native woody plants to bloom; its yellow flowers appear in October and November as the leaves are falling. The name is derived from the use of forked branches of witch-hazel as divining rods to locate water,

Witch-hazel—bark   *Witch-hazel*

a practice known as water-witching. This large shrub or small tree is usually found in moist, cool woods, especially on rocky slopes. It is common throughout the state, although severe browsing by deer has caused a decline in some areas as new shoots from the base are prevented from growing tall enough to replace the older stems. The range of witch-hazel extends from Nova Scotia to Florida and west to Minnesota and Oklahoma.

The fragrant flowers are insect-pollinated. The fruits, which mature the next autumn following flowering, burst open when mature, propelling the seeds for a distance of several yards. Witch-hazel leaves frequently bear small cone-shaped galls on the upper surface caused by the witch-hazel leaf gall aphid; another insect, the witch-hazel bud gall aphid, converts the capsules into spiny galls.

Native Americans valued witch-hazel for a variety of medicinal purposes and its use continues today. An extract of the leaves and bark is used as an astringent, a gargle, and in manufacturing numerous cosmetic products. Grouse and squirrels eat the seeds.

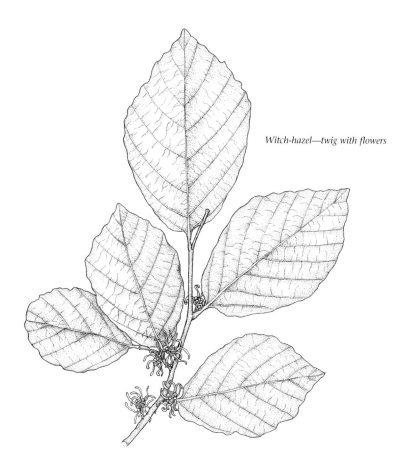

Witch-hazel—twig with flowers

WITCH-HAZEL 355

Witch-hazel—flowers

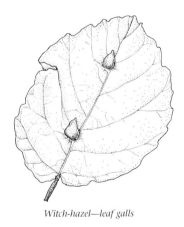

Witch-hazel—leaf galls

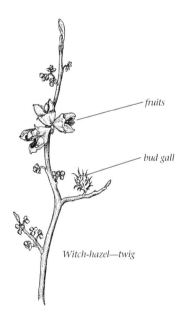

fruits

bud gall

Witch-hazel—twig

YELLOW-POPLAR—SEE TULIPTREE

Chapter 4. How to Identify Trees

It is possible to identify trees by comparing an unknown with the pictures and descriptions contained in this book. However, a more systematic method of identifying an unknown specimen is by the use of a dichotomus key. The key presents the user with a series of choices in the form of pairs of descriptive statements. By selecting the statement that best describes the plant being identified, a user can move through the key and evaluate all the characteristics necessary for accurate identification.

A few tips will help the novice key user. Select a representative sample of the plant in question. Examine it carefully; don't dwell on the odd exception, but rather focus on the typical characteristics. For example, if most of the leaves of a tree have 3 lobes, don't worry about the few that have 5 or 7 lobes.

Read each pair of statements carefully and thoroughly before deciding which one best fits the plant you are looking at; pay particular attention to the connecting words such as "and" or "or." Be sure you understand the botanical terminology; use the glossary if necessary.

After reaching a tentative identification, consult the descriptions and illustrations to confirm that you have made a correct identification.

KEYS TO PENNSYLVANIA TREES

Key 1. Trees with needle- or scale-like leaves, or leaves fan-shaped

1. trees deciduous
    2. leaves fan-shaped . . . . Ginkgo (*Ginkgo biloba*)
    2. leaves needle-like
        3. cone scales 15–20, smooth and shining on outside; needles light green to blue-green, with inconspicuous white bands beneath . . . . American larch, tamarack (*Larix laricina*)
        3. cone scales >40, smooth or hairy on the outside; needles blue-green, with faint to conspicuous white bands beneath
            4. cone scales reflexed at the apex, not hairy on the outside . . . . Japanese larch (*Larix kaempferi*)

    4. cone scales straight or slightly incurved, hairy on the outside . . . .
. . . . European larch (*Larix decidua*)

1. trees evergreen
    5. leaves opposite or in whorls of 3, scale-like or subulate
        6. branchlets forming more or less flattened sprays
            7. individual branchlets nearly rounded in cross section; cones (if present) spherical . . . .
. . . . Atlantic white-cedar (*Chamaecyparis thyoides*)
            7. individual branchlets strongly flattened in cross section; cones (if present) oblong or ovoid
. . . . Arbor-vitae (*Thuja occidentalis*)
        6. branchlets not forming flattened sprays . . . . Eastern red-cedar (*Juniperus virginiana*)
    5. leaves needle-like, borne singly or in clusters of 2–5
        8. needles borne singly
            9. twigs roughened by persistent raised, peg-like leaf bases
                10. needles square in cross section, sessile
                    11. twigs hairy; cone scales fan-shaped, broadest near the margin; cones ¾–2 in. long
                        12. needles ⅓–1 in., mostly sharp-pointed, yellow-green to dark green; cones 1–2 in.
long . . . . Red spruce (*Picea rubens*)
                        12. needles ¼–½ in., mostly blunt-tipped, blue-green; cones ½–1 in. long . . . .
. . . . Black spruce (*Picea mariana*)
                    11. twigs not hairy or only slightly hairy; cones 1½–6 in. long
                        13. needles dark green; branchlets strongly drooping on mature trees; cones 3½–8 in.
long . . . . Norway spruce (*Picea abies*)
                        13. needles blue-green, whitened; branchlets not drooping; cones 1–4 in. long
                            14. cone scales fan-shaped, margin entire . . . . White spruce (*Picea glauca*)
                            14. cone scales diamond-shaped, margin toothed or ragged . . . .
. . . . Colorado blue spruce (*Picea pungens*)
                10. needles flat in cross section, tapering to a short leaf stalk . . . .
. . . . Canada hemlock (*Tsuga canadensis*)
            9. twigs smooth or nearly so
                15. leaf scars slightly raised on one side; 3-lobed bracts of the cone scales conspicuously
longer than the scales . . . . Douglas-fir (*Pseudotsuga menziesii*)
                15. leaf scars flush with the twig surface; bracts of the cone scales shorter than the scales . . .
. . . . Balsam fir (*Abies balsamea*)
        8. needles borne in clusters of 2–5
            16. needles 5 per fascicle . . . . Eastern white pine (*Pinus strobus*)
            16. needles 2–3 per fascicle
                17. needles <3½ in., mostly in 2s
                    18. cone scales spineless
                      19. bark of upper trunk and larger branches orange; needles blue-green; cones symmet-
rical, persisting on the branches after opening . . . . Scots pine (*Pinus sylvestris*)
                      19. bark of upper trunk and branches brown; needles yellow-green; cones asymmetri-
cal, persisting on the branches mostly in a closed condition . . . .
. . . . Jack pine (*Pinus banksiana*)
                  18. cone scales with a definite spine
                    20. cones 2½–3½ in. with very stout, spreading or upwardly curving spines . . . .
. . . . Table-mountain pine (*Pinus pungens*)
                    20. cones 1¼–3 in. with slender, straight spines . . . . . . Virginia pine (*Pinus virginiana*)
                17. needles 2¾–7 in., in 2s or 3s
                  21. needles in 3s
                    22. needles twisted; cones persistent, armed with definite spines . . . .
. . . . Pitch pine (*Pinus rigida*)
                    22. needles mostly in 2s (rarely 3s), not twisted; cones deciduous, bearing short spines
. . . . Short-leaf pine (*Pinus echinata*)

21. needles in 2s
    23. fresh needles breaking cleanly if bent; cone scales without spines . . . .
    . . . . Norway pine, red pine (*Pinus resinosa*)
    23. fresh needles not breaking cleanly if bent; cone scales with a short spine
        24. twigs whitened; needles 2¾–5 in.; cones dull brown . . . .
        . . . . Short-leaf pine (*Pinus echinata*)
        24. twigs not whitened; needles to 7 in.; cones glossy yellow-brown . . . .
        . . . . Austrian pine (*Pinus nigra*)

Key 2. Trees in flower (with or without leaves)

1. flowers perfect
    2. flowers in a small cluster surrounded by 4 showy white or pinkish bracts . . . .
    . . . . Flowering dogwood (*Cornus florida*)
    2. flowers not surrounded by showy bracts
        3. flowers > ½ inch wide and/or with a conspicuous, white or colored corolla
            4. petals completely separate and distinct
                5. flowers with bilateral symmetry
                    6. trees with spines or prickles on trunk or branches . . . .
                . . . . Black locust (*Robinia pseudoacacia*)
                    6. trees unarmed
                        7. flowers appearing on bare branches before the leaves have emerged . . . .
                    . . . . Redbud (*Cercis canadensis*)
                        7. flowers appearing with or after the expansion of leaves
                            8. leaves palmately compound
                                9. petals white with red or yellow markings . . . .
                          . . . . Horse-chestnut (*Aesculus hippocastanum*)
                                9. flowers yellow-green, yellow, or reddish
                                    10. petals yellow or reddish, as long or longer than the stamens . . . .
                              . . . . Yellow buckeye (*Aesculus flava*)
                                    10. petals yellowish-green shorter than the stamens . . . .
                              . . . . Ohio buckeye (*Aesculus glabra*)
                            8. leaves pinnately compound
                                11. petals yellow . . . . Goldenrain tree (*Koelreuteria paniculata*)
                                11. petals white
                                    12. twigs and branches green, leaves lacking a garlic odor . . . .
                              . . . . Japanese pagoda-tree (*Sophora japonica*)
                                    12. twigs and branches brown, leaves and young shoots with the odor of gar-
                                    lic . . . . Chinese-cedar (*Cedrela sinensis*)
                5. flowers with radial symmetry
                  13. flowers with > 5 petals
                      14. flowers appearing before the leaves emerge
                          15. petals pink or white, flowers opening upward or outward; flower buds densely
                          hairy
                              16. petals pink . . . . Saucer magnolia (*Magnolia soulangeana*)
                              16. petals white . . . . Kobus magnolia (*Magnolia kobus*)
                          15. petals dark maroon, flowers drooping . . . . Pawpaw (*Asimina triloba*)
                    14. flowers appearing after the leaves have expanded
                          17. petals green with an orange blotch at the base . . . .
                          . . . . Tuliptree (*Liriodendron tulipifera*)
                        17. petals white or pale greenish-yellow
                            18. leaves thick and leathery, shiny above and whitened beneath . . . .
                          . . . . Sweetbay magnolia (*Magnolia virginiana*)

18. leaves thinner, not whitened beneath

    19. leaves leaves 6–10 inches long, spaced along the twigs; petals greenish-yellow . . . . Cucumber-tree (*Magnolia acuminata*)

    19. leaves 12–20 inches long, clustered at the ends of the branches; petals white . . . . Umbrella-tree (*Magnolia tripetala*)

13. flowers with 4 or 5 petals

  20. flowers with 4 petals

    21. flowers with 2 stamens . . . . .White fringetree (*Chionanthus virginicus*)

    21. flowers with 4 stamens

      22. petals yellow, linear or strap-shaped . . . Witch-hazel (*Hamamelis virginiana*)

      22. petals white, not strap-shaped . . . . Alternate-leaf dogwood (*Cornus alternifolia*)

  20. flowers with 5 petals

    23. trees with spines or thorns on the trunk and/or branches

      24. thorns occurring as short lateral branches with sharp tips

        25. flowers with an inferior ovary, fruit a pome . . . . Apple or crabapple (*Malus* spp.)

        25. flowers with a superior ovary, fruit a drupe (plums)

          26. leaf teeth with marginal glands (or a scar where the gland had been) . . . . Allegheny plum (*Prunus alleghaniensis*)

          26. leaf teeth without marginal glands

            27. hypanthium hairy . . . . Beach plum (*Prunus maritima*)

            27. hypanthium not hairy

              28. petals > 3/8 inch long . . . . American plum (*Prunus americana*)

              28. petals < 3/8 inch long . . . Chickasaw plum (*Prunus angustifolia*)

      24. simple thorns present at the nodes of the branches and often branched thorns also present on the trunk . . . . Hawthorn (*Crataegus* spp.)

    23. trees without spines, thorns, or prickles

      29. flower stalk fused to a long strap-shaped bract . . Basswood (*Tilia americana*)

      29. flower stalk not fused to a bract

        30. flower with a single style and a superior ovary, fruit a drupe

          31. inflorescence a raceme

            32. raceme with < 12 flowers . . European bird cherry (Prunus padus)

            32. raceme with 20 or more flowers

              33. leaf teeth rounded at the tips . . . . Wild black cherry (*Prunus serotina*)

              33. leaf teeth with a fine hair-like tip . . . . Choke cherry (*Prunus virginiana*)

          31. inflorescence an umbel-like cluster

            34. flowers pink, appearing before the leaves . . . . Higan cherry (*Prunus subhirtella*)

            34. flowers white, appearing with or after the leaves

              35. large tree to 60 feet; branches ashy gray . . . . Sweet cherry (*Prunus avium*)

              35. small tree to 30 feet; branches reddish-brown . . . . Pin or Fire cherry (*Prunus pensylvanica*)

        30. flower with 2–5 styles and an inferior ovary, fruit a pome

          36. flowers appearing before the leaves have expanded or as they are beginning to expand

            37. styles 5, free or fused at the base, mouth of the hypanthium open

              38. flowers in racemes

39. leaves at flowering time just beginning to expand, green, densely hairy, folded along the midrib .... Shadbush (*Amelanchier arborea*)

39. leaves at flowering time about one-half expanded, not folded along the midrib, reddish .... Smooth shadbush (*Amelanchier laevis*)

38. flowers not in racemes

40. flower stalks and hypanthium densely hairy .... Apple (*Malus pumila*)

40. pedicles and hypanthium not hairy to slightly hairy .... Sweet crabapple (*Malus coronaria*)

37. styles 2–5, separate to the base, mouth of the hypanthium closed around the styles

41. styles 2–3 .... Callery pear (*Pyrus calleryana*)

41. styles 5 .... Pear (*Pyrus communis*)

36. flowers appearing after the leaves have expanded

42. leaves compound

43. leaves once-pinnate, flowers white

44. inflorescence branches and hypanthium not hairy

45. leaflets long-acuminate, 3–5 times as long as wide .... American mountain-ash (*Sorbus americana*)

45. leaflets short-acuminate or acute, 2–3 times as long as wide .... Showy mountain-ash (*Sorbus decora*)

44. inflorescence branches and hypanthium densely covered with dense white hairs .... European mountain-ash (*Sorbus acuparia*)

43. leaves twice-pinnate, flowers pink .... Mimosa (*Albizia julabrissin*)

42. leaves simple .... Oriental photinia (*Photinia villosa*)

4. flowers with petals fused, at least at the base

46. flowers with radial symmetry

47. stamens 5 .... Blackhaw (*Viburnum prunifolium*)

47. stamens more than 5

48. stamens 10

49. corolla urn-shaped, narrowed toward the tip .... Sourwood (*Oxydendrum arboreum*)

49. corolla not urn-shaped

50. corolla lobes 5, ovary superior .... Japanese snowbell (*Styrax japonica*)

50. corolla lobes 4, ovary inferior .... Carolina silverbell (*Halesia carolina*)

48. stamens 30 or more .... Sapphire-berry (*Symplocos paniculata*)

46. flowers with bilateral symmetry

51. flowers purple, appearing before the leaves ..... Empress-tree (*Paulownia tomentosa*)

51. flowers white or pale yellow with brown or purple markings inside the tube, appearing after the leaves have expanded

52. flowers 1¼–1½ inches wide; apex of the leaf abruptly acuminate .... Southern catalpa (*Catalpa bignonioides*)

52. flowers 2–2½ inches wide; apex of the leaf long-acuminate .... Northern catalpa (*Catalpa speciosa*)

3. individual flowers < ½ inch wide, corolla absent or inconspicuous

53. trees armed with spines or prickles, flowers in a compound umbel

54. leaves doubly compound

55. inflorescence with a single erect central axis .... Hercules'-club (*Aralia spinosa*)

55. inflorescence lacking a single central axis, rather divided near the base into several paniculate branches . . . . Japanese angelica-tree (*Aralia elata*)

54. leaves simple . . . . Castor-aralia (*Kalopanax pictus*)

53. trees without spines or prickles

56. flowers appearing early in the spring before the leaves have emerged

57. leaves alternate

58. flowers appearing in the early spring

59. flowers on long, slender, drooping flower stalks . . . . American elm (*Ulmus americana*)

59. flowers on short stalks, not drooping

60. calyx hairy . . . . Slippery elm (*Ulmus rubra*)

60. calyx not hairy . . . . Siberian elm (*Ulmus pumila*)

58. flowers appearing in the fall . . . . Chinese elm (*Ulmus parvifolia*)

57. leaves opposite

61. flowers on long drooping stalks . . . . Sugar or black maple (*Acer saccharum* or *A. nigrum*)

61. flowers not on long drooping stalks

62. flowers red, ovary not hairy . . . . Red maple (*Acer rubrum*)

62. flowers brown, ovary hairy . . . . Silver maple (*Acer saccharinum*)

56. flowers appearing with or after the leaves

63. flowers in a panicle or a raceme

64. flowers in a raceme

65. flowers in an upright raceme . . . . Mountain maple (*Acer spicatum*)

65. flowers in a drooping raceme

66. bark dark brownish-gray . . . . Sycamore maple (*Acer pseudoplatanus*)

66. bark striped green and white . . . . Striped maple (*Acer pensylvanicum*)

64. flowers in an upright or drooping panicle

67. petals and young twigs hairy; panicle upright . . . . Staghorn sumac (*Rhus typhina*)

67. petals and young twigs not hairy, panicle drooping

68. leaves simple . . . . Amur maple (*Acer ginnala*)

68. leaves trifoliate . . . . Bladdernut (*Staphylea trifolia*)

63. flowers in an umbel-like corymb

69. leaf and flower stalks oozing milky sap when cut or broken

70. large tree with a single trunk . . . . Norway maple (*Acer platanoides*)

70. shrub or small tree, often multistemmed . . . . Hedge maple (*Acer campestre*)

69. leaf and flowers stalks not oozing milky sap . . . . Japanese maple (*Acer palmatum*)

1. flowers unisexual

71. male flowers in erect, spreading, or drooping catkins or catkin-like racemes

72. female flowers also in erect, spreading, or drooping catkins or dense, catkin-like racemes

73. male and female flowers on separate trees (dioecious)

74. milky sap present . . . . Mulberry (*Morus* spp.)

74. milky sap not present

75. male flowers with 1–9 stamens, nectar gland present . . . . Willows (*Salix* spp.)

75. male flowers with 8–40 stamens, nectar gland absent . . . . Poplars (*Populus* spp.)

73. male and female flowers on a single tree (monoecious)

76. flowers appearing before the leaves

77. female catkins persisting after the seeds are shed and resembling small pinecones

78. female catkins erect . . . . Speckled alder (*Alnus incana* ssp. *rugosa*)

78. female catkins bent downward . . . . Smooth alder (*Alnus serrulata*)

77. female catkins not persisting after the seeds are shed

79. bark brownish, rough and flaky . . . . Hop-hornbeam (*Ostrya virginica*)

79. bark smooth or becoming platy with age
    80. bark smooth and gray, not exfoliating . . . . . . Hornbeam (*Carpinus caroliniana*)
    80. bark dark reddish brown, white, yellowish or tan, often peeling horizontally in papery layers
        81. bark dark reddish-brown, not peeling horizontally . . . . Sweet birch (*Betula lenta*)
        81. bark lighter, peeling off in thin papery layers
            82. twigs strongly aromatic . . . . Yellow birch (*Betula alleghaniensis*)
            82. twigs not strongly aromatic
                83. bark tan to light brown . . . . River birch (*Betula nigra*)
                83. bark white
                    84. branches strongly pendulus . . . . European white birch (*Betula pendula*)
                    84. branches erect to only slightly drooping
                        85. twigs hairy . . . . European white birch (*Betula pubescens*)
                        85. twigs not hairy
                            86. twigs bearing many glands . . Gray birch (*Betula populifolia*)
                            86. twigs not bearing many glands . . . . Paper birch (*Betula papyrifera*)
76. flowers appearing after the leaves . . . . Honey-locust (*Gleditsia triacanthos*)
72. female flowers not in a catkin or catkin-like raceme
  87. female flowers in a globose cluster; flowers appearing after the leaves have expanded
    88. female flowers in one or more spiny clusters at the base of the upper male catkins
      89. leaves not hairy beneath . . . . American chestnut (*Castanea dentata*)
      89. leaves hairy beneath
        90. small, native understory tree or shrub to 15 feet . . Chinquapin (*Castanea pumila*)
        90. cultivated tree to 50–60 feet . . . . Chinese chestnut (*Castanea mollissima*)
    88. female flowers in globose clusters borne on separate stalks . . . . Paper mulberry (*Broussonetia papyrifera*)
  87. female flowers in the axils of newly emerging leaves
    91. male catkins in 3s on a common stalk . . . . Hickories (*Carya* spp.)
    91. male catkins solitary
      92. leaves simple, pith continuous . . . . Oaks (*Quercus* spp.)
      92. leaves pinnately compound; pith hollow with partitions
        93. pith dark brown . . . . Black walnut (*Juglans nigra*)
        93. pith tan . . . . Butternut (*Juglans cinerea*)
71. male flowers not in catkins or catkin-like racemes
  94. trees armed with spines or prickles, at least on the juvenile branches
    95. flowers in small umbel-like clusters, axillary; sap not milky . . . . Toothache tree (*Zanthoxylum americanum*)
    95. flowers in stalked spherical heads; sap milky . . . . Osage-orange (*Maclura pomifera*)
  94. trees not armed
    96. male and female flowers present on the same tree (monoecious)
      97. male flowers in spherical heads
        98. female flowers also in dense spherical heads
          99. male flowering heads clustered in an upright raceme with a single female head at the base . . . . Sweetgum (*Liquidambar styraciflua*)
          99. male flowering heads on drooping stalks,male heads spaced along on stalks that also bear 1-3 female heads
            100. female heads mostly 1 per stalk . . . . Sycamore (*Platanus occidentalis*)
            100. female heads 2–3 per stalk . . . . London planetree (*Platanus* x *acerifolia*)

98. female flowers on separate stalks . . . . American beech (*Fagus grandifolia*)

97. male flowers borne singly or in small clusters but not in dense spherical heads

    101. flowers borne singly or in small clusters along the new branchlets; leaves simple . . . . Hackberries (*Celtis* spp.)

    101. flowers in a large terminal panicle; leaves twice pinnate . . . . Kentucky coffeetree (*Gymnocladus dioicus*)

96. male and female flowers borne on separate trees (dioecious)

    102. flowers with both petals and sepals

        103. leaves opposite

            104. flowers appearing before the leaves

                105. flowers on slender drooping stalks . . . . Box-elder (*Acer negundo*)

                105. flowers in small sessile clusters . . . . Red maple (*Acer rubrum*)

            104. flowers appearing after the leaves have expanded

                106. stamens longer than the petals; fruit a drupe

                    107. bark thin . . . . Japanese corktree (*Phellodendron japonicum*)

                    107. bark thick and corky . . . . Lavalle corktree (*Phellodendron lavallei*)

                106. stamens shorter or equaling the petals; fruit a cluster of follicles . . . . Bee-bee tree (*Tetradium danielii*)

        103. leaves alternate

            108. flowers with 4 petals

                109. petals fused at the base; stamens 8 . . . . Persimmon (*Diospyros virginiana*)

                109. petals distinct; stamens 4

                    110. flowers in short branched clusters; leaves deciduous . . . . Hoptree (*Ptelea trifoliata*)

                    110. flowers borne singly or in small unbranched clusters; leaves evergreen . . . . American holly (*Ilex opaca*)

            108. flowers with 5 or more petals

                111. flowers (and leaves) borne on short lateral shoots

                    112. male flowers solitary on the stalks . . . . Mountain holly (*Ilex montana*)

                    112. male flowers clustered at the ends of the stalk . . . . Blackgum (*Nyssa sylvatica*)

                111. flowers not borne on short shoots

                  113. petals hairy

                    114. inflorescence terminal; twigs hairy . . . . Staghorn sumac (*Rhus typhina*)

                    114. inflorescence lateral; twigs smooth . . . . Poison sumac (*Toxicodendron vernix*)

                113. petals smooth, lacking hairs

                  115. inflorescence lateral; petals and stamens each 3–5 . . . . Hoptree (*Ptelea trifoliata*)

                  115. inflorescence terminal; petals 5; stamens 10 . . . . Tree-of-heaven (*Ailanthus altissima*)

    102. flowers lacking petals, sepals present or absent

        116. sepals lacking

            117. male flowers with 10–20 stamens . . . . Katsura (*Cercidiphyllum japonicum*)

            117. male flowers with 2–4 stamens . . . . Black ash (*Fraxinus nigra*)

        116. sepals (or tepals) present . . . .

            118. flowers with 6 greenish-yellow tepals; leaves alternate . . . . Sassafras (*Sassafras albidum*)

            118. flowers with small 4-lobed calyx; leaves opposite . . . . Ashes (*Fraxinus* spp.)

Key 3. Trees with opposite or whorled simple leaves

1. leaves 8–16 in. long, usually some whorled
  2. leaves entire
    3. apex of leaf abruptly acuminate; flowers 1¼–1½ in. wide, conspicuously purple-spotted . . . . Catalpa, Indian-bean (*Catalpa bignonioides*)
    3. apex of leaf long-acuminate; flowers 2–2½ in. wide, faintly purple-spotted . . . . Catalpa, cigar-tree (*Catalpa speciosa*)
  2. leaves toothed . . . . Empress-tree (*Paulownia tomentosa*)
1. leaves generally <8 in. long, all opposite
  4. leaves toothed or lobed
    5. leaves 3–5-lobed
      6. broken leaf stalks clearly showing milky juice
        7. leaves 4–8 in. across, not hairy below, teeth and lobes rounded . . . . Norway maple (*Acer platanoides*)
        7. leaves 2–4 in. across, hairy below, teeth and lobes pointed . . . . Hedge maple (*Acer campestre*)
      6. broken leaf stalks not showing milky juice
        8. leaves 3-lobed and finely double-toothed; bark of young trunk and branches striped . . . . Moosewood, striped maple (*Acer pensylvanicum*)
        8. leaves 3–5-lobed and coarsely toothed; bark of young trunk and branches not striped
          9. sinuses between the lobes extending about b of the way (or more) to the midvein
            10. large trees; leaves distinctly whitened below . . . . . Silver maple (*Acer saccharinum*)
            10. small trees or shrubs; leaves green below (or sometimes reddish)
              11. shrubs; leaves 3-lobed (or occasionally with some leaves 5-lobed) . . . . Amur maple (*Acer ginnala*)
              11. small trees; leaves 5–9-lobed . . . . Japanese maple (*Acer palmatum*)
          9. sinuses between the lobes extending halfway (or less) to the midvein
            12. bases of the sinuses between the principal lobes rounded
              13. stipules present (often stalked and resembling tiny leaves); sides of leaf blades turned under giving the leaves a claw-like appearance . . . . Black maple (*Acer nigrum*)
              13. stipules absent; leaf blades essentially flat . . . . . . Sugar maple (*Acer saccharum*)
            12. bases of the sinuses between the principal lobes forming a sharp angle
              14. leaves essentially not hairy below . . . . . . Sycamore maple (*Acer pseudoplatanus*)
              14. leaves whitened or hairy below
                15. shrubs or small trees; leaves generally hairy below . . . . Mountain maple (*Acer spicatum*)
                15. large trees; leaves whitened below, pubescence, if present, confined to the principal veins . . . . Red maple (*Acer rubrum*)
    5. leaves toothed but not lobed
      16. leaves pinnately veined . . . . Black-haw (*Viburnum prunifolium*)
      16. leaves palmately veined . . . . Katsura (*Cercidiphyllum japonicum*)
  4. leaves entire
    17. lateral veins of the leaves curving strongly toward the leaf apex; bases of the leaf stalks joined by stipule scars . . . . Flowering dogwood (*Cornus florida*)
    17. lateral veins of the leaves not curving strongly toward the leaf apex; bases of the leaf stalks not joined by stipule scars . . . . Fringetree (*Chionanthus virginicus*)

Key 4. Trees with opposite or whorled compound leaves

1. leaves palmately compound
   2. winter buds sticky; leaves mostly with 7 leaflets . . . . Horse-chestnut (*Aesculus hippocastanum*)
   2. winter buds not sticky; leaves mostly with 5 leaflets
      3. bark light grayish-brown, smooth; fruit not prickly; leaflets widest above the middle; petals yellow or reddish, of varying lengths, as long as or longer than the stamens . . . . Yellow buckeye (*Aesculus flava*)
      3. bark dark brownish-black, scaly; fruit prickly; leaflets widest at the middle; petals yellowish-green, similar in length, shorter than stamens . . . . Ohio buckeye (*Aesculus glabra*)
1. leaves pinnately compound
   4. branches remaining green for 3–4 years . . . . Box-elder (*Acer negundo*)
   4. 3–4-year-old branches gray or brown
      5. twigs lacking a terminal bud
         6. lateral buds hidden in the leaf stalk bases
            7. bark thick and corky; leaflets broadly tapered at base . . . . Corktree (*Phellodendron lavallei*)
            7. bark thin; leaflets truncate or slightly heart-shaped at base . . . . Japanese corktree (*Phellodendron japonicum*)
         6. lateral buds not hidden in the leaf stalk bases . . . . Bladdernut (*Staphylea trifolia*)
      5. twigs bearing a conspicuous terminal bud; lateral buds not hidden in the leaf stalk bases
         8. crushed leaves having a foul odor . . . . Bee-bee tree (*Tetradium daniellii*)
         8. crushed leaves not having a foul odor
            9. leaflets sessile; calyx absent; samaras flat throughout, winged to the base . . . . Black ash (*Fraxinus nigra*)
            9. leaflets definitely stalked; calyx present and persistent in fruit; samaras with a distinct subterete body and a flat wing
               10. stalks of the middle and lower leaflets with a wing extending from the blade nearly to the rachis; wing of the samara extending halfway or more down the body . . . . Green ash (*Fraxinus pennsylvanica*)
               10. stalks of the middle and lower leaflets wingless or nearly so; wing of the samara extending ⅓–½ the length of the subterete body
                  11. leaflets pale or whitish and papillose beneath; twigs, leaf stalks, and rachis usually not hairy . . . . White ash (*Fraxinus americana*)
                  11. leaflets green or tawny beneath, not papillose; twigs, leaf stalks, and rachis hairy . . . . Pumpkin ash (*Fraxinus profunda*)

Key 5. Trees with alternate simple leaves

1. evergreen tree; leaf margins armed with spines . . . . American holly (*Ilex opaca*)
1. deciduous trees; leaves unarmed
   2. leaves lobed (sometimes also toothed)
      3. leaves palmately lobed
         4. leaves aromatic when crushed
            5. leaves toothed as well as lobed . . . . Sweetgum (*Liquidambar styraciflua*)
            5. leaves lobed but not also toothed
               6. leaf apex obtuse to rounded . . . . Sassafras (*Sassafras albidum*)
               6. leaf apex truncate to indented . . . . Tuliptree (*Liriodendron tulipifera*)
         4. leaves not aromatic when crushed
            7. leaves strongly whitened below . . . . White poplar (*Populus alba*)
            7. leaves not strongly whitened below
               8. lateral buds hidden in the bases of the leaf stalks
                  9. branches armed with scattered prickles . . . . Castor-aralia (*Kalopanax septemlobus* var. *septemlobus*)
                  9. branches not armed

          10. bark white; fruiting heads borne singly ...... Sycamore (*Platanus occidentalis*)

          10. bark yellowish-gray; fruiting heads 2–3 per stalk ....

          .... London planetree (*Platanus* x *acerifolia*)

      8. lateral buds not hidden

          11. broken leaf stalks showing milky juice

            12. mature bark furrowed; twigs orangish

              13. leaves hairy beneath; fruit red then purplish-black ....

              .... Red mulberry (*Morus rubra*)

              13. leaves not hairy beneath except on the larger veins; fruit white, pink, or rarely purple .... White mulberry (*Morus alba*)

            12. mature bark smooth; twigs grayish ... Paper-mulberry (*Broussonetia papyrifera*)

          11. broken leaf stalks not showing milky juice ...... Tuliptree (*Liriodendron tulipifera*)

3. leaves pinnately lobed

    14. leaves with shallow tooth-like lobes

        15. leaf blades distinctly asymmetric at the base .... Witch-hazel (*Hamamelis virginiana*)

        15. leaf blades essentially symmetric at the base

          16. trees armed with thorns

            17. Leaves with some of the lateral veins extending to the sinuses as well as the lobes of the leaf

              18. leaves more or less tapered at the base, not rounded or heart-shaped ....

              .... English hawthorn (*Crataegus monogyna*)

              18. leaves rounded to heart-shaped at the base ....

              .... Washington hawthorn (*Crataegus phaenopyrum*)

            17. leaves with the lateral veins running only to the points of the lobes or teeth

              19. leaves of the flowering branches not lobed, broadest beyond the middle

                20. upper leaf surface very glossy; stalks of the flowers and fruits not hairy ....

                .... Cock-spur hawthorn (*Crataegus crus-galli*)

                20. upper leaf surface dull; stalks of the flowers and fruits hairy ....

                .... Dotted hawthorn (*Crataegus punctata*)

              19. leaves of the flowering branches broadest near or below the middle; leaf margin shallowly lobed or strongly doubly-toothed

                21. leaves broadly rounded, heart-shaped, or flattened at the base

                  22. mature leaves hairy beneath, at least on the veins

                    23. lower surface of the leaves hairy only on the veins at maturity; stamens about 10 .... Pennsylvania hawthorn (*Crataegus pennsylvanica*)

                    23. lower surface of the leaves hairy throughout; stamens about 20 .....

                    .... Downy hawthorn (*Crataegus mollis*)

                  22. mature leaves not hairy

                    24. leaf teeth/lobes short and blunt; fruit with a bluish-white waxy coating .... Frosted hawthorn (*Crataegus pruinosa*)

                  24. leaf teeth/lobes sharply pointed; fruit lacking a waxy coating

                    25. mature leaf stalk more or less hairy

                      26. fruit spherical ..... Red-fruited hawthorn (*Crataegus coccinea*)

                      26. fruit distinctly longer than wide ....

                      .... Holmes' hawthorn (*Crataegus holmsiana*)

                    25. mature leaf stalk not hairy

                      27. leaf stalk lacking glands ....

                      .... Broad-leaf hawthorn (*Crataegus dilatata*)

                      27. leaf stalk with a few scattered glands ....

                      .... Large-seed hawthorn (*Crataegus macrosperma*)

              21. leaves more or less tapered at the base

                28. leaves as wide or wider than they are long ....

                .... Dodge's hawthorn (*Crataegus dodgei*)

      28. leaves mostly longer than wide

          29. mature leaves not hairy beneath; leaves 1–2 inches long . . . .
            . . . . Round-leaf hawthorn (*Crataegus chrysocarpa*)

          29. mature leaves more or less hairy beneath, at least on the veins; leaves
            mostly more than 2 inches long

            30. leaf stalk and inflorescence branches hairy . . . .
              . . . . Pear hawthorn (*Crataegus calpodendron*)

            30. leaf stalks and inflorescence branches not hairy

               31. leaf stalk and leaf base with scattered glands; prominent gland-
                  bearing bracts present in the inflorescence . . . .
                  . . . . Biltmore hawthorn (*Crataegus intricata*)

               31. leaf stalk not hairy, inflorescence lacking gland-bearing bracts
                  . . . . Long-spine hawthorn (*Crataegus succulenta*)

16. trees unarmed

    32. tips of the teeth ending in a bristle; acorns maturing in one year . . . .
    . . . . Sawtooth oak (*Quercus acutissima*)

    32. tips of the teeth rounded, acute or with a short cusp, but not ending in a bristle

       33. stalk of acorn ¾ in. or more; lower surface of leaves densely hairy and soft to the
       touch, usually whitish or pale gray; in poorly drained habitats . . . .
       . . . . Swamp white oak (*Quercus bicolor*)

       33. stalk of acorn <¾ in.; lower leaf surface not hairy or variously hairy (hairs often
       not visible without magnification), green, pale green, or somewhat whitened; in
       well-drained habitats

          34. small tree or shrub; leaf teeth mostly 4–7 on each margin . . . .
          . . . . Dwarf chestnut oak (*Quercus prinoides*)

          34. tree; leaf teeth 8 or more on each margin

             35. leaves with rounded teeth, the hairs of the lower surface (under magnifi-
             cation) mostly 2–4 branched, branches ascending; mature bark dark gray,
             deeply ridged and furrowed; acorn cup funnel-shaped, the nut ¾–1¼ in.
             long . . . . Chestnut oak (*Quercus montana*)

             35. leaves with acute or incurved teeth, the hairs of the lower surface (under
             magnification) mostly 6- or more branched, the branches appressed or
             spreading; mature bark light gray, scaly; acorn cup bowl-shaped, the nut
             ⅜–¾ in. long . . . . Chinquapin oak (*Quercus muhlenbergii*)

14. leaves more deeply lobed

  36. leaf apex truncate or indented . . . . Tuliptree (*Liriodendron tulipifera*)

  36. leaf apex rounded or pointed

    37. leaves aromatic when crushed . . . . Sassafras (*Sassafras albidum*)

    37. leaves not aromatic when crushed

      38. tips of the lobes ending in a bristle; acorns maturing in 2 growing seasons

         39. lower surface of mature leaves not hairy or with tufts of hairs in the vein axils,
         or if hairy throughout, then the hairs easily removed by light rubbing with a
         finger

           40. mature buds densely hairy (usually whitish or grayish) throughout their
           length; scales around rim of the acorn cup loose at their tips . . . .
           . . . . Black oak (*Quercus velutina*)

           40. mature buds not hairy, or densely hairy only on the upper half or near the
           tip; scales around rim of the acorn cup appressed

             41. sinuses between lobes of the leaf relatively shallow, mostly ½ or less the
             distance to the midrib . . . . Red oak (*Quercus rubra*)

             41. sinuses between lobes relatively deep, >½ (often ¾ or more) the distance
             to the midrib

               42. upper scales of mature buds densely hairy and contrasting with the

not hairy or sparsely hairy lower scales; acorn cup covering about ½ of the nut; upland species . . . . Scarlet oak (*Quercus coccinea*)

42. upper scales of mature buds mostly not hairy, similar to the lower scales; acorn cup covering ½–⅓ of the nut; lowland species

    43. bud scales red-brown, relatively lustrous; nut about ⅜ in. long; leaf lobes 5–7, tending to narrow to the tip with relatively few teeth and secondary lobes . . . . Pin oak (*Quercus palustris*)

    43. bud scales brownish or grayish, relatively dull; nut ½–1 in. long; leaf lobes mostly 7, tending to enlarge to the tip with relatively numerous teeth and secondary lobes . . . .
. . . . Shumard oak (*Quercus shumardii*)

39. lower surface of mature leaves densely and closely hairy, the hairs crusty-granular or soft and felt-like, not easily removed by light rubbing with a finger

    44. shrub; leaf blades mostly <4 in. long, white or light gray below . . . .
. . . . Scrub oak (*Quercus ilicifolia*)

    44. tree; leaf blades usually >4 in. long, green, yellow-green, rusty, or grayish below

        45. leaves widest near the tip, often with 3 shallow lobes, the hairs of the lower surface crusty-granular; acorn cup covering ½ of the nut . . . .
. . . . Blackjack oak (*Quercus marilandica*)

        45. leaves widest below to above the middle, with 3–7 mostly narrow, often curved lobes, the hairs of the lower surface relatively soft and felt-like; acorn cup covering ⅓–½ of the nut . . Southern red oak (*Quercus falcata*)

38. tips of the lobes rounded; acorns maturing in 1 growing season

    46. leaves not hairy beneath . . . . White oak (*Quercus alba*)

    46. leaves hairy beneath (hairs may not be evident without magnification)

        47. leaves variously lobed, the upper half tending to be coarsely toothed; scales around the rim of the acorn cup elongate and curly, the cup covering ½ or more of the nut . . . . Burr oak (*Quercus macrocarpa*)

        47. leaves, or many of them, tending to be cross-shaped; scales around the rim of the acorn cup loose, the cup covering ⅓–½ of the nut . . . .
. . . . Post oak (*Quercus stellata*)

2. leaves toothed or entire

  48. leaves toothed

    49. trees armed

      50. spines or thorns occurring only on the branch tips

        51. lenticels on the stems absent or (if present) not horizontally oriented

          52. upper surface of leaves somewhat glossy; terminal buds pointed; flowers white

            53. fruit pear-shaped, >1½ in. in diameter; calyx lobes persistent; styles 5 . . . .
. . . . Pear (*Pyrus communis*)

            53. fruit globose, ⅜ in. or less in diameter; calyx lobes deciduous; styles 2–3 . . . . . .
. . . . Callery pear (*Pyrus calleryana*)

          52. upper surface of leaves not glossy; terminal buds rounded; flowers usually pink or pinkish-tinged

            54. hypanthium, flower stalks, and young twigs densely hairy . . . .
. . . . Apple (*Malus pumila*)

            54. hypanthium, flower stalks, and young twigs not densely hairy, although sometimes somewhat hairy

              55. hypanthium and flower stalks not hairy or with some long, soft hairs; sepals persistent in fruit . . . . Sweet crabapple (*Malus coronaria*)

              55. hypanthium and flower stalks hairy; sepals deciduous in fruit . . . .
. . . . Crabapples (*Malus* hybrids)

51. lenticels on the stems prominent and horizontally oriented
    56. leaf teeth glandless; sepals lacking marginal glands
        57. leaves ovate, oval, or obovate, acute to obtuse; lower leaf surfaces, flower stalks, and hypanthium hairy . . . . Beach plum (*Prunus maritima*)
        57. leaves lanceolate to ovate, long acuminate; lower leaf surfaces slightly hairy to becoming smooth; flower stalks and hypanthium not hairy
            58. leaves abruptly long-acuminate; petals ¼–½ in. long . . . .
            . . . . American plum (*Prunus americana*)
            58. leaves gradually acuminate; petals ⅛–¼ in. long . . . .
            . . . . Allegheny plum (*Prunus allegheniensis*)
    56. leaf teeth gland-tipped (or with a scar where the gland had been); calyx without marginal glands . . . . Chickasaw plum (*Prunus angustifolia*)
50. thorns abundant on the branches
    59. leaves with some of the lateral veins extending to the sinuses as well as the lobes of the leaf
        60. leaves more or less tapered at the base, not rounded or heart-shaped . . . .
        . . . . English hawthorn (*Crataegus monogyna*)
        60. leaves rounded to heart-shaped at the base . . . .
        . . . . Washington hawthorn (*Crataegus phaenopyrum*)
    59. leaves with the lateral veins running only to the points of the lobes or teeth
        61. leaves of the flowering branches not lobed, broadest beyond the middle
            62. upper leaf surface very glossy; stalks of the flowers and fruits not hairy . . . .
            . . . . Cock-spur hawthorn (*Crataegus crus-galli*)
            62. upper leaf surface dull; stalks of the flowers and fruits hairy . . . .
            . . . . Dotted hawthorn (*Crataegus punctata*)
        61. leaves of the flowering branches broadest near or below the middle; leaf margin shallowly lobed or strongly doubly-toothed
            63. leaves broadly rounded, heart-shaped, or flattened at the base
                64. mature leaves hairy beneath, at least on the veins
                    65. lower surface of the leaves hairy only on the veins at maturity; stamens about 10 . . . . Pennsylvania hawthorn (*Crataegus pennsylvanica*)
                    65. lower surface of the leaves hairy throughout; stamens about 20 . . . .
                    . . . . Downy hawthorn(*Crataegus mollis*)
                64. mature leaves not hairy
                    66. leaf teeth/lobes short and blunt; fruit with a bluish-white waxy coating
                    . . . . Frosted hawthorn (*Crataegus pruinosa*)
                    66. leaf teeth/lobes sharply pointed; fruit lacking a waxy coating
                        67. mature leaf stalk more or less hairy
                            68. fruit spherical . . . . Red-fruited hawthorn (*Crataegus coccinea*)
                            68. fruit distinctly longer than wide . . . .
                            . . . . Holme's hawthorn (*Crataegus holmsiana*)
                        67. mature leaf stalk not hairy
                            69. leaf stalk lacking glands . . . .
                          . . . . Broad-leaf hawthorn (*Crataegus dilatata*)
                            69. leaf stalk with a few scattered glands . . . .
                          . . . . Large-seed hawthorn (*Crataegus macrosperma*)
            63. leaves more or less tapered at the base
                70. leaves as wide or wider than they are long . . . .
                . . . . Dodge's hawthorn (*Crataegus dodgei*)
                70. leaves mostly longer than wide
                    71. mature leaves not hairy beneath; leaves 1–2 inches long . . . .
                    . . . . Round-leaf hawthorn (*Crataegus chrysocarpa*)

71. mature leaves more or less hairy beneath, at least on the veins; leaves mostly more than 2 inches long
  72. leaf stalk and inflorescence branches hairy . . . . Pear hawthorn (*Crataegus calpodendron*)
  72. leaf stalks and inflorescence branches not hairy
    73. leaf stalk and leaf base with scattered glands; prominent gland-bearing bracts present in the inflorescence . . . . Biltmore hawthorn (*Crataegus intricata*)
    73. leaf stalk not hairy, inflorescence lacking gland-bearing bracts . . . . Long-spine hawthorn (*Crataegus succulenta*)
49. trees unarmed
  74. leaf blades asymmetric at the base
    75. teeth rounded and irregular; buds naked . . . . Witch-hazel (*Hamamelis virginiana*)
    75. teeth pointed; buds covered by scales
      76. lateral leaf veins extending into the teeth
        77. leaf blades about as wide as long, heart-shaped . . . . Basswood (*Tilia americana*)
        77. leaf blades longer than wide, not heart-shaped
          78. leaves and twigs very rough to the touch; buds rusty, densely hairy . . . . Slippery elm (*Ulmus rubra*)
          78. leaves and twigs not hairy or only slightly rough to the touch; buds not hairy or somewhat pale-hairy
            79. leaves mostly single-toothed . . . . Chinese elm (*Ulmus parvifolia*)
            79. leaves mostly double-toothed . . . . American elm (*Ulmus americana*)
      76. lateral leaf veins branching and curving before reaching the teeth
        80. leaves toothed to below the middle; fruiting stalks longer than the leaf stalks . . . . Hackberry (*Celtis occidentalis*)
        80. leaves entire or with only a few scattered teeth above the middle; fruiting stalks about as long as the leaf stalks . . . . Dwarf hackberry (*Celtis tenuifolia*)
  74. leaf blades essentially symmetric at base
    81. leaves palmately veined
      82. mature bark furrowed; twigs orangish
        83. winter buds ¼–⅓ in.; leaves hairy beneath; fruit red then purplish-black . . . . Red mulberry (*Morus rubra*)
        83. winter buds about ⅛ in.; leaves not hairy beneath except on the larger veins; fruit white, pink, or rarely purple . . . . White mulberry (*Morus alba*)
      82. mature bark smooth; twigs grayish . . . . . . Paper-mulberry (*Broussonetia papyrifera*)
    81. leaves pinnately veined
      84. lateral leaf veins extending into the teeth
        85. one lateral vein extending into each tooth, the number of lateral veins equaling the number of teeth
          86. terminal buds ⅜–1 in., sharp pointed . . . . American beech (*Fagus grandifolia*)
          86. terminal buds generally <⅜ in.
            87. terminal buds clustered at the tips of the twigs
              88. tips of the teeth ending in a bristle; acorns maturing in one year . . . . Sawtooth oak (*Quercus acutissima*)
              88. tips of the teeth rounded, acute or with a short cusp, but not ending in a bristle
                89. stalk of acorn ¾ in. or more; lower surface of leaves densely hairy and soft to the touch, usually whitish or pale gray; in poorly drained habitats . . . . Swamp white oak (*Quercus bicolor*)

89. stalk of acorn <¾ in.; lower leaf surface not hairy or variously hairy (hairs often not visible without magnification), green, pale green, or somewhat whitened; in well-drained habitats
  90. small tree or shrub; leaf teeth mostly 4–7 on each margin . . . .
    . . . . Dwarf chestnut oak (*Quercus prinoides*)
  90. tree; leaf teeth 8 or more on each margin
    91. leaves with rounded teeth, the hairs of the lower surface (under magnification) mostly 2–4-branched, branches ascending; mature bark dark gray, deeply ridged and furrowed; acorn cup funnel-shaped, the nut ¼–1¼ in. long . . .
    . . . . Chestnut oak (*Quercus montana*)
    91. leaves with acute or incurved teeth, the hairs of the lower surface (under magnification) mostly 6- or more branched, the branches appressed or spreading; mature bark light gray, scaly; acorn cup bowl-shaped, the nut ⅜–¾ in. long . . . .
    . . . . Chinquapin oak (*Quercus muhlenbergii*)
87. terminal buds solitary at the tips of the twigs
  92. pith star-shaped in cross section
    93. mature leaves green and not hairy below; branches and buds not hairy; nuts usually 2–4 per bur . . . .
    . . . . American chestnut (*Castanea dentata*)
    93. mature leaves whitish- or grayish-hairy below
      94. shrub or small tree to 17 ft. tall; nut usually 1 per bur . . . .
      . . . . Chinquapin (*Castanea pumila*)
      94. tree to 65 ft. tall; nuts 2 or 3 per bur . . . .
      . . . . Chinese chestnut (*Castanea mollissima*)
  92. pith round in cross section . . . . Siberian elm (*Ulmus pumila*)
85. teeth more numerous than the lateral veins
  95. leaves deeply heart-shaped at the base . . . . Basswood (*Tilia americana*)
  95. leaves, rounded, truncate, or shallowly heart-shaped at the base, not heart-shaped
    96. small trees or shrubs
      97. tall, multistemmed colonial shrubs; leaves with 8–14 principal veins on each side, acute to short acuminate at apex; female catkins ⅜–½ in.
        98. leaves doubly toothed; teeth irregular in size; female catkins bent downward . . . . Speckled alder (*Alnus incana* ssp. *rugosa*)
        98. leaves finely toothed; female catkins erect . . . .
        . . . . Smooth alder (*Alnus serrulata*)
      97. upright small trees; leaves with 5–8 principal veins on each side, rounded or notched at apex; female catkins ½–1¼ in. . . . .
      . . . . European alder (*Alnus glutinosa*)
    96. medium to large trees
      99. bark brownish, rough and flaky . . . .
      . . . . Hop-hornbeam (*Ostrya virginiana*)
      99. bark smooth or becoming rough and platy with age
        100. bark smooth and gray, not exfoliating; lenticels not obvious . . . .
        . . . . Hornbeam (*Carpinus caroliniana*)
        100. bark dark reddish-brown, white, whitish-tan, or yellowish, often papery and exfoliating; lenticels obvious
          101. mature bark white or creamy

102. leaves triangular or rhombic with an acuminate tip
    103. branches not pendulous; leaf tip long-acuminate . . . . Gray birch (*Betula populifolia*)
    103. branches pendulous; leaf tip acuminate . . . . European white birch (*Betula pendula*)
102. leaves ovate with an acute tip
    104. leaves 2–3 in. long; branches erect to slightly drooping . . . . Paper birch (*Betula papyrifera*)
    104. leaves 1¼–2 in. long; branches stiffly erect . . . . European white birch (*Betula pubescens*)
101. mature bark light reddish-brown, yellowish-gray, or dark blackish-brown, but not white
    105. twigs slightly to strongly aromatic when scraped or crushed; bark dark and tight or yellowish-gray and exfoliating; leaves rounded to heart-shaped at the base
        106. bark blackish-brown, not exfoliating but becoming rough and platy in age; twigs strongly aromatic . . . . Sweet birch (*Betula lenta*)
        106. bark yellowish-gray, exfoliating in papery layers; twigs weakly aromatic . . . Yellow birch (*Betula alleghaniensis*)
    105. twigs not aromatic; bark light reddish-brown, exfoliating in irregular papery layers; leaves tapered at the base . . . . River birch (*Betula nigra*)
84. lateral leaf veins branching and curving before reaching the teeth
  107. leaf stalk distinctly flattened toward the base of the blade
    108. leaf stalk markedly flattened near its apex
      109. leaf margin minutely hairy, especially on the teeth
        110. large leaves notably broader than long, without glands at the base of the blade . . . . Lombardy poplar (*Populus nigra*)
        110. large leaves no broader than long, with 0–6 glands . . . . Eastern cottonwood (*Populus deltoides*)
      109. leaf margin without hairs
        111. teeth 3–15 on each side, coarse . . . . Big-tooth aspen (*Populus grandidentata*)
        111. teeth >15 on each side, fine
          112. leaves hairy beneath, with 2 cup-shaped glands at the base of the blade . . . . Big-tooth aspen (*Populus grandidentata*)
          112. leaves not hairy beneath, without glands at the base of the blade . . . . Quaking aspen (*Populus tremuloides*)
    108. leaf stalk only slightly flattened top to bottom
      113. mature leaves not hairy or hairy only on the veins below
        114. leaves obtuse to rounded at apex, heart-shaped at base, hairy on the veins below . . . . Swamp cottonwood (*Populus heterophylla*)
        114. leaves acute to acuminate at apex, tapered to slightly heart-shaped at base, not hairy below . . . . Balsam poplar (*Populus balsamifera*)
      113. mature leaves densely hairy below . . . . White poplar (*Populus alba*)
  107. leaf stalk rounded or grooved
    115. buds covered by a single scale
      116. bud scale margins free and overlapping; buds sharply pointed
        117. leaf blades not whitened beneath, shiny above . . . . Black willow (*Salix nigra*)

117. leaf blades whitened beneath, dull or highly glossy above . . . .
. . . . Peach-leaved willow (*Salix amygdaloides*)
118. leaves dull above, broadly to narrowly lanceolate, 3–6 times as
long as wide; stipules lacking or rudimentary, leaf-like only on
vigorous or late-season shoots
118. leaves highly glossy above; leaves lanceolate to very narrowly so,
5–10 times as long as wide; stipules leaf-like . . . .
. . . . Carolina willow (*Salix caroliniana*)
116. bud scale cap-like, its margins fused; buds blunt
119. leaves not whitened beneath
120. stipules leaf-like . . . . Shining willow (*Salix lucida*)
120. stipules lacking or rudimentary
119. leaves whitened beneath or the lower surface obscured by dense hairs
121. branches strongly pendulous . . . .
. . . . Weeping willow (*Salix babylonica*)
121. stems erect or drooping
122. leaves dull above, remaining silky in age; branches flexible to
somewhat brittle at the base, epidermis flaky . . . .
. . . . White willow (*Salix alba*)
122. leaves shiny or highly glossy above (sometimes dull in S. x
rubens); soon becoming smooth; branches highly brittle at the
base, epidermis not flaky . . . . Crack willow (*Salix fragilis*)
115. buds covered by multiple scales
123. lenticels on the stems prominent and horizontally oriented
124. inflorescence a raceme
125. leaves with a conspicuous hairy zone along the midrib toward the
base beneath; leaf teeth rounded at the tips; calyx lobes persistent
in fruit . . . . Wild black cherry (*Prunus serotina*)
125. leaves lacking hairs along the midrib beneath; leaf teeth with fine
hair-like tips; calyx lobes deciduous in fruit
126. petals twice as long as the stamens . . . .
. . . . European bird cherry (*Prunus padus*)
126. petals as long as or only ⅓ longer than the stamens . . . .
. . . . Choke cherry (*Prunus virginiana*)
124. flowers in umbel-like clusters
127. bark smooth with prominent horizontal lenticels; branchlets
never thorny; stone globose
128. leaves finely toothed, not hairy; fruits ¼ in. in diameter . . . . .
. . . . Pin cherry (*Prunus pensylvanica*)
128. leaves toothed or doubly toothed
129. leaf stalks 1–1½ in. long; fruits ½–¾ in. in diameter . . . . . .
. . . . Sweet cherry (*Prunus avium*)
129. leaf stalks ⅜–¾ in. long; fruits ⅛–⅜ in. in diameter . . . .
. . . . Higan cherry (*Prunus subhirtella*)
127. bark rough and scaly, lenticels not prominent; branchlets sometimes ending in thorns; stone flattened, with lateral ridges
(plums)
130. leaf teeth glandless; sepals lacking marginal glands
131. leaves ovate, oval, or obovate, acute to obtuse; lower leaf
surfaces, flower stalks, and hypanthium hairy . . . .
. . . . Beach plum (*Prunus maritima*)

131. leaves lanceolate to ovate, long acuminate; lower leaf surfaces slightly hairy to becoming smooth; flower stalks and hypanthium not hairy

132. leaves abruptly long-acuminate; petals ⅓–½ in. long .... American plum (*Prunus americana*)

132. leaves gradually acuminate; petals ⅛–⅓ in. long .... Allegheny plum (*Prunus allegheniensis*)

130. leaf teeth gland-tipped (or with a scar where the gland had been); calyx without marginal glands .... Chickasaw plum (*Prunus angustifolia*)

123. lenticels on the stems absent or (if present) not horizontally oriented

133. leaves with branched hairs below

134. pith hollow with partitions .... Carolina silverbell (*Halesia caroliniana*)

134. pith solid .... Japanese snowbell (*Styrax japonica*)

133. leaves not hairy or pubescence not stellate

135. broken leaf stalk showing milky juice

136. mature bark furrowed; twigs orangish

137. winter buds ⅛–⅓ in.; leaves hairy beneath; fruit red then purplish-black .... Red mulberry (*Morus rubra*)

137. winter buds 1/16–⅛ in.; leaves not hairy beneath except on the larger veins; fruit white, pink, or rarely purple .... White mulberry (*Morus alba*)

136. mature bark smooth; twigs grayish .... Paper-mulberry (*Broussonetia papyrifera*)

135. broken leaf stalk not showing milky juice

138. neither stipules nor stipule scars present

139. leaves acute to rounded at base .... Sourwood (*Oxydendrum arboreum*)

139. leaves tapered at base .... Sapphire-berry (*Symplocos paniculata*)

138. stipules or stipule scars present

140. leaf scars with 1 vein scar .... Mountain holly (*Ilex montana*)

140. leaf scars with > 1 vein scar

141. leaves mostly obovate, tapered at the base .... Oriental photinia (*Photinia villosa*)

141. leaves mostly ovate to elliptic, rounded to acute at the base

142. flowers and fruits mostly in racemes

143. leaf undersurface densely hairy to densely covered with long, straight hairs, although some hairs are shed early, hairs always present on leaf undersurface at base of midrib at leaf abscission; young leaves green .... Shadbush (*Amelanchier arborea*)

143. amount of hair on the leaf undersurface variable, but undersurface completely smooth by the time of leaf abscission, and frequently before; young leaves frequently copper-colored, red pigment also evident in fall coloration .... Smooth shadbush (*Amelanchier laevis*)

142. flowers and fruits not in racemes

    144. upper surface of leaves somewhat glossy; terminal buds pointed; flowers white

        145. fruit pear-shaped, >1½ in. in diameter; calyx lobes persistent; styles 5 . . . . Pear (*Pyrus communis*)

        145. fruit globose, ⅓ in. or less in diameter; calyx lobes deciduous; styles 2–3 . . . . Callery pear (*Pyrus calleryana*)

    144. upper surface of leaves not glossy; terminal buds rounded; flowers usually pink or pinkish-tinged

        146. hypanthium, flower stalks, and young twigs densely hairy . . . . Apple (*Malus pumila*)

        146. hypanthium, flower stalks, and young twigs not densely hairy, although sometimes somewhat hairy

           147. hypanthium and flower stalks not hairy or with some long, soft hairs; sepals persistent in fruit . . . . Sweet crabapple (*Malus coronaria*)

           147. hypanthium and flower stalks hairy; sepals deciduous in fruit . . . . Crabapples (*Malus* hybrids)

48. leaves entire

  148. tree armed . . . . Osage-orange (*Maclura pomifera*)

  148. trees unarmed

    149. leaves averaging >6 in. long

      150. stipules or stipule scars encircling the twigs

        151. buds not hairy . . . . Umbrella-tree (*Magnolia tripetala*)

        151. buds hairy . . . . Cucumber-tree (*Magnolia acuminata*)

      150. stipules or stipule scars absent . . . . Pawpaw (*Asimina triloba*)

    149. leaves averaging <6 in. long

      152. leaves palmately veined . . . . Redbud (*Cercis canadensis*)

      152. leaves pinnately veined

        153. leaves aromatic when crushed

          154. stipules or stipule scars encircling the twigs

            155. leaves semi-evergreen, thick and leathery, strongly whitened beneath . . . . Sweetbay magnolia (*Magnolia virginiana*)

            155. leaves promptly deciduous, thin, green beneath

              156. large tree to 100 ft.; flowers appearing with the leaves, greenish-yellow . . . . Cucumber-tree (*Magnolia acuminata*)

              156. smaller tree to 35 ft.; flowering before the leaves emerge

                157. flowers white . . . . Kobus magnolia (*Magnolia kobus*)

                157. flowers purple . . . . Saucer magnolia (*Magnolia soulangeana*)

          154. stipules or stipule scars absent . . . . Sassafras (*Sassafras albidum*)

        153. leaves not aromatic when crushed

          158. pith star-shaped in cross section; terminal buds clustered at the tips of the branches

            159. leaves mostly ¾–1½ in. wide, densely hairy beneath . . . . Shingle oak (*Quercus imbricaria*)

            159. leaves mostly ⅜–¾ in. wide, usually smooth or nearly so beneath . . . . Willow oak (*Quercus phellos*)

158. pith round in cross section; terminal buds borne singly at the tips of the branches
 160. broken leaf stalk showing milky juice ... Osage-orange (*Maclura pomifera*)
 160. broken leaf stalk not showing milky juice
  161. carefully torn leaf blade remaining connected by fibrous threads .....
  .... Alternate-leaf dogwood (*Cornus alternifolia*)
  161. carefully torn leaf blade not remaining connected by fibrous threads
   162. pith solid; buds dark brown, rounded at the apex ....
   .... Persimmon (*Diospyros virginiana*)
   162. pith with darker cross walls; buds greenish, acute at the apex ......
   .... Blackgum (*Nyssa sylvatica*)

Key 6. Trees with alternate compound leaves

1. trees armed with thorns, spines, or prickles
 2. leaves twice-pinnately compound
  3. stems and leaves armed
   4. inflorescence with a distinct central axis; leaf stalk and rachis bearing prickles; veins of leaflets not running to the teeth .... Hercules'-club (*Aralia spinosa*)
   4. central axis of the inflorescence very short or lacking; leaf stalk and rachis lacking prickles; veins of leaflets running into the teeth .... Japanese angelica-tree (*Aralia elata*)
  3. stems only armed .... Honey-locust (*Gleditsia triacanthos*)
 2. leaves once compound
  5. leaves and twigs aromatic when crushed .... Toothache-tree (*Zanthoxylum americanum*)
  5. leaves and twigs not aromatic when crushed .... Black locust (*Robinia pseudoaccacia*)
1. trees unarmed
 6. leaves twice-pinnately compound
  7. leaflets rounded at the apex .... Honey-locust (*Gleditsia triacanthos*)
  7. leaflets more or less pointed at the apex
   8. leaflets coarsely and irregularly toothed or lobed ... Goldenrain tree (*Koelreuteria paniculata*)
   8. leaflets entire
    9. main vein of leaflets near margin .... Mimosa (*Albizia julibrissin*)
    9. main vein of leaflets near center .... Kentucky coffeetree (*Gymnocladus dioica*)
 6. leaves once compound
  10. leaves with 3 leaflets .... Hoptree (*Ptelea trifoliata*)
  10. leaves with > 3 leaflets
   11. leaflets toothed or lobed
    12. leaflets coarsely few-toothed near the base of the blade, each tooth bearing a black gland at the tip .... Tree-of-heaven (*Ailanthus altissima*)
    12. leaflets toothed or lobed along all or most of margin
     13. leaflets coarsely and irregularly toothed or lobed ....
     .... Goldenrain tree (*Koelreuteria paniculata*)
     13. leaflets regularly toothed
      14. pith hollow with partitions
       15. pith dark brown; upper margin of the leaf scars not notched, with a prominent hairy fringe all the way across; fruit oblong-ovoid, pointed ....
       .... Butternut (*Juglans cinerea*)
       15. pith tan; upper margin of the leaf scars notched, sometimes with a pad of hairs at the center, but not hairy all the way across; fruit subglobose, not at all pointed
       .... Black walnut (*Juglans nigra*)
      14. pith solid

16. stipules present

    17. twigs, leaves, inflorescence branches, and hypanthium not hairy; winter buds sticky

        18. leaflets long-acuminate, 3–5 times as long as wide; fruit ⅛–¼ in. thick . . . . Amerian mountain-ash (*Sorbus americana*)

        18. leaflets short-acuminate or acute, 2–3 times as long as wide; fruit ¼–⅓ in. thick . . . . Showy mountain-ash (*Sorbus decora*)

    17. twigs, lower leaf surfaces, inflorescence branches, hypanthiums and winter buds with dense white, long, soft hairs; buds not sticky . . . . European mountain-ash (*Sorbus aucuparia*)

16. stipules absent

    19. pith occupying more than ½ the diameter of the stem

        20. twigs densely long-hairy . . . . Staghorn sumac (*Rhus typhina*)

        20. twigs not hairy or short-hairy . . . . Chinese-cedar (*Cedrela sinensis*)

    19. pith occupying less than ½ the diameter of the stem

        21. buds bright yellow; bud scales 4–6, not overlapping; leaflets 7–9(11); husk winged along the sutures . . . . Bitternut hickory (*Carya cordiformis*)

        21. buds brown or gray; bud scales >6, overlapping; leaflets 5–7(9); husk not winged

            22. terminal buds <⅓ in.; twigs not hairy; leaflets mostly not hairy beneath . . . . Pignut hickory (*Carya glabra*)

            22. terminal buds ⅓–1⅛ in.; twigs hairy; leaflets hairy beneath, at least on the veins

                23. mature bark deeply furrowed but not shaggy; outer bud scales deciduous; husk of fruit <¼ in. thick . . . . Mockernut hickory (*Carya tomentosa*)

                23. bark exfoliating in long shaggy strips; outer bud scales persistent; husk of fruit to ⅜ in. thick

                    24. leaflets 7–9, dense lower surface pubescence persisting at maturity; fruit oblong, ⅛–⅓ in. long, nut flattened; apices of outer bud scales prolonged into stiff, spreading points . . . . Shellbark hickory (*Carya laciniosa*)

                    24. leaflets 5, lower surface pubescence mostly limited to veins and tufts of hairs in the teeth at maturity; fruit subglobose to ovoid, 1½–2 in. long, nut not flattened; apices of outer bud scales prolonged, but not stiff and spreading . . . . Shagbark hickory (*Carya ovata*)

11. leaflets entire

    25. once compound and twice-pinnately compound leaves on the same tree . . . . Honey-locust (*Gleditsia triacanthos*)

    25. all leaves once compound

        26. lower leaflets coarsely few-toothed near the base of the blade, each tooth bearing a black gland at the tip . . . . Tree-of-heaven (*Ailanthus altissima*)

        26. all leaflets strictly entire

            27. base of the leaf stalk not conspicuously swollen . . . . Poison sumac (*Toxicodendron vernix*)

            27. base of the leaf stalk prominently swollen . . . . Japanese pagoda-tree (*Sophora japonica*)

Key 7. Leafless trees with leaf scars opposite or whorled

1. vein scars several in a straight or curved line, crowded or joined to appear as 1
  2. large trees
    3. leaf scars mostly with a concave upper margin, indented by the bud . . . . White ash (*Fraxinus americana*)
    3. leaf scars with a truncate or only slightly concave upper margin, not strongly indented by the bud
      4. twigs hairy
        5. widespread in moist woods and floodplains . . . . Green ash (*Fraxinus pennsylvanica*)
        5. only in vernal ponds and wet woods along Lake Erie . . . Pumpkin ash (*Fraxinus profunda*)
      4. twigs not hairy
        6. terminal bud wider than long . . . . Green ash (*Fraxinus pennsylvanica*)
        6. terminal bud as long as or longer than wide . . . . Black ash (*Fraxinus nigra*)
  2. small tree or shrub . . . . White fringetree (*Chionanthus virginicus*)
1. vein scars 3 or more and distinct
  7. terminal buds absent
    8. leaf scars nearly or completely surrounding the lateral buds
      9. bark thick and corky . . . . Lavalle corktree (*Phellodendron lavallii*)
      9. bark thin . . . . Japanese corktree (*Phellodendron japonicum*)
    8. leaf scars clearly below the lateral buds
      10. vein scars 3
        11. stipule scars absent . . . . Katsura (*Cercidiphyllum japonicum*)
        11. stipule scars present . . . . Bladdernut (*Staphylea trifolia*)
      10. vein scars 7 or more
        12. tree to 50 ft.; fruit ¼–⅜ in. thick . . . . Southern catalpa (*Catalpa bignonioides*)
        12. tree to 100 ft.; fruit ⅜–½ in. thick . . . . Northern catalpa (*Catalpa speciosa*)
  7. terminal buds present
    13. terminal buds naked or bud scales impossible to distinguish . . Bee-bee tree (*Tetradium daniellii*)
    13. terminal buds clearly covered by scales
      14. bud scales not overlapping
        15. leaf scars raised on persistent leaf stalk bases . . . . . . Flowering dogwood (*Cornus florida*)
        15. leaf scars not raised on leaf stalk bases . . . . Blackhaw (*Viburnum prunifolium*)
      14. bud scales overlapping
        16. vein scars close and nearly joined in a C- or U-shaped line
          17. large trees
            18. leaf scars mostly with a concave upper margin, indented by the bud . . . . White ash (*Fraxinus americana*)
            18. leaf scars with a truncate or only slightly concave upper margin, not strongly indented by the bud
              19. twigs hairy
                20. widespread in moist woods and floodplains . . . . Green ash (*Fraxinus pennsylvanica*)
                20. only in vernal ponds and wet woods along Lake Erie . . . . Pumpkin ash (*Fraxinus profunda*)
              19. twigs not hairy
                21. terminal bud wider than long . . . . Green ash (*Fraxinus pennsylvanica*)
                21. terminal bud as long as or longer than wide . . . . . Black ash (*Fraxinus nigra*)
          17. small tree or shrub . . . . White fringetree (*Chionanthus virginicus*)
        16. vein scars clearly separate and distinct
          22. vein scars 5 or more (usually in 3 groups); terminal buds often >½ in.
            23. winter buds sticky . . . . Horse-chestnut (*Aesculus hippocastanum*)
            23. winter buds not sticky

24. bark light grayish-brown, smooth . . . . Yellow buckeye (*Aesculus flava*)
24. bark dark brownish-black, scaly . . . . Ohio buckeye (*Aesculus glabra*)
22. vein scars 3 (rarely 5); terminal buds usually <½ in.
    25. buds stalked, covered by 2 exposed not overlapping scales
        26. twigs and buds not hairy; bark white striped . . . .
            . . . . Striped maple (*Acer pensylvanicum*)
        26. twigs and buds hairy; bark not white striped . . . .
            . . . . Mountain maple (*Acer spicatum*)
    25. buds sessile, covered by >2 exposed overlapping scales
        27. buds densely covered with white hairs . . . . Box-elder (*Acer negundo*)
        27. buds not densely covered with white hairs
            28. terminal buds usually ¼–½ in.
                29. buds reddish; opposite leaf scars meeting . . . .
                    . . . . Norway maple (*Acer platanoides*)
                29. buds green; opposite leaf scars not meeting . . . .
                    . . . . Sycamore maple (*Acer pseudoplatanus*)
            28. terminal buds usually <¼ in.
                30. terminal buds rounded or blunt pointed; 4 or fewer pairs of bud scales visible
                    31. bud scales not hairy
                        32. terminal buds ⅛–¼ in.
                            33. twigs foul smelling when broken; bark flaking on older trunks
                                . . . . Silver maple (*Acer saccharinum*)
                            33. twigs not foul smelling when broken; bark rough but not usually flaking on older trunks . . . . Red maple (*Acer rubrum*)
                        32. terminal buds ¹⁄₁₆–⅛ in. . . . . Amur maple (*Acer ginnala*)
                    31. bud scales hairy, at least toward the tips . . . .
                        . . . . Hedge maple (*Acer campestre*)
                30. terminal buds acutely pointed
                    34. 4–8 pairs of bud scales visible
                        35. buds brown; hairs at upper edge of leaf scar brown . . . .
                            . . . . Sugar maple (*Acer saccharum*)
                        35. buds dark brown to almost black; hairs at upper edge of leaf scar pale . . . . Black maple (*Acer nigrum*)
                    34. fewer than 4 pairs of bud scales visible . . . .
                        . . . . Japanese maple (*Acer palmatum*)

Key 8. Leafless trees with leaf scars alternate

1. stems armed with thorns, spines, or prickles, or some branches with thorn-like endings
    2. some branches with thorn-like endings
        3. terminal buds present; stipule scars absent . . . . Apple or Pear (*Malus* spp. or *Pyrus* spp.)
        3. terminal buds absent; stipule scars present . . . . Cherries and Plums (*Prunus* spp.)
    2. stems with thorns, spines, or prickles, but not with thorn-like endings
        4. stems armed with irregularly scattered prickles
            5. unbranched or seldom-branched tree to 65 ft. growing clonally; stem densely prickly . . . . . .
                . . . . Hercules'-club or Japanese angelica-tree (*Aralia* spp.)
            5. much-branched tree to 100 ft.; not clonal; young stems somewhat prickly . . . .
                . . . . Castor-aralia (*Kalopanax septemlobus* var. *septemlobus*)
        4. stems with spines definitely associated with the nodes (internodal prickles sometimes also present)
            6. stems mostly with 2 spines at each node, spines never branched
                7. crushed twigs aromatic . . . . Toothache-tree (*Zanthoxylum americanum*)

       7. crushed twigs not aromatic . . . . Black locust (*Robinia pseudoaccacia*)

     6. stems usually with 1 spine at each node or spines absent from some nodes, spines sometimes branched

        8. spines never branched

           9. terminal buds absent . . . . Osage-orange (*Maclura pomifera*)

           9. terminal buds present . . . . Hawthorns (*Crataegus* spp.)

        8. at least some spines branched . . . . Honey-locust (*Gleditsia triacanthos*)

1. stems unarmed

   10. stipule scars encircling or nearly encircling the twigs

      11. leaf scars encircling the lateral buds

         12. bark white; fruiting heads borne singly . . . . Sycamore (*Platanus occidentalis*)

         12. bark yellowish-gray; fruiting heads borne in 2s or 3s . . . . London planetree (*Platanus* x *acerifolia*)

      11. leaf scars not encircling the lateral buds

         13. terminal buds sharp-pointed, enclosed by several outer scales . . . . American beech (*Fagus grandifolia*)

         13. terminal buds not sharp-pointed, enclosed by 1 or 2 outer scales

           14. terminal buds more or less flattened, enclosed by 2 non-overlapping outer scales . . . . Tuliptree (*Liriodendron tulipifera*)

           14. terminal buds not flattened, enclosed by 1 outer scale

              15. pith with darker cross walls; leaves often persistent . . . . Sweetbay magnolia (*Magnolia virginiana*)

              15. pith not with darker cross walls; leaves deciduous

                16. buds not hairy . . . . Umbrella-tree (*Magnolia tripetala*)

                16. buds hairy

                  17. young twigs not hairy

                    18. youngest twigs dark brown above, greenish on side away from sun . . . . Kobus magnolia (*Magnolia kobus*)

                    18. youngest twigs uniformly red-brown . . . . Cucumber-tree (*Magnolia acuminata*)

                  17. young twigs hairy . . . . Saucer magnolia (*Magnolia soulangeana*)

   10. stipule scars absent or not nearly encircling the twigs

      19. leaf scars 2-ranked (occurring alternately on opposite sides of the twigs)

         20. buds clearly naked

            21. stipule scars absent; buds not stalked . . . . Pawpaw (*Asimina triloba*)

            21. stipule scars present; buds stalked . . . . Witch-hazel (*Hamamelis virginiana*)

         20. buds covered by scales or the nature of their covering difficult to determine

           22. vein scar 1

              23. pith with darker cross walls . . . . Persimmon (*Diospyros virginiana*)

              23. pith solid

                24. buds more than one per node . . . . Japanese snowbell (*Styrax japonica*)

                24. buds one per node

                  25. young twigs bearing recurved hairs . . . . . Sapphire-berry (*Symplocos paniculata*)

                  25. young twigs not hairy . . . . Mountain holly (*Ilex montana*)

           22. vein scars 3 or more

              26. pith irregularly triangular or star-shaped in cross section

                27. pith irregularly triangular in cross section

                  28. mature bark white or creamy

                    29. buds <³⁄₁₆ in.; bark close, not easily separable . . . . Gray birch (*Betula populifolia*)

                    29. buds ³⁄₁₆–⅜ in.; bark separating into papery layers

30. branches erect to slightly drooping
    31. bark spontaneously peeling into papery layers, often yellowish or pinkish . . . . Paper birch (*Betula papyrifera*)
    31. bark usually not spontaneously peeling, white . . . .
    . . . . European white birch (*Betula pubescens*)
30. branches pendulous . . . . European weeping birch (*Betula pendula*)
28. mature bark light reddish-brown, yellowish-gray, or dark blackish-brown, but not white
    32. twigs slightly to strongly aromatic when scraped or crushed; bark dark and tight or yellowish-gray and exfoliating
        33. bark blackish-brown, not exfoliating but becoming rough and platy in age; twigs strongly aromatic . . . . Sweet birch (*Betula lenta*)
        33. bark yellowish-gray, exfoliating in papery layers; twigs weakly aromatic . . . . Yellow birch (*Betula alleghaniensis*)
    32. twigs not aromatic; bark light reddish-brown, exfoliating in irregular papery layers . . . . River birch (*Betula nigra*)
27. pith star-shaped in cross section
    34. mature bark gray, smooth; buds with several scales . . . .
    . . . . Hornbeam (*Carpinus caroliniana*)
    34. mature bark brownish, rough, buds with 2 or 3 scales
        35. mature branches not hairy . . . . American chestnut (*Castanea dentata*)
        35. mature branches hairy
            36. tree to 65 ft. . . . . Chinese chestnut (*Castanea mollissima*)
            36. small tree or shrub to 17 ft. . . . . Chinquapin (*Castanea pumila*)
26. pith round in cross section
    37. stipule scars absent . . . . Redbud (*Cercis canadensis*)
    37. stipule scars present
        38. buds mostly with 2 scales . . . . Basswood (*Tilia americana*)
        38. buds mostly with 3 or more scales
            39. bud scales clearly in 2 ranks
                40. vein scars 3
                    41. buds densely rusty-brown hairy; inner bark mucilaginous . . . .
                  . . . . Slippery elm (*Ulmus rubra*)
                    41. buds not rusty-brown hairy; inner bark not mucilaginous
                        42. bud scales with darker margins . . . .
                      . . . . American elm (*Ulmus americana*)
                        42. bud scales uniformly colored . . . . Siberian elm (*Ulmus pumila*)
                40. vein scars > 3
                    43. buds ⅛–⅓ in. . . . . Red mulberry (*Morus rubra*)
                    43. buds ¹⁄₁₆–⅛ in. . . . . White mulberry (*Morus alba*)
            39. bud scales not in 2 ranks
                44. buds closely appressed to the stem; pith often with darker cross walls or hollow with partitions
                    45. tree to 110 ft. . . . . Hackberry (*Celtis occidentalis*)
                    45. small tree or shrub to 17 ft. . . . . . . Dwarf hackberry (*Celtis tenuifolia*)
                44. buds not closely appressed to the stem; pith solid
                    46. axillary buds directed to one side of the twig . . . .
                    . . . . Chinese elm (*Ulmus parvifolia*)
                    46. axillary buds not directed to one side of the twig
                      47. twigs not hairy or nearly so . . . Hop-hornbeam (*Ostrya virginiana*)
                      47. twigs densely hairy . . . . Oriental photinia (*Photinia villosa*)

19. leaf scars not 2-ranked
    48. drooping clusters of white or whitish berries persisting through the winter; generally confined to swamps, fens, or marshes .... Poison sumac (*Toxicodendron vernix*)
    48. fruit (if present) not drooping clusters of white or whitish berries; habitats variable
        49. twigs aromatic when crushed
            50. vein scar 1 .... Sassafras (*Sassafras albidum*)
            50. vein scars > 1
                51. vein scars 3 .... Hoptree (*Ptelea trifoliata*)
                51. vein scars > 3
                    52. aroma of crushed twigs spicy, pleasant .... Sweetgum (*Liquidambar styraciflua*)
                    52. aroma of crushed twigs garlic-like, unpleasant ....
                    .... Chinese cedar (*Cedrela sinensis*)
        49. twigs not aromatic when crushed
            53. most (if not all) leaf scars on abundant short lateral shoots
                54. vein scar 1; cones generally persistent
                    55. cone scales 15–20, smooth and shining on outside .. Tamarack (*Larix laricina*)
                    55. cone scales >40, smooth or hairy on the outside
                        56. cone scales reflexed at the apex, not hairy on the outside ....
                        .... Japanese larch (*Larix kaempferi*)
                        56. cone scales straight or slightly incurved, hairy on the outside ....
                        .... European larch (*Larix decidua*)
                  54. vein scars 2; cones never present .... Ginkgo (*Ginkgo biloba*)
            53. leaf scars spaced more or less normally along the twigs; short lateral shoots may be present but not as abundant
                57. pith star-shaped in cross section .... Oaks (*Quercus* spp.)
                57. pith more or less rounded, somewhat angled, or difficult to distinguish in cross section
                    58. pith with darker cross walls or hollow with partitions
                      59. vein scar 1 .... Carolina silverbell (*Halesia caroliniana*)
                      59. vein scars 3
                        60. pith hollow with partitions
                          61. pith tan to light brown .... Black walnut (*Juglans nigra*)
                          61. pith dark brown .... Butternut (*Juglans cinerea*)
                      60. pith with darker cross walls .... Blackgum (*Nyssa sylvatica*)
                  58. pith solid or the pith difficult to distinguish
                    62. lateral buds partially or completely buried in the leaf scar and rupturing the leaf scar upon expanding in the spring
                      63. branches remaining green for 2–4 years ....
                      .... Japanese scholar-tree (*Sophora japonica*)
                      63. branches not remaining green for 2–4 years
                        64. bark on older branches light gray, smooth, with prominent horizontal lenticels .... Mimosa (*Albizia julibrissin*)
                        64. bark on older branches dark gray, rough, lenticels not evident ......
                        .... Honey-locust (*Gleditsia triacanthos*)
                  62. lateral buds not buried in the leaf scar
                      65. leaf scars surrounding or nearly surrounding the lateral buds
                        66. pith occupying ½ or more of the diameter of the stem ....
                      .... Staghorn sumac (*Rhus typhina*)
                        66. pith occupying < ½ the diameter of the stem ....
                      .... Hoptree (*Ptelea trifoliata*)
                  65. leaf scars not nearly surrounding the lateral buds

67. first or only scale of the lateral bud located directly above the leaf scar
 68. buds with only 1 scale . . . . Willow (*Salix* spp.)
 68. buds with >1 scale
  69. buds resinous
   70. resin yellow or tan on brown buds . . . .
   . . . . Eastern cottonwood (*Populus deltoides*)
   70. resin orange or red on reddish-brown buds
    71. resin with balsamic fragrance when warm . . . .
    . . . . Balsam poplar (*Populus balsamifera*)
    71. resin, if fragrant, not balsamic . . . .
    . . . . Lombardy poplar (*Populus nigra*)
  69. buds not resinous
   72. buds not hairy . . . . Quaking aspen (*Populus tremuloides*)
   72. buds hairy
    73. twigs yellowish; pith orange . . . .
    . . . . Swamp cottonwood (*Populus heterophylla*)
    73. twigs not yellowish; pith whitish to light brown
     74. buds with short, straight hairs . . . .
     . . . . Big-tooth aspen (*Populus grandidentata*)
     74. buds densely hairy . . . . . White poplar (*Populus alba*)
67. first scale of the lateral bud not directly above the leaf scar
 75. pith salmon-pink . . . . . . Kentucky coffeetree (*Gymnocladus dioica*)
 75. pith whitish, greenish, brownish, or difficult to distinguish
  76. vein scar 1
   77. vein scar linear . . . . Persimmon (*Diospyros virginiana*)
   77. vein scar not linear . . . . . Sourwood (*Oxydendrum arboreum*)
  76. vein scars 3 or more
   78. buds apparently naked, sulfur-yellow or brown . . . .
   . . . . Bitternut hickory (*Carya cordiformis*)
   78. buds covered by scales
    79. buds borne on stalks
     80. female catkins ½–1¼ in. . . . .
     . . . . European alder (*Alnus glutinosa*)
     80. female catkins ⅓–½ in.
      81. female catkins bent downward . . . .
      . . . . Speckled alder (*Alnus incana* ssp. *rugosa*)
      81. female catkins erect . . . .
      . . . . Smooth alder (*Alnus serrulata*)
    79. buds not stalked
     82. lateral buds with 2–3 scales
      83. pith occupying ½ or more of the diameter of the
      twigs . . . . Tree-of-heaven (*Ailanthus altissima*)
      83. pith occupying <½ the diameter of the twigs . . . .
      . . . . Goldenrain tree (*Koelreuteria paniculata*)
     82. lateral buds with 4 or more scales
      84. true terminal bud lacking . . . .
      . . . . Osage-orange (*Maclura pomifera*)
      84. true terminal bud present
       85. leaf scars large, triangular or 3-lobed
        86. terminal buds <⅓ in. . . . .
        . . . . Pignut hickory (*Carya glabra*)

86. terminal buds >⅓ in.
    87. mature bark deeply furrowed but not shaggy . . . . Mockernut hickory (*Carya tomentosa*)
    87. mature bark exfoliating in long shaggy strips
        88. tips of outer bud scales prolonged into stiff spreading points . . . . Shellbark hickory (*Carya laciniosa*)
        88. tips of outer bud scales prolonged but not stiff and spreading . . . . Shagbark hickory (*Carya ovata*)
85. leaf scars smaller, not triangular or 3-lobed
    89. terminal buds generally >⅓ in. long and 3–4 times as long as broad
        90. pith whitish; vein scars mostly 3 . . . . Shadbush (*Amelanchier* spp.)
        90. pith brownish; vein scars mostly 5 . . . . Mountain-ash (*Sorbus* spp.)
    89. terminal buds generally <⅓ in. long and <3–4 times as long as broad
        91. twigs (and often branches) with prominent horizontally elongated lenticels; crushed twigs often with a bitter almond aroma . . . . . . Cherries or plums (*Prunus*)
        91. lenticels (if present) not prominent or horizontally elongated; crushed twigs not aromatic
            92. leaf scars mostly crowded near the ends of the current year's growth; twigs glossy reddish or copper-brown; terminal buds much larger than the lateral buds . . . . Alternate-leaf dogwood (*Cornus alternifolia*)
            92. leaf scars more evenly spaced; twigs brownish or grayish; terminal buds and lateral buds of about equal size . . . . . Apple or pear (*Malus* or *Pyrus*)

Glossary

achene   a single-seeded fruit that does not split open

Allegheny Front   the slope that marks the eastern edge of the Allegheny Plateau

allelopathy   inhibition of the growth of one plant by another through the production and release of chemicals

alluvial   deposited by running water, as alluvial soil

alternate   having one leaf or branch per node

angiosperms   the flowering plants

apical dominance   control of the growth form of a plant through hormones produced in the uppermost branch tips

aril   a fleshy layer present on the seeds of some plants

astringent   a drug that has a drying effect

barrens   plant communities characterized by sparse trees and a landscape dominated by grasses or shrubs. Barrens usually occur on low-nutrient, often droughty soils and sites that burn frequently.

bottomlands   lowlands along streams or rivers, floodplains

branch spur   a short lateral branch with numerous nodes, but lacking internodes; usually bears both flowers (and fruits) and leaves; see also short shoot

bristle   a stiff hair-like projection of the epidermis of plants

browse line   a horizontal line below which all vegetation has been consumed, when caused by white-tailed deer the browse line is approximately 5 feet from the ground

browsing   consumption of twigs of woody plants

bundle scar   scar left where the vascular connections between leaf and twig are severed

calcareous   containing abundant calcium

callus   wound tissue formed by plants where they are injured or cut

calyx   a collective term for the sepals, the outermost whorl of flower parts

cambium   a layer of actively dividing cells located beneath the bark of trees and shrubs, the cambium is responsible for increase in girth of trunks and branches of woody plants

canopy   the uppermost layer of the forest

capsule   a dry fruit that opens spontaneously at pores or seams

cathartic   a drug that causes evacuation of the bowels

catkin   a dense, erect or drooping, elongate cluster of flowers

clone   a group of organisms that are genetically identical

compound leaf   a leaf composed of 2 or more separate blade segments

conifer   a seed-bearing but nonflowering plant that produces its seeds in cones; the leaves of conifers are needle-like

corolla   a collective term for the petals of a flower

cultivar   a form of a plant that has been selected and maintained by humans

deciduous   a plant that retains it leaves for only a single growing season

decoction   a drug prepared by extracting the plant parts in boiling water

dendrochronology   the study of past events through the record preserved in tree rings

diabase   an intrusive rock that is dark in color and finely to coarsely crystalline

dioecious   with male and female flowers on separate plants

dormant   alive but not actively growing

drupe   a fruit, such as a plum or cherry, in which the seed(s) are enclosed in a bony stone that is surrounded by a fleshy layer

emetic   drug that causes vomiting

endangered species   a plant that is at risk of extinction

entire   referring to a leaf edge that lacks teeth

evapotranspiration   the process of water loss from the surface of leaves and other plant parts

evergreen   retaining a given set of leaves for more than one growing season

extirpated, extirpation   gone locally, but not totally extinct

fertilization   fusion of egg and sperm cells

follicle   a fruit that splits open along one side

gall   an abnormal plant growth induced by another organism such as an insect, fungus or bacterium

girdled   a condition in which the bark, down to and including the cambium, is stripped from the entire circumference of a woody stem

gland   an area or structure on a plant that secretes a sugary or oily liquid

gymnosperms   a group of plants that includes the conifers and related groups

hedgerow   a narrow strip of trees and other vegetation at the edge of a field

hypanthium   a cup-shaped structure formed by the fused bases of the sepals and petals; characteristic of the rose family; remaining flower parts are borne on the rim of the hypanthium

inferior ovary   an ovary that appears to be located beneath the other floral organs

inflorescence   a cluster of flowers on a plant

infusion   a drug prepared by steeping plant parts in cold or hot water

internode   the portion of a stem between nodes

juvenility   referring to an initial period of growth of many trees during which flowering does not occur

lateral bud   a bud produced in the angle between a leaf and the stem

leaf scar   a mark remaining on a twig after a leaf has fallen

lenticel   a corky growth on the surface of a twig through which gas exchange occurs

mesophytic   growing conditions that are medium in terms of moisture availability

monoecious   having separate male and female flowers on the same plant

mycorrhizae an association of fungi with the roots of plants that facilitates absorption of water and minerals

naturalized a non-native plant that has established itself in a new geographic region and has become self-perpetuating

node a point along a stem where leaves, flowers, buds, or branches occur

nodules swellings on the roots of plants formed by nitrogen-fixing bacteria

native present in Pennsylvania prior to European exploration and settlement, or having arrived since through natural means of dispersal

old growth forest that has not been cut, cleared, or subjected to other human-caused major disturbance

opposite occurring in pairs at each node or joint on a stem

palmate radiating from a central point

panacea a cure-all

panicle a branched inflorescence that matures from the bottom up

parasitic deriving nourishment directly from another living organism

pathogen an organism that causes disease

perfect flowers flowers that contain both stamens and pistil(s)

phloem a specialized plant tissue that transports sugars from the site of photosynthesis to other areas within the plant

photosynthesis the process by which plants make sugar and oxygen from carbon dioxide and water using energy from the sun; the green pigment chlorophyll is necessary for photosynthesis

pinnate arranged longitudinally along opposite sides of a central axis

pistil the female organ in a flower; the pistil includes the ovary, style, and stigma

pistillate containing a pistil; female

pollination movement of pollen from anther to style

pome an apple-like fruit with a fleshy outer layer and a cartilaginous core

poultice a drug that is held against the skin

purgative a drug that causes evacuation of the bowels

resin a clear, yellowish-brown, gummy material produced by conifers and a few other trees; resin often develops a white crust when exposed to air

riparian occurring along a stream or river

samara a single-seeded winged fruit that does not split open

sepals the outermost whorl of flower parts, collectively the sepals comprise the calyx

serpentine barrens plant communities found on serpentinite

serpentinite a greenish metamorphic rock that is high in magnesium

sessile lacking a stalk, attached directly to the stem

shale barrens sloping, south-facing sites with finely broken shale rock on the surface and very sparse vegetation

short shoot a short lateral branch with numerous nodes, but lacking internodes; usually bears both flowers (and fruits) and leaves; see also branch spur

simple leaf a leaf with a single blade segment

sinus the indented area between lobes along a leaf edge

spine   a stiff, sharp needle-like structure on the stem of a plant; spines are modified leaves or stipules and occur singly or in pairs at the nodes

staminate   containing stamens; male

stigma   the area of the pistil that is receptive to pollen

stipule   one of a pair of leafy organs located at the base of the leaf stalk in some plants

storax   an aromatic gum produced by some trees, also referred to as styrax

succession   the natural replacement of one plant community by another

successional species   sun-loving plants that colonize an open site but eventually are replaced by more shade-tolerant species

superior ovary   an ovary that is located above the point of attachment of other floral organs

tannin   a chemical found in plants; tannins have astringent qualities

temperate   having a moderate climate

terminal bud   the bud that occurs at the end of a branch

thorn   a sharp, stiff, needle-like, branched or unbranched plant structure derived from a modified branch; thorns always occur at nodes

threatened species   a plant that may become endangered if critical habitat is not maintained

tincture   a drug that is prepared by extracting plant parts in alcohol

umbel   an arrangement of flowers in which the individual flower stalks arise from a common point

umbo   the thickened portion at the tip of the cone scales in conifers

understory   the herb, shrub, and small tree layers that occur under a forest canopy

unisexual flowers   flowers that contain only male or female parts, but not both

vascular   specialized plant tissues that conduct water and dissolved materials; vascular tissues in plants contain xylem and phloem

vegetative reproduction   formation of new plants through means other than flowering and production of seeds; vegetative reproduction results in new plants that are genetically identical to the parent

xylem   specialized tissues in plants that conduct water from the roots to the leaves and other parts

Tree Lists

NATIVE TREES THAT ARE IMPORTANT FOOD SOURCES FOR MOTHS AND BUTTERFLIES

alder	*Alnus serrulata, A. incana* ssp. *rugosa*
black cherry	*Prunus serotina*
American elm	*Ulmus americana*
slippery elm	*Ulmus rubra*
white fringetree	*Chionanthus virginicus*
hackberry	*Celtis occidentalis*
hawthorn	*Crataegus* spp.
black locust	*Robinia pseudoacacia*
oak	*Quercus* spp.
pawpaw	*Asimina triloba*
American plum	*Prunus americana*
trembling aspen	*Populus tremuloides*
redbud	*Cercis canadensis*
staghorn sumac	*Rhus typhina*
sweetgum	*Liquidambar styraciflua*
tuliptree	*Liriodendron tulipifera*
black walnut	*Juglans nigra*
choke cherry	*Prunus virginiana*

SMALL- TO MODERATE-SIZE NATIVE TREES WITH CONSPICUOUS FLOWERS

blackhaw	*Viburnum prunifolium*
flowering dogwood	*Cornus florida*
alternate-leaved dogwood	*Cornus alternifolia*
white fringetree	*Chionanthus virginicus*
hawthorn	*Crataegus* spp.
mountain-ash	*Sorbus americana, S. decora*
redbud	*Cercis canadensis*
shadbush	*Amelanchier arborea, A. laevis*
sourwood	*Oxydendrum arboreum*
sweetbay magnolia	*Magnolia virginiana*
witch-hazel	*Hamamelis virginiana*

NATIVE TREES WITH EDIBLE FRUITS

blackhaw	*Viburnum prunifolium*
butternut	*Juglans cinerea*
American chestnut	*Castanea dentata*
chinquapin	*Castanea pumila*
sweet crabapple	*Malus coronaria*
mockernut hickory	*Carya tomentosa*

shagbark hickory	*Carya ovata*
shellbark hickory	*Carya laciniosa*
pawpaw	*Asimina triloba*
persimmon	*Diospyros virginiana*
American plum	*Prunus americana*
Chickasaw plum	*Prunus angustifolia*
beach plum	*Prunus maritima*
shadbush	*Amelanchier laevis, A. arborea*
black walnut	*Juglans nigra*

NATIVE EARLY SUCCESSIONAL TREES (SUN-LOVING)

white ash	*Fraxinus americana*
big-tooth aspen	*Populus grandidentata*
trembling aspen	*Populus tremuloides*
gray birch	*Betula populifolia* (southeast only)
blackhaw	*Viburnum prunifolium*
pin cherry	*Prunus pensylvanica*
sweet crabapple	*Malus coronaria*
black locust	*Robinia pseudoacacia*
red maple	*Acer rubrum*
Virginia pine	*Pinus virginiana*
American plum	*Prunus americana*
eastern red-cedar	*Juniperus virginiana*
sassafras	*Sassafras albidum*
staghorn sumac	*Rhus typhina*
sweetgum	*Liquidambar styraciflua*
tuliptree	*Liriodendron tulipifera*

NATIVE TREES OF RIPARIAN FORESTS

green ash	*Fraxinus pensylvanica*
river birch	*Betula nigra*
bladdernut	*Staphylea trifoliata*
box-elder	*Acer negundo*
eastern cottonwood	*Populus deltoides*
American elm	*Ulmus americana*
slippery elm	*Ulmus rubra*
shellbark hickory	*Carya laciniosa*
honey-locust	*Gleditsia triacanthos*
hoptree	*Ptelea trifolia*
hornbeam	*Carpinus caroliniana*
silver maple	*Acer saccharinum*
sycamore	*Platanus occidentalis*
black walnut	*Juglans nigra*
black willow	*Salix nigra*

NATIVE WETLAND TREES

smooth alder	*Alnus serrulata*

speckled alder	*Alnus incana* ssp. *rugosa*
black ash	*Fraxinus nigra*
pumpkin ash	*Fraxinus profunda* (northwest only)
Atlantic white cedar	*Chamaecyparis thyoides* (southeast only)
swamp cottonwood	*Populus heterophylla* (southeast only)
balsam fir	*Abies balsamea* (sphagnum bogs only)
shagbark hickory	*Carya ovata*
American holly	*Ilex opaca* (southeast only)
sweetbay magnolia	*Magnolia virginiana* (southeast only)
red maple	*Acer rubrum*
pin oak	*Quercus palustris*
swamp white oak	*Quercus bicolor*
willow oak	*Quercus phellos* (southeast only)
black spruce	*Picea mariana* (sphagnum bogs only)
red spruce	*Picea rubens* (glaciated area only)
poison sumac	*Toxicodendron vernix*
sweetgum	*Liquidambar styraciflua* (southeast only)
tamarack	*Larix laricina* (sphagnum bogs only)
black willow	*Salix nigra*
Carolina willow	*Salix caroliniana*
peach-leaf willow	*Salix amygdaloides*

TREES AT OR NEAR THE SOUTHERN LIMIT OF THEIR NATURAL RANGE IN PENNSYLVANIA

speckled alder	*Alnus incana* ssp. *rugosa*
gray birch	*Betula populifolia*
paper birch	*Betula papyrifera*
balsam fir	*Abies balsamea*
showy mountain-ash	*Sorbus decora*
red pine	*Pinus resinosa*
black spruce	*Picea mariana*
red spruce	*Picea rubens*
tamarack	*Larix laricina*

TREES AT OR NEAR THE NORTHERN LIMIT OF THEIR NATURAL RANGE IN PENNSYLVANIA

pumpkin ash	*Fraxinus profunda*
river birch	*Betula nigra*
yellow buckeye	*Aesculus flava*
chinquapin	*Castanea pumila*
white fringetree	*Chionanthus virginicus*
Hercules'-club	*Aralia spinosa*
sweetbay magnolia	*Magnolia virginiana*
blackjack oak	*Quercus marilandica*
Shumard oak	*Quercus shumardii*
post oak	*Quercus stellata*
southern red oak	*Quercus falcata*
willow oak	*Quercus phellos*

pawpaw	*Asimina triloba*
short-leaf pine	*Pinus echinata*
Table Mountain pine	*Pinus pungens*
Virginia pine	*Pinus virginiana*
Allegheny plum	*Prunus alleghaniensis*
sourwood	*Oxydendrum arboreum*
sweetgum	*Liquidambar styraciflua*
umbrella-tree	*Magnolia tripetala*

TREES AT OR NEAR THE EASTERN LIMIT OF THEIR NATURAL RANGE IN PENNSYLVANIA

trembling aspen	*Populus tremuloides*
Ohio buckeye	*Aesculus glabra*
yellow buckeye	*Aesculus flava*
bur oak	*Quercus macrocarpa*
shingle oak	*Quercus imbricaria*
Shumard oak	*Quercus shumardii*
redbud	*Cercis canadensis*

PENNSYLVANIA TREES LISTED BY FAMILY

Maple Family—Aceraceae

hedge maple	*Acer campestre*
Amur maple	*Acer ginnala*
box-elder	*Acer negundo*
black maple	*Acer nigrum*
Japanese maple	*Acer palmatum*
striped maple, moosewood	*Acer pensylvanicum*
Norway maple	*Acer platanoides*
sycamore maple	*Acer pseudoplatanus*
red maple	*Acer rubrum*
silver maple	*Acer saccharinum*
sugar maple	*Acer saccharum*
mountain maple	*Acer spicatum*

Cashew Family—Anacardiaceae

staghorn sumac	*Rhus typhina*
poison sumac	*Toxicodendron vernix*

Custard-Apple Family—Anonaceae

pawpaw	*Asimina triloba*

Holly Family—Aquifoliaceae

mountain holly	*Ilex montana*
American holly	*Ilex opaca*

Ginseng Family—Araliaceae

Japanese angelica-tree	*Aralia elata*

Hercules'-club	*Aralia spinosa*
castor-aralia	*Kalopanax septemlobus* var. *septemlobus*

Birch Family—Betulaceae

European alder	*Alnus glutinosa*
speckled alder	*Alnus incana* ssp. *rugosa*
smooth alder	*Alnus serrulata*
yellow birch	*Betula alleghaniensis*
sweet birch	*Betula lenta*
river birch	*Betula nigra*
paper birch, canoe birch	*Betula papyrifera*
European weeping birch	*Betula pendula*
gray birch	*Betula populifolia*
European white birch	*Betula pubescens*
hornbeam, ironwood	*Carpinus caroliniana*
hop-hornbeam	*Ostrya virginiana*

Trumpet-creeper Family—Bignoniaceae

southern catalpa, Indian-bean	*Catalpa bignonioides*
northern catalpa, cigar-tree	*Catalpa speciosa*
empress-tree	*Paulownia tomentosa*

Caesalpinia Family—Caesalpiniaceae

redbud	*Cercis canadensis*
honey-locust	*Gleditsia triacanthos*
Kentucky coffeetree	*Gymnocladus dioica*

Honeysuckle Family—Caprifoliaceae

blackhaw	*Viburnum prunifolium*

Katsura-tree Family—Cercidiphyllaceae

katsura-tree	*Cercidiphyllum japonicum*

Dogwood Family—Cornaceae

alternate-leaf dogwood	*Cornus alternifolia*
flowering dogwood	*Cornus florida*
blackgum, tupelo	*Nyssa sylvatica*

Cypress Family—Cupressaceae

Atlantic white-cedar	*Chamaecyparis thyoides*
eastern red-cedar	*Juniperus virginiana*
arbor-vitae, northern white-cedar	*Thuja occidentalis*

Ebony Family—Ebenaceae

persimmon	*Diospyros virginiana*

Heath Family—Ericaceae

sourwood	*Oxydendrum arboreum*

Bean Family—Fabaceae

black locust	*Robinia pseudoacacia*
Japanese pagoda-tree, scholar-tree	*Sophora japonica*

Beech Family—Fagaceae

American chestnut	*Castanea dentata*
Chinese chestnut	*Castanea mollissima*
chinquapin	*Castanea pumila*
American beech	*Fagus grandifolia*
sawtooth oak	*Quercus acutissima*
white oak	*Quercus alba*
swamp white oak	*Quercus bicolor*
scarlet oak	*Quercus coccinea*
southern red oak	*Quercus falcata*
scrub oak, bear oak	*Quercus ilicifolia*
shingle oak	*Quercus imbricaria*
bur oak	*Quercus macrocarpa*
blackjack oak	*Quercus marilandica*
chestnut oak	*Quercus montana*
chinquapin oak, yellow oak	*Quercus muhlenbergii*
pin oak	*Quercus palustris*
willow oak	*Quercus phellos*
dwarf chestnut oak	*Quercus prinoides*
red oak	*Quercus rubra*
Shumard oak	*Quercus shumardii*
post oak	*Quercus stellata*
black oak	*Quercus velutina*

Ginkgo Family—Ginkgoaceae

ginkgo, maidenhair tree	*Ginkgo biloba*

Witch-Hazel Family—Hamamelidaceae

witch-hazel	*Hamamelis virginiana*
sweetgum	*Liquidambar styraciflua*

Horse-chestnut Family—Hippocastanaceae

yellow buckeye	*Aesculus flava*
Ohio buckeye	*Aesculus glabra*
horse-chestnut	*Aesculus hippocastanum*

Walnut Family—Juglandaceae

bitternut hickory	*Carya cordiformis*
pignut hickory	*Carya glabra*
shellbark hickory	*Carya laciniosa*
shagbark hickory	*Carya ovata*
mockernut hickory	*Carya tomentosa*
butternut, white walnut	*Juglans cinerea*
black walnut	*Juglans nigra*

Laurel Family—Lauraceae

sassafras   *Sassafras albidum*

Magnolia Family—Magnoliaceae

tuliptree   *Liriodendron tulipifera*
cucumber-tree   *Magnolia acuminata*
kobus magnolia   *Magnolia kobus*
saucer magnolia   *Magnolia soulangeana*
umbrella-tree   *Magnolia tripetala*
sweetbay magnolia   *Magnolia virginiana*

Mahogany Family—Meliaceae

Chinese-cedar, Chinese toon *Cedrela sinensis*

Mimosa Family—Mimosaceae

mimosa   *Albizia julibrissin*

Mulberry Family—Moraceae

paper-mulberry   *Broussonetia papyrifera*
osage-orange   *Maclura pomifera*
white mulberry   *Morus alba*
red mulberry   *Morus rubra*

Olive Family—Oleaceae

white fringetree   *Chionanthus virginicus*
white ash   *Fraxinus americana*
black ash   *Fraxinus nigra*
green ash, red ash   *Fraxinus pennsylvanica*
pumpkin ash   *Fraxinus profunda*

Pine Family—Pinaceae

balsam fir   *Abies balsamea*
European larch   *Larix decidua*
Japanese larch   *Larix kaempferi*
tamarack   *Larix laricina*
Norway spruce   *Picea abies*
white spruce   *Picea glauca*
black spruce   *Picea mariana*
Colorado blue spruce   *Picea pungens*
red spruce   *Picea rubens*
jack pine   *Pinus banksiana*
short-leaf pine   *Pinus echinata*
Austrian pine   *Pinus nigra*
Table Mountain pine   *Pinus pungens*
red pine, Norway pine   *Pinus resinosa*
pitch pine   *Pinus rigida*
white pine   *Pinus strobus*
Scots pine   *Pinus sylvestris*
Virginia pine   *Pinus virginiana*

douglas-fir	*Pseudotsuga menziesii*
Canadian hemlock, eastern hemlock	*Tsuga canadensis*

Planetree Family—Platanaceae

sycamore, buttonwood	*Platanus occidentalis*
London planetree	*Platanus* x *acerifolia*

Rose Family—Rosaceae

shadbush, serviceberry, Juneberry	*Amelanchier arborea*
smooth shadbush, smooth serviceberry	*Amelanchier laevis*
Brainerd's hawthorn	*Crataegus brainerdii*
pear hawthorn, black-thorn hawthorn	*Crataegus calpodendron*
round-leaf hawthorn	*Crataegus chrysocarpa*
red-fruit hawthorn	*Crataegus coccinea*
cockspur hawthorn	*Crataegus crus-galli*
broad-leaf hawthorn	*Crataegus dilatata*
Dodge's hawthorn	*Crataegus dodgei*
Holmes' hawthorn	*Crataegus holmesiana*
Biltmore hawthorn	*Crataegus intricata*
large-seed hawthorn	*Crataegus macrosperma*
downy hawthorn	*Crataegus mollis*
English hawthorn	*Crataegus monogyna*
Pennsylvania hawthorn	*Crataegus pennsylvanica*
Washington hawthorn	*Crataegus phaenopyrum*
frosted hawthorn	*Crataegus pruinosa*
dotted hawthorn, white hawthorn	*Crataegus punctata*
long-spine hawthorn, fleshy hawthorn	*Crataegus succulenta*
sweet crabapple	*Malus coronaria*
apple	*Malus pumila*
crabapple	*Malus* sp.
Oriental photinia	*Photinia villosa*
Allegheny plum	*Prunus alleghaniensis*
American plum	*Prunus americana*
Chickasaw plum	*Prunus angustifolia*
sweet cherry, European bird cherry	*Prunus avium*
beach plum	*Prunus maritima*
European bird cherry	*Prunus padus*
pin cherry	*Prunus pensylvanica*
black cherry	*Prunus serotina*
Higan cherry	*Prunus subhirtella*
choke cherry	*Prunus virginiana*
callery pear	*Pyrus calleryana*
common pear	*Pyrus communis*

American mountain-ash	*Sorbus americana*
European mountain-ash	*Sorbus aucuparia*
showy mountain-ash	*Sorbus decora*

Rue Family—Rutaceae

corktree	*Phellodendron japonicum*
corktree	*Phellodendron lavallei*
hop-tree	*Ptelea trifoliata*
bee-bee tree	*Tetradium daniellii*
prickly-ash, toothache tree	*Zanthoxylum americanum*

Willow family—Salicaceae

white poplar	*Populus alba*
balsam poplar	*Populus balsamifera*
eastern cottonwood	*Populus deltoides*
big-tooth aspen	*Populus grandidentata*
swamp cottonwood	*Populus heterophylla*
Lombardy poplar	*Populus nigra*
trembling aspen	*Populus tremuloides*
white willow	*Salix alba*
peach-leaf willow	*Salix amygdaloides*
weeping willow	*Salix babylonica*
goat willow	*Salix caprea*
Carolina willow	*Salix caroliniana*
crack willow	*Salix fragilis*
shining willow	*Salix lucida*
black willow	*Salix nigra*

Soapberry Family—Sapindaceae

goldenrain tree	*Koelreuteria paniculata*

Quassia Family—Simaroubaceae

tree-of-heaven	*Ailanthus altissima*

Bladdernut Family—Staphyleaceae

bladdernut	*Staphylea trifolia*

Storax Family—Styracaceae

Carolina silverbell	*Halesia carolina*
Japanese snowbell	*Styrax japonica*

Sweetleaf Family—Symplocaceae

sapphire-berry	*Symplocos paniculata*

Linden Family—Tiliaceae

basswood, American linden	*Tilia americana*

Elm Family—Ulmaceae

hackberry	*Celtis occidentalis*
dwarf hackberry	*Celtis tenuifolia*

American elm	*Ulmus americana*
Chinese elm	*Ulmus parvifolia*
Siberian elm	*Ulmus pumila*
slippery elm	*Ulmus rubra*

Index

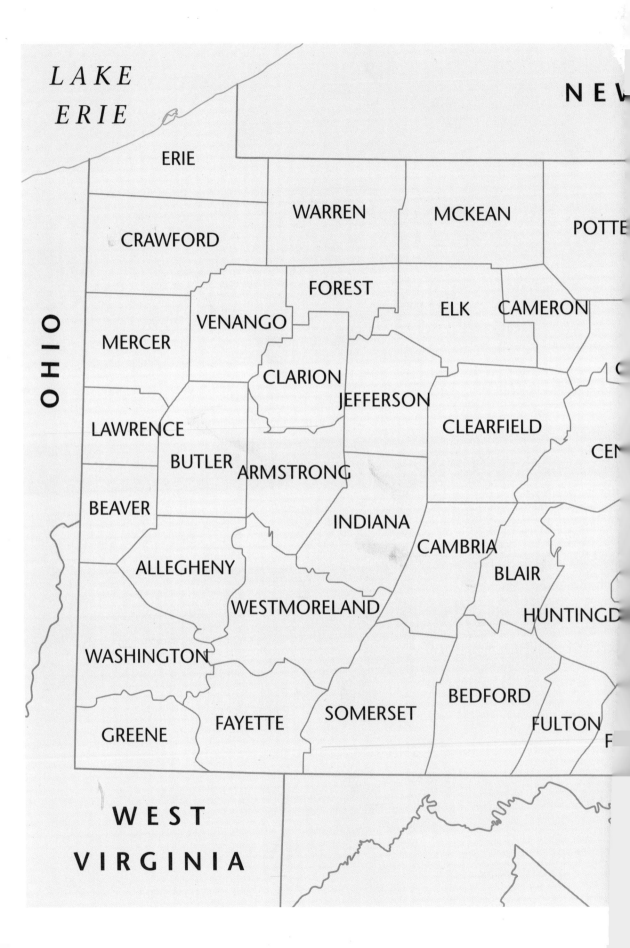